Praise for

GIVE ME THE WORLD

"An unorthodox odyssey, Mrs. Hadley writes with a facile, feminine touch, an attractive curiosity for places and people, as well as a natural enterprise and enthusiasm." —*Kirkus Reviews*

"She took with her on a two-year voyage only those durable qualities with which it is evident that she is blessed—a mind bright as a magpie's eye, and the sure love of life that finds reassurance in the sudden grin on the face of a stranger."
—Nadine Gordimer, for *The Observer*

"This . . . reissue of a 1958 memoir . . . wears well, thanks to Leila Hadley's spirited sophistication and keen eye for detail."
—*USA Today*

"*Give Me the World* enchants the reader with the beauty and clarity of the writing, its confiding tone, and the author's honesty and enthusiasm." —*Herald Sunday*

". . . *Give Me the World* is an entertaining companion to one's first armchair journey to the East." —*New York Herald Tribune*

"Written with great wit and passion, constructed as seductively as the spider's web, this is a romance about a young mother's liaison with the world, which taught her all the real and deep feelings of a life fully lived."
—Andrew Solomon, author of *The Noonday Demon*

"*Give Me the World* possesses, in tumbling abundance, the qualities that make wonderful travel writing—charm, vitality, curiosity, an uncomplaining, resilient energy, humor (it's a very funny book), and a kind of eager transparency, the traveler's eye being open, alert, almost clairvoyantly intelligent." —Lance Morrow

Leila Hadley/by Philippe Halsman

GIVE ME THE WORLD

LEILA HADLEY

SEAL PRESS

GIVE ME THE WORLD

© 1958 by Leila Hadley
Foreword © 2003 by Leila Hadley

First Seal Press paperback edition 2003

Seal Press
An Imprint of Avalon Publishing Group Incorporated
161 William Street, 16th Floor
New York, NY 10038

Errata

Due to the fact that this book was published in 1958 using different printing
technology, we were unable to make the following corrections within the text:

Page 58: "by men" should appear as "by then"

Page 145: "dumfounded" should appear as "dumbfounded"

Page 198: "gusty" should appear as "gutsy"

"Bagdad" should appear as "Baghdad" throughout

"sirup" should appear as "syrup" throughout

Reprinted by arrangement with Thomas Dunne Books,
an imprint of St. Martin's Press, LLC, New York, NY.

Library of Congress Cataloging-in-Publication Data is available.

ISBN 0-58005-091-3

9 8 7 6 5 4 3 2 1

Printed in the United States of America
Distributed by Publishers Group West

For my husband

"Give me the world if thou wilt, but grant me an asylum for my affections."

—*From the Icelandic* Tulka

Contents

GIVE
ME THE
WORLD

CHAPTER ONE

Castles in the Air

I HAD WANTED to get away.

Now, after the letters and telegrams had been read, after the steward had placed vases and bowls of flowers on the bureau, and my son Kippy had converted his bunk and the contents of the bon-voyage baskets into an extravagant barricade of outsized jars of caviar, hothouse fruit and chocolate bars, I took off my earrings, my beaded hat from Mr. John's and the scarlet coat from Trigère that still wasn't paid for. I lay down on the other bunk and was dispirited because I derived from the stateroom little of the rapture I had anticipated.

As a child, I had traveled almost every year with my family to England for the summer, and I remembered how each cabin then had seemed more enchanting than the last. Now that I was twenty-five, with a six-year-old child of my own, perhaps I shouldn't have expected to be charmed instantly by a stateroom. But perhaps, I thought, all my preconceived ideas would turn out the same way, flattening with experience into dim shadows, like Mr. Eliot's shadows that fell so gloomily between the idea and the reality.

I wished that I were more like Kippy, artless, untroubled and reacting in accord to a single heart and a single mind. I wondered whether there would ever come a time when I could reconcile what I wanted to do and what I felt I should do with what I did. I hoped that by going away, by being alone with the added stimulation of alien people, sights and customs, I would in some way be able to disentangle myself from the octopus of my doubts and fears and misgivings.

I had wanted to leave New York—not the city, which I loved—but the life I lived there, which seemed to claim from me barely more than an acceptance. I wanted to be a stranger in a world where everything I saw, heard, touched and tasted would be fresh and new, because wonder and awareness seemed to have disappeared from my life, leaving an excessive familiarity with an existence of routine.

Each day had been as undistinguished as the next. I got up, dressed, went to the office, worked, left the office, stayed home or went out, and fell asleep knowing the whole process would be repeated the following day.

It had started five years before. Disillusioned as one can only be at twenty, having by then already been married and divorced, I wanted to get as far away as possible from my own background and experience. Public relations had seemed to be the answer. But the work that once had offered such scope and excitement had eventually become contained and diminished in the tools of the trade—a typewriter, two telephones with push-buttons, and a rotary index, the Wheeldex.

I particularly disliked the Wheeldex. It symbolized all that disturbed, all that irritated. Attached to its polished steel frame were a thousand cards, detachable, each bearing a name, address and telephone number. They were small rectangular cards classified by color into the categories of Radio, Television, Newspapers, Magazines, Manufacturers, Advertising Agencies, and a mass of palegreen cards set aside for Friends—a rough and wistful designation for a group of people who were mostly acquaintances and business associates. It seemed to me that I spent most of my time riffling through the Wheeldex calling people I didn't care for who in turn called other people I didn't know to arrange things that meant nothing to me at all.

I became an executive, and for a while I delighted in my job. When the delight wore off, I was afraid to exchange the known devils for the unknown, because by then I had come to terms with the Wheeldex and the thousand people whose names I knew, whose telephone voices were familiar and whose faces I seldom saw.

By planning publicity campaigns, planting stories, sending forth publicity releases, setting up advertising tie-ins, organizing public appearances and guest spots on radio and television, I tried to achieve a state of public awareness and acclaim for clients who rewarded me generously for my efforts.

No matter how much I made, however, I was always in debt. I ran up preposterous bills that took months to pay off. Strangely enough, I bought, I imagined, only what I needed. I just happened to need a lot of things—clothes, books, records, flowers, presents for this friend's birthday and that friend's wedding. The rent for my Fifty-seventh Street apartment was high, and every month there was an irreducible pile of envelopes with cellophane windows billing me for groceries, cleaning, laundry, the telephones—I had three —gas and electricity, the window-cleaner, the doctor, the dentist, the drugstore, the newsstand, and besides all these there would be a mountain of accounts payable to department stores and various shops. I never quite knew how it happened, but I found myself in the comfortless predicament of working at a job I didn't like for the money to pay for a lot of things I didn't need.

Wonderful Mary Greig, who loved Kippy and me as though we were her own, looked after Kippy while I worked. Beset with unknown longings and a hunger for the indefinable, I would often turn to Mrs. Greig and say I was unhappy and that nothing seemed to interest me any more. "No wonder," she would reply tartly, "leading the rat-race you do. You should find yourself a good man and get married." And then as the telephone rang, she would add humphingly, "I suppose this means another late night. Well, enjoy yourself."

And off I would go with someone who perhaps also suffered from a vague, unshakable malaise and feelings of dissatisfaction. Either we would set off on a perpetual scavenger hunt for the new—the new restaurant, the new play, the new game, the newfangled and featured, all of which might have been new but which were never different—or we would chant our troubles back and forth at each other. While agreeing that we needed a change of some sort, we would ruefully condemn ourselves for our apathy and go on living the same old way.

One day, after an infuriating morning at the office, when the susurrus of the air-conditioning machine had interchanged sticky humidity with damp chill; when the cardboard container of black coffee had overturned and flooded the desk; when a publicity campaign I had worked on for seven weeks was rejected, I finally felt, after months of irresolution, that I had reached the breaking point. Something had to be done.

It was too late to cancel my lunch appointment. I went along to the restaurant and waited morosely for the arrival of a man I'll call James. James was late and, having experienced an unproductive morning of work, he was also in a cantankerous mood. We picked at the antipasto and idly guillotined a few acquaintances, and by the time we had drunk two glasses of Orvieto and eaten too much manicotti, we had decided that New York was a hateful place inhabited by hateful people. James, who had just returned from the Far East, was contemplating a trip to Africa.

"I've always wanted to go to the Far East," I said mournfully. "It's one of my favorite castles in the air."

"Well, why don't you go then?" James asked. "At the risk of being a bore, may I quote you something from the last chapter of *Walden?*" This was a favorite piece of reading of his, and now one of mine, and I believe he knew it almost word for word. " 'If you have built your castles in the air, your work need not be lost; that is where they should be. Now put your foundations under them.' "

"Oh, James," I protested, "you know it's not as simple as that. I don't have any money."

"You make enough," he said.

"I know," I said wearily, "and I spend it."

"Well, if you take my advice," he said, "you'll book your passage now and worry about money later."

Another glass of Orvieto added weight to his suggestion. I telephoned my secretary and told her I wouldn't be back for the rest of the afternoon. At James's direction, I floated off to the offices of the American President Lines and emerged an hour or so later a little more knowledgeable about the Far East than I had been before, with the assurance of a cabin for Kippy and myself on a cargo ship sailing in three months' time for Manila and Hong Kong.

It was astonishing how much better I felt once I had settled on a definite course of action. I embarked on a reading jag about the Orient, plunging into reference books with all the intensity of a schoolchild determined to get the best marks in the class. Having a passion for notebooks, I started a fresh one for recording arbitrary and agreeable information about Far Eastern culture patterns, concepts, whimsies and phenomena. I brooded over the doctrinal complexities of Hinduism and Buddhism, and delighted in the knowledge that birds' nest soup is actually made from birds' nests. I discovered that a *bêche de mer* is a sea slug and *ginseng* an aromatic herb, and that both are esteemed by the Chinese as great delicacies. I found that a *nilgai* is a blue cow indigenous to India, that Far Easterners don't like shaking hands and that in Siam, silver-plated tiger skulls are sold for ashtrays.

I devoted another section of my notebook to more practical agenda—reminders to get a joint passport for Kippy and myself, to get visas, to get a tenant for my apartment, to get inoculations against plague, cholera, typhoid and tetanus. It was somewhat discouraging to find out that the process of escape was largely a matter of routine paper work and visits to the doctor.

At the same time that I was entering pages of medical advice into my notebook, I gathered together introductory letters and addresses of people that I might call upon.

A month from my departure there remained only one uncompleted detail: the apartment had to be rented. After that I would pack, and Kippy and I would leave for the coast, and at last be on our way.

A real-estate agent produced a host of prospective tenants who for three weeks traipsed through the apartment, finding it alternately too large, too noisy, inadequately furnished, overly furnished, too small, overpriced, anything and everything, but never right. Then, *mirabile dictu*—tenants, and I began to pack.

In a pandemonium of blue tissue paper and lists, overturned boxes and cartons, the dining-room table awash with a chaotic hodgepodge, Mary Greig and I faced supreme decisions.

Ought Kippy to have six pairs of shoes, or would four be enough? Where was the extra socket for the traveling iron? Was there room for my black silk suit? Should I take Kleenex and camera film, or would I be able to buy them along the way?

Were there any books I wanted to take that I could do without? Finally, the luggage was packed. All was in order.

I went to my last farewell party in New York.

And three days later Kippy and I were aboard the *President Madison,* a cargo ship sailing from San Francisco, bound for Manila and Hong Kong.

CHAPTER TWO

Getting Away from It All

It was beginning—the departure and the escape that I longed for.

There was an air of seedy festivity about the paper serpentines writhing and catching at each other and tangling in the sharp wind. From the deck, Kippy and I threw unwinding rolls of dingy pink and green paper to the people on the pier below. A representative of the ship's company was the only person I recognized in the pale sunlight where the crowd stood in front of the gray pier shed. From time to time, he would look up at Kippy and me and wave and shout good-by. I would wave back at him and smile until it felt awkward, and then we would both invent something to look away at.

The gangway was clankily secured alongside. The hawsers were hauled in and the cables cast loose. The ship's siren blasted. And then the engines were going. Everyone waved more vigorously than before. The paper streamers broke and fell in the water as the ship began to slip slowly away from the pier. As the space widened between us and the people we were leaving behind, I felt weary, relaxed and relieved, and somewhat downcast that I felt no great elation at departure. I stayed on deck with Kippy until the fog closed in, and the Golden Gate Bridge was only a series of pyramiding supports, its glamorous superstructure lost in the haze. And then I went back to the stateroom and its bright baskets of fruit and flowers.

For three months I had planned and worked and prepared for

one future moment, until I was so filled with the thought of it that
I could think of nothing else. Even more than I imagined depended
upon this moment's coming into being. It was a moment that would
turn my living to another direction. It was a moment of singular
importance, this moment of departure, and yet it had come and
gone, and I had scarcely sensed its passing. Lying on the bunk,
absent-mindedly eating sweet, seedless grapes, I felt unsure of myself, uneasy that perhaps I had done the wrong thing, a little
worried that the change and escape I had ardently contemplated
might, after all, not turn out as I hoped.

But the fit of the blues I thought I was in for was soon gently
dissipated by the soothing routine of ship's life. Living was at once
simplified. As there were only eight other passengers, there were no
attempts at organized entertainment, no committees, no competi-
tions. With set limits on what I could do and see, I felt deliciously
free from the pull of guilt at doing nothing much at all. I walked
around the deck, looked at the sea, read desultorily, slept and ate.
This exterior simplification of living seemed to bring about a cor-
responding interior one. Forgetful of the past and quite mindless of
the future, I experienced a sort of languor and calmly surrendered
myself to the idling progression of time.

The other passengers were all paired off and quite content to
stay that way. There were two squat, bespectacled Japanese businessmen with fat, jiggling bottoms. They picked their teeth at the
table and sucked their breath in sharply when they spoke, and
marched round and round the deck with bent heads.

There were two spinsters who were missionaries. For the most
part, they sat on deck, the pages of their open Biblical commentaries whipped by the wind to a frenzied flapping. They were both
middle-aged women with large, clumsy bodies and thick buns of
braided brown hair. One had a prim, girlish face ending with a
small mouth and falling away into a ruddy wattle. The other wore
pince-nez spectacles and looked like a myopic squirrel. She had gone
up to all the passengers on the first day out and said, "My name
is Miss Slater, and I'm pleased to meet you." But her aggressive
friendliness had met with no response, and although she chatted
volubly to her companion, after the second day she hardly spoke to
anyone else.

There was a Filipino lady and her American husband. She was so stout and ungainly that it was almost impossible to imagine that she had ever been a child who could skip and run. Her husband, a retired Navy man, had the blotchy, purple-veined skin of an alcoholic. They spent most of their time in their cabin and only appeared for meals during calm weather.

Then there was a Mrs. Fulton and her mother; they sat at our table. Mrs. Fulton was a divorcee from Nashville with eyes like a hungry bird's, a fussy little person doted upon by her tiny gray mother. They were on a six-weeks' vacation trip and they were both disappointed that they hadn't chosen a larger ship. It was a shame, the mother said, that there was no dressing up for dinner and that there were neither horse races nor movies to pass the time. Mrs. Fulton said that she wished there were some nice men aboard, and she and her mother baaed back and forth to each other like tired sheep. I was relieved beyond measure when the rough weather came and drove them back to their cabin.

Fortunately, in between meals, Mrs. Fulton and her mother kept to themselves. So did the rest of the passengers, each couple aware of the others only for the sake of politeness. Our relationship, for the whole voyage, resembled nothing so much as the close-range remoteness of passengers traveling in an elevator. This was fine with me. There was no one around to claim my freedom, no one for me to disoblige or avoid, and, better yet, there was no disarming soul to pry from me confidences that afterward I would wish had gone unsaid.

I was not lonely, however, for in their off hours there were always the ship's officers to talk to. They were generally bursting with information of an intensely nautical character and willingly explained the ship's appointments and radar equipment to Kippy and me. They were good men, efficient, sensible and considerate, and unaffectedly nice in their manner and bearing. They seemed so sure of themselves as they spoke of meteorology and walked about leaning without stumbling against the roll of the ship. Johnny, the second mate; Dick, the third mate; and Mike, the wireless operator —I liked them best.

Kippy portioned his time equally among the Captain, a hearty Irishman, who bounced him on his knee and talked to him about

boxing; Mike, under whose tutelage he filled a copybook with letters in Morse code and "I love my Mom" and "I will be a good
boy" written over and over again; and José, our roly-poly Filipino
waiter, who taught him phrases in his native Tagalog and gave him
a Japanese cigarette box that ground out a tweedling tune as the
lid clicked up to release a wooden bird with a cigarette in its bill.
Kippy cherished the box and carried it with him everywhere. "Cigarette, Johnny?" he would ask. "Cigarette, Joe?" "Cigarette, Mike?"
And when he saw the Captain, he would jump from one foot to
the other with excitement, for the Captain always wanted a cigarette.

"Cigarette?" the Captain would boom delightedly. "Why you
must have read my mind. Yes, indeed, I'll have one, my boy." As
Kippy would press the catch so enthusiastically that his fingernail
would go quite purple, the box would squeak and tweedle and up
would pop the wooden bird with the cigarette. The Captain never
failed to express surprise and pleasure.

The voyage lasted twenty-one or twenty-two days. I was never
certain which, for we lost a day when we crossed the 180th Me-
ridian. One day it was Tuesday and we were in the Western
Hemisphere, and the next it was Thursday and we were in the
Eastern Hemisphere, and Wednesday was completely gone, mysteriously made to disappear by the legerdemain of time operative
at the International Date Line. To have a day suddenly thieved
away gave me an uneasy feeling, and it seemed odd to me that all
the others, who undoubtedly would have complained rather testily
had a hat or a book blown overboard, should accept the loss of a
whole Wednesday with such stoical reserve. But then, as Johnny
had said, I was lacking the scientific turn of mind necessary to
understand such matters.

Until the Tuesday that had been followed so precipitately by a
Thursday, the wind had been sharp and cold, the sunshine thin,
the sea relentlessly gray and rolling. There would be a brief show
of color in the sky when the sun rose, a corrugated banner of pink
and red mottled like the feathers of a Plymouth Rock hen. Then
the color would fade into fogginess, and sky and sea would blend
with each other in grayness until the sun set, pale and pink. Then

would come a dark night with few stars. Lying in my bunk, trying to read, I would see out of the corner of my eye the measured sliding of Kippy's hairbrush from one raised edge of the bureau to the other and find myself waiting for my shoes to skate across the cupboard floor and thump in time with the lurching of the ship. I could usually hear faint music below. On relatively calm nights, Dick would play *The Barber of Seville, Faust, Madame Butterfly* or something of Beethoven's on his gramophone. On less calm nights, Johnny would play a lilting Swedish folk song called "Nicolina" over and over again on his tape recorder, and on some nights I could hear a metallic orchestral outburst before the news came through on the ship's radio. But on nights when the hairbrush leaped over its barriers and the chair fell on its back and slithered aimlessly about the floor like a toppled turtle, I could only hear the clamorous creaking and straining of the ship, the clattering in our cabin, and the muffled noise of the sea hurling itself against us.

Thursday had been such a night, and I woke up Friday to the clanking of buckets and the brushing sibilance of deck-scrubbing. I poked my head out of the porthole expecting to see another slate-colored day, but the sky was lustrous and pearly, and the water that sloped out of sight and then wallowed up again was sapphiric and sparkling in the light. By noon the day had warmed, and the sky was a dazzling blue. The warmth lasted and in the next few days intensified to summery heat. Arms and legs were bared. The officers put on white shorts. Cold glasses left wet circles on the tablecloth at mealtimes. Fans were turned on. At night the stars were diamond bright, the wind indolent and gentle. In the ambient heat it was strange not to hear the humming of cicadas and only the throbbing of the engines as we steamed along.

I saw my first school of flying fish and was astonished to see how little they were. I had expected them to resemble creatures from a medieval bestiary, to be as big as marlin, with great wing fins, and I was a bit disappointed to see instead how modern and utilitarian they looked, unlike either bird or fish, more like small aluminum rockets skimming across the sea toward the dark line of the horizon. Yet I could watch them endlessly. Isolated in a world where we were always in the center of a floor of water beneath the radiant emptiness of the sky, any sign of life in the surrounding void produced a trancelike state of wondering contemplation. With the same musing concentration of someone watching a pot of water and waiting for it to come to a boil, I would gaze out at the puff of smoke or the glimmer of lights of a distant ship, or stare at a lone black frigate bird until it disappeared, a thousand miles from land, gliding and swooping in the wind. Five days before we reached Manila, I saw a tropic bird of almost enameled whiteness, with two extraordinarily long yellow tail feathers, and that night, for the first time, I saw the four stars of the Southern Cross.

The night before we were to arrive in Manila, I hardly slept at all, and by five-thirty I was up and looking out the porthole.

The rim of the porthole smelled of salt and brass polish. There was no land in sight.

"Are we in Manila yet?" Kippy asked in a soft voice.

In the early morning his voice was always soft, his eyes gentle, his gestures leisurely. I loved Kippy especially in the morning. It was the only time of day when his whole being was as flowing and artless as a curve. In an hour or so he would tauten to tense angularity, and by noon he would be transformed into a flying wedge, charged with curiosity, bristling with energy, a missile that more than likely I would feel like dodging.

"Are we there yet?"

"No," I said, tugging a comb through my hair. "Mind you don't step on the suitcase. I've just got everything straightened out."

Kippy mumbled about and said I had packed his belt and that his pants wouldn't stay up without it. I discovered I had also packed my sneakers, and had to drag forth one of the strapped suitcases, unlock it and burrow through three layers of tissue paper and belongings before I found them. And then another search to dig up Kippy's belt. I relocked the suitcase, tucked Kippy's shirt temporarily in his trousers and mislaid the luggage keys several times before we were ready to go down to breakfast.

Miss Slater, looking more like a myopic squirrel than ever, was the only other passenger still eating. She nodded good morning and continued chewing rhythmically on a piece of buttered toast.

I tried to be calm and promptly upset my coffee cup.

Mike glanced over from the officers' table. "Guess you have channel fever," he said, grinning. He explained to Kippy that channel fever had nothing to do with being sick. "It's a nice feeling," he said. "Sort of like waiting for your birthday to come."

Miss Slater pushed her chair back scrapingly and nearly collided with José, who was bringing me a fresh cup of coffee.

"*Salamat po,*" Kippy shrilled.

José beamed. "That's a smart boy, that kid."

"Ah, he's my pal," Mike said. "Hey, Kip, tell Joe how you say pretty girl."

"*Magandang dalaga,*" Kippy said. "*Ini ibi kita,*" he added.

José rolled his eyes in mock astonishment. Mike winked at me. "See? Pretty girl and he loves her. Kip'll be all right. Kip can keep me company in the radio shack any time."

Kippy looked at Mike with adoration.

At eight o'clock Johnny came down from the watch and slid into place. Kippy reported that I had channel fever. "Oh, that." Johnny smiled. "Two eggs over easy, Joe." He shook out his napkin with a flap and spread it over his knees. "Channel fever, hey? You should've seen how steamed up I was on my first trip around. But hell, after ten years, one port's the same as another." He shrugged. "Manila's just another cargo to work." He began to discuss stevedores with Mike.

The Captain strode into the saloon, and Kippy and he went into their cigarette routine. I felt a little left out, alone in my jitters and excitement.

Before going on deck, I looked once more at the wardroom chart. The route of the day before had been inked in. Now where were we? It was only eight-fifteen. Hours yet before we were scheduled to dock. Dishes rattled in the pantry. Someone down the passageway was stropping a Rolls Razor. A murmur of conversation came from the saloon. An aria from *Madame Butterfly* trilled from Dick's gramophone. The minutes seemed to be passing in slow motion.

I was still staring at the chart when Johnny strolled along and explained that we had passed Cape Bolinao and Palauig Point the night before and were now nearing the Scarface Islands, which we would be passing any minute off to port. He started to walk away and then turned suddenly. "Hey," he said gruffly. "I didn't mean to be a wet blanket this morning. It's really great to see someone all hopped up about coming into port. I wish to hell this was my first taste of the old East." Off he went with his sailor's angling gait. Half way down the passageway he stopped. "Good luck, kid," he called over his shoulder.

I went out on deck. At first I could see nothing but the South China Sea, calmer and greener than it had been earlier. Then a rocky cluster of islands appeared almost magically out of the haze. Craggy and barren, bearded with sooty scrub, the mountains somberly surveyed the sea, a scarf cloud suspended over the highest peak accentuating their jutting harshness. Far away, on a narrow spit of land, I could see a lighthouse, a shining white cube which was blocked from view when a rusty red and black cargo ship steamed by, its Plimsoll mark high off the water. As we sailed closer inshore, land appeared on the starboard side as well. The haze lifted and Bataan Peninsula came as a surprise. All of a sudden there was land—substantial hills, thickly wooded, looking extravagantly green after three weeks at sea.

Crested combers rolled sensuously toward the shore and broke over black rocks in a delicate shower of foam and spray. Beyond, on the astonishingly vivid island slopes, I could see tousled palms and marshy rice fields and sugar-cane plantations, and across the land a sprinkling of pale and tiny thatch huts.

The sounding lead swung past me in a silver arc.

The purser passed out red pasteboard landing tickets.

Kippy tugged me from the rail to go below for lunch.

Just after lunch the engines stopped, a launch swung alongside, and the pilot, immigration officer and quarantine inspector came aboard. The examination of visas, health certificates and passports was reassuringly simple. We started to move toward Manila Bay.

Across the harbor, Manila was a long low sweep of red-roofed white buildings. The water was a brilliant emerald and clouds were outlined like steel in a cobalt-blue sky. Launches and tugs swirled around us. The hulls of foundered Japanese and American battleships pierced the water to thrust their rigging at us like bayonets. The passengers were now all out on deck.

We drifted slowly past the breakwater. Windrift and garbage

floated by. It was half past five by the customs clock tower when
the *Madison* eased into its berth, flanked by the *Straat Makassar,* a
Dutch passenger ship, and a Pacific Far East Line freighter with an
Indian bear trade-mark on its funnel. On either side of us, smokestacks stretched in an erratic line as far as I could see. Plank
shacks, tilting recklessly, perched on the sterns of the loading
barges. Through the door of one of them I could see a mother
suckling her baby, while two children in magenta polo shirts played
tag around a flapping clothes line.

A friend of James's, Paul Wood, a lean, gray-haired man with
an air of authority, bustled Kippy and me down the gangway and
through customs. Then Kippy and I were whisked into a limousine
with white linen seat covers and driven off to a hotel furnished
with all the comforts air conditioning, modern plumbing and
functional furniture provide. I suppose the knowledge that American culture had been firmly rooted in the Philippines for over fifty
years should have prepared me for this, but such was not the case,
and I felt rather let down to have the doors shut so suddenly on
my first glimpse of the East.

Paul treated us to a dinner of local specialties—*lapu-lapu* fish
swimming in a sweet and sour sauce of pimientos, onions and green
peppers; roast suckling pig garlanded with hibiscus; rum-soaked
pineapple—I was certain Kippy would have nightmares all night,
but he didn't.

The following morning, after breakfasting on coffee so permeated
with chicory that I had to drink water instead ("It is boiled, isn't
it?"), and fresh unseeded papaya which I naïvely mistook for a slice
of cantaloupe spread with large-grained caviar, Kippy and I set off
to see what we could of Manila.

As we wandered along colonnaded streets lined with doorless
shops in a city which otherwise seemed structurally like most Western cities, vendors jogged after us rattling trays of shoelaces, candy,
cough drops and combs. Child beggars, many no older than Kippy,
coaxed and wheedled and reached after us with curving hands,
looking at us beseechingly, their eyes luminous, large and dark, like

the eyes of young animals, with only the faintest trace of white beyond the iris.

The streets were crowded with people whose skin tones ranged from shades of creamy bister and buff to cinnamon, bronze and raisin color. There were Chinese women with hair so neatly arranged that it seemed glazed to their heads. There were picture-book Indians wearing geranium-pink turbans and Malays wearing velvet fezzes. And there were many Europeans—a term which outside America and Europe is applied indiscriminately to all whites.

Four small boys, as darkly handsome as Murillo gamins, top-heavy with shining black hair, squatted in a circle on the sidewalk playing dice, looking as if they would be engulfed by the crowd, but the crowd surged up to them, parted infinitesimally, passed them, and closed together again.

I spied some bolts of *piña* cloth in a shopwindow. The cloth was lovely stuff, made from pineapple fiber, filmy and woven with complex and delicate designs, and I bought enough of it for a dress.

"Why didn't you bargain, Mummy?" Kippy asked. "Johnny said you should never buy anything without bargaining first." The sales-girl smiled thinly. For the purchaser's lagniappe, customary in the East, Kippy was given a miniature outrigger.

Lingering in the shop a while to admire the array of tourist merchandise, I experimentally struck a set of Moro gongs. Satisfied that the five small gongs of copper chimed melodiously, I struck the two heavier gongs, which thundered and echoed and flung sound waves at me until I quivered like a tuning fork. Somewhat abashed, I hurried Kippy out of the door as if he were the culprit.

We hailed a jeep-taxi with a dashboard embellished by paper flowers and crucifixes, and we jounced away over cobbled side streets until we came to the wide promenade bordering the harbor. Seen through clumps of graceful palms, the emerald water dotted with launches, steamers, cutters and native outriggers was a tableau that would have achieved the exaggerated perfection of a travel poster had it not been for the scrawny untidiness of the war wrecks. We drove around an old Spanish fort which was now a ruin of plaster and rusting barbed wire, and then we returned to the hotel where the room boys shook their heads over the price I had paid for the *piña* cloth and groaned when the boat Kippy had been given sank on its trial run in the hand basin.

After lunch, Paul drove us on a fast tour of the environs of Manila. At almost every turn there would be a roadside stall massed with oval yellow pomelos, fleshed like grapefruit but sweeter, each segment sealed with white rind so that the fruit was often sold by the slice instead of the whole. We drove past cassava fields and rice *padis* waded in by carabaos with curving horns and protruding hipbones; through little palm jungles where thatched huts standing tall on stilts were secreted; and then out again, as you might come from a tunnel, into parkland fragrant with frangipani and bright with hibiscus.

"I love Manila," Paul said. "People go home to America and say that they're going to retire, but six months later they come back and tell everyone that they're just going to stay for a little while. Two years later they return again to America. The next time they come back, they don't tell anyone. They just arrive without ceremony and settle down and spend the rest of their lives here. Once you've ever lived here, you usually stay. It gets you. The life's easy, you can do as you please, there's no rush, little tension. When you go back to the States you find you can't talk to your old friends any more. They're different, and somehow you're different, and it just doesn't work out. I've tried it."

Two men trudged before us along the dusty road shooting at pigeons, and on the horizon the scaffolding of a new hospital rose like a trial sketch by Mondrian. We stopped for a moment to watch the sun slide from the sky and balance on the crest of a wooded hill—an extravagant, metallic panache. In the distance I could see three small boys marching in single file along the valley path, the leader playing a mouth organ. Its clear, sweet tremolo was suddenly muted as an old man trudged past us driving three belled carabaos before him. The sun slipped behind the hill, the boy with the mouth organ vanished, and the man and his clinking carabaos changed to animated silhouettes as they went on their way with the sound of the bells growing fainter and fainter, the last tinkling notes lingering indefinitely in a stillness broken only by the thrumming of cicadas.

My time in Manila had almost run out. With a surge of acceleration, the car shattered the quiet as Paul turned to race back to the hotel.

I repacked the suitcase, paid the hotel bill. I recited the catechism of departure that was to become so familiar. Have I got my passport? Money? Luggage keys? Travelers' checks? Kippy-go-to-the-bathroom. Kippy-please-tuck-in-your-shirt.

At the quay, the air was filled with a racketing clamor of grinding and wheezing machinery and the din of voices as trucks and trailers were unloaded and cargo was swung aboard. The tumult of sound crashed around us as we said good-by to Paul and followed the porter up the gangway. We sailed late that night, steamed in the morning along the lush green coast of Luzon, and in the afternoon glided into Subic Bay for a brief stop-over.

The jungley hills embracing Subic Bay shimmered in the heat and from them came a heavy exhalation, a curious odor, like the pungent, damp-earth smell of a hothouse. A possible paradise for a shipwrecked sailor, it was hardly the place for an American naval installation, and yet there it was—tankers, floating drydocks, Quonset huts and all.

The base had been laid out with military precision. Quonset huts were centered on rectangles of lawn, and the acacias bordering the avenues were self-consciously equidistant one from the other. The officers' club was an oasis of modern air conditioning, movies every night and a well-stocked bar. Inside the commissaries and the Post Exchanges you could buy ice-cream sodas, milk shakes and whisky out of bond at ridiculously low prices. Here dance tunes bounced brightly out of juke boxes, and scrip, looking for all the world like toy money from a Monopoly set, replaced dollar bills.

Kippy drank Coca-Cola, ate hot dogs and stared at a juke box bubbling with green and lavender lights. We didn't take photographs and we didn't walk on the grass because signs told us not to. We were careful not to get in the way of men in olive-green coveralls who were working against desperate odds with DDT

sprays and pruning shears and motorized lawn mowers to resist
the dominance of the jungle.

In the cabin, Kippy and I lay on our bunks. Even with the vent
and forward port opened wide and the fan on, it was crazily hot.
Kippy stretched out in lax, wet nakedness. I had come back to
the boat to fetch a bottle of citronella, had bathed Kippy and
myself, put on sandals with the intention of getting dressed and,
finding this too much of an effort, had collapsed on the bunk,
spineless and sodden. Perspiration, like a column of insects, cease-
lessly trickled its way down and across my body.

Kippy neither whined nor complained. He assumed the protective
coloration or, rather, the colorlessness of inertia and docilely waited
for me to take notice of him.

"Come on, Kipperoo," I said at last, "let's go get something to
eat."

Heat rose in suffocating layers as we went down to the gangway
on the crew deck. The last of the cargo consigned to the base was
being discharged. Waves of sound, as throbbingly insistent as those
heard in an ether dream, pounded through the ship.

We went down the gangway, onto the quay, and over to the
commissary for a quick and early supper. Then we went to sit on
the sea wall along the path overlooking the bay. Mrs. Fulton
sauntered past us, clinging to the arm of an unknown sailor in
whites. Two men from the naval base walked by from the other
direction, and then we were quite alone.

The sun retired hastily from the sky as it does in the tropics. The
hills were purple waves rising to a crest above the bay immobilized
at the point of breaking. Hardly riffling the surface, a gar fish
propelled itself through the water. The air was hot and heavy; the
sky now plumed with crimson, now shot with gold, tautened with
a parting fiery glow and crumpled into darkness. Night came in a
dark rush.

Immediately beneath us, the bay burned green in the light reflected from the street lamps, the luminous, clear water flickering
with little fish that flittered and skittered with dizzying rapidity
until they trembled past the boundaries of brightness into obscurity.

The moon was fever-bright, its reflection pyramiding from the horizon through the pass in glittering, writhing frenzy across the water. The *Madison* had gone berserk with the heat and had climbed from the bay to rest on wavering pillars of light. Beyond the bay, the water was the black of anthracite, and the sky was the black of velvet of the deepest dye and the thickest texture imbedded with the brilliance of a million stars.

I had seen beautiful nights, ecstatic, tender and tranquil nights, but never a night so vaunting and wanton, a night so ostentatious that it fascinated rather than pleased.

Walking back to the ship, I saw Mrs. Fulton and the sailor lying beneath an acacia tree. I drew Kippy close to me so that he couldn't see what they were doing.

CHAPTER THREE

Hong Kong and the Wickedest City of the Far East

WE LEFT LATE AT NIGHT, and by morning we were centered in a blue-toned world of our own. In unbroken motion the horizon rose above the taffrail, paused for a few seconds and then descended, to rise again with slow deliberation.

The carpenter and the oiler were up on deck for a bit of fresh air. "Angie ain't much for dancing," the oiler was saying. "But you take Margie now, she's okay."

They bobbed their heads toward me. "Morning," they said, as I went by. "How's the little shaver?"

"He's fine," I said.

In the radio shack, in free and cheerful counterpoint with the peremptory ticking of incoming weather reports, Mike was singing the "Jolly Tars' Lament." He had got to the part where

> *Besotted they slump to the floor ah,*
> *Ere they drown in the beer's fatal foam,*

when I passed the screen door.

Below, Johnny was in his cabin with Dick, hunched over a hydrographic chart the size of a small bathroom rug, the two of them muttering about the sun's azimuth and declination. The tape of "Nicolina" unwound from the reels of the recorder. *Yah yike yah heem err air err Nicolina.* Could Swedish really sound like that?

There was a gush of soapy, warm, apple-smelling air from the entrance to the dining saloon where the first mate and the purser were whiling away their coffee break in a discussion of the best places to eat and drink along the coast of the Western Pacific. Kippy was sitting tailor fashion on a banquette in the corner, offering himself cigarettes and gravely refusing them, just for the pleasure of hearing his cigarette box tweedle and deedle.

"He's practicing up for the Captain," the first mate said with a wink. And, yes, sure enough, there was the Captain striding down the corridor.

"Good morning, Kippered herring," said he.

"Good morning, sir. Cigarette, sir?"

"How did you read my mind?" The Captain was joviality itself. "Just what I wanted. . . ."

His voice trailed away as I climbed the companionway to our cabin, where the luggage was ticketed for Hong Kong with yellow labels pranced across by red dragons. After almost a month, the voyage and its calm, simple routine were coming to an end. I felt a gentle and momentary pang of regret when the next day brought the first glimpse of the southeastern coast of China.

We had sailed far enough north for the air to have cooled considerably. The sky was a more temperate blue and, far off on the starboard side, a rind of land appeared, as pale and translucent as porcelain. Ahead of us, a three-masted, square-sterned junk bound for Swatow, one of the sailors said, crossed our track. Silently she glided before us, her chrysanthemum-colored sails billowing and ribbed with bamboo sprits; changing her tack as she passed us, she coursed away to the north. She curved so close that I could see her helmsman, a tiny figure in black pajamas and a conical bamboo hat.

We slipped along slowly, the land taking on substance, and suddenly the sea was heaped with bare, blue islands. Gradually, as the high-centered island of Hong Kong came in sight, the water became winged with the russet sails of fishing junks and the single pink sails of sampans with tiny cabins like barrel halves lying on their sterns. As we sailed close to the mouth of Joss House Bay, thousands of gulls and ospreys flew out to greet us with creaking calls. The cook dumped the garbage overboard for them.

Away to the left, above the starched white ruffle of buildings bordering the mainland, the shadows deepened over the ancient blue hills of Kowloon, and on our right, the British crown colony of Hong Kong reared from the water, proud and typhoon-blown, the lights beginning to wink on in the town at the base of the Peak. As the *Madison* swung into her berth on the Kowloon side, the evening settled swiftly and delicately, and an autumn moon, glowing orange-gold like a poppy, drifted up in the mild night sky.

On our way to the hotel, I looked out the taxi window as wonderingly as though we had just landed on another planet. We were driving along Queen's Road, one of the main thoroughfares, which was choked with traffic. The sidewalks were colonnaded with roofed-over white pillars, the pillars at shop entrances striped with crimson Chinese characters as complex as snow crystals. Overhead were suspended rows of narrow, vertical neon-lighted signs, some ending with a horizontal explanation in English such as Glory Medicine or Hercules Bicycles, and many others untranslated, decorative mysteries. Streams of people in black and blue and white pajamas surged beneath the covered archways, spilling into the street to evade with almost bored indifference the oncoming tide of trolleys, bicycles, cars and rickshaws. Many women wore their hair in single hip-length plaits that swung as they walked. Most women carried babies bound to their backs. I saw one woman untie her baby and hold him out over the gutter. After he had done what he had to, she tied him up again in his cloth sling, very carefully, as if he were an egg that might break. People surged before us and behind us and around us. The musky, moldy, gingery odor that is the pervasive smell of the East clung to my nostrils with the same tenacity that it did later to my clothes and books and luggage. My ears, as though exclusively attuned to the new and foreign, shut out the rattle of the trolleys and the drone of car engines, and registered instead a polytone of chanting Cantonese voices, the *clip-clopping* on the pavement of coolie women's clogs, and shrill Chinese music broadcast, I discovered later, over the Oriental equivalent of Muzak.

When we got to the hotel, the desk clerk said that he had taken the liberty of engaging for us an amah, a servant-nursemaid, who he hoped would be suitable for our needs. She was in our room waiting for us, and when we arrived she immediately began to take off Kippy's clothes and to fold them neatly on a chair. She was twenty-seven years old, minus a year by American count, for the Chinese reckon age from the moment of conception, and her name was Ah Ling.

She was short and slim and wore her coal-colored hair in a lacquered chignon. She had a low, rather flat bosom, a torso disproportionately long for her slightly bowed legs, and a smooth, honey-colored face made immoderately charming by features testifying to the Chinese passion for small, delicate, harmonious details. She was dressed in white, pencil-striped pajamas, the jacket fastened at the side with little looped embroidery frogs, the sleeves cuffed back to show fine-boned wrists and quite the most beautiful hands and nails I had ever seen.

She fixed her eyes solemnly on me. "Missy tired? Missy want tea?"

She pressed the bell for the "loom boy," who came padding to the door in plump-footed black silk slippers. Tea and fruit were quickly brought, and I signed a chit for them, getting a nice sense of joy from watching the room boy add up the bill in Chinese. Ah Ling peeled a mango for me in one long, even paring, letting the skin spiral and fall into glinting circles on my plate.

While I was eating, she bathed Kippy and put him to bed. I sat back in a wicker armchair watching her move about the room, regally and gracefully, beginning now to unpack my things, putting clothes away in the bureaus, hanging up clothes in the armoire, laying aside the laundry and the sewing. I picked up a cigarette and Ah Ling was there with a match, and the ashtray had a wet tissue folded in it so that the ashes wouldn't blow.

Ah Ling went home about ten and returned the next morning about seven, bringing with her a bamboo suitcase containing her toothbrush, soap, comb and a change of clothing. She pulled back the curtains, opened the jalousies, and ran me a bath liberally laced with a disinfectant solution called Dettol. She warned me not to drink the tap water and pointed out the carafe of boiled water that was to be used for teeth-brushing purposes.

Breakfast was wheeled in by a different room boy from the one of the previous evening, this one elderly and given a rather sinister appearance by a wart on his cheek sprouting four hairs easily an inch long. There is a tenet of Confucius which states that hair belongs to one's parents and therefore must not be cut off, and an unshaved wart, like the outmoded pigtail, is a symbol of filial piety and ancestor worship much in evidence in southern China. Not knowing this at the time, I saw the beetle of brown skin clinging to his cheekbone as a blemish quite in keeping with the villainous character I supposed him to be. I couldn't have been more wrong. This room boy, like all the other room boys—and there must have been dozens of them to the floor—turned out to be pleasant and solicitous and bloomed with friendliness when Kippy asked him to teach him Cantonese.

The room boys delighted me. They coached me in the fine art of bargaining and patiently tried to teach me Cantonese, and they were ever ready to bring bowls of fruit and fresh carafes of water. They appeared with such alacrity that it was as though the buzzer sprang a trap to release them on the threshold, like marbles in a pinball machine. My clothes were swept away to be washed, pressed and returned in a matter of hours; my shoes were polished; everything was done for my comfort with no suggestion from me, and it was done almost playfully, as though it weren't a chore at all. This was my first taste of the fabled service of the East, and I liked it. Being waited upon hand and foot required no apology, no explanatory aside, only the acceptance and the knowledge that it was all *de rigueur* and dirt cheap (Ah Ling's wages, for instance, amounted to about eighty cents a day). I felt too light-headed and too comfortable to reflect philosophically on the social implications of cheap labor.

I loved Hong Kong, the island and the town. The town is officially called Victoria, but this is a name which appears only on maps and in guidebooks, and, for its size, the town retains a curious anonymity, being rarely referred to by any name but that of its island matrix, a name meaning Fragrant Lagoon, pronounced nasally, Cantonese fashion, as Hawng Kawng.

The broad, level streets of the town run parallel to the shore and are cut across by steep and narrow lanes that wind up the hillsides and come to a halt at a respectful distance from the first level of small villas, garden-fortified bungalows and apartment buildings housing government personnel. As the buildings sidle from the volcanic promontories toward the high center of the island, they become larger and grander. Only the rich can afford to live on Taipan Row and the Peak.

The area around and about our hotel was also *taipan* territory. By eight, dressed in gleaming sharkskin suits, most of the *taipans* were down from their hills ready to conduct the day's business from the baroque administrative offices, the neo-Hellenic houses of commerce, and the banks along the bourse of Queen's Road, Connaught and Des Voeux, where the shops were freighted with an exquisite cargo of jade, ivory, porcelain, rosewood, rose quartz and brocade.

Hong Kong has the most wonderful shops in the world, and in every section of the city I found pleasing things to behold—a caged myna bird in a firecracker shop; smoking wands of incense at almost all the doorways; a shop in Upper Lascar Row selling nothing but ink and brushes, the ink made of pine soot and gum in thick, gilded sticks, and the brushes made of camel's hair stuck into bamboo reeds; the animal and bird market near Mercer Street where you could buy lemurs and crickets and doves; the ivory chops or seals that the Chinese use as name stamps (with the blandest of flattery a chop vendor assured me that the Cantonese translation of my name was *Beautiful Flower*); shops that sold ancestor portraits, each portrait a seated figure with elaborate robes and a blank face to be filled in with features to the purchaser's liking; shops selling white-soled silk slippers (I couldn't resist buying a pair and was not a little disconcerted when Ah Ling told me that this was footwear reserved only for corpses); shops selling coats of Swatow embroidery woven with Buddhist emblems—the supply of pleasure was inexhaustible.

Watching the merchants click up the total of my purchases on their abacuses, I never quite got over the feeling that it was all part of a charming, conspiratorial jest—that somewhere in a back room they had made their computations using ordinary Western numbers and a scratch pad.

I wondered, of course, as every foreigner must, at the food. Centuries of famine and overpopulation have driven the Chinese to experimental extremes in nourishment which originally must have been abhorrent but which are now acceptable and, in many cases, delicacies for the refined Chinese palate. I found there were readily available in the market such things as sharks' fins, dried swifts' nests, stuffed lotus roots, dried lilies, dried bats, dehydrated tentacles of squid, black seaweed and trepangs that looked like fossilized caterpillars—the *béches de mer* I had heard so much about. There were flat, salted ducks lacquered a bright red. There were cockroaches and locusts preserved in sirup. There were also three kinds of eggs: small, but quite ordinary hen's eggs; duck eggs preserved in lime, aged for a hundred days, not years, as I had previously been told; and duck eggs cured by salting which had chooey-booey red and white insides. Nevertheless, apart from eccentric extremes, I prefer Chinese food to French—it's prettier, the flavor is more subtle, and it's much less fattening.

The autumn days were warm, but early in the morning and late at night the wind was sharp and chilly. Ah Ling had only one sweater, and having noticed that when she washed it she had to go without it until it dried, I gave her a sweater of mine. She in turn gave Kippy a bamboo and paper kite. I was astonished at the kite's unfolded splendor. It was a dragon, eight feet long and, like everything the Chinese made, of superlative craftsmanship. The best place of all for kite-flying is the Peak, and so one morning we took the little funicular train to the top. As Kippy let the string unwind, the dragon soared into the air, the wind swishing its tail and moving its paws and fluttering its bright red tongue. There were other children with kites like centipedes and like goldfish, but the dragon was by far the most spectacular kite in the sky. For a moment we all stood together, Ah Ling with her toes pointing in, Kippy with his toes pointing out, the three of us silently enchanted. Then Kippy began to run tirelessly back and forth, with the dragon galloping above him. Ah Ling and I settled ourselves on a stone wall to watch. Near by, there was a bauhinia tree full of deep pink flowers, and hiding in its fragrant podded depths, bulbuls, the Oriental nightingales, trilled and trilled.

Like a landscape on a painted scroll, each register of the perspective seemed equally important, equally charming: Ah Ling glancing watchfully at Kippy; the absurd baronial mansions on the hill slopes; here and there the crimson of a flame-of-the-forest tree or the tender green of a clump of bamboo; the town; the harbor; and the mountains of the mainland that by evening would have changed from red-brown to shimmering blue.

I thought I had never seen a lovelier place than Hong Kong, with its autumnal radiance, its tininess opening out to space, the water always fanning away; hills and water, a lovely sense of space and traveling distances on all sides. To the west were the harbor and the mainland; to the east, the bays—Stanley, Repulse and Deepwater—and between them and the long, wide stretch of the South China Sea, an island-studded channel, and always sailing past, close by or silhouetted on the horizon, a high-sterned junk with billowing sails.

Kippy was in tears when the string broke and the dragon kite drifted into the sky out of sight. As a consolation, he was promised an afternoon at the Tiger Balm Gardens. The Gardens, the enterprise of Aw Boon Haw, a patent medicine tycoon who had amassed millions of Hong Kong dollars from the sale of a mentholated salve called Tiger Balm (especially recommended for bunions, asthma, dysentery and tuberculosis), were whimsically decorated with statuary—painted phoenixes, chimeras, dragons and baleful monkey gods —and further tricked out with mazes, grottoes, pagodas and humpbacked bridges across water-lily ponds—the whole extraordinary shebang swarming with shoeshine boys.

Kippy rarely could be coaxed from the frescoes that depicted the fates in the hereafter of the blessed and the damned—mostly the damned—opium smokers, gamblers, voluptuaries, gluttons, thieves and murderers, all of whom were shown being whipped, beheaded, disemboweled by fiends, dismembered, roasted on spits, devoured by tigers and tortured by other horrifying means.

Believing that each religion has its value and subscribing impartially to the doctrines of Lao-tse, Buddha, Christ and Confucius, the Chinese had acquired a terrifying interdenominational Hell, and the pictorialization of it was certainly not for the squeamish. For Kippy, the murals had the wonderful fascination of the forbidden: they were the synthesis of all the horror comics I had ever withheld. These sensationally graphic murals also had a great fascination for the Chinese, and whenever I visited the gardens I saw groups of people standing about them laughing uproariously. I had been told that the Chinese regard laughter as a protective medium through which an emotional balance can be sustained. Intellectually, I'm ready to admit there is much to be said for this concept; but in practice (Ah Ling, for instance, chuckling over the spectacle of a man being hacked to bits by a meat cleaver) I found it faintly disturbing.

Not in the mood to see the gardens, I said that I would go along with Kippy and Ah Ling as far as the entrance and that I would then go back to town by myself.

Near the hotel was a line of down-tilted rickshaws with their pullers alertly squatting between the handle shafts. Ah Ling and Kippy took the first rickshaw in line. I took the second. My rickshaw boy helped me into the narrow seat, thrust the cedarwood fan he had been waving before his face down the back of his collar, grasped the handle shafts and jogged after the other rickshaw. His legs were thin, and as he paced along the veins wriggled beneath his muscle-swollen calves like little blue adders.

We turned down a narrow road lined with the dark, spicy-smelling caverns of carpenters in sandalwood, where laundry impaled on bamboo poles thrust from upper windows provided an overhead population of fluttering scarecrows, and where at the corner there were two blind beggars, one with a three-stringed violin, the other with a tiny drum suspended on a worn-out bandolier.

We came to Causeway Bay, a cove used as a typhoon shelter for fishing junks and sampans. Farther along, up on the bank, were refugees from Red China who lived in a rubbishy mess of mats and rubble thrown together into a squatters' encampment, and beyond these pustular shacks glittered the pagodas and the painted phoenixes of the Tiger Balm gardens.

I waved good-by to Kippy and Ah Ling and asked the rickshaw boy to turn back and take me to Wanchai. He bit the tip end from a black watermelon seed, pushed it farther into his mouth, tongued out the shell and smiled the appeasing smile of one who wants to understand but doesn't. After circling several times and stopping at various wrong destinations, I was set down where I wished. Wanchai, the raffish quarter of Hong Kong minus a red-light district's customary guilty archness, whether seen at night in the glare of kerosene lamps or during the day in clear sunlight, is a place teeming with people, a place of almost stunning vivacity.

There were any number of ambulant kitchens peddling congee, a rice gruel odorous with salted fish.

There were sugar-cane vendors and purveyors of lethal-looking balls of mashed lotus seeds.

There were herbalists with their wares set out on the pavement before them: dried snakeskin for rheumatism; powdered deers' horn and dried sea horses for circulatory ailments; rhinoceros horn for boils; sandalwood chips and the bottled gall of boa constrictors for asthma; and to add an up-to-date element to their merchandise, a few tins of Tiger Balm.

There were astrologers, palmists, diviners and phrenologists. Seated before sandwich boards and back cloths of astrological charts and magnified sketches of eyes and hands and jigsaw-puzzle skulls, these soothsayers met the demand for the revelation of the future and predicted auspicious and unlucky days in the horoscopes of the prostitutes, pimps, thieves, coolies, bunny-suited schoolchildren and servant girls who pressed about them.

I quickly acquired a waist-high convoy of children whose narrow eyes, set shallowly under faint little eyebrows, followed me intently wherever I went. With upper lashes hidden beneath the full Mongoloid epicanthic fold, their eyes were defenseless as they gazed up at me, their expressions sober and curious as though I were a magician on trial at a party.

Together with my entourage, I strolled through the clamorous streets, stopping to listen to coolies chanting something that sounded like the "Volga Boat Song" as they hoisted bamboo scaffolding into place; stopping to have my skirt patched where a hole had been burned in it by a smoking stick of incense; stopping to watch a game of mah-jongg. There were four men playing, all with the classic features of ancient philosophers, high cheekbones, wispy white beards and creased foreheads. As they selected their ivory-coated tiles marked with the suits of flowers and seasons and bamboo, or threw the dice, or delightedly laid down a set, their faces were beautifully happy, their features composed in an expression of infinite wisdom and spiritual serenity. This expression is marvelously common among the aging Chinese, who truly believe that their declining years are their best.

It was a long time before the crowds thinned and I was in familiar territory, walking past the imperial, curlicued marble lions of the Hong Kong and Shanghai Bank and the severe, rectangular-toothed lions of the People's Bank of Red China. At both banks, the bushy-bearded Sikh watchmen on duty had fallen asleep on their wooden Indian cots.

That week I met a Chinese journalist who had Westernized his name to John Chiu, or a name much like it. He had endeavored to Westernize his personality as well, but I suspected that some quality of the original had been lost in the process, for he had a manner so good-natured, a deportment so irreproachable, an intent to please so determined that he often assumed the one-faceted aspect of a character in a morality play enacting the role of Amiable Sociability.

Shortly after I had met him he took me for a day's outing in the New Territories so that I could get a general idea of the Chinese countryside. We started off early in the morning and drove onto the Star Ferry to cross the harbor to Kowloon. Once away from the ugly industrial settlement of Kowloon, we climbed into hills of bristly scrub that rolled away to steeper hills terraced with a patchwork of vegetable gardens seamed with gray stone and came out on an escarpment high above a swarm of fishing junks sheltered in Tide Cove. The boats below looked bright and silvery, the beach thin and fawn colored, and the wind blew up the scent of the sea to mingle with the smell of the road's damp earth.

After a while, the road curved inland through an uncluttered landscape delicately sketched in subdued colors. The hills had dived underground and reappeared worn, old and somber in the distance, footed with long spinneys of dark banyans and rosewood. On either side of the road, black-trousered Hakka women were helping their men plow and harrow dry rice *padis* to make them ready for planting. Seen from the roadside, the women were distinguishable from the men only by their headgear, for while the men wore knobby-crowned, wide-brimmed coolie hats of plaited bamboo, the women had cut the crown from theirs, replaced it with a piece of black cloth, and trimmed the brim with a loose and broad black ruffle, the effect being the inappropriate but not unbecoming one of garden-party frivolity.

There were a few rice *padis* that had been harvested up which had not dried up, and in these, domestic carabaos wallowed and snortled. Audacious ricebirds perched on their shoulders, and sometimes, hopeful for a frog or a rat, there would be a pond heron or two nearby. Pensive and preening, the herons stood about on one frail long leg, rubbing their bills against their fluffy white breasts. They were large birds with reddish heads and necks, and were beautiful when they flew away on slow-beating wings.

The road ribboning ahead was planted with candlenut and spider trees, and there was always a walking, black-clad figure in sight— a Hakka woman shouldering a carrying pole stuck with two enormous pompons of hay; a minute child, his head shaved except for a center tuft, making his way in skipping staggers under the weight of a wicker net filled with cabbages; a man with a bundle of sugar cane on his back and a hen in a bamboo cage slung over one arm— goblin-sized creatures beneath the pale blue of the sky, a sky so high that the car we sat in seemed no larger than a tortoise.

The landscape, all grays and blues and muted browns and greens, was occasionally flecked with the bright color of a pond-side clump of pink lotus, or by a parakeet in the bare branches of a spider tree. Once an exquisite yellow butterfly alighted on the windshield wiper and was blown away. Once we saw a red bird preening itself among the waxy blossoms of a wild plum tree. In a few small villages glided over by magpies there was a murmur of color from the fly-mottled fruit in the market place, and the tiny bursts of brilliance where the sun struck a tin pail or a brass bowl, but generally, away from the villages all was visually quiet. The road unfurled across land that was chaste and strangely definite in its understated beauty, and came to an end—for me, at any rate—with the black and white striped gates and sentry boxes, the barbed-wire barricades and the uniformed guards stationed at the border of Communist China.

John had another attractive suggestion to put forward. Later in the week he was going to Macao. Did I want to come along? I did. The idea of going to this Portuguese island colony of vice and opium intrigued me, but the getting there had been problematic. If Macao was, as it was acclaimed, the wickedest city in the Far East, it was hardly the place to take Kippy, and, thinking ahead to lonely, embarrassingly suspect meals in restaurants, I hadn't particularly wanted to go there on my own. John, who made frequent pilgrimages to Macao to see a Eurasian dance hostess with whom he had a comfortable and convenient arrangement, was just the escort I had in mind—a pleasant male, helpful, unobtrusive and preoccupied.

The morning we were to go, I was awakened by the sound of Ah Ling singing in Chinese the saddest of the three songs she usually sang while giving Kippy his morning bath. Not that the songs were actually sad; they weren't. One was about two fighting grasshoppers, another was about the dragon-boat festival, and this one, a mournful crooning quavering that never quite was resolved, had to do with the joys of eating meat dumplings and bean sprouts. When I watched Ah Ling, I could tell the song was happy—the humorous tranquillity of her eyes, the smile lifting the corners of her mouth, hooking it up like a little pink hammock—the arrangement of her features transposed the key of what she was singing from minor to major. But as I sat up in bed, the disembodied song came to me only as a lament accompanying the early morning shadows of passers-by scissoring along the laddered stairs beyond the balcony window.

The terrace doors were open, and the soft, smoky air bubbled past the blue portière curtains and blew gently about the room. The laundry lists had been blown from the desk, and I got out of bed to pick them up. Even in laundry lists the artistry of the Chinese was reflected. On slips of paper columned from right to left, my dresses and Kippy's shirts appeared as masterpieces of intricate penmanship. I could tell what was what from the numbers alongside. I knew the Chinese numerals from one to ten because they were inscribed on the telephone dial. Four and five were the nicest—four was like a child's drawing of a curtained window, and five was a bird standing on a top hat, although Kippy thought it looked more like a television antenna.

Leaving Kippy in Ah Ling's lap listening to a story about the Mo, an animal that eats up bad dreams, I set out with John for the iniquities of Little Portugal.

The coastal ferry that was to take us there, the motor vessel *Tai Loy*, was scheduled to leave at ten in the morning. Time being the flexible matter it is in the Orient, we left closer to noon. The *Tai Loy* was small, painted a dazzling white, and armed against pirates with guns and an iron net spread around and across the top deck. To my dismay, she was also equipped with a public-address system that was blasting forth "You Are My Sunshine" when we first climbed aboard.

A tally man was collecting number sticks from a procession of coolies working to unload bottle-necked baskets filled with dried fish from the junk on our left. A group of women with babies tied to their backs had formed a human chain to pass along trays of cucumbers and red peppers from another junk to a truck waiting farther on down the line. On either side of us, fishing and cargo junks huddled to the quay side, clapping slowly against the water, showing bleached gray hulls and a tangle of tall masts and archaic rigging.

The deck of the junk to our right was heaped with iron-bound crates, burlap sacks, gasoline drums and plaited bamboo hampers; a pig was tethered to the mainmast; squawking chickens were caged on the stern, and the single clear space on deck had been spread with newspapers and set aside as the field of operations for a mah-jongg game. The players crouched over the rectangular ivory pieces, apparently unconcerned that they were plunk in the middle of traffic. A young girl stepped as delicately as a cat around them, moving back and forth with dirty clothes which she attached to a hooked bamboo pole and swished about in the water; the clothes were hauled in, looking miraculously clean, and hung on the rigging.

Four children, none over a yard high, and one barely walkable, frisked and tumbled about the crates and hampers, and for one

dreadful moment the baby looked as though he would topple
from a gasoline drum and fall into the circle of mah-jongg players.
The players remained imperturbable, just as if they knew he would
be rescued by one of the other children, grabbed around his naked
bottom and lugged off in the nick of time.

The game was interrupted when one of the players got up to
make use of an open privy jutting over the gunwale. Anticipating
his purpose, he rolled up the leg of his wrap-around black trousers
as he left the game to cross the deck. I was still new enough in the
East to be mildly startled by these deviations from Western con-
ventions of privacy. I had been more startled to discover that for
all their exquisite civilization the Chinese had none of our evasive
refinements of conversation, none of our reticences, none of our
unmentionables. That morning, for example, I had asked John
how he was.

"Not too good," he said. "I've a hemorrhoid that's been acting
up." And then, lapsing into his pre-Westernized character, eager
as only an Oriental can be to discuss a physical liability, he had
gone on to give me an intimate medical account of the cause and
cure of his ailment. Afterward, it had taken an effort on my part
to think of him in any but this context, and at a loss for nonclinical
conversation, I had turned my attention to the mah-jongg players
on the neighboring junk.

The game had been finished, the pieces shuffled rattlesomely and
another game begun when "Anchors Aweigh" blared from the
public-address system, and at the same time the *Tai Loy* hooted and
began to back off from the quay. The tall masts of the junks merged
together, saw-toothed rudders blurred beneath patterned sterns,
and almost without knowing it, we were out in the harbor. We
sailed due west into the South China Sea, slipping between Cheung
Chau Island and the headlands of twin-humped Lantao, and then
we were outside the Bocca Tigris, the wide lower mouth of the
Pearl River, for centuries the crossroads of a rich river and sea
traffic in silk and tea and opium.

A few wooded islands appeared. A portly comprador in a white
drill suit, who had been silently sipping a gimlet and studying the
South China Post folded back to the shipping pages, looked up and
pointed them out to me. They were piratical strongholds, he said,

as well as the sites for Communist gun emplacements. So far, the Communists had fired upon only three ships for sailing too close to the islands, but the pirates attacked frequently. Only the day before, a ferry bound for Hong Kong had been looted and several passengers killed. The few other passengers about received this information with the indifference of good Taoists. I seemed to be the only person who was not a fatalist, and I was certainly the only one who showed relief—I could feel the muscles in my face relaxing —when there were no signs of forthcoming aggression.

We put into the Porto Interior of Macao in the middle of the afternoon and moored between two black-canopied brothel boats from Canton that appeared to be deserted. For a town which profits hugely from the smuggling of gold, opium, arms and ammunition, a town famous as a sink of iniquity, Macao seemed curiously innocent, a little, fair Mediterranean-looking town with villas of flaking pink, white, blue and yellow plaster shaded by the wavy boughs of big, dark trees. Back from the quilted blue silk of the harbor, the ruins of old chapels and the moldering culverins of crumbling forts were peaceful and sun-warmed, the basking places for velvety geckos with eyes that never closed. There was a garden with black-crested bulbuls and sparrows flying through it, where Camoëns was supposed to have written the *Lusiad* sixty years after Vasco da Gama, besting the Adamastor, the dreadful phantom of the Cape of Good Hope, had discovered a new route to India.

In the town, cobbled alleys and wide *avenidas* centered with the diamond spray of fountains were named for Portuguese saints and heroes. But the blood that coursed through these arteries, the blood that gave life to the island and to the town, was pure Chinese.

Along the *avenidas*, coolies pedaled bicycle rickshaws around the marble pomp of statues of Portugal's great men, and the Sacred Heart College, conducted by Canossian nuns, was flanked by a Chinese bazaar. The squalor of a refugee squatter's camp encroached upon the grounds of a Dog's Home; and there was a confusing propinquity of firecracker factories and monasteries, incense-stick factories and orphanages, churches and joss houses. Where the businesslike Chinese had converted villas into stores, bamboo awnings painted with vermilion ideographs hung from the wrought-iron complicacies of early nineteenth-century balconies, and the bright-colored splash of these cryptic signs was giddily incongruous against a backdrop of fading rose and amber façades.

This was the operative incongruity of Macao, the commingling of the European old with the Oriental new, decrepitude and vitality fusing together as pleasantly as the tinkling shrill of bicycle-rickshaw bells and the sound of clocks chiming in broken church towers. In the drowsing afternoon, Macao was believably what the guidebook said—an island of peculiar charm, and the ideal place for a quietly entertaining holiday. Then the darkness, so quick to come in the East, leaped down.

I returned to the hotel, where I had left my suitcase, had a bath, dressed and went down to the lobby, where a few dapper Chinese were fanning themselves with bamboo fans, not so much to keep cool but as a practical measure against swarms of flies and mosquitoes. I waited for John and his dance-hostess friend to show up.

They came at last, John leading the way, followed by a sulky-looking girl in green satin whom he introduced as Miss Fereira. She gazed at me appraisingly. My jewelry was not as sumptuous as hers, my nails not as long or so brilliantly painted, my dress of a duller color and a less extravagant cut. Miss Fereira permitted herself a thin little smile. And then the three of us went outside into the dusty night-glitter of the street.

"Where shall we go?" John asked. "A Portuguese place?"

"Oh, no," Miss Fereira protested. "Why don't you take us to Fat Siu Lan's? The food's so different there."

"All right," John said, hailing two bicycle-rickshaws. "All right, Fat Siu Lan's."

From her tone and from his, I presumed that Fat Siu Lan's was expensive and wrongly supposed that it would turn out to be a clip joint with nothing to recommend it but the cachet of expensiveness.

Bicycle bells shrilling, our rickshaws joined the company of other rickshaws rattling along the principal thoroughfare of the Avenida Almeida Ribeiro. At a corner, solemnly regarded by a plaster bust of an unsmiling saint, we turned and headed down another avenue. The faces of pedestrians were ghastly in the whitish glare of the street lamps, the banyans lining the way frenzied by the wind blowing from the sea, and all at once the town seemed strangely malignant. We turned from the broad *avenida* into a narrower street, and from the street into a lane, and from the lane into Rua da Felicidado, an alleyway between cavernous stone shelters, a hellish little Street of Happiness inhabited by prostitutes costing two patacas (about thirty cents) an hour.

Soliciting for them were foul old women who set up a maniacal shrieking the moment our rickshaws came in sight. As there was only a flapping curtain before each entrance hole, the coupling taking place inside the shelters was carried on unhidden from passers-by. To be certain that I should miss nothing of this dreadful show, the rickshaw boy stopped pedaling, pointed to a cavern where the cotton curtain had been blown completely aside, and roared with laughter from the sheer prurient amusement of it all.

Mercifully, Rua da Felicidado branched off into a cobbled lane, and it was here that the establishment of Fat Siu Lan was located, a dilapidated three-storied wooden house given the appearance of a pet shop by the piled-up cages and tanks outside containing lobsters, turtles, mice, monkeys, poultry, fish and snakes. Three shaven-headed children, scarcely bigger than dolls, were poking a straw through the interstices of a cobra's cage. After having told them not to—much to their delight—I stepped around buckets of excreta and a barrelful of garbage placed for collection, and followed John and Miss Fereira inside.

To the left of the first landing of a steep and shaking flight of stairs was the kitchen, a square room with a mammoth coal stove built of brick and tile. Two cookboys in blood-stained aprons stood side by side at a center table and slivered frog meat and bean sprouts into matching shreds, while another helper, with the same painstaking accuracy, measured a smidgin of ginger against a candareen weight resting on the pan of a brass scale.

Unaware of the gastronomic surprises in store, I continued up the stairs to the private dining rooms (the Chinese shun the barbarous custom of eating before strangers) and found myself in the midst of a great brouhaha. John had run into a friend of his, the kingpin of the local firecracker industry. The Kingpin had already ordered a slap-up dinner for himself and eight friends, and he insisted that we join them.

The eight friends, all shouting jovially, swarmed into the corridor and swept us through a beaded curtain into a room festooned for the occasion with ropes of multicolored paper flowers. The room was hot and smoky. A naked light bulb and a push-button bell dangled on two long wires twisted together from the center of the ceiling, and as I came in, someone rang the bell, pushing it in a way that caused it and its companion light bulb to swing back and forth, the penduluming bulb filling the room with rocking shadows.

A covey of attractive singsong girls floated forward with trays of melon seeds and almonds. Other singsong girls materialized with butterfly pianos which they hammered with drumsticks to produce a gonging con brio, a form of music so unfamiliar that it didn't appeal to me in the least.

A small boy with a face as flat as a kitten's wandered from guest to guest rattling a begging-box. Around his neck was a placard which said, "Ladies and gentlemen and soldiers and sailors, through no fault of mine I am an orphan. Please give me money. Thank you."

I helped myself to some melon seeds, and then wished I hadn't because the husks were as much of a problem to get rid of as olive pits. There were spittoons provided just for this exigency—large brass affairs embossed with dragons and peonies—but I couldn't bring myself to use them. Somewhat self-consciously, I balled the wet husks in my hand and dropped them from the window.

Glasses were briskly filled and emptied and the finger game was played to determine who should pay for the next round. The finger game is more or less like the nursery sport of wood-paper-scissors-stone done to the count of ten in Mandarin and ending with a lot of mysterious finger waggling by the participants. The chorus bears no trace of the unmeasured rhythms and the intonational vagaries associated with Eastern music. On the whole, I thought it sounded like what you find yourself, or at least I find myself shouting at a football game.

Since no one spoke to me, I stood by one of the singsong girls and stared with mindless fascination at the flexible drumsticks whirring against the wires of the zitherlike butterfly piano. The

drumsticks were tipped with triangular pads and looked as if they
would make perfectly functional shoe trees.

A man on my left offered me a gimlet and a card that identified
him as Li Fook Wo, a director of the Au Pit Seng Trading Company and the vice-president of the Hang Tai Match Factory. "What
brings your husband to the East?" he asked. I said that I had no
husband, that I was just traveling about with my young son.

"Ah," he said thoughtfully, fingering a gold Parker pen clipped
to his breast pocket. "Do you want to sell your passport?"

No, I didn't, I said, pleased as Punch to have been mistaken for
an adventuress and quite unconcerned with his suggestion, which
was too disconnected from reality even to bother thinking about.

"Well, if you change your mind, let me know," Mr. Wo said—or
perhaps his name was Mr. Li: the Chinese have a baffling practice
of reversing the customary order of given names and surnames.

"You're sensible not to sell your passport in Macao," said the
gentleman on *his* left. "You can get double for it in Bangkok. Permit me to give you the name of a friend of mine."

"Please don't bother," I said quickly. I was sorry to give up my
short-lived role as an adventuress, but it was beginning to make me
feel uncomfortable. "I really don't want to sell my passport at all."
Was it my fancy, or did Mr. Wo wink at me? "I'm sure that we can
more than meet any Bangkok offers," he murmured.

I saw a wolfish old man, fat and mincing, like a doll on an
elastic string, walk over to Miss Fereira and pat her on the bottom.
He was a *ham sup lo,* she told me later—a Cantonese slang word
which, literally translated, means a wet and salty one.

We sat down finally at a large round table spread with a plastic
cover on which had been placed ivory chopsticks, porcelain soup
spoons, small dishes of soy sauce and at each place a rice bowl, a
soup bowl and a shallow bowl for bones. The singsong girls laid
aside their butterfly pianos and, stationing themselves behind us in
demure and smiling complaisance, wiped our hands and brows
with steaming almond-scented towels.

Tea was served, brewed in individual lidded cups, pale green Iron
Goddess tea from Fukien. Everyone agreed that it was excellent,
perfectly cured and with a fragrance far superior to that of the
Dragon Well and chrysanthemum varieties. Presumably for my

benefit, some talk about the weather in English followed, and then the conversation was resumed in Cantonese.

Snake soup was served next, and since it would have been disgracefully rude to have refused it, I sipped at the verbena-perfumed broth and tried to overlook the parings of yellow-striped snakeskin swimming about my spoon. The broth had an odd, almost pleasant taste. Although the snakeskin strips undulating in the bowl killed any enjoyment I might have had from it, I managed to keep up the pretense of eating until the waiter came to take the bowls away.

The guests, murmuring approval, picked judiciously at subsequent dishes of fried shrimp and glistening coral-colored lima beans. In deference to me as the only foreigner present, the choicest morsels were pinced together with chopsticks and courteously deposited in my bowl. Until I had almost eaten the last of them, I didn't realize that the lima beans were newborn mice coated with honey.

Then in came a blue and white rice-patterned platter heaped with transparent globules resembling giant Vitamin A capsules. With the suppressed pride of one offering a soup tureen of caviar, the Firecracker Kingpin identified these as brandied snakes' eggs. Marvelous for one's glands. "The best you can buy," John sang out fulsomely to me from the other end of the table. "They're imported from Singapore."

I shall throw up, I thought, I shall certainly throw up if I eat one, but I ate two, swallowing them whole, and nothing happened except that for the rest of the evening I was haunted by the idea that they were going to hatch inside me.

There were successive courses of roast pigeon, ricebirds and abalones, and the excellence of these, combined with a taste of the hot rice wine everyone was drinking, gave me, for the first time in the evening, a momentary sense of well-being. After each course tea was rebrewed, and the handmaidens performed their swabbing operations with steaming towels.

I comforted myself with the thought that the worst was over and helped myself to some more chopped abalones. The beaded curtains were pushed aside, and a waiter padded in carrying before him a monkey in a basket. The monkey, wedged so tightly in the oval-shaped basket that only its wrinkled, rather querulous little face was showing, was passed about the table for our inspection. I surmised that we were in for some sort of entertainment, although I hadn't expected to see a performing monkey. When the subtle intelligence of the Chinese is expended upon amusement, a trick animal is just not the sort of thing you expect.

I waited for the monkey to dance or whatever it was going to do, but instead the waiter sliced off the top of its head with a meat cleaver. The monkey gave a dying scream, twitched for a few seconds, and its basket was then set in the middle of the table. Everyone stood to scoop a teaspoon of steaming brains from its grisly half-head.

I went back to Hong Kong, to my large, clean, bright room, with the curtains blowing and the steps outside laddering up to the base of the Peak and Ah Ling's gentle voice saying, "Missy tired? Missy want fruit?"

I am an indiscriminate eater of fruit, and after I had eaten all the lichee nuts there were in the fruit bowl—not as greedy as it sounds, because these stark little balls, halfway between the prickly cup of a thistle and a strawberry, have little to them except a sweet slippery coating for a largish pit—I dug into a big green custard apple with a soft, creamy inside that I could eat with a spoon.

Ever since I discovered that I had been using Ah Ling's toothbrush instead of my own, my germ-consciousness had evaporated, and I suppose that I must have carelessly eaten a bit of contaminated fruit skin, for I promptly came down with enteric fever.

After two weeks I was able to get up and walk around the block, and by the end of the month I made arrangements to go on by cargo boat to Siam.

On our last day in Hong Kong, Ah Ling gave me a tissue-wrapped package. In it was a brass dragon with a bell on the tip of its tail for Kippy, and for me there was a silk-covered jewelry box embroidered with swags of plum blossoms and a prancing phoenix.

Ah Ling said very carefully, as though she had rehearsed it many times, "These are for Missy and the little master so you may limember Hom Koms and your Ah Ling, and so you may liturn vay soon."

CHAPTER FOUR

Bangkok, the City of the Gods

THE *Szechuen* was a small coastal vessel with a British master and a Chinese crew. Having completed the circuit of Japanese ports, she was now bound for Bangkok and Singapore carrying a crowd of Chinese deck passengers, a few passengers traveling first class and eleven hundred tons of cargo that included two and a quarter tons of fountain pens, one ton of harmonicas, a quarter of a ton of "Night Skin" prophylactics, a quarter of a ton of glass syringes (presumably for heroin addicts), and an assorted tonnage of portable gramophones, cotton piece goods, hat ribbon, spark plugs, desk fans, hair nets, calendars, sun glasses, sewing machines, bicycle parts and iron plate.

Having expected to meet a mixed bag of talkative characters straight out of Somerset Maugham, I was depressed to find that besides Kippy and myself the only other first-class passengers were two French Catholic nuns traveling to Macassar, and a pockmarked Chinese trader bound for Singapore. If they had tales to tell, the opportunity never presented itself to tell them. The nuns, clinging to each other and trailing a scent of soap and camphor, emerged from their cabin only to walk about the deck, and never set foot in the dining saloon. The trader, isolated at mealtimes at a separate table because the Captain believed him to be of an inferior race, slept most of the day on deck in a hammock chair.

Kippy was the only child aboard, and since no one loves to have children about more than the Chinese, he was the ship's communal

43

pet. The cook made him a big purple kite from the paper used for wrapping apples, and the sailors helped him to fly it from the stern. The deck passengers let him hold their fishing lines, and the steward was always ready to supply him with Chinese comic books and firecrackers.

But for me, as the cabin became hotter and hotter, the voyage became more dreary, more dismal. Somewhere in the Gulf of Siam, along the Cambodian coast, we ran aground on a sand bar, and there we stayed and sweltered for a day until we were eased off by the tide. There was a further delay while we moored in the roadstead off Paknam, the lower port of Bangkok on the yellow river mouth of the Chao Phya Menam, and waited for the lighters to come to unload cargo. After we had waited half a day in the rabid sun, two great barns of boats lumbered alongside; winches started grinding, and the unloading began. When at last the holds had been emptied and the lighters had gone wallowing away and we had docked at the quay, there was still more waiting to be done for the medical officers and customs officials to make their inspection.

I filled out a customs declaration stating that I had in my luggage no firearms, ammunition, explosive articles, harmful habit-forming drugs, implements of war, playing cards, pathogenic microorganisms or venoms, radio sets, opium or opium pipes.

And then, set down on a bedraggled landing stage, a glimpse of a slatternly settlement beyond, I felt a little forlorn when I saw that none of the people I had written to were there to meet us. Nor was there any sign of transport, nor anyone about who could speak English. Bangkok was seventeen miles away. I glanced around uneasily, not sure what to do, and remembered with sudden relief that I had in my passport folder a Siamese phrase book I had bought in Hong Kong.

Believing that I had the situation well in hand, I found the phrase I wanted and muddled confidently through it.

"MEE ROAT! DO EE-sahNmah ee." Is there a bus?

The business in the phrase book about capital and small letters indicated the tone and pitch in which each word should be singingly spoken. Plainly, I had got the tone and pitch wrong, for as I looked at the coolies ringed about us, I saw that their sallow, glistering faces were expressive of nothing but amiable curiosity.

I tried again. "ja'jahp ROAT! DO EE-sahn DAH ee Tee-nah EE." Where can I get a bus?

The coolies switched on enameled, uncomprehending smiles.

I began again, my voice noticeably louder and sharper than it had been before.

The coolies began to chuckle. Their bewildered expression changed to a look suggesting that I was just about the funniest thing they had seen in a long time. I pointed out to the coolies the meanings written in Siamese script in my book. I expected them to read, did I? That was too much. Ignoring the restraint of their traditional politeness, they laughed delightedly.

In a black rage, I shouted at them in English, quivering with the shame and pleasure of being offensive. In the midst of this abominable scene, my pleasure in my own temper evaporated and, calming down, I looked with anxiety at the faces about me. They were suddenly emptied of all expression.

A truck appeared, with two coolies standing on the running board pointing at me. The driver dismounted, a man small as all Siamese are small. Unlike the coolies who wore lampshadelike raffia hats and a length of checkered cloth about their waists, he was wearing a white shirt, white duck trousers, a Panama hat and battered white sneakers, his toes sticking out of the holes in them. He knew enough English to explain that he would take Kippy and me to Krung Thep for a reasonable fare. I might have guessed that Krung Thep was the Siamese way of saying Bangkok, but the conversation dragged on for some time before I found out.

Watching the coolies heave the luggage into the back of the truck, I felt their dislike for me. I tipped them all lavishly. They accepted the money silently and looked away. As we drove off in the truck, I felt the pain of humiliation spread like a stain from my throat to the pit of my stomach.

The cab of the truck was doorless. Sitting on the outside, with Kippy squeezed between the driver and myself, my arms and face were quickly coated with dust, my legs pecked by flying pebbles. The rays of the sun bore down almost vertically, producing a flesh-astonishing heat. The countryside bowed down beneath the heat, swooned beneath the heat, and lay flat and quiet—a quiet that was like deafness. We drove along a corrugated dirt road across open rice land, *padis* of rice ready to be harvested on either side; bamboo scrub and reed jungle in the distance; an occasional umbrella-crowned acacia or camphor tree with sinewy, contorted roots growing by the roadside. White egrets perched on the backs of drooping-eared, long-horned carabaos browsing along shallow canals. Fishermen cast their nets into muddy canals and raised them filled with tin-bright fish. Children stood beside huts perched on stilts, their tiny figures flattened against the landscape like book-pressed flowers.

Far away a gold temple spire stabbed against the sky, but the heat produced a sort of hardening and dulling sclerosis that over-took my imagination and perception, and folding leg over leg, feeling each tickled with perspiration and stinging with grit, I closed my eyes against the dust, opening them from time to time to see if the landscape had changed, closing them again when I saw that it hadn't. Kippy was jolted into sleep. The driver, drowsily keeping his eyes on the road, was silent.

We reached Bangkok, the City of the Gods. The city looked shabby, chaotic and improvised, hardly a city at all but a vast, sprawling village of two-storied buildings filled in with wooden and tin shacks, the whole crisscrossed with canals—*klongs,* they were called—more traffic-crowded than the pot-holed dirt roads. Momentarily, I felt lifted out of myself by the sight of golden towers and temple spires rising above a sea of roof tops. Then the road jittered away into another pattern and we arrived at the Oriental Hotel.

Kippy came to life to blow several blasts on a quartermaster's whistle that the steward on the *Szechuen* had given him and, with a match provided by the driver, he set off his last string of inch-long firecrackers. Wearily, I filled out the forms that a receptionist handed me, and we were led upstairs to our room.

You don't travel for the sake of duplicating the conveniences and experiences of your own home, and you expect, while traveling, a certain challenge to your adaptability. There are times, neverthe-less, when your precious sense of strangeness, discovery and enthusiasm simply sinks beneath the strain of petty physical discomforts and general irritation. My stay in Bangkok was one of these disheartening times.

Although it was the cool season and presumably more pleasant than the hot or rainy season, it was still steaming hot. For one like myself, who had said so easily in the past that I loved the heat, the inferno of Bangkok was a Dante-esque comeuppance.

There were mosquitoes. The room boy, morning, afternoon and night, sprayed bedroom and bathroom with Flit. Waiters at restaurants, the moment you were seated, rushed to spray Flit under the table. I slept beneath a tent of mosquito netting. I oiled myself with Skeetofax. I still felt there was a good chance of my being bitten to death.

There was the language barrier. Many Siamese spoke excellent English and French, but those of them to whom I had letters of introduction were all away when I arrived. Consequently, in the beginning, the only Siamese I came in contact with were room boys, *samlohr* boys and shopkeepers.

The room boys spoke no English at all. Not that there was any reason that they should; it was just inconvenient that they didn't. "Please," I would say in my phrase-book Siamese, "bring me some coffee." Always the boy would nod and smile. Sometimes he would remember to bring the coffee, sometimes he wouldn't. Absentmindedness, a Buddhist trait prized by the Siamese, was an outstanding quality of the room boys at the Oriental. Sometimes the room boy would appear to understand and would then return, taking his time about it, with soap or a candle.

I got along better with the *samlohr* boys. Bangkok swarmed with *samlohrs*, comical little contraptions with the back of a rickshaw and the front of a bicycle. The *samlohr* boy peddled in front, and behind him, on a seat with springs straining for escape beneath a dingy cover, the passenger sat, shaded by a white cotton awning. There was a set tariff for an hour's trip, so that haggling over the fare was eliminated. Freed from the conscience-stricken feeling that I had paid too little, and from the prickling feeling of annoyance that I had paid too much, it was impossible for me to lean back in the carriage without lazily crossing one leg over the other and feeling privileged and superior. At such times, since confidence is the key to proficiency in a foreign language, I was generally able to match sound and tone and say something intelligible.

I never established this sort of pleasant communication with the shopkeepers. By nature gentle and unaggressive, the Siamese shopkeepers had none of the Indian or Chinese love of bargaining, and if they chanced to speak English, they overcame the local distaste for directness by asking why the price should matter to me, a rich American? With a queer feeling of chagrin, I saw myself regarded as a rich American and a target for dupery; and I came to expect and to listen for the muted, disrespectful giggle that would follow me as I left the darkness of the store for the brightness of the street.

I would return to the Oriental Hotel, lie down upon the bed, yank on the pulley that let down a canopy of mosquito netting around me, and turn to another page of Siamese words and phrases. I struggled with the phonetic niceties of the thirty-two vowel sounds used in common speech and yearned for a fluency I never acquired. But I gave up completely on the written language. Learning to recognize such simple signs as DANGER, WOMEN and EXIT was as difficult as memorizing the patterns in filigreed silver.

At night, to be reading and to have the town's electrical generating system fail (never at the time it had failed the evening before), the lights going off and the fan running down at the moment least expected; to have neither proper shower nor bath, but to bathe with murky, mosquitoey water ladled with a tin dipper from an Ali Baba jar—the reserve of philosophic tolerance I thought I had dwindled, and these minor miseries became major exasperations.

Then why did I stay? I was curious about the country. Like birds'-nest soup, I thought that the taste for Siam might be a slowly acquired one. On the other hand, there was always the satisfaction of making the worst out of a bad job, and if I were going to dislike Siam, I wanted to stay there long enough to see the record of its unpleasantness firmly established. I would stay for a couple of months, I thought, and then, one way or the other, I would know how I felt.

But I never did know. I never felt a deep emotional response to Bangkok or to what I saw of the rest of Siam. I felt like a shell stirred by the sea, stirred by sudden loathings of the heat, inconveniences and discomforts, stirred by sudden pleasures. My feelings were never on sure ground, and my impressions were fragmentary.

Sometimes I awoke early, the morning pale and misty in the room, the bare floor barred with the light dustily filtering through the jalousies. The room was always heavy with that peculiar Far East smell, with the over-smell of charcoal smoke from kitchens and from street braziers, and the moldy smell of the bedclothes and the long Dutch Wife bolster, and the disinfectant odors of Flit and Dettol.

There was the fugue of small noises that came as a coda to the night and as a prelude to the day—the rustling of cockroaches in the wastepaper basket where Kippy had thrown a piece of candy; the murmur of the room boys down the hall; the yelping of pye dogs (if one of them bit you, you rushed to the hospital to have fourteen injections in your stomach for hydrophobia); the clinking of silver against silver as the tables were set for breakfast; the hoarse, admonitive cries of the room's guardian gecko.

I would look to see where the gecko was—I had a horror of coming upon him unexpectedly—but usually he was pattering on polished pink feet along the top of the jalousies, or lying on his belly along the molding, swirling his tail and snapping at flies. The chinchooks, who were only finger-length lizards, kept out of his way and settled themselves in the bathroom, where they ate ants. Never enough, unfortunately. There was a ribbon of ants forever wavering along the toothpaste tube, which was labeled Pepsodent in Siamese and Chinese.

Once, when Kippy and I left the hotel shortly before six, there had been some commotion about a cobra that had been discovered coiled on the rim of the striped awning just outside the dining terrace, but generally the hotel was barely stirring by the time we set off.

Outside, some of the owner-drivers of *samlohrs* would still be sleeping, lying on the seats of their vehicles with their feet propped on the handle bars. One would wake up and pedal us off to the sampan-ferry station on the river. It was not particularly surprising, in a country where nothing was wholly everyday, to see that the trade label was sewn on the outside—right rear pocket—of the *samlohr* boy's khaki shorts. It was not particularly surprising, somehow, to find that *all* trousers and shorts in Siam had labels sewn on the outside.

By six, the Buddhist monks were already making their rounds, each with his feet bare, his head and eyebrows shaved, his right arm left uncovered by a toga of saffron cotton. They walked with the imperturbable dignity of royalty, holding before them wooden offering bowls into which rice and fruit were heaped by housewives eager to acquire merit. Some were professional monks, others were laymen, temporarily detached from the turmoil of life by a sort of spiritual draft which requires all Buddhist males to spend at least three months of their lives in a monastery.

When we came to the long market sheds and godowns near the Customs House, Kippy and I transferred ourselves from *samlohr* (three wheels) to *sampan* (three boards), and were sculled across the river by a sampan girl wearing an ankle-length *panung* of bright-colored cotton fastened in a roll at her waist, and a low-cut bodice of imminent, but never realized, immodesty.

In the early morning, the river, the Chao Phya Menam, the Siamese called it, The Mother of Life, was at its height of animation.

A great part of Bangkok's population lives on the water. There would seem to be no reason for living anywhere else. A sampan is as cheap to build as a shack. Ground rent is done away with, the laundry problem made easy, and moving is simplified to a matter of inclination.

Sitting on the far bank of the Menam, Kippy and I watched whole communities float by. There were floating shops of all kinds: hardware peddlers in a blaze of brass and tin; greengrocers and fruiterers; charcoal sellers; a general store, bright with the irremediable vulgarity of pink plastic combs pinned to plaques of cardboard; a cloth merchant, surrounded by Siamese silks and cottons, with a bolt of magnificent Chinese tribute silk done up in a newspaper parcel on the bow. Rafts of teak logs from Central Siam drifted downstream on their way to Bangkok sawmills.

There were river-borne astrologers, barbers, doctors and magicians.

There were masses of restaurant boats with strings of bottled carbonated drinks and Tiger beer trailing from the stern to cool. There were tea boats. There were fleets of houseboats.

The whole of life was there to see. The newly born, with saffron paste smeared on their heads, bobbles of flies spangling their eyes and ears, held to suckle at the breast; the young, the old, the sick, the dying. Women, when not looking after their children, or cooking, or doing the laundry, washed themselves, stepping from the shore to the water, raising their *panungs* and then their bodices as they went so that never more than an inch of flesh was exposed between cloth and water, their bathing operation as modest as it was thorough.

Girl children wore a *cache-sexe* of silver mail suspended from a chain about their waists; boys wore shirts and nothing below the waist; and together they took to the water as easily as baby beavers.

I could feel my stomach grow queasy, and the saliva would well in my mouth, as I watched a man on a tea boat washing dishes in water only a foot away from where a child was being held out to relieve himself; or when I looked at children splashing in water scummed by the city's sewage, littered with garbage scraps and slimy weeds and afloat with dead rats, whose gray feet stood as stiff as bedposts above the bloated white counterpanes of their bellies.

But if I looked away from the sluggish, olive-green water and the bubbles perpetually forming and loosening about the patina of slime, and if I were careful to be selective in the range of my vision, the scene was infinitely enjoyable. Beautiful the greens along the bank, the fanlike palms, the groves of bamboo; the lush, broad leaves of plantain; pandanus and rattan; the silvery gray of the sampans, and the plaids and stripes of *panungs* vibrant in the sun. Lovely the abundance of food waiting to be sold on the river banks and in the sampans—a glowing, shining profusion of purple mangosteens, pale green custard apples, rose apples, coconuts, spiky rambutans, and orange mangoes that tasted like turpentine and roses; loquats, pineapples, prickly-skinned durians the size of footballs, basket pans of bananas, baskets of shiny grains, papayas, pomelos, papers spread with the daffodil yellow of egg-yolk sweetmeats, and baskets of silvery fish. Although Siamese, as good Buddhists, do not believe in taking life, they see nothing wrong in rescuing fish from drowning. If the creatures die on the bank or in a net, it is probably from exhaustion due to their long immersion, they say, and surely there can be no harm in eating them.

Once, I had peered into a fishing basket, and a Puckish-faced boy had obligingly pulled out a greeny-orange fish and laid it on the ground. I could hardly believe my eyes when the fish scrambled away crablike on its flippers. The boy laughingly hared after it, waving his net, and after several misses, he recaptured it and threw it back in the basket. That was the first time I had ever seen a climbing perch, but from then on I came across them frequently, and once, to my joy, I happened to see one that was actually climbing up the slanting bole of a palm tree.

One heat-weighted day I returned from the river to the hotel feeling that I had been buffeted with more severity than usual by dust, heat and mosquitoes. Discomfort had anesthetized me to the point where I was aware of nothing but the pressing desire for a glass of ice water and a hot bath. There was nothing relaxing about pouring dippersful of murky water from the Ali Baba jar over myself, nor any fun in sitting in an inch of hot water decanted from a bucket that took the room boy an hour to cart upstairs. I wanted a hot bath deep enough to float in.

I made a grand tour of Bangkok's hotels, determined to find one with running hot water. After spending a day hanging about managers' offices listening to a standardized line of patter about the water shortage and plumbing that I was assured confidently would be repaired the next day, and that I knew with equal confidence would not, I happened upon the Rajdhani Hotel in the Hua Lampong railway station. The hotel consisted simply of a lobby, a dining room, a staircase and a dozen or so rooms-with-bath. If, as I had every reason to believe, the water was siphoned from the boilers of passing locomotives, at least there was plenty of it, and it was voluptuously hot.

I changed hotels at once. My room, like the rest, was accessible only from a balcony directly above the indoor station platform, no more than fifteen feet above the train tops, so that when a train departed for Chiengmai or arrived from Pitsanuloke I had the momentarily startling sensation of being aboard. There was no

advance warning except for a cloud of spunk-smelling smoke. It
was an experience that took some getting used to.

I was lucky, though, to have hot water, and I was further comforted by the presence of Pranee, the daughter of the proprietor.
She was eighteen, with the kittenlike features of most Siamese girls
—short chin, snub nose, small face wide across the cheekbones and
large, oblique eyes. Like many Siamese girls, she had bobbed her
hair and had had the ends waved into a curly ruffle which fluffed
above the tip of her ears and ended as neatly as a topiary bush at
their lobes. Only men, she told me, rice farmers and peasants, and
sometimes elderly women, wore their hair like mine—long and
straight and drawn into a bun at the back. She frequently brought
me little wreaths of jasmine and yellow flowers like morning
glories to wind about my bun to "pretty it up."

"There," she would say, covering up the last hairpin. "Now you
are resembling a bona fide glomma girl."

Pranee had taught herself English in the hope that she would
someday be able to go to Hollywood. She kept herself informed of
the idyllic lives of the stars by subscribing to *Modern Screen*. She
had become a member of a fan club, and this had led to a correspondence with an American pen pal who was president of the
John Wayne Fan Club of Titusville, Pennsylvania.

She had committed Mr. Wayne's private life to memory and
spoke often about him as she amiably attended to the odd jobs that
came her way. She wrote out the menus and supervised the room
boys. When the lights failed, she went from room to room, with
an armful of candles, giving every occupant two candles, to be
mounted, wherever desired, each in a pool of its own wax. Since I
already had an oil lamp, my two candles were placed in the bathroom, one on either side of the basin. The tutelary gecko stationed
beneath the basin would sit up for the better part of the night,
looking wickedly crocodilian and self-important as he enjoyed the
limelight and the tiled echo of his own utterances.

In her spare time Pranee tried to find companionable young girls
to amuse Zulfi Salik, who occupied the room next to mine.

Mr. Salik—I think that was his name—was a cabinet minister
from Pakistan and a delegate to a conference on Asiatic manpower
that was going on in Bangkok at the time. He was a man of forty

or so—it was hard to tell—swarthy, with short-cropped dark hair, a thick body and a lean face with shining brown eyes set close together above a drooping, fleshy nose. He suffered from some sort of dropsical ailment which had caused his ankles and wrists to swell considerably, and he spent most of his time in his room, where, when I passed the open door, I could see him lying beneath the mosquito net being fanned by the room boy. He gave the impression of being as pathetically and grandly out of place at the Rajdhani as a desert sultan stranded in a Midwest farm town. As though to leave no doubt that he was accustomed to some luxuriously remote existence, he had embarked on the conversion of the room boys to pet slaves.

The important thing in breaking in a servant to new duties, I had thought, was to be calm, impersonal and explicit, but Mr. Salik took the opposite tack. He made no attempt to speak Siamese. "Darling, my love, my sweet," he would say in Oxford-accented English to the room boy. "Do this little thing for me. Get me some ice water."

"I am your friend," he would say, with no trace of friendliness in his tone. "But, God damn you, get me some ice water!"

The first time I had heard these commands of Mr. Salik, I had smiled knowingly. "Fat chance," said I to Kippy. "You be timekeeper and see what the boy brings."

"Six minutes," Kippy reported. "Ice water."

"A fluke," I had said. "Pure luck."

I was bound to admit later on that I was wrong. With increasing envy and amazement, I had glimpses through the open door of Mr. Salik seated with an expression of monarchial complacency in the window chair while the room boy shaved him; of Mr. Salik having his shoes fastened, his feet washed, his back rubbed and powdered, his thick body massaged with hot towels.

The sight of Mr. Salik so pampered and indulged piqued me, and I felt rather pleased when Pranee confided to me that his pleasures were incomplete. He craved a female companion, and Pranee declared that she was having a terrible time trying to find one for him. In the beginning, matters had been simple enough. She had merely to lean over the veranda and beckon to one of the girls standing in a purposeful cluster across the street. The trouble was that word had got around about Mr. Salik, Pranee said. He was hard to please. She sighed.

"And the girls, they are no liking Indians, so I am having to go three, four, five blocks away to find other girls who will visit him. I get tired looking."

"That's a shame," I said.

"That's a shame," I heard Pranee saying to Mr. Salik later in the day. "Miss Pranee, it was dreadful." Mr. Salik's Oxford voice floated into my room. I gathered that he was standing close to the window opening onto his veranda, which adjoined mine. "Miss Pranee, this girl came into my room, and before she even greeted me, she removed all her clothes. I assure you, in all my experience, Miss Pranee, I have never seen such bestiality. Do, please, I beg of you, locate for me next time a person of a little more dignity."

That evening Pranee tapped at my door. I recognized her knock and told her to come in. "Pardon, please," she said, looking as though she were about to cry. "It's Mr. Salik. He is so displeased with me, and I try so hard to find him a little girl friend and I cannot. My father says I must render service to our guests, make them all be happy." She regarded me with plaintive, wistful eyes. "Mr. Salik is a nice gentleman. He is needing a nice girl like me. But I cannot help him. I am too busy. I must write the menus. When the room boys call 'Miss Pranee, Miss Pranee,' I must come fast as a wink. So I am thinking to give Mr. Salik this."

She extended a frail arm, and held between her thumb and first finger was a copy of *Black Shadow,* a pamphlet widely distributed in Bangkok, containing the addresses and descriptions of all the brothels in town and providing detailed information as to cost, service and repertoire.

"I'm sure Mr. Salik would appreciate it very much," I said. "If I were you, I'd leave it on his bureau where he would be sure to see it."

The tiny furrow that had appeared between Pranee's penciled eyebrows vanished. "Then all problems is solved, is it not?" She smiled at me gaily and, turning at the door, steepled the palms of her exquisitely manicured hands together before her face, and bowed. *"Savadi,"* she said. ("May Buddha touch you.")

"Savadi," said I, following suit.

And Pranee was gone, leaving behind her a scent of fresh jasmine.

I don't suppose that a spirit of sexual revelry is anywhere more pervasive than it is in Bangkok. For a man whose hormones are in an uproar, I guess Bangkok comes pretty close to being the romantic paradise the guidebooks say it is. But for me, Bangkok often had the peculiar quality of a carnival burlesque—a naïve and exhibitionistic spectacle that was sometimes entertaining and frequently embarrassing.

Drugstores and market places stocked a bewildering inventory of aphrodisiacs, hormone vitalizers and contraceptives. Displayed among the requisite shopwindow décor of faded crepe-paper streamers and paper flowers were weird apparatuses guaranteed to render the utmost in sexual titillation. Booksellers plastered their walls with pin-up girls of every race and carried what appeared to be the full complement of pornography current in the world market.

To make sure that one missed nothing of Bangkok's sexual wonderland, the Siamese had thoughtfully provided a Baedeker—*Black Shadow,* edited by Dream Lover, the pamphlet that Pranee had left on Mr. Salik's bureau. As Dream Lover said in the preface, "This pocket book is somewhat inevitable to be kept ready at hands."

Wishing his readers "good luck and good love," Dream Lover warmed to his subject with the introduction of dancing shows. Nai Lang's dancing show, taking place nightly at Bampen Boon market, he proclaimed as "the most sexual inflammation at all times. . . . He has many elegant feminine youth of experience . . . the dances being sexual inflammation because of his dancers almost naked provoke the sex to the superlative degree. . . . Show is decisively second to none."

And then, with exultant cries in mangled English, he launched into a description of the thirty-nine brothels he wished to recommend—"those many rendezvouses of very sweet, intense and hot paradise where await you young, showy nightingales of the night ready to be the best of your night companion to guide you into and through the Land of Aden, the place of bliss."

"Gentlemen," he continued, "should there be indescribable

dreams arising out of your disquieting sexuality, these paradisaical rooms vividly adorned by beautiful, young, smart, charming women in attendance will undoubtedly be your best. To what extent your mind may wander, it is so far a matter of fact for those young, showy nightingales to do their duty in attending and fulfilling your wish."

Occasionally Dream Lover would inject a cautionary note—"The actual condition of these night lovers is having been widely known to men night roamers"—but in general his references to the "feminine youth of loving service" were lyrical.

These "larks of the night," "maidens of the Blue Danube," "Chinese girls of today and tomorrow," were prepared, he said, "to lay fanciful service to their visitors, to render secret magic charm, extreme paradise, happy love"; and to "sing songs of sweet love through the murmuring of the eastern night wind."

Terms for service 10 to 100 tics. (Twenty ticals to a dollar.)

Slightly higher charges were quoted for feminine youth regarded as "extraordinary," "very special," "extra," and "upper class"; private terms for the "girls of loving service nightly to be seen roaming along the street. One by one has her own loving affairs. You may have her engaged at any hour you like."

Mr. Salik evidently found a lark to comfort him, for he took to spending the nights away from the hotel, and Pranee reported that he had given her a satin-covered box of expensive French chocolates with a deckle-edged card tucked under the ribbon inscribed "To Miss Pranee, the Rose of the Rajdhani, with affectionate regards from Zulfi Salik." Pranee pasted the card into her scrapbook.

One afternoon I went with Pranee to the Silpakorn Theater to see a *khon* drama, or masked play. The theater was a barnlike building with a strong smell inside of bananas, copra and oranges. We arrived early and were allotted two wooden folding chairs second row center. The theater hall was as dusky as a room at twilight, everything seeming to have been touched with a gray-blue wash and freckled with the yellow light that sieved down from the holes in the roof. The condition of the roof made it impossible for plays to be presented during the rainy season.

The audience, with the informality typical of Eastern theatergoers, had brought both food and babies to the theater with them. The man next to me, his lips stained crimson and his teeth black from betel chewing, had begun to munch his way through a small basket of thumb-sized bananas. The man in front of me dipped alternately into a paper cornucopia filled with roasted peas and a punnet of shredded dried prawns that looked like pipe tobacco. Pranee produced some of the chocolates Mr. Salik had given her which she had transferred to a spillet of newspaper.

Members of the orchestra trooped in to take their places in front of the stage. I was charmed by their instruments. There was a boat-shaped xylophone of bamboo and a carved circular frame containing sixteen brass gongs graduated to scale. There was a drum that looked like an African tomtom, and three that resembled miniature beer kegs; two flageolets and an oboe. The oboe carried the melody, the gongs sounded the cadence, and the rest of the instruments chimed and wailed and banged with high-spirited vivacity. The music was almost wholly dissonant, a frenzy of unreconciled sharps and flats, but, by men having heard enough Eastern music to have acquired some taste for it, the sound seemed rather pleasing as it furrowed a path through my mind.

The footlights came up, and there was a hiss of excitement as the curtains were jerkily drawn aside to reveal the interior of a castle in Ceylon, presided over by Thotsakan, the Demon King of Lanka. Above his grotesque mask and sumptuous crown, a courtier held a gilt and brocade umbrella, the symbol of royalty. Other attendants were grouped around him, each richly costumed in a close-fitting blouse and knee breeches of heavy brocade stiff with jeweled embroidery, each glittering with ornamental chains, bracelets, anklets and uptilting epaulettes of gold.

And so the play began. The story was based on an incident in the Rama-Kien, the Siamese version of the Ramayana, an Indian epic which chronicles, in sixty thousand verses, the adventures of its eponymous hero Rama, and the comings and goings of the Hindu pantheon.

A chorus group, seated to the right of the stage in front of the curtain, began the prologue, telling us where we were and what was going to happen next.

Pranee, who knew every detail of the whole Rama cycle, briefed me on the story. Thotsakan, worried that a group of hermits might cause trouble for him, was going to dispatch an ogress and her army of crowlike myrmidons to vanquish them.

The ogress and her followers rushed off stage accompanied by the wailing obbligato of their signature tune. They were then shown in a truly dreadful battle scene with the hermits. The battle, a ballet, waged to an orchestration of traditional action tunes of anger and fear, went on for some time, every movement watched by the audience with tense enjoyment.

The actors who weren't playing feminine roles wore head masks which rendered each as mute as a clock beneath a bell jar, and their lines had to be recited for them by the chorus. But whether they spoke their lines or had the chorus speak for them, all the actors expressed themselves by gesture language, a pantomime of extraordinary refinement and encyclopedic range.

The story was hard to follow, but I loved the play for the sheer sensuous feel of it; the purples and hot pinks, the reds, greens and gold of the costumes and the fine grace of the actors' movements spilled from my eyes into my mind like water over a weir.

The audience groaned when the hermits were defeated by the ogress and her evil band. Pranee said that it was now up to the child-prince Rama to kill the ogress. His role was played by a young girl, a tiny doll-like creature dressed in gold brocade, who was greeted by shouts of joy from the audience. She didn't wear a mask, but the oval perfection of her face had been emphasized with white powder, her eyes and brows had been darkly outlined, her mouth incarnadined so that her features might attain the desired quality of superbness and nobility. Up she leaped, as though she had been blown into the air, and came to rest on the stage as a leaf might, before she leaped again.

Lightly, lightly, she danced, performing with extraordinary grace, now balancing on one leg with the other bent backward and held at a right angle while she executed serpentine movements with her head, now poised with one leg outstretched, expressive foot bent back, as though there were no other way of standing, while she interpreted long musical passages with delicate gesticulations of her hands and arms. One of her specialties was to thrust her arms out in such a way that her elbows appeared to be dislocated; another

was her ability to curve her fingers up and back, sometimes almost
to her wrists, in a tilting curve which echoed the motif of the
courtiers' winged epaulettes and the curve of the gilded gables
painted on the backdrop.

The lovely Rama creature danced away and reappeared, heralded by a marching tune, to kill the ogress. After this *pas de deux*
was over, on came two gloriously caparisoned ogre chieftains—one
in a white mask, one in a terra-cotta mask—vowing to revenge their
mother's death by slaying Rama. They exited in a gilded chariot
inlaid with mother-of-pearl and equipped with a tiered, gilded
canopy—the sort of lavish stage property the Siamese adore. The
final scene was their battle with Rama.

There was a terrible smacking of swords, but Rama had a
weapon the ogres didn't have—a bow and arrow—and, holding the
bow with an arm bent in the artistic elbow-dislocated position, he
let the arrow fly and killed the ogre with the terra-cotta mask. With
the aid of another player, Prince Rama now appeared to have four
arms, indicating that he was the incarnation of Vishnu. Off scuttled
the white-masked ogre, terrified by the miracle that had come to
pass.

The audience roared with approval as gods and heavenly nymphs,
crowned with multi-tiered helmets, flocked upon the stage to dance
with joy and to shower Prince Rama with popped rice and flowers.
Some of the blossoms—paper, of course; real ones would have been
too ordinary—fluttered out to the audience and were greatly prized
souvenirs.

There was a last burst of cacophony from the orchestra, and the
performance ended. The audience gathered up its babies and, leaving behind a carpet of eggshells, papers and peelings, slowly left the
theater.

It was dark when we went outside. Pranee turned to steeple her
hands in greeting and introduced me to a man called Suchitr, the
publisher of one of the leading Siamese newspapers. Oddly enough,
it turned out that I had had a letter of introduction to Suchitr, but
he had been out of town when I first arrived. He insisted that we
join him for dinner at Chez Eve, which was the only European-
style night club in town and, as far as I knew, the one place in all
of Bangkok which was air conditioned. Apart from the air condi-

tioning, the only other attraction of Chez Eve was that it was frequented by King Phumiphol, who liked to stand in with the band and improvise blues on the saxophone.

When we got there, and as soon as the waiter had sprayed Flit beneath the table, I looked curiously about the room to see if his Royal Highness was there. And, sure enough, there he was, sitting alone at a table next to the band, a thin, owlish-looking young man wearing spectacles and a white linen suit.

It seemed incredible that no one was making a fuss over him, and I remarked on this to Suchitr.

"When he's off duty, he likes it that way," Suchitr said. "We're a democratic people."

"He's sweet," Praneee said. "He is also dancing very well. He danced with me twice last month. A rumba and a fox trot."

"He often dances with pretty girls," Suchitr said, in answer to the look of surprise I hoped I had managed to hide. "He loves pretty girls."

In a way it was a shame, I thought, that an age of democracy had swept grandeur aside. It didn't seem right that the man worshiped as the descendant of Buddha should have an eye for pretty girls, nor, as the Brother of the Moon and the Half-Brother of the Sun, that he should dance on a crowded floor to the tune of "Chiquita Banana" and "I Wanna Be Evil."

Phumiphol's father had been considered too sacred to be addressed directly or even looked at by a commoner. His subjects had approached him in a flattened crawl, working themselves along with their elbows and their toes, their eyes fixed on the dust. The last of a dynasty of absolute monarchs, Phumiphol's father had been surrounded by a court which echoed the incomparable splendor and pomp of the medieval Orient.

In comparison, his son appeared lusterless and déclassé. In my mind's eye, I saw this thin, bespectacled young man, cheeks puffed out, playing the saxophone, with his subjects jigging all about him at eye level—a regrettable image of the Lord of Life, the Supreme Arbiter of the Ebb and Flow of the Tide.

There were times in Siam when I was made disconsolate by that special loneliness which seems peculiar to traveling. Petty discomforts and irritations had given a curious intensity to my sense of geographic and emotional isolation. The worst of it was that there was no one really to talk to. Kippy talked for hours to Shabobbus, a spaceman with whom he discussed secret interplanetary military maneuvers. But with me, Kippy's conversational sphere was limited to facts—"I like mangosteens"; "I want to see a movie"; "It's hot" —and questions—"Why do durians smell so awful?" "Why don't the priests have any hair?"

I talked to Pranee, but since the things which interested me about Siam seemed as hackneyed to her as her interests in Ameria—movie stars, high buildings, cowboys, gangsters, John Wayne, Hollywood —were to me, our conversation tended to lapse into perfunctory interludes between questions; because of the language barrier, our talk was superficial, and at moments when significance seemed closest, our words had the maddening habit of turning into mere vocables, and our talk would trail off into uncertainty and blank smiles.

On the few occasions when the opportunity presented itself to speak to Mr. Salik, I found that he didn't talk: he made depressing pronouncements. One time, in the early evening, when I was sitting in the lobby sipping lemonade with chunks of brownish ice floating in it, my legs encased in a *panung* sewn into a bag as a protection against mosquitoes, Mr. Salik came over and sat next to me. He lowered himself gingerly into the chair and propped his sandaled feet on the table top. "The heat is terrible," he said. "Believe you me, I can hardly wait to get back to Lahore."

A shaded light bulb dangled on a cord above our heads, so that as we sat across from each other we were separated by a cone of light moted with mosquitoes. He gestured toward the light. "I may never reach Lahore. I may die instead of malaria." He closed his eyes dramatically, as though they were already closed by death. "Or," he continued, still with his eyes closed, "I may pass away with the ruddy fever that causes this." His eyes popped suddenly open as he thrust out his swollen wrists and wagged a swollen ankle for my inspection. He let his hands fall to the table. "The doctors say they can do nothing."

He lifted his hand wearily to salute Pranee and Kippy when they returned from a Wild Western they had gone to, and then he limped off, saying that it was time for him to take his medicine and to have a "pre-dinner lie-down."

Suchitr's appearance upon the scene was a blessing. He was kind and knowledgeable and spoke fluent American-English. I don't mean that to be as patronizing a description as it sounds. Unfortunately, personality tends to lose its identity when strained through the mesh of a foreign language, forfeiting, like applesauce, the solidity, texture and much of the flavor of its origin. Consequently, I never really knew much more about him.

In the custody of Suchitr, Kippy and I went to the Pasteur Institute, where visiting Indians and Europeans hunched with their ciné cameras over a stone-walled, moated snake pit to watch a barefooted attendant pull out cobras, hamadryads and Russell's vipers from beneath their small igloo shelters. A loud *urrr* of sucked-in breaths came from the crowd as the attendant stood in his minute of distinction, smiling toward the cameras' click and purr, with a bunch of snakes grasped by their tails in each of his shiny-knuckled fists. The snakes writhed in twisting arcs, all agitated to a sinuous frenzy, the naked nerves of their tongues flickering with the terrible suggestion of primordial evil.

There was a moment of fascination when the tableau seemed richer than life, when the snakes, like those that Lawrence saw in Taormina, seemed like demigods, like kings in exile, uncrowned in the underworld. Then the moment melted, as the doctor, all brisk and bustling, came along with his laboratory saucers to extract venom for antitoxin.

I had heard that Bangkok was teeming with opium dens and, trying to sound worldly and casual, I asked Suchitr if he would take me to one.

"Certainly," he said. "Would you care to go tonight?"

"Fine," I said. "Have you ever smoked opium?"

"Why, of course," Suchitr answered, as though smoking opium were the most natural thing in the world, which, of course, in Siam it was.

I thought ahead to the times when, back in New York, I would say, "By the way, I once had an interesting experience in an opium den," or even, "Opium? Why, of course, I smoked it in Bangkok."

Doubting that anyone would believe me without some substantiating evidence, I asked Suchitr to lend me a newspaper flash camera.

We set out that evening in Suchitr's car, Suchitr driving in typical Siamese fashion with one hand on the horn and the other busy for the most part with the rear-view mirror and the ashtray. We slipped away from the *samlohrs,* the trolleys and wildly swerving cars, and parked in a dead-end street somewhere near Yawaraj Road. We walked into a thin triangle of vapory moonlight edged by a litter of straw and a tumble of crates flung up against the low black backs of godowns and chandlers' warehouses. There was a sudden rustle of small movement as shadowy shapes of rats streaked into deeper shadow.

The river was near, but its sharp odor of oil and mold and copra was only an underbreath beneath a heavier scent, a little like burning sugar, bittersweet, smoky, sickly, unmistakably the concentrate of an exhalation I had often noticed whiffling from alleyways and open doors, a familiar but unidentifiable Eastern smell. I asked Suchitr what it was.

"*Yafin,*" he said, "opium," as he turned to lead me down a dark and dank lane rustling with rats I couldn't see.

"Don't worry. They won't bite you," Suchitr said with the universal lordliness of the male confronted by skittish feminine fears.

We got to the end of the alley, rounded the corner, dodged past two skinny pye dogs heckling and barking at each other, and walked a few paces to an entranceway lighted by an overhead lamp beneath which were two metal signs. The one inscribed with Siamese characters said that opium was smoked inside, the other, in English, simply said Coca-Cola.

There were opium houses all up and down the rubbish-strewn lane. The smoky, bitter-sweet smell of opium was nauseating. We went inside. On the left, screened off with chicken wire from the tiny, unlighted foyer in which we stood, was a large, shadowy chamber papered with newspaper and magazine covers—*Life* seemed to be the most popular selection—and crowded with double-decker bunks, all but a few of which appeared to be occupied by loudly snoring patrons. The "workingmen's special," Suchitr had explained. Twenty tics a night.

We waited for an old woman carrying a tray of teacups to come creakingly down the steep staircase, and then we groped our way in the darkness to the second floor.

On the landing, at the right of the entrance to a dim and smoke-filled room, pipes for hire were arranged in racks behind a broad counter, each of the hundred or so pipes a thick, straight tube of bamboo stained by smoke to a dark copper color, the shaft about two feet long and fitted with a doorknoblike bowl of red earthenware fixed to a brass plate that was set closer to the end plug of ivory than to the pierced mouthpiece. There were more pipes in a glass-fronted wall cabinet, and an attendant, fitting a key to its Chinese lock, brought out one of them, handsomely chased with gold and silver, which he handed to Suchitr. Suchitr, in turn, presented it to me, saying that it was his for me to smoke and that he would use one of the common pipes instead. The desire to experiment bounded up inside me, eager for a new experience, and then, like a timid animal, warily backed away and lay down again.

"Let me just look around a bit first," I said evasively. But my conscience had informed me of my choice and, as a result, I was already beginning to suffer from a pang of regret, as distracting and painful as a toothache, for whatever it was I would miss by being an observer rather than a participant.

Stalling for time, I asked what all the things were for on the counter—the brass jeweler's scale, the countless little pots and tins. The manner of the attendant changed. He dropped his respectful, at-your-service attitude and assumed in its place the air of indulgent patronage called for by such a touristy question. He lifted the lids of the various pots to show me that they contained opium, a black and tarry substance which, he patiently explained, was nothing more than dried poppy juice that had been boiled, purified and evaporated. He scooped up a blob of it with his long thumbnail, deftly rolled it into a pellet and counterbalanced it on the scale with a two-gram weight.

"Just right for a nice smoke," he said. "Very nice painkiller. Very pleasurable."

Suchitr said that one had to smoke at least three pipes before one felt any noticeable effect, and that he usually smoked anywhere from twenty to thirty pipes in an evening. Moderation, he said, was the main thing. Smoking forty or fifty or even sixty pipes, as some people did in a night, was just asking for trouble, but thirty was a safe limit. Unless, he added, examining the contents of one of the tins, one was given bad stuff.

He flicked the tin with his thumb and third finger and sent it sliding across the counter toward the attendant.

The attendant glanced at the tin, shrugged and smiled culpably. Suchitr spoke to him sharply and then, turning to me, said, "They all do it. That was a tin of dregs—opium that has been smoked before. It gives you a frightful head and makes you vomit."

"But never mind." He smiled at me reassuringly, "I'll see that he gives us good stuff. No dregs, no Indian chandoo, nothing but the best."

Nor would we spend the evening in the room we were in. "Not this forty-tic dump," he said emphatically. Such a place was only for the rank and file of patrons. We would go to the separate salons —one for ladies, one for gentlemen—that cost a hundred tics a night. The price included the rental of a silk *panung*, hot rice wine and as much tea as we wanted. He made the declaration grandly, and I smiled wanly in response.

That sounded fine, I said, continuing my face-saving sham, but I thought it would be better to look around the room we were in first and take a few pictures. Would anyone mind?

No, no, the attendant said. I could take as many pictures as I wanted. No one would mind in the least—the opium smokers were all quiet, happy people. A gold-toothed smile broke easily in his face, and he summoned a girl-child who was one of a corps of female attendants, seemingly comprised of grandmothers and granddaughters, whose job was to prepare the opium for the clientele and to tidy up the place in what little spare time they had. Suchitr said that he would stay at the counter and have a drink while I made notes or took pictures.

I followed after the little girl who walked sedately before me as though her life depended upon not jiggling the tray she was carrying. A double row of opium tables divided the large, dim room and lined three of its shabby, smoke-impregnated walls. Furnished with a brass spittoon, a rush mat and two mottled porcelain head rests, each table consisted of a smooth platform of teakwood raised from the floor and separated from the adjoining table by a partition, half solid, half slatted, about four feet high, the total effect being rather similar to a series of exhibitors' stalls at a dog show.

We walked past ancient men whose skin was pulled to the color of tallow where it stretched over their cheek and breast bones, their flesh gone so thin that it looked as though light would shine through it as through a fragile cup. Languidly they lay on their tables, some snoring dryly, their lamps gone out; some dozing and muttering to themselves; some awake, drinking tea, and talking to their neighbors in the soft tones one uses in a library or a museum.

We walked past younger addicts whose excessive indulgence had dwarfed them and given them the coarse and ugly look peculiar to retarded children. We walked past other smokers who showed no sign at all of being harmfully affected.

At the table of a man who had the countenance and bearing of a merchant, the little girl set down her tray on which was arranged a spirit lamp, a round box containing the measured dose of opium, a long needle and an ivory-ended bamboo pipe. She climbed on the table and, squatting back on her heels, began to perform the preparatory ritual. She lighted the lamp and held the needle over its flame. When the needle glowed red, she dipped it into the opium paste and gathered on its point a pendant drop which she held above the lamp, twirling and toasting it into a sizzling black ball. Then she kneaded the ball against the exterior of the pipe's earthenware bowl, stabbed the needle into the bowl's tiny eyelet, released the ball, inverted the bowl above the flame and handed the pipe to the merchant. With a great, sucking breath he inhaled the pipe in one draught, held the smoke back for a long moment and then exhaled it in a gray-blue cloud.

He nodded to the little girl, and she bent over again to prepare a second pipe, the lamplight making her oval face and her long child's hands golden. Would it be all right if I took a picture? The merchant leaned back on his porcelain head rest and posed amiably; the little girl, squatting sentinel above the lamp, remained as she was; and, raising the camera, I congratulated myself on a fine photograph. I flicked the lever, the flash went off with a burst of white light, and after that events happened with a rush. There was an angry shout from the back of the room, and I saw a man in a red-checkered *panung* and a white shirt jogging toward me with a knife in his hand.

I raced back to Suchitr, the camera hitting awkwardly against me. "Quick!" he said. "Go down the stairs." I rattled down the staircase, bumping against the wall and the banisters, stumbled through the doorway into the lane, and then I leaned against the building's rough wooden side and tried to catch my breath. A few minutes later, hearing the sound of footsteps coming down the stairs, I turned quickly, my alarm melting when I saw that it was Suchitr.

"It's all right," he said. "The attendant hit him on the head with a chair, so he'll be quiet for a couple of hours."

I listened to him with the numbness that follows a crisis. He just couldn't understand it, he kept saying over and over again. Opium didn't usually make you violent. The man must have been a lunatic to have come after me like that with a knife.

Oddly enough, I realized then, for the first time, the enormity of what might have happened, but the incident as a whole made little sense to me: it had none of the tidiness of fiction, no neat beginning, no neat conclusion, no details, no motivation. And yet, if its inconclusive brevity made it an unsatisfactory adventure to retell, it had been a strangely satisfying experience which had set me free from the regret and humiliation I had felt earlier in the evening. Being an observer hadn't been so tame after all, and by the time I returned to the Rajdhani I was riding high in the triumph of this unexpected ransom.

Shortly afterward, Suchitr left for a business meeting in Burma. Pranee left to visit her relatives in Chiengmai, and at just about the same time Mr. Salik's conference in Bangkok ended and he departed for Lahore. Kippy and I waved good-by to him from the veranda as he boarded the dawn bus for the airport.

"Now we don't have any more friends here," Kippy said.

"Well, maybe we have," I said. "We'll see." Irwin, an American owner of a Bangkok restaurant, was back in town, and we were to meet him at the Oriental after lunch. In the meantime, we had the whole morning to ourselves.

The gecko lay on the rim of the bathtub, his throat palpitating, in a state of saurian torpor. Standing well back, I flicked a towel at him, and he scurried up the wall and glowered at me all the time I was in the bath. I ran a fresh bath for Kippy, and when we were both dressed, we went downstairs. Pranee's father was sitting in the lobby concentrating his attention upon the section of the newspaper given over to information concerning local commodities.

"Savadi," he said, and then went back to studying the folded page as though the greatest sin in the world was ignorance of the market prices of sticklac, lotus seeds, sago and shellac.

We hailed a *samlohr,* and the driver pedaled us away. The little foot grille of the carriage part was ornamented with the clumsily enameled figures of a blond pin-up girl in a bikini and a cowboy riding a bucking bronco. That this sort of western novelty should be regarded with such high favor throughout the East, where the level of artistic craftsmanship is superlative, was an Oriental caprice that puzzled me only a little less than the fact that our *samlohr* boy, like many Siamese, had both his upper front teeth capped with gold, a cut-out of a tiny heart on one and a tiny playing-card club on the other disclosing the whiteness of the tooth beneath.

We drove through Ban Moh, the silversmiths' district, where the shopwindows displayed an exuberant fantasy of *repoussé* silver, and then we turned from a small street into a cloistered, tamarind-lined lane bordered on one side by cinnamon-brown houses sequestered in walled compounds, and on the other side by a *klong* and the myriad of sampans that drifted along its milky olive surface. A woman, relieving herself behind a bush on the bank, heard our approach and swiftly flung up her *panung* so that her head and not her bottom was covered, an inversion of modesty from our viewpoint but not from hers: unseen, we were nonexistent. We passed a boy cockily riding on the humped back of a carabao, and a wandering priest carrying a parasol of oiled paper. We turned back again into a main avenue. Everywhere above the sequences of shabby roof tops rose the annulated finials and shimmering golden spires of temples. It was hard to imagine that so many temples existed: Wat Po, which housed a gilded reclining Buddha the length of a ferryboat and with barn-high foot soles of mother-of-pearl; Wat

Saket, dazzling in its golden excesses, the glittering expanse of its *chedi* enshrining a chip of Gautama's bone which Buddhist pilgrims by the thousand annually journeyed to worship; Wat Benjamabopit, with its gallery of bronze Buddhas and its white marble chapel; Wat Arun, the Temple of the Dawn, with its flamboyant pinnacles—and hundreds of others.

But of all the temples, there was none like Wat Phra Keo, the Temple of the Emerald Buddha. Here, as nowhere else, the blazing extravagance and the prodigious glamour of the fabled East endured and was wonderfully alive. I don't know how many pavilions there were. I always felt too overwhelmed and exalted to count them, but there seemed to be a large number faced with jewels set in elaborate designs, a pretension only revealed at close range to be a mosaic of a million bits and pieces of glass, earthenware and china, incredibly lovely in their total effect. Window frames and doors were lacquered and exquisitely inlaid with pearl shell. The loving attention the Siamese confer upon roofs had blossomed here into a passionate affair of polished green, blue, orange, red and yellow tiles, tiered, uptilted, spired and towered, each of scores of gables lacily inlaid and framed with glittering moldings shaped like a reedbuck's horn. There was a great spire-capped *chedi* glazed with gold that gave off a trembling glare like a fire, and a jeweled forest of smaller reliquaries.

Fabulous beasts crouched in the shadow of bo trees with little green valentine hearts for leaves in a courtyard thronged with top-hatted plaster giants, tusky-toothed demons arrayed in armor of imbricated china mosaic and complacently fierce bronze lions.

"Wat Phra Keo," I said to the *samlohr* boy. It seemed a waste of time to go anywhere else.

Outside the temple walls proprietors of fruit and sweetmeat stalls drew attention to their wares by ringing gongs and bells. Vendors dispensed stamp-sized patches of gold leaf to be applied by the faithful to their favorite images, and hawkers were doing a thriving business selling stiff stalks of pink lotus, caged finches and wands of incense for devotional offerings. Kippy bought a paper cornucopia of raisins and a spillet of unroasted peanuts. Then, in deference to the sanctity of the temple courtyard, we removed our shoes at the gate and, holding them in our hands, padded across the blistering hot stone.

In the back of a covered gallery painted with scenes from the Rama-Kien I came across four discarded Buddha heads piled higgledy-piggledy under a rosewood tree where a Siamese family were picnicking. Three of the heads were sat upon by children, who were impiously drumming their heels against august stone noses and ancient limestone eyelids while they refereed a cockroach race staged by a younger brother. The fourth head was used as a back rest by their great-grandmother, whose flesh hung in wrinkled folds from her bones. One breast, thin and flat as a spaniel's ear, left uncovered by a length of calico twisted over her shoulder, sagged grotesquely to the waistband of her *panung*. To attract attention, one of her great-granddaughters reached up to tug at the dark, puckered nipple. Another child considerately disengaged her fingers and gave her some raisins that had spilled from Kippy's cornucopia.

Kippy insisted that he wanted to stay and watch the cockroach races, so I left him with the children and went across the way to enjoy the dreamlike sensation of sitting in the central shrine, leaning against a pillar, with my mind like an open net through which sights and sounds and almost no thoughts swam. The cool marble floor was crowded. New arrivals brushed past me searching for a place to sit, and having found an open spot, they knelt down, touched their foreheads to the floor in prayer, and then sat back on their heels, ready to chat, eat, chew betel, or to while away time as I was, by doing nothing at all.

The fragrance of incense and tuberoses and the not unpleasant smell of hard-boiled eggs and bananas the woman next to me was eating settled over me like a fog. Through the open doors I could hear the tinkling-tonkling of the sweet-toned little bells hung beneath the eaves, one of the most restful, time-effacing sounds in the world. High up on a golden pillar, protected by a golden canopy, the Emerald Buddha was enthroned. The image was not carved from emerald but from jasper, a technicality that in no way detracted from its impressive appearance. The image had three seasonal costume changes; as it was then the cool season, it was suitably bundled up in rubies, sapphires, emeralds, diamonds, pearls and beaten gold.

A profligate squandering of gold in the ornamentation of the frescoed walls, the pillars, the Buddha's tiered altar pillar and the mountainous central altar had created a world so aesthetically dazzling that gold and silver bo trees, the former tribute of Lao vassal princes and Malay rajahs were, by comparison, a simple, almost modest display of precious metal.

The floor space not occupied by pillars, people, altars and gilded sculpture was taken up by an exhibition of gifts from foreign dignitaries and by what presumably was the overflow from the Royal Attic. Looking at the extraordinary jumble of marble statuary, grandfather clocks and crystal chandeliers, you could imagine queens in a spring-cleaning quandary coming across treasures too good to throw out but for which there was simply no place. What to do? Why, the Royal Temple, of course. Where else? And off the bric-a-brac would go by the chariotload.

I squinted at this glittering bowerbird collection, seeing the multitude of objects, by some optical illusion, outlined with a white aureole, then seeing them without form, like vivid pigments congealed at random on a palette, until a blink of my eye restored them to their proper focus. There was a prince's cradle of gold and ivory. There were music boxes, enameled birds designed to sing in gilded cages, an animated bear and other mechanical follies, for which, in all probability, the keys had been lost. There was the glorious paraphernalia attaching to elephants and elephant travel: jeweled accouterments of the royal war elephant; a scale model of the apartments of a white elephant (like all white elephants regarded as an avatar of Gautama in previous existences) complete to the last elaborate detail of a miniature orchestra ready to entertain at the flick of an ear or the twitch of a trunk; and a golden howdah surmounted by a seven-tiered canopy.

There were marquetry commodes, Venetian chairs, a solid gold, gem-encrusted spittoon. There was a jade walking stick and a rose paperweight made from Burmese rubies. To conceive of a stage sufficiently grand to mount these royal properties made my imagination ache from stretching, and I got up and went outside.

In front of the steps, two little boys strolled back and forth, flying kites equipped with whistles that made bird-warbling sounds. They were gently told to move out of the way by a company of saffron-togaed priests wishing to be photographed against a faultlessly sacrosanct background by one of their party who had brought along a Brownie camera.

CHAPTER FIVE

The Schooner

THAT AFTERNOON, as planned, Kippy and I met Irwin at the Oriental. Irwin turned out to be a middle-aged American who liked to think of himself as the official greeter for all other Americans who came to Bangkok. Since he also liked to think of himself as an entrepreneur—"I'm a better entreprenooer than I am a restauratooer, and I'm the best damn restauratooer in town!"—he preferred Americans with projects in mind or money to spend. I fitted into neither category, but as it was an off season for tourists and as I was protected by a small child instead of a husband, Irwin decided to overlook my shortcomings and develop what he referred to as a "real, nice friendship."

I made the mistake of telling him that I was writing notes for a travel diary, and he hounded me with story ideas. I could use none of them, but Irwin never gave up trying. "Well, dear," he would say, "if you can't use the suggestion, how's about a drink this afternoon, or maybe you'd like to go out for dinner, huh?" Usually I would refuse, but with Suchitr and Pranee away, there were times when I welcomed even Irwin's company.

One day, when I was sitting on the Oriental's determinedly green lawn (the Rajdhani had no lawn), Irwin bounded from a near-by patio and slid into the chair opposite mine. "Hello, dear," he said, giving me a bright, V-shaped smile.

I said hello, and hoped he wouldn't stay long.

"Wait until you hear the story I have for you this time, dear."

Irwin slapped his knee and leaned forward toward me. "You know what I did? I bought eighty-five pounds of honey for thirty bucks! Yessir! Only thirty smackers for real Stateside honey." He chuckled and, shooting the cuffs of his nylon shirt, settled back to tell me all the details of the transaction. Apparently, there were four young men on a sailboat who had been so short of cash that they had agreed to part with a barrel of honey for far less than the current market price.

Irwin described the boat vaguely as being small, three-masted and named *California* after the crew's home state. He said that the four Californians aboard had sailed across the Pacific and were intending to sail around the world, and that he didn't know much else about them except that they obviously were no businessmen. He crowed with laughter at this pleasantry, then added, "I'm supposed to go down to the docks round about now and pick up the honey. Care to join me?"

Well, why not? Having collected Kippy from the shadows of a flame-of-the-forest tree where he was trying to corner a large lizard, the three of us crowded into the front seat of a jeep and jolted off down the New Road toward the East Asiatic Docks.

A quarter of an hour later Irwin parked the jeep alongside a godown. "There," he said, pointing. "There's the boat."

About ten yards ahead a three-masted schooner was moored to the wharf. In comparison to a barge anchored off her stern, she looked very small and slight. "Yop," Irwin said. "That's the *California,* your story and my honey." He sidled awkwardly aboard and hallooed. After a muffled reply from somewhere below, Kippy and I followed him down the ladder of an open hatchway into what was apparently the main cabin.

It was rectangular in shape, larger than I had expected, clean, compact and orderly. Flanking both sides of the cabin, low storage chests, well padded with mattresses and pillows of faded yellow, had been converted into couches, with ample headroom provided for cabinets above one and a substantial bookrack over the other. The far wall was completely taken up with a large double cabinet, the lower half of which projected a little farther than the adjacent oil stove, which, with a sink and cupboard unit, evidently made up the galley. In the center of the cabin twin barrels with yellow leather seat cushions were tidily stowed out of the way beneath a drop-leaf mahogany table spread with a jaguar skin.

Not much light came through the skylight above the cabinet, and hardly any filtered past the four curtained portholes, so that the cabin was gently illuminated, the light falling in such a way that the three shirtless men inside looked gleaming and golden. One was softly strumming a guitar, another was loading a movie camera, and the third was sitting in front of the cabinet cleaning a shotgun. They looked up at us inquiringly and continued with what they were doing. I suddenly felt out of place, queerly embarrassed—as though somehow I had blundered into someone else's dream.

"Well, hiya, fellas," Irwin greeted them loudly.

"Hi," they answered, and although all three of them spoke at once, their reply was hardly more than a murmur.

Irwin introduced Kippy and me, said that he had come to pick up the honey and asked where the skipper was.

"Vic isn't here just now," the man with the camera said. "But you can pick up the honey and pay us if you want."

Irwin said quickly that that was fine with him. There was a pause, and then the man with the guitar looked up at me. "I'm Yvor," he said. "Glad to have you aboard."

The man with the camera said that he was Art.

"My name's Hal." The third man wiped the gun grease from his hands on a piece of cotton waste and asked if we wanted a drink.

"Fine," Irwin said. Hal opened the lid of the lower half of the cabinet, reached in and brought out a bottle of rum. He poured a generous amount into five thick white Navy mugs, slugged some water into each from the sink pump, and passed the cups around. Kippy decided that it was too hot below and went up on deck. Irwin sat down heavily on the couch and engrossed himself in the act of drinking. Then there was only the sound of breathing, of water lapping against the hull and of the strange, sweet melody of the guitar.

The three men and I sipped our drinks and said nothing. They were around my age, somewhere in their middle twenties, although it was difficult to know, for their faces were sun-lined and darkened by a day or two's growth of beard. They had an air of self-assurance and poise. Seemingly unconscious of my appraisal, the three of them remained silent. Hal was dark; Yvor was blond; and Art was somewhere in between.

The notes of the guitar slipped from major to minor, and, speaking gently, afraid to set sound in motion in the stillness of this cabin where there seemed to be no room for voices, I asked Yvor the name of the tune he was playing. " 'Isa Lei,' " he said. "Old Fijian song."

Irwin jabbed a forefinger at me. "Hey," he said, slapping his empty mug on the table, "Fijis, that's a romantic name for you all right. Whyn't you ask the fellas some questions, get a story together like?" His voice and the sharp sound of the mug rapped on the table exploded the quiet haze. Reluctantly I produced a notebook and pencil, rather afraid that the over-all impression of romance would vanish when reduced to terms of who, what, why, when and where.

The crew answered my questions briefly and factually. There were just the four of them aboard as owner-crew, each with an equal investment in the schooner. The responsibilities of captaincy were rotated, although for the sake of convenience and convention Vic was the paper, or titular, skipper. Vic, at the moment, was at the local airport collecting information for an article he was writing. They told me that three and a half years before, they had left Los Angeles with blithe self-confidence, a hundred and fifty dollars apiece, and the firm intention of not returning until they had sailed around the world. During the war Vic had been a Marine pilot, the others officers in the Navy. At the start none of them knew much about sailing.

"But we learned," Hal said, laying his gun aside to point out the route they had taken on the world chart mounted on the left of the cabinet. Los Angeles to Acapulco to Panama. The island archipelagoes of the South Pacific—The Galápagoes, Marquesas, Tuamotus, Societies, Cooks, Tokelaus, Tongas, Fijis, and the Solomons. New Hebrides. New Guinea. Indonesia. Siam. Another week and they would be on their way again. Singapore, and after that they weren't sure. It was a question of trade winds and monsoons.

Irwin succumbed to the heat and the rum, and fell asleep breathing heavily.

"Your friend's asleep," Yvor said.

"He's not my friend." I disowned Irwin without a qualm.

"Then get rid of him," Hal growled.

"Do you know he's swindling you on that barrel of honey?" I asked.

"Ah," Yvor said, smiling. "It's not to worry." He laid his guitar across his knee. "He's just another gyp artist who thought he had us skinned." He paused to tune his guitar. "We tried to tell him—" he plucked a string tentatively—"but he wouldn't listen." He struck a chord. "That honey's so old it's half crystallized, and there are at least five pounds of cockroaches in the bottom of the barrel. Irwin is getting just about what he's paying for." Yvor leaned back and started to play *"Isa Lei"* for the third time.

Hal gave the shotgun a final polish and with a sigh of satisfaction replaced it in the gun rack in the top half of the cabinet. Even though he stooped, his dark hair brushed against the overhead. He wakened Irwin, and the barrel of honey was put in the jeep in place of Kippy and me.

I think it was when I was looking through the photograph album Art showed me that I first began to think about sailing on the *California.* It was such an undefined hope that I'm not certain when it first came, but I think it was then, looking at the photographs of Bora Bora, and pearl divers in Manihi, and the valleys of Hiva Oa and Haka Maii. The schooner rocked like a cradle as a barge passed by, and I thought how wonderful it must be to pursue far horizons, away from the insistent clocks and schedules of regular routes, passenger steamers and air terminals. How wonderful to travel with uncertainty, dependent upon the whim of the sea and the wind, unsure of times of arrival and departure, to come slowly and quietly to places where there were things you did not know, never to arrive in a rush of other people and other people's baggage.

Hal thumbed some tobacco into the bowl of a yellowed meerschaum pipe. As he lighted the pipe and drew on it, making the flame spurt up and down, I thought what an astonishing-looking man he was, a dark giant with a melancholy, fierce, scholarly face that made me think of El Greco, Arabs and Richard Burton.

"The schooner's nice, all right," Hal said, "but anyone could have done what we did if they had been able to, or wanted to. We don't have wives and we don't have children and we were free to pack up and go. We wanted to. A lot of people don't. Maybe they think they do, but when they really get down to it, they don't. Otherwise they would. Nothing to it."

"Except a lot of hard work," Art put in. "People look at us and say how they envy us and how they wish they could take time off from their jobs and loaf about the way we do all day. They seem to have the idea that this is just one long, happy round of fun and games. Just one happy, adventurous cruise."

"Which at times it is," Yvor said mildly.

"Sure," Art agreed. "But it's still a hell of a lot of hard work just the same."

Yvor turned to me. "Do names like Hiva Oa and Haka Maii make you starry-eyed? They do me. You should go there. They're great."

Hal knocked out his pipe into the garbage bucket and then refilled our mugs with tepid rum. Mosquitoes buzzed about the still, heated darkness of the cabin. I wished that I could have gone to the Marquesas or, for that matter, anywhere aboard the schooner. I tilted the barrel I was sitting on so that my head rested against the mainmast. "Do you," I asked carefully, "take passengers?"

"Sometimes. We chartered out the *Cal* once to some Australian lumbermen who were scouting for kauri pine in the New Hebrides. Once we took on a Norwegian writer, and once, for a couple of weeks, we took on a husband and wife team who were working on a lecture-travelogue deal." Art pushed a scalloped shell across the table to me. "Put your ashes in this and not on the deck."

"You leave for Singapore at the end of the week?"

"I guess."

"Would you take Kippy and me as passengers?"

Hal sighed. Yvor's eyebrows slanted upward in a quizzical expression. Art got up and went over to the cabinet to pour himself another drink.

"Would you?" I repeated.

"Why?" Hal asked. "Why do you want to go?"

"Why did you want to sail around the world?" I countered. "I don't know *why*. It's just something I'd like to do."

"And I suppose you always get your own way. Well, lady, not

this time," Hal said. "We've got a strict rule. We don't take lady passengers."

"You took that husband and wife," I argued. "Why not a mother and son combination?"

He looked at me for a moment. "It's hardly the same thing," he said dryly. "And what about your husband? What would he say?"

"I'm divorced."

"Divorced!" Art repeated loudly. "Lady, think of our reputations!" He lighted the Coleman lamp on the table and instantly the glass chimney was assaulted by a host of mosquitoes. "I'm sure the yacht clubs wouldn't approve of clean-living American boys with a divorced woman aboard. What do you think, Hal?"

"That Mrs. Hadley doesn't appreciate your humor very much."

"Look," Hal said to me. "Seriously, it's out of the question. No lady passengers. Women cause trouble." The subject was temporarily closed because at that moment Kippy came down the ladder.

"I've finished playing," he announced. "I'm hungry."

"Chow. That's an extra good idea." Yvor beckoned to Kippy and, catching hold of his striped polo shirt, tucked it beneath the waistband of his white duck trousers. "There," he said, giving him a friendly spank. "Just for being so good, you and your mother can join us for dinner ashore." Kippy looked pleased. "You accept?" Yvor turned to me. "Fine." He glanced at the twenty-four-hour clock fastened to the bulkhead to the left of the world chart. "Nineteen hundred. We'd better get under way."

Sliding off the couch, he followed Hal and Art to the forward cabin. "Wait while we change," he called back to me. "We won't be long."

Kippy curled up on the couch, his fair hair dark and wispy with perspiration, his shirt sticking to his back so that his shoulder blades looked like wings. There was the sound of bureau drawers being opened and closed, and after a while the three men reappeared.

We went up on deck and I was surprised to find that it was dark. Clumps of tangled river grass floated darkly downstream past the hull. Silhouettes of sampans glided by. Across the river a freighter was pulling up anchor, the chain rattling in her hawsepipe, the steam winch sending up clouds of smoke like a billowing banner into the clear night air. The *California,* fettered by her moorings, her sails furled neatly on the booms, quietly but restlessly protested the great Siamese heat. I suddenly felt intemperate about sailing on the *California.* I was surprised that my offer to come along had been turned down so bluntly. I wasn't used to being rejected.

That night I lay on the bed stubbing out one Abdullah Imperial cigarette after another in an ashtray advertising Mekong gin, staring up through the mosquito netting at the teakwood squares on the ceiling, reliving the day, and wondering how I was going to get aboard the schooner. Vic, the fourth member of the crew, might be more reasonable than the others. He had to be, that was all there was to it.

I set off again the next morning for the East Asiatic Docks. I had no trouble finding the *California.* I felt that I would have recognized her tall masts and clipper bow anywhere. Hal was working on the mainsail. "Hi," I called. "What are you doing? Putting on the sails?"

"Bending them on, lady, bending them on," he said, looking over his shoulder at me. "Glad you showed. We're going to leave earlier than we expected. Tomorrow or the day after. Heard the weather is blowing up around the Gulf area. We want to get started soon. No sense in running into a typhoon."

Oh, no! That gave Kippy and me only a day to get aboard.

"Well," Hal said, turning to face me, "can't you make it from the wharf to the deck? You want me to help you?"

"No, thanks," I said, tossing my high-heeled sandals onto the deck. I caught hold of the mainshroud and pulled myself aboard. I sat down on the hatch and looked about. The deck and hatches were painted gray; the trim gunwale caps and standing rigging were black. There seemed to be endless lines secured to the pin rails. It was blazing hot, and the deck burned my bare feet. Another man, whom I hadn't seen before, was scraping the old varnish from a dinghy stowed forward on the starboard side.

"That's Vic," Hal said, following my glance. "And that's Scupper, our pooch." He pointed to a panting brindle heap lying in the shade of the dinghy. "Now you've met us all." He rubbed the palms of his hands on his ragged dungarees and then sat down beside me on the hatch and offered me a cigarette from a crumpled package. He seemed disinclined to talk, and nothing much was said until Vic joined us.

So much depended on Vic. If he approved of me, then I might very well find myself sailing to Singapore on the schooner, rather than flying on to India as I had planned. My mind leaped up to meet the possibilities and the complications of the situation. I said hello, carefully measuring him. He was thin, small boned and wiry and had an air of bold impertinence—like a cocksparrow, I thought. Just like a cocksparrow.

"Hi, kiddy," he said, calmly inspecting me, and then right away he began to fire off questions. Where had I come from? Where was I going? Where did I live in America? New York? How could I stand living in such a crummy place? What a bunch of phony jokers New Yorkers were!

This wasn't the way I had expected the conversation to go at all. "Would you—" I hesitated, then began again, taking hold of myself. "Would you let Kippy and me come along with you as passengers to Singapore?" The question seemed to me so important that I could scarcely bring myself to say the words.

"Nope," he said. "No lady passengers. This is a man's boat, kiddy. When we're at sea we don't want any women aboard mucking things up."

"Oh, really," I said impatiently. "You're not being fair at all. I won't get in the way. Why don't you give me a chance?"

"We just can't do it, kiddy," Vic said. "No lady passengers. You can't go. We're glad to have you aboard today, though, so if you want, stick around."

I stuck around. Maybe they would change their minds at the last minute. I spent the rest of the day exploring the schooner and trying my best to be ingratiating and helpful. I was like Browning's Last Duchess, who smiled at everything she saw and whose looks went everywhere. I admired the utilization of space, the almost severe cleanliness and order. I knelt on the couch in the lounge and examined the bookrack with its row of mold-bleached books. There was, as I was sure there would be, a good deal of Melville, Conrad, Stevenson and Maugham. The rest was a diversified collection: Joyce, Kant, Plutarch, Cook's *Voyages* and a two-volume set of Havelock Ellis which Scupper had apparently chewed on; *Anna Karenina, Green Mansions,* several anthologies of science fiction, a grease-stained copy of *The Joy of Cooking.* There was an abundance of technical and scientific literature on oceanography, seamanship, sociology and philosophy. There were more bookshelves and racks in the forward cabin, and another library in the chart-room.

I looked at the wheelhouse and imagined myself at the wheel. I peered briefly into the engine room, which smelled pungently of oil and gasoline. I talked a good deal with the four men, and I felt overwhelmed by the longing to sail with them to Singapore. It was as if I were watching clouds formlessly mounting and assembling in the sky at last take on shape. It was like a childhood game, spotting cloud people and cloud animals, to see in my mind's eye my daydreams sharpen and particularize into the image of this schooner on which I wanted to sail. The very thought that I had a daydream in my grasp and might not be able to realize it was a torment.

"Look," I said. "Don't make it so difficult. I'm coming along with you to Singapore. I must. That's all there is to it."

"Sorry," Hal said sharply. "You're not. For the last time, you're not coming. It's not because we don't like you. It's just that we have a no-women-on-board-at-sea policy that we've stuck to for three and a half years. Anyway, you couldn't take it if you did come. There's no fresh water aboard except for drinking and cooking. Salt-water baths only."

I shrugged. "I don't care."

"Uncomfortable quarters."

"That doesn't matter."

"No privacy."

"I'm sure I could manage."

"Personal safety. Kippy or you might fall overboard. If you fell over at night or in rough weather, you'd have had it. We couldn't rescue you. The boat would just have to go on without you."

"I'd be careful. I'd watch out for Kippy."

"You'd be underfoot all the time. You'd be no help at all if there were any trouble."

"Well, I'd stay out of the way, and what would it matter if I

weren't any help? For three years you've managed pretty well on
your own."

"Look, kiddy," Vic broke in. "Has anyone ever told you about
the bees and the butterflies?"

"How crude," Yvor murmured.

"Crude, hell. We're all red-blooded American boys," Vic said.
"Let's not beat about the bush. A girlie aboard would be murder."

"Let's not club the subject to death," Hal said. He reached
behind him, felt along the shelf and pulled down a rusty harmonica.
"You can't come, lady, that's that." He began to play "You Are
My Sunshine."

"Well," I said, as evenly as I could, "if you ever change your
minds, will you let me know?"

"Sure," Hal said. "Sure, we'll let you know."

When I went down to the docks the next day, the *California*
was gone.

Two weeks later I received a cable from Hal saying that they
had arrived safely in Singapore. The crew must have changed their
minds. Why else should Hal have cabled me? Usually nothing is
ever done immediately in Siam, but, joyously sweeping aside protocol and convention, I somehow managed to get Kippy and myself
aboard the next morning's flight for Singapore.

At noon the lights above the cockpit door blinked on. NO SMOK-
ING. FASTEN YOUR SEAT BELTS. The stewardess made a trilingual
statement in Hindustani, Malay and Siamese to the same effect.
Beneath the clouds I could see the dense jungle of the Malayan
Peninsula rising to meet us and, as the plane banked steeply, a
glimpse of the roof tops of Singapore Town and a patch of sea.
The plane leveled off and came in for a landing at Kallang Air-
port.

Like most airports, Kallang had an aura of cosmopolitan indis-
tinction. The terminal buildings, the administrative offices, the
magazine kiosks, and the queues of passengers with harried and
bewildered expressions gave no key to the essence of what lay
beyond. Seen against this setting, the people not dressed in Western
costume looked out of place and a little garish, like partygoers in
evening clothes coming home at breakfast time. I went through

Immigration and Customs sandwiched between an Indian lady swathed in a green silk sari and a Malay businessman wearing a black velvet fez and a sarong made up in pin-striped serge to match his tailored jacket. I retrieved our luggage, and there Kippy and I were, on the edge of Singapore, a town I knew nothing about and that I had come to only so that we might sail on a three-masted schooner whose exact whereabouts were unknown.

Marshaling an ancient taxicab and cramming luggage, Kippy and myself into it, I started off on a search for the *California*. The Yacht Club seemed the most likely place for the schooner to be, but no, she wasn't there. However, a British port official volunteered to take us out in the club launch to see if we could find her. Leaving a red-sashed servant guarding our luggage, we chugged away in the launch and zigzagged across the immensity of Keppel Harbor past cargo boats from every port in the world, past Arab dhows, past Macassar *prahus,* past Cantonese junks with their batswing sails, but nowhere was there a sixty-three-foot, gaff-rigged schooner with a white hull and *California* lettered in black on her transom.

After an hour's search our British samaritan said that he was inclined to believe that the schooner might be in for repairs at the Empire Docks, some four miles away. We returned to the shore, woke up the driver, gave him a new set of directions, and with a "Cheerio. Best of luck" from the officer, Kippy and I drove off again. Two hours later we were still meandering through the Empire Docks—a labyrinth of canals, piers, alleyways and godowns. I saw a hundred *Californias,* only to have them turn out to be trading vessels or sailing coasters when we rounded the corner. But at last, miraculously, I found her.

I clattered aboard joyfully and sang out the good news that I had arrived. Hal and Yvor appeared from below.

"Well, what do you know," Hal said, looking at me with incredulous eyes. "Where in God's name did you come from?"

"Well, I'll be damned," Yvor said. "What brings you here?"

I must say that I had expected a less casual welcome but I was so pleased to be there, so filled with delight to see the two men, so eager for them to understand that the reason I was there was because I was in love with the schooner, which, to me, was all the

wonder and mystery and adventure in the world, so hopelessly
wound up with excitement and relief that nothing could have
lessened my enthusiasm. I chattered wildly, breathlessly, almost
incoherently.

"Lady, lady," Hal interrupted after a while, shaking his head
and smiling. "I never meant you could come with us. I only sent
you the cable because I thought you'd read about the storm that
hit the Gulf—you know, the one I told you I thought we'd miss,
but which we didn't—and that you'd think we were all drowned or
something."

"Oh," I said, hearing my voice faint and far off.

"Judas Priest!" Yvor said. "You don't have to look like that. It's
not the end of the world," and he began to laugh. Then Hal joined
in, and then, suddenly, we were all laughing. A small band of
barefooted dock workers collected around us, giggling like children,
and even the cab driver came over to see what was happening.

Hal clapped me on the shoulder and helped me off the boat saying it was high time for Kippy and me to get settled somewhere
and that he and Yvor would go back with me to town to see about
a hotel.

I was longing to stay at the celebrated Raffles Hotel, but as there
were no rooms to be had there, I went instead to the Adelphi. It
was a substantial and stolid hotel, with a dark lobby cooled by
punkah fans. I was given a two-room suite with a terrace and a
large, old-fashioned bathroom which had, as a *pièce de résistance,*
a huge iron bathtub with curlicue claw feet. After Bangkok, this
was unparalleled luxury.

"Ah," Hal said, gazing at the bathtub approvingly. "Mind if we
use it?"

"We have to pay fifty cents American for a bath at the dock
hostel," Yvor said apologetically. He went on to explain that he
and the rest of the crew were very short of cash. The storm they
had encountered in the Gulf of Siam, apart from blowing out
eleven sails, had caused a good deal of damage all around, and
paying for new sails and repairs was costing the crew almost all the
money they had.

"Of course," I said. "Use the bath any time."

Art and Vic also cheerfully accepted the use of the bathtub and, strangely enough, the use of my bathtub seemed to be the main-spring of our friendship. It was rather an odd friendship. The crew's attitude toward women was one of condescension and bio-logical attention. They treated me as one might a precocious child, as someone quite droll and a little bit off. "Hadley, you're 'nuts" was a standard remark of Vic's. I was no longer Mrs. Hadley, but "Hadley," which sounded like the name of a stage butler, and I was obviously nuts because I used an eyelash curler (Vic found it in the bathroom while he was taking a bath) and had a hat made of beads.

That the crew were different from anyone I had ever known before made them all the more charming and attractive to me. What other people thought didn't bother them. They regarded emotion with suspicion. They didn't talk merely for the sound it makes, nor trickily maneuver the conversation for the sake of wit, nor formulate serpentine discussions of non-problems. I wasn't particularly impressed by their discussions of navigational com-plexities, but I never tired listening to all the stories they told with casual, stark humor—"D'you remember the time the shark almost got Vic?" "Remember when Yvor got hit by lightning?" "Then there was a fer-de-lance that crawled into Hal's sleeping bag, and Hal had to lie there without moving all the time we were trying to smoke the brute out."

They were full of such anecdotes. What anecdotes of physical courage could I offer in return? The time my sister dropped a garter snake down my back? The time I had stepped into a hornets' nest? I had behaved shamefully both times. They listened, but were not terribly interested in what I had to say about my life in New York and the time I had spent in Europe. They were skeptical that anything good could emerge from such an environment as mine and I, so eager to prove myself an exception to their prejudice, could think of no way to impress them.

I did what I could to help out—what Art acidly described as a "mother-hen routine"—searching Singapore for cheap laundries adept at removing rust stains, picking up their mail when I went to get mine at the Consulate, and running whatever errands they would trust me with. I kept hoping that all this helpfulness would

melt the crew's collective heart and that they would change their
minds and take me with them when they left.

I don't believe I was getting very far with this mollifying process
until an unexpected ally showed up—Woody Wirsig, a magazine
editor whom I had known in New York. I told him, of course,
about the *California,* how I had begged to sail aboard her as a
passenger, and how I had flown from Bangkok only to be rejected.
Woody thought this was extremely funny and said that he would
like to see the men who could turn me down. "It would be a great
story," he said musingly. "One girl and four men on a boat."

"And a six-year-old child and a dog," I said.

"Yes, that's real material," he said. "Tell you what. Let me meet
the boys and let's see what can be done about it."

Art thumbed slowly through the pages of the *California's* worn
photograph album, with Woody looking over his shoulder. Vic
and Yvor sat opposite, and Hal stretched out on the couch. Patiently, I tended the Primus stove, waiting for the coffee to perco-
late.

Art pointed out the pictures he had taken in Papua of tribal
widows who wore necklaces of their deceased husbands' bones; and
pearl divers in Penrhyn; the Big and Little Nambu tribes of Male-
kula. Hal raised his head sleepily and, propping himself on his
elbow, murmured something about village virgins and *kava* ceremonies in Samoa. Vic spoke casually of storms they had pulled
through. I poured the coffee and passed it around.

Until then I don't believe the crew fully realized the extraordinary quality of their story. They had been skeptical when I told
them that an account of their adventures illustrated with photographs was a valuable commercial property ("Lady, don't run off
at the mouth so!"), but now Woody told them exactly what I had.

"Submit sample photographs," he said. "Outline the story."

"I could outline the story," I suggested hopefully.

"Of course," Woody said. "That's the idea. Let her do it. Take
her along with you. Then you've got the added interest of one girl
on a boat with four men. Any magazine would be interested in
that." He paused to sip his coffee. "You'd all stand a chance of
making some money," he added coaxingly.

I was as careful of the situation as if it had been a newborn baby. "I'll pay my passage," I said. "Whatever you think it should be."

"Well," Vic said slowly. "We'll think it over."

They thought it over until the night of the Chinese New Year, when Kippy, the crew and I went to the Happy World amusement park to celebrate the coming Chinese Year of the Dragon. We stopped at the gate to watch a man in a monkey mask throw a handful of bamboo divining sticks into the air for those who wanted their fortunes predicted, and an Indian snake charmer who was wearily serenading a sleepy cobra. We walked past a cinema marquee topped by a giant-size figure of Esther Williams in a bathing suit inscribed "HAPPY CHINESE NEW YEAR TO MY FANS." We rode on the merry-go-round, tried our luck at the shooting galleries, and finally ended up at an all-night eating place where the proprietor's small son was curled contentedly on the doorstep, a plate of melon seeds beside him and his lap filled with a heap of small scarlet packets containing his New Year's gifts of money.

"We've got good news for you," Yvor said, as we all sat down. "We've decided to let you come with us on the *Cal*. We're sailing in three days."

It was said at last. All the warmth of feeling I had for the schooner engulfed me, and I felt like a piece of driftwood caught in a whirlpool, going around and around and around.

Hal grinned wryly. "You won, lady," he said. "Consider it a deal." He ordered another round of coffee and a plate of cakes cut into butterfly shapes. "Here," he said to Kippy. "Eat now, while you have a chance, before you're a cabin boy."

Hal paid the bill, and when the change was returned, he sorted it out carefully, separating the square Malayan pennies from the rest. "Look at them," he said with faint disgust. "They're out of proportion. They're not even symmetrical." The talk drifted into a discussion between Yvor and Hal of the statistical probability of consecutively throwing twenty heads or tails.

The next morning I bought the crew a case of beer and took it down to the schooner. Toni, a Malayan girl friend of Vic's, was standing on the deck. I said hello, but she didn't answer, and I started down the ladder to the lounge.

"Look out, Hadley. Papa doesn't have his *pareu* on," Yvor shouted.

I stopped midway, awkwardly balancing myself and the crate of beer on the narrow treads of the ladder.

"All right. Come on down." Hal took the beer crate from my arms, placed it in the galley sink, and said that I was a hero for bringing it. I felt a glow of pleasure at this tribute.

Vic handed me a sheet of the *California* stationery. It was headed *Schooner California,* and there was a printed blue silhouette of the schooner in the left-hand corner. "It's the crew list. Look at it," Vic said, grinning. I looked at the sheet of paper.

William W. V.	Master
Yvor H. S.	Navigator
Arthur T.	Engineer
Hal D. M.	Sail maker
Arthur Hadley III	Cabin Boy
Leila E. B. Hadley	Cook

I read it several times, savoring the sound of it.

"I don't know how it will go down with the local pillars of society, but that's it," Vic said. "That's the list. You're signed on officially."

"Your coming along may cause some comment," Yvor said.

I shrugged. The possibilities of What People Would Say were too remote at that point for me to consider seriously.

"Our personal relationships have been too good to have you jeopardize them," Art said formally. "To eliminate ill feeling and jealousy, we'll make every effort not to chase you up the mainmast and round the deck, and we'll expect you to do the same for us. Okay?"

"Okay," I replied meekly.

The four men had grouped themselves around the table while I sat facing them on the couch, a humble candidate before a tribunal. The situation would have been farcical if we hadn't all been so serious.

"First of all, the boat comes first." Hal puffed on his meerschaum pipe. "You've got to do everything we tell you to. No girlish temperament on your part.

"Secondly, whatever inconveniences there are, you'll have to put up with them. We won't change our way of life for you. You'll have to make the effort to fit in.

"Thirdly, and most important, we've decided to take you along on the basis of a temporary paying partner. We've voted you on board not as a passenger but as a working member of the crew. Seeing as how you're going to work on our story, we didn't feel right about soaking you a fancy fare, but this means you'll also have to work on the boat and do your share just the same as the rest of us. We've decided to go to Ceylon, but, of course, if we don't get along, we'll put you off wherever it's convenient for us. All clear? Understand?"

I said yes, and wrote out a traveler's check to pay for Kippy's and my share of the food and the running expenses as far as Penang, the first stop en route to Ceylon.

That night we were all invited to a farewell party arranged by an old school friend of mine who had happily turned up in Singapore.

I was the guest of honor and stood for a long time saying how-do-you-do to Bill-of-Caltex, Tom-of-Coca-Cola, Joe-of-Stanvac, Charlie-of-Goodrich Rubber and all the other American businessmen whose names were welded to those of their companies. The news of my sailing on the *California* had created quite a stir, and as I was shaking hands with the newly arrived guests I was aware that there was considerable reaction to my going. The men confined their opinions chiefly to a roguish wink at the crew and a refined and knowing leer at me, while the ladies said, in quite audible whispers, what the men had the grace only to imply. To my face, however, they presented a united smiling front, saying with tigerish smiles, "What fun your little boy will have," and "Goodness, how adventurous you are!"

The Naval Attaché of Singapore thumped his glass smartly down on its cork coaster. "I think it's all damn nonsense," he said. "I think the men are out of their minds to take you. But if you're going to go and don't want to get thrown overboard, you better listen to me." He then proceeded to give me swift and tart instructions on the course of my future behavior.

"Be productive," he said. "Do your fair share of the work. Don't *ever* kibitz. Don't complain about their cooking. Don't complain about *anything*. Don't get in their way. See that your little boy doesn't get in their way. Keep your mouth shut as much as you can. Don't ask a lot of silly questions. Take along some packages of Dreft. It lathers even in salt water. Get down to breakfast early and stay below, for the boys might want a little privacy at that hour. And remember above all else, that the boys have got along very well so far, and if anything goes wrong, it's your fault. Do you understand?" He peered at me searchingly. I nodded. "All right, then," he finished up. "Good luck and good sailing." I felt that I should salute, click my heels and walk backward out of the room.

Caught between the cross fires of the Naval Attaché and the gossipy ladies, I wasn't sure that the evening was going to be tolerable.

I turned warily to acknowledge the introduction of an American, the captain of a round-the-world cruise ship. "I envy you your sailing on the schooner," he said. "Nothing in the world like sailing. Hard work, but infinitely rewarding."

Suddenly I liked the Captain very much. He said that he had heard I was doing some writing. He also wanted to write a book— *Captain, My Captain,* he thought he would call it—and it would be about his life at sea and about the eccentricities of some of the passengers he had carried. Did I think that a man who couldn't stand his cabin mate and insisted that a wooden partition be built across his stateroom would make a good anecdote? And what about a man who had to have his eggs boiled exactly three minutes and eighteen seconds? Or an elderly woman who wore transparent shorts and a T-shirt and whose only apparent purpose in going on a cruise had been to see the "dirty pictures" at Pompeii?

We went back to talking about ships, and, supposing quite accurately that there would be little room on the *California* for my bulky suitcases, the Captain offered to take them along with him on his ship as far as Ceylon. He also insisted on giving me an oilskin sou'wester and a seaman's knit pull-over since "a little bit of foul-weather gear might come in handy." He waved aside my thanks. "Think nothing of it," he said. "We seafaring folk always stick together." This was the first insight I had into the camaraderie shared by all lovers of the sea. "We seafaring folk," he had said—

and to me, it was as though he had given me a membership card for the only club I had ever wanted to join.

The next night, my last in Singapore, I spent packing. Vic had come up to the hotel for a bath and was stretched on the bed watching me sort out the things I would take from the things I would send ahead with the Captain to Ceylon.

CHAPTER SIX

The Voyage to Penang

IT WAS A FINE DAY for sailing. The sun gleamed upon the masts of the *California* so that they shone like three golden spears poised against the sky. Along the docks there was a pervasive smell of copra, like a compound of coconut oil and burnt almonds. I climbed aboard. Yvor helped me with my luggage, and together we went below to the lounge, where Hal was stretched out on the couch reading a three-week-old issue of *Time* and Vic sat on the cushioned barrel, paring his toenails with a penknife.

"When do we sail?" I asked Vic.

"Whenever we're ready," he answered, picking up a nail paring from the deck and placing it carefully in the garbage pail.

Yvor took up his guitar and strummed a few chords and softly and slowly began to sing a song about a pretty quadroon who, like a flower, had faded too soon. He continued to play for a while. Hal kept on reading. Vic finished cutting his toenails and began to clean them with the point of the knife blade. There was a sudden thump on deck, followed by the sound of someone coming aboard and the patter and click of dog's feet.

"Art's back," Vic said. He turned to me. "Go help him put the chow away."

I hurried up on deck, where I found Art surrounded by wicker crates and wooden boxes containing what appeared to be adequate provisions for a small army. "Here—" Art indicated the vegetable locker. "You put the fresh stuff away here, and I'll stow the rest of it below." Scupper pawed the lid of the vegetable locker and whined eagerly. "He wants to get at the cockroaches," Art explained, smiling indulgently. I lifted the lid of the locker gingerly, and a giant cockroach scuttled out. Scupper trapped it between his paws and played with it a while before he ate it. "Good doggie." Art patted him and then went off with a bushel basket of tinned food.

Potatoes. Onions. Bananas. Cabbage. Carrots. Tomatoes. Peas. Pineapples. I wedged them as carefully as I could in the space allotted. I noticed a cluster of dock hands watching me, and I tried to look as casual as possible, as if stowing away provisions were something I did every day of my life. For their benefit I ostentatiously coiled and uncoiled a few lines before I returned below.

The jaguar skin had been removed from the dining table and seagoing parallel boards had been placed along each edge and inserted down the center. There was an authoritative and rapid exchange between the four men.

"Lounge all secured?"

"Head valve closed?"

"Ports closed?"

"Stores stowed?"

"Well, let's get under way."

"Okay. I'll turn off the generator then. We ought to have enough juice by now to start up the silly engine."

Inquisitively I followed them on deck to see what would happen next. Hal descended into the dark hole that was the engine room, shut off the generator and switched on the Diesel. There was a violent roar, a grinding, shuddering cough, and then silence.

"Goddamn silly bastard," Hal snarled. There was a rattle and a rather uncertain roar, as if the engine were trying to please but hadn't the strength to do so. A splutter and silence.

"Dear, sweet Jesus." It sounded as if Hal had kicked the engine. Immediately there was an angry racketing which leveled off into a clamorous throbbing. The *Cal* vibrated like a tuning fork.

Hal bellowed reassuringly, "It looks like she'll run for a while." I perched on top of the hatch and watched Vic and Yvor casting off the bow and stern lines. The *Cal* began to rock. Vic climbed hastily into the wheelhouse, and Yvor shoved the bow out from the dock. Slowly we began to edge away.

"Well, we're off at last," Yvor remarked carelessly. Hal emerged from the engine room, his face smudged with grease, his back and chest dripping with sweat. He glanced at me approvingly. "That's a girl," he said. "Stay there out of the way until we get the sails up." He swung himself into the wheelhouse next to Vic, and we powered slowly out along the docks, past the berths where cargo ships from Rotterdam, Vladivostok, London and Marseilles towered above us; past a fleet of fishing boats, cutters and ketches; and then out into the entrancing panorama of Keppel Harbor, the gateway to the Indian Ocean, and the entrepôt of traders. Fascinated, shielding my eyes against the burning sun, drinking in the variety and the movement around us, I turned this way and that. Wallowing *tonkangs* transferred cargoes of oil and rubber, tin and copra to rusty, beaten-up freighters. Macassar *prahus* with needle-sharp bowsprits and masts stepped tripod-fashion on their beamy decks swept past clumsy, transom-sterned *twakows,* loaded down with firewood from the mangrove belts. Steersmen vigorously swung the long bowsprits of Borneo *bugis* back and forth to avoid seemingly inevitable collisions with junks and dhows and peddlers' sampans.

Hal sat on the gearbox behind the wheelhouse and guided the wheel with his feet. He chewed gum and anxiously surveyed the harbor. "We'll never make it out of here without hitting at least one of them," he said, gesturing to the *twakows* and *bugis* surrounding us.

Vic shrugged. "It's not to worry." He had the air of a bantam rooster out to reassure a rather morose eagle. Sauntering up to the bow, he signaled directions to Hal, who continued to chew gum with a painfully distressed expression. A launch raced by, churning up the water and crossing our bow dangerously close.

Hal protested strongly. "All right, all right," Vic shouted back. "We had the right of way."

We passed the breakwater. Then the engine began to throb irregularly. Yvor lunged for the engine room and reappeared shortly with the news that something was wrong with the engine and that it was high time anyway to get the sails up. I offered to help but was told firmly not to move unless otherwise instructed. Obviously,

I was considered a menace. With a lot of chatter about vangs and booms—meaningless to me—the mizzen was hoisted, and then the main and the fore. With the engine cut off, there was a sudden quiet, the peaceful sound of water rushing and gurgling around the hull interrupted only by curt commands of "Sheet her out" and "Slack the lazy jack!"

Kippy, looking very cowed—Art had just told him to shut up and get out of the way—crawled up on the hatch and sat beside me. It was comforting to find him in the same state that I was—bewildered, out of place and enormously excited.

The wind caught in the sails, billowing them out, and we passed the governor's island with the ornate Residency on its crown. We headed off toward the Malacca Straits, and now that open water was in sight, the boys dropped their terse, efficient manner and replaced it with an air of breezy indifference. Hal slid off the gearbox and dropped comfortably into the seat alongside the wheel. Bracing his knee against the wheel, he began to read a water-stained copy of *Tales of the Supernatural.* I followed the others below, where they poured themselves generous slugs of lukewarm rum.

The conversation drifted around to the South Seas. "You know," Yvor said reflectively, "the South Pac is the best damn place we've ever seen. There's no place like it. We've never had it so good."

For my benefit he described the specialized environment of the islands—the lagoons and the barrier reefs, the outstanding hospitality and the good life, and then lightly he began to talk about the women. "Bora Bora," he said dreamily, "was an extra good place for women. It was a big army base during the war. A spectacularly beautiful island, by the way—frangipani all over the place. Well, only one sailor ever came back after the war to marry his girl, but the other girls didn't seem to care. They just went along, mighty proud of their half-American babies, which they took much better care of than they did their pure Polynesian kids. In fact, everyone seemed to want to have a blond baby in the Societies." He lit a cigarette and, having paused to concentrate on blowing three perfect smoke rings, said musingly, "There isn't much intellectual stimulation in the islands, but between the food and the women you don't really care what the political situation is or what's on André Gide's mind now. You just sit at Quinn's Bar, or any one

of the other honky little tonks and think what a fine life it is and
how damn lucky you are to be alive. It's a special sort of paradise,
and if you're in the mood for it, there's nothing to touch it. We got
tired of it after a while, but if there's one place we all want to go
back to, that's it—*tiare tahiti* and all."

I asked what a *tiare tahiti* was. Vic pointed to a flower design in
his *pareu* which was barely discernible beneath the dirt and grease.
"It's kind of like a wild gardenia which grows all over the islands.
The girls wear them behind their ears. If you wear one behind
your left ear, it means you've found your man; behind your right
ear, you're still looking. Some girlies, of course, wear flowers behind
both ears. Those are bad girlies." Vic raised one dark and shaggy
eyebrow. "Very bad girlies."

Art had said little during this discussion, busying himself instead
with the preparation of dinner. I watched him deftly peel and slice
potatoes. I asked him if he needed any help. "You can if you want,"
he answered without looking up. "But we all take turns. Each of
us has a Cook Day. You'll have yours . . . let's see—" he hesitated
—"you'll have yours after Hal's, I suppose." He stacked a pile of
thick, white plates on the table. He had set the Primus stove to one
side and had turned on the Diesel stove, which was already generating enough heat to make the lounge uncomfortably hot.

I wandered up to the wheelhouse, where Hal was alternately
reading and looking up at the sails. Scupper was curled at his feet,
and Kippy was stretched out on the cushioned seat opposite Hal.
I sat down cautiously on the windward side on the ledge of the
wheelhouse next to Kippy.

"Feel sick?" Hal asked. I assured him I never got seasick.

"I get seasick," he said, looking solemn. as people always do when
they speak of themselves or their habits, no matter how trivial.

"Are you sick now?"

"No, it's not rough enough, but I always feel punk the first day
out."

I said it was odd that after almost four years at sea he should
still feel seasick. The topic of seasickness seemed ridiculously prosaic at such a time. The sky was pearly, pinkening in the west, and
a fresh breeze had sprung up, ruffling the water. Singapore had
completely disappeared, and far off I could see the coast of Sumatra,

like a vague blue cloud bank on the horizon. The sun set with a beauty that was staggering—all golden and fiery and molten crimson which faded into the brief, glowing serenity of twilight, before it darkened and the first few stars were visible.

"Chow," Art shouted up to us. "Chowsie-wowsie!" Slowly Hal climbed out of the wheelhouse. He braced the wheel against the seat cushion, and we went below to the lounge, which was like a furnace. I had never felt such heat concentrated in any room before. Even though we were not exerting ourselves, we all perspired in an alarming way. Yvor and Art had changed from khakis to *pareus*, Tahitian cotton sarongs, which were the standard wearing apparel aboard the schooner.

After supper I helped Art wash the dishes. He heated a pan of salt water and added it as needed to the water in the sink. While he washed, I pumped the dirty dishwater out and pumped in fresh salt water for rinsing, a process that had to be repeated frequently. The pump was stiff, and my arm was aching by the time the last plate was rinsed and put away. I started forward toward the crew's quarters, a cabin which they referred to as the yo-yo room because of the way it bounced around in heavy weather.

"Where are you going?" Art demanded. I replied that if it were all right with him I was going to use the bathroom. "The head," I amended as casually as possible.

"Well, it's not all right," Art said. "You can't go until I've shown you how." I stared at him suspiciously as he preceded me into the minute cubbyhole situated well up in the fo'c'sle.

"If you're going to use the head, you might as well know how to use it right, or there'll be—" He cut himself short and changed whatever he was about to say to, "a damned mess on the overhead." He pointed out various valves affixed to the head and, referring to a diagram on a piece of paper pinned to the bulkhead, showed me what was meant by petcock A and valve C. "You have to turn this one, petcock A, on to fill the bowl. Then you pump the water in like this. Now you turn— Are you watching me?"

I nodded glassily.

"Now you turn this valve here, Valve C, so you can flush it. Now you just pump up and down until the bowl is empty and *clean*," he concluded meaningfully. "Now *you* see if you can fill up the bowl and flush it." I went through the procedure awkwardly several times before Art felt confident enough to leave me to whatever shreds of privacy remained. The door to the head was of plywood and was fitted so loosely in the frame that I was sure every rustle would be clearly audible in the lounge. There was a small basin alongside, and modestly I turned on the faucet. Instantly there was a shout of fury from the lounge. "Leave the water alone, for God's sake! That's *fresh* water. That's not for washing; it's for drinking!" There was a second's pause. "Did you hear me?" Art roared.

"Yes," I said faintly, heartily wishing that bodily functions were nonexistent. To make matters even worse, I thought that the pump handle had stuck. It hadn't—I had turned the wrong valve, that was all—but it seemed like hours before I had fulfilled all the necessary instructions. I emerged panting and triumphant and was attempting to sneak up on deck unnoticed when I saw Art standing in the companionway smirking. "Everything come out all right?" he asked. Wordless, I fled up the ladder to the sanctuary of the wheelhouse.

Yvor was on watch, and although he must have been aware of the incident below, he made no reference to it. He pointed out a light intermittently flashing off on the portside which marked the Lingga Archipelago, and then sociably began to brief me on the various constellations overhead. Orion, of course, with his glittering belt, and the Big Dipper, which was coming up low on the horizon, the Southern Cross, Taurus and Gemini—I picked these out with no trouble, which encouraged Yvor to locate a half dozen or so other navigational stars whose names I promptly forgot. But there was plenty of time to learn to identify them, and I lay back on the cushion contentedly looking up at all the stars which were beautiful and nameless until I descended sleepily to the chartroom.

The chartroom was a brief and narrow channel between a broad, built-in chart table and a bunk, bounded on the forward end by the engine room and by a raised platform aft which served as the lazaret. All possible space had been utilized. The lazaret was a dark hole crammed to the overhead with spare anchor chains, coils of line, Art's rusting golf clubs, stacks of discarded books, spare sails and packing cases of emergency rations. The wild jumble was partially concealed by a wooden honeycomb arrangement for holding charts at the foot of the bunk and by the chart table on the other side of the cabin. Cabinets and bookshelves backed the chart table, which, was bare except for a rolled-up chart and a goose-necked lamp. Drawers beneath the table held the rest of the charts. The overhead was painted white and was quilted with rusty rivets, and on the ledge over the bunk a sextant was pegged. The base of the mizzenmast came down close by the head of the bunk, and between the partition that divided the engine room from the chartroom, and the mast, a table had been bracketed, just large enough to hold an ashtray, a Hamilton chronometer set in a gimbaled case, and a framed photograph of a Polynesian girl with a flower tucked behind her left ear. (What was it Vic had said that meant? She had found her man—that was it.) I picked the photograph up and examined it. The girl was very pretty and she had inscribed the portrait with meticulous Spencerian calligraphy to Hal, with affection. Replacing the picture, I continued my survey.

A built-in series of cabinets and bookracks ran along the inside edge of the bunk, backed by a large black radio panel which looked complicated and mysterious. There were three portholes—one over the chart table, one over the bunk bookrack, and one above the goose-necked lamp, which looked out on the deck. Above the chronometer hung a kerosene lamp, greenish-black with corrosion, and a small light bulb with a piece of dirty string dangling from it was fixed to the overhead at the foot of the bunk. Lying on the bunk, I discovered that I could switch it on by grasping the string with my toe and jerking it. The bunk itself was covered with a rust-stained sheet, two olive-drab Army blankets and a dark green poncho as a counterpane. The most that could be said for the chartroom was that it was serviceable and orderly, but because it was temporarily allocated to Kippy and me, I loved it. I stowed my suitcase and duffel bag in the lazaret and stuffed the rest of my belongings in the bunk cabinets. Kippy had fallen asleep at the foot of the bunk; he was barefoot, but otherwise fully clad in T-shirt and blue jeans. I decided to sleep in my underwear, but I couldn't sleep much that first night.

There were too many odd noises to become accustomed to: there was an over-all creaking, like the sound of a rusted gate swinging to and fro in the wind, and then there was the rattle of the blocks on the travelers as the booms shifted back and forth, and a myriad of other unidentifiable noises. There was a hole in the overhead of the lazaret in which the binnacle port was set, and through it I could hear occasional murmurs, and once, for about an hour, the plink-plinking of Yvor's guitar.

I awoke groggily. A large, hard, cold hand was gripping my shoulder. I wriggled sleepily. "Time to get up, lady. Chow. Chow." I sat up in the bunk, knocking my head smartly on the overhead, and slid uncertainly to the deck. It was a full minute before I realized that I was clad only in the briefest of underwear and that Hal was leaning against the ladder looking at me appraisingly. I scrambled back into the bunk, yipping with confusion.

"Chow," Hal repeated without changing his expression. Slowly and deliberately he climbed up the ladder. Thinking of all the things I should have said and hadn't, I yanked on a pair of shorts and a shirt, braided my hair and managed to get from bunk to deck without stumbling or cracking my head, my annoyance dissolving when I climbed on deck and saw the sun shining on the sea and the diamond turmoil of the wake rippling behind us.

It was Vic's Cook Day, and breakfast was a tempestuous affair. Vic darted about the lounge scaling coffee mugs at us, swearing at the stove, in a pother that the biscuits were burned on the bottom and raw on top, rattling and banging pans, and all the while keeping up a running flow of conversation about an article one of the men's adventure pulps had ordered him to rewrite, about the things he wanted to do—all wildly impractical things like walking from Cairo to Morocco, chartering a dhow to explore the Baluchistan coast, leading an archaeological expedition to Alaska, and then his talk coursed off onto the subject of women and their extraordinary behavior.

This last topic restored him to rollicking good humor. It was a little difficult to imagine Vic as the Lothario he said he was. Standing by the stove, he looked like an unlikely and seedy cavalier. His hair was rumpled, his face unshaven and a large hole in his *pareu* disclosed rather more than a quarter of one lean and hairy buttock.

But he was, remarkably enough, exactly what he purported to be. Vic considered life a personal challenge and with rash imprudence pursued whatever took his fancy, never bothering with a *should I* or *should I not*. He would, or he wouldn't, and, like Fiddler Jones, he would probably die with a thousand laughs and not a single regret. At times his cockiness and brashness might make him a figure of fun, but he had two rare and patent qualities—honesty and courage.

Hal was not so easy to assess. He sat hunched over his food like a predatory animal, magnificent in his size, his darkness and the strength of his features. He was moody and restrained, a man of controlled emotions and a pessimistic outlook. When the rest of the crew rejoiced over a freshening breeze, Hal would gaze mistrustfully at the sails and say he hoped they wouldn't blow out. When the rest of the crew were impatient to get Customs clearance over with so that they could go ashore, Hal would announce that he wasn't coming, that he was going to read a book instead, that there probably wasn't much to see anyway but another "bunch of happy, dancing, chiseling gooks." But I am anticipating the story and telling more about Hal than I knew then. At that moment I was puzzled by him and somewhat intimidated by his severity.

Yvor was not as much of an enigma as Hal, but he defied any quick and easy classification. His closely cropped blond hair and china-blue eyes gave him rather a childlike appearance, a look of innocence that probably made every woman he met want to mother him. I felt like protecting him too—from what, I didn't know; it was just a feeling, and I wanted to kick myself for having it because it seemed so ridiculous. Presumably as a defense against the feelings he engendered, Yvor made a point of denying any physical weakness in himself, a trait I admired excessively because it was one I couldn't imagine possessing. When I'm sick, for instance, I want everyone to make a big fuss about me—flowers, presents, the works —so I marveled at the story of Yvor, the lightning and the jaguar.

When the *California* had to put in at Panama for extensive repairs, and when the crew had had to take on employment to pay for these expenses, Yvor had worked as a geodetic surveyor, charting the unexplored reaches of the Darien jungle. The work had entailed long, isolated encampments, usually on the tops of mountains, and it was on one of these stays that the camp he was occupying had been struck by lightning and completely destroyed. Severely burned and partially paralyzed, he had crawled down the mountainside with another member of his party who died later on from a combination of malaria and the burns he had received. Yvor dragged him, delirious and half-conscious, twenty-three miles to the nearest village, where an ambulance was summoned to drive them both back to civilization and a hospital. Yvor's version of the story passed lightly over the agonizing descent and journey and stressed instead the encounter with a jaguar who had blocked their trail along the way.

"He was a big brute," Yvor said, "and there he sat, twitching his tail, right in the middle of the path, about fifteen yards away. The other guy (the one with malaria) looked at the jaguar and it was just too much, and he sat down and cried. And the funny thing about it all was that the jaguar looked at us for a long time and then turned his back to us and wandered away into the jungle."

Why? Yvor shrugged. He didn't really know, but it was lucky, wasn't it, he asked with a smile, that the jaguar had been so amiably disposed? Other men might have made much of the jaguar as a symbol of terror, a snarling beast who was not fifteen yards away, but five, and ready to spring. But Yvor never embellished his stories with histrionics, and their calm, factual nature gave them a credibility which some of Vic's hair-raising tales did not always have.

Art had no idiosyncrasies. He was the most predictable and dependable member of the crew. From all appearances, he had managed to regulate his life as carefully as he had his personal habits. Even on the boat, he observed the amenities much as he would have at home. In comparison to the others, Art was radiantly clean. His face, which had a collegiate youthfulness, was freshly shaved. His hair was combed. His shirt and trousers, if not laundry fresh, were at least twice as presentable as the ragged, sloppy assortment the other three were wearing. Yvor had a diversity of talent; Hal had an erratically brilliant mind; Vic had a lust for adventure. Art was distinguished by his reliability and conscientiousness.

What amazed and impressed me most about these four men was their lack of a common bond other than their ability and willingness to travel. Having united their time, resources and effort to sail the *Cal* around the world, they had surrendered their personal feelings to achieve optimum efficiency and harmony aboard. That they had been able to do this as successfully as they had was, I felt, if not quite a miracle, something not very far from it.

After three years and a half of their living constantly together, it was not easy to tease apart the separate personalities from the collective whole that had made me first think of the crew as "they," "the boys," and not as individuals. Their personalities had acted one upon the other, strengthening and toning down individual characteristics, so that as their attempts to surrender personal feelings for the sake of unity aboard had succeeded, their individuality had become less noticeable. Their gestures and mannerisms were similar and their everyday vocabularies strikingly alike. But these were superficial likenesses and, as individualities emerged, I was astonished at the way they bridled temperament and developed tolerance to maintain the co-operative harmony which existed. Everyone had told me that I would upset the balance. Naturally, I didn't want to and was absurdly eager to help.

When Art suggested after breakfast that the decks should be scrubbed down, I volunteered to lend a hand and discovered that the job was in no way as easy as I had expected. There was a tin bucket with a length of rope attached to the handle. It was an art to swing the bucket over the side, fill it with water and haul it up on deck again. I had to be very careful to swing the bucket ahead of me; if I had allowed the bucket to swing back, the force of the water would have ripped the bottom out. Then, having filled the bucket, I had to swing it up over the side without letting it scratch the hull. The bucket was heavy, and after I had hauled up the fourth bucketful, my arms hurt, and I exchanged places with Art, scrubbing the decks with a stiff-bristled brush and letting him haul the water and wet down the deck. The deck was blistering hot, my feet burned, the deck and woodwork all seemed inordinately grease-stained, and by the time the job was accomplished to Art's satisfaction—no spot was too small to escape his attention—I was dripping with perspiration and achingly tired.

"Have a bath," Hal suggested from the wheelhouse.

"I suppose you want me to haul up the water for you," Art grumbled. He set the bucket down with a thump beside me and flipped me the brush we had been using to scrub the deck. Reaching through the skylight, he plucked a box of Dreft from the galley shelf and told me to use it sparingly as the supply was short. Faced with water, soap and a brush, all of which suddenly seemed quite unsuitable to the purpose I had in mind, I did what I could with the materials on hand.

"Now," Art said, "stand up and hold onto the lines." I did as I was told, and Art, who was standing about six feet behind me, hurled a bucket of water at my back, and while I was still spluttering from the shock, hurled another bucket at me from the front. Having been initiated to my first bath at sea, I lay down on the chartroom hatch and let the hot sun do its work—drying both me and my clothes.

I was relaxed and steaming pleasantly when Hal ordered me to the wheelhouse for my first lesson in helmsmanship. It started off badly. I bruised my shin climbing to the wheelhouse, and, receiving no sympathy from Hal, I sat on the ledge seat, nursing my leg and eying him and the wheel reproachfully. The wheel had eight spokes, and the mainspoke was distinguished from the rest by a twist of leather braid on the handle. Hal said that this was called a Turk's-head knot, snorted when I said it was pretty and, pointing to the binnacle, brusquely got down to business.

"It's all very simple," he said. "That's the compass dial and that's the lubber's line, and all you have to do is to keep the lubber's line on the compass setting. We're now on northwest three hundred and twenty degrees." He indicated the point with his index finger. "Now," he said, "you try." I seized the wheel, and for a few seconds we remained on course. Then the lubber's line deserted the black triangle marking the NW 320-degree point and wobbled wildly between an assortment of other black triangles marking other points and directions. Hal snatched the wheel away from me and, after a great deal of sail flapping, aligned the lubber's line once more with the desired compass point.

With infinite patience he began all over again, guiding my hand, encouraging me, rebuking me— "Don't strain yourself experimenting with all three hundred and sixty degrees. Be content with just one or possibly five of them"—but never losing his temper or raising his voice, until finally I got the "feel" of the wheel. With a good deal of concentration and a great deal of manipulation I was able to steer with fair accuracy.

"You're up too high," Hal said suddenly. I didn't quite know what he meant, but I swung the wheel so that the compass dropped from 310 to 300. This was obviously the wrong thing to do because the booms started to rattle and the sails began fluttering. I looked at Hal blankly as he took over the wheel and the compass came to a jiggling halt at 320 degrees. "But that's higher than it was," I protested.

"Judas Priest!" Hal exploded. "Don't you know *anything?*" Before I had a chance to do anything more than look hurt and indignant, he had launched into an illogical and confusing lecture. The gist of it was that we were on the port tack, and the wind was coming from the left so that the sails billowed out on the starboard side. When he had said that I was up too high, he wasn't referring to the numbers on the compass, as I had supposed, but rather to the fact that I was pointing the bow too high into the wind. To remedy the situation, the schooner had to shift her course slightly to the right or starboard side. "So that when we're on the port tack and someone says you're up too high you run the compass up a few degrees instead of back. Is that it?" I asked Hal. That was it, he said, but it was without question the least scientific explanation he had ever heard.

I gathered from the rest of his explanation that the only time the directions jibed with the points on the compass was when the schooner was on the starboard tack, with the sails therefore on the port side. Instantly, I developed an affinity for the starboard tack as it seemed so much more rational than the port tack. I made the mistake of telling this to Hal and was informed coldly that he had seen a better head on a boil and that there were two ways of looking at things: one from the nautical, scientific viewpoint, and the other from the hopeless confusion of a flatlander and that I was about as flat a goddamned lander as he had ever come across. It was a new experience for me to be rebuffed with such scorn, but by the end of the day both Kippy and I were more or less accustomed to it.

Kippy was treated with a highhanded severity which, surprisingly enough, he didn't seem to mind. He trotted cheerfully back and forth from lounge to wheelhouse, transporting innumerable cups of coffee and cigarettes. He mastered the intricacy of the valves and petcocks in the head. He cleaned up after Scupper with a rag and a spoon and a putty knife, and when Hal draconically insisted that he remain silent during all meals, he submitted with resignation, and although he looked a little wistful, he didn't complain.

I was commanded, on the other hand, not to scatter ashes on the deck in the lounge, not to stuff my clothes haphazardly into the cabinets in the chartroom for fear I might spring the door hinges but to roll them up neatly instead, and if I were going to practice tying bowlines and square knots, half tangles and tight snarls though they might be, I must not, unless I wanted to be smacked, leave the lines where anyone might trip over them. I was curiously happy, though, padding about the deck with bare, grease-soled feet, wearing an old shirt and shorts. I was sunburned and itching with prickly heat, but I had an enormous sense of accomplishment from the fact that I could steer after a fashion, operate the Primus stove without more than two false starts and cope almost casually with the convolutions of the head.

In the afternoon, the light, flat sea turned green and luminous and the sky purplish blue with a curving line of dark marking the horizon; a light squall blew up, the rain breaking in a shower of silver over the water. We all gathered on deck, letting the rain sluice over us, rinsing the dirt from our clothes and dissolving the gray patches of crystallized salt from our skins.

As they took turns steering and stood by the gunwales splashing the water over their backs and arms, the crew assumed an almost godlike presence. Their sun-darkened bodies and brightly figured *pareus* gave them a pagan, unreal appearance, which was heightened by the glowing half-light of the squall. Even Kippy, with his blue jeans hiked up with a rawhide thong, looked like some impish faun bent on all manner of mischief, quite unlike a mortal child. They clustered together on the far side of the deck, leaving me on the other side feeling somewhat alien and lonely before this display of supernatural maleness.

The clipper bow tapering into a shearing deck plunged up and down in endless motion. My momentary pang of loneliness was displaced by an exultant delight in being alive and the sudden consciousness that I had been right after all; that nothing *did* matter as much as being aboard this remarkable schooner. We were allied in our femininity, and if she submitted with good grace to masculine domination, so then would I. Having come to this conclusion, I was relieved of all misgivings concerning the boys' attitude toward me and descended to the chartroom, where I wrapped myself in a spare *pareu* hanging on a hook beneath two ragged Navy jackets and covered myself with the poncho to keep off the drips of water which leaked through the overhead. I lighted a cigarette with a wooden kitchen match, striking the match carefully on the underside of the bunk-side table so that the scratch mark wouldn't show. I lay there, lazily smoking, knowing that what I had most wanted had eventually come to pass, coveting this moment of realization in a state of dreamlike contentment.

The chartroom dimmed as if it hadn't quite expected night to come so soon; patches of daylight quivered tenuously in the center of the cabin and on the chartroom table until they were blotted out in shadow. With the *pareu* knotted beneath my armpits I made my way up the ladder and lurched across the slippery deck down to the lounge where the scene was identical with that which had taken place in the morning, except that now Vic was preparing chicken *cacciatore,* not biscuits. By heaping on spoonfuls of rosemary and oregano, he was trying to disguise the fact that the chicken was tinned. Used pots and pans slid back and forth, clinking and clanking across the bar, and Hal and Yvor were playing a guitar and harmonica duet of *"Isa Lei":*

> *Isa, Isa, vulangi lasadina*
> *No mulako au na rara wakina*
>
> (Isa, you are my only treasure
> Must you leave me so lonely and forsaken)

Vic continued to attack dinner, his actions automatic but far from smooth. Between the table centerboards he slapped down an apothecary jar half filled with speckled, dingy castor sugar, a dented tin shaker of pepper, a dark blue tin of Cerebos table salt, a kilo container of waxy margarine which was made in Indonesia and tasted vile, a tin of Australian processed cheese and a jar of Heinz mayonnaise, part of the original supply with which they had left Los

Angeles. He punched two holes viciously in the top of a rusty tin of evaporated milk and set it down with a bang next to the margarine. This accomplished, he brought forth a stack of thick white Navy crockery and a yellow plastic tray filled with utensils and announced belligerently that chow was on and to come and get it. The chicken *cacciatore* was only slightly overseasoned and so was judged a success.

After dinner it was decided that I could handle the dawn watch, from five until eight in the morning, if we didn't arrive in Penang before then. Yvor relieved Art in the wheelhouse so that Art could have what was left of the dinner and Yvor went aft to the chartroom to ponder over our position. The squall had delayed our progress, and no one was quite sure exactly where we were.

"Better hang out the lights. Don't want anything bumping into us." Hal brought out the kerosene lamps, red glass for port and green glass for starboard. Filling them with the precise somnambulism of habit in every motion, he lashed them onto stands in the shrouds and then went below to pore over the unrolled chart of the Malacca Straits with Yvor. I lay on the bunk listening to them talk about star fixes and zenith angles, sextant readings and reefs, and, thinking it all very mystifying, dozed off to sleep and was groggily disbelieving when I was shaken out of the bunk and told that it was time to go on my first watch.

Yvor handed the wheel over to me, warning me to keep a sharp lookout for ships and to wake up Hal or Vic if anything went wrong. Then I was left alone; I was terrified at the responsibility of keeping the schooner on course.

There was no light in the wheelhouse other than the faint glow of the binnacle light. The compass was a demon of flickering, jumping triangles, and I strained forward nervously, my hands clamped to the wheel, peering at the compass, anxiously trying to keep the lubber's line aligned on the NW diamond. I kept watching for lights of other ships and was panicky when I saw one. Mercifully it faded out shortly thereafter. There was little wind and the blocks rattled angrily, the sails listlessly flapping on the restive booms. As the blackness of the night began to lift, so did my tension. There was a lingering chill, a sort of pause before the dawn, the sea gray and pearly and the sky the same color. There was a whitening in the east, and the great golden sun began to ascend. I felt more confident now and gripped the mainspoke less tightly, so that the leather Turk's head no longer bit deep into my palm.

Scupper curled like a fat comma on the opposite ledge, stirred, shivered slightly and wrinkled his nose so that a pink spot twitched beneath his right nostril. He stretched his four white paws out, indolently scratched on the cushion, and fell asleep again. I wondered how he managed to keep his chest and throat and paws so white. When I rubbed or scratched my skin anywhere, the skin rolled off in tiny black threads of dirt.

I heard the faint hum of a motor and, looking out, saw far off across the water the silhouette of a junk sailing parallel to us, and then the sunlight began to flicker in little steely points on the windowpanes. The wheelhouse assumed its familiar form and shape. Half of the wheelhouse was enclosed with woodwork, and the covering tarpaulins for the remaining sides and back were rolled up in orderly sausage shape. There was a barometer and a stopwatch and a thermometer pegged on the woodwork between the two front panes of glass. The thermometer read 70 degrees and would probably rise to 105 degrees around noon. Beneath the windows was a built-in flag locker, the top of which served as a catchall for a variety of objects: a tightly furled American flag; a pair of Navy binoculars; an alarm clock; a small, black airplane compass which Vic had kept as a souvenir of the time when he was a fighter pilot; a flashlight which didn't work; the chart which Hal and Yvor had been studying the evening before; and a limp roll of toilet paper—the boys used the facilities of the bow basket rather than those offered by the head below. The two side ledge seats were furnished with grease-stained cushions, quilted with buttons, but most of the buttons were missing, and all that remained were the rusty circles marking the places where they had once been.

At seven-thirty the sun felt hot on my back and Vic came up on deck, looked over the sails and retrimmed the mizzen. Then he casually pulled up his *pareu* and relieved himself over the side. He sauntered back to the wheelhouse, looked rather surprised to find me there, climbed in, shoved Scupper off on the deck, and said that we should have been at Penang by this time if the wind had been

any good. It was now improbable that we would arrive before tomorrow morning.

"You're not going to put me off in Penang, are you?" I asked.
"Hell, no, lady. You've been a good and solid passenger." He
grinned at me jauntily. He reached under the cushion and brought
out a notebook. "Diary," he said by way of explanation. He wrote
in it for a while. Scupper suddenly bounded out of the cockpit
and started racing back and forth on the deck barking excitedly.

"Porpoises," Vic said, without looking up. I blocked the wheel
with the cushion and scrambled out to have a look at a pair of
sleek, fat porpoises slipping through the water alongside. Scupper
whined and barked, his claws clickety-clicking on the deck, and the
porpoises rolled and tumbled about the hull, shiny and black and
sharp-finned. "Oh, oh, oh, Scup, good doggie," Vic encouraged
Scupper mildly, and the dog bounded back and forth in a frenzy
until the porpoises swam away.

Hal, dark, shaggy and grim, emerged from below, a cigarette
dangling from the corner of his mouth. He emptied the pail of
garbage overboard. "Leave a few burned pans around, why don't
you," he said, scowling at Vic. Vic gave Hal a slightly grating smile
and said deprecatingly, "Just a few pans I left soaking overnight.
Nothing to blow your stack about."

"It's a hell of a thing to do," Hal said, eying Vic accusingly as
he scoured the left-over pans.

The morning had begun, the third day out.

After breakfast I began on a reading lesson with Kippy. It was
a ridiculous book, full of the activities of two small children, Dick
and Jane, who spent most of their time helping Mother or carrying
on a dialogue with their dog confined mostly to such remarks as,
"Oh, Spot. See the ball. See the red ball, Spot. Run and get the
ball, Spot." Kippy twisted about impatiently on the hatch beside
me and showed no interest in Dick or Jane or Spot. Vic watched
Kippy and me with an expression of amusement. "How can you
expect the poor kid to be interested?" he asked. "How can he care
about all that tripe when he's making a trip like this?" Encouraged
by this show of sympathy, Kippy sought sanctuary in the wheelhouse and I closed *Fun with the Family* with a snap.

"That's right," Vic said, nodding approvingly. "Now you're

showing some sense." He had already begun to demonstrate to Kippy how a Magnus hitch should be tied.

Hal had solved the worrisome problem of what to eat, which faced everyone on Cook Day, with the simple solution of two menus for which ingredients were always available. Menu A—corned beef hash, mashed potatoes and tinned string beans—was for lunch. Menu B—mashed potatoes, Spam and tinned peas—was for supper. Occasionally he relented and alternated the two, and we had Menu A for supper. Neither menu was ever greeted with enthusiasm by the crew.

"Christ, How Dog, this scarcely looks fittin'," Yvor exclaimed, as he slid into his place for lunch. (Hal was nicknamed How Dog, just as Yvor was often called Yoke, both names having originated from the Navy alphabet of code words.)

"Well, as usual it looks as if it had all been eaten before," Art said, with a gusty sigh.

"What is it?" Vic asked. "Menu A or Menu B for a change?"

"All right, you bastards," Hal said. "If you don't like it, you know what you can do with it."

The wind freshened in the afternoon, and Art and Hal spent long spells in the engine room trying to repair whatever was wrong, swearing loudly, reappearing long enough on deck to pour a bucket of water over themselves and then returning to the furnace heat. I took two bucket baths and wished fervently that a refrigerator had been included in the general equipment as the lukewarm water out of the fresh-water pump was not particularly refreshing. The wind slackened by sundown, and since we made little progress, it was decided to heave to for the evening.

At dawn Hal started up the engine, which literally blasted me out of my bunk, and we powered into Georgetown Harbor. The island of Penang, about two and a half miles distant from the Malayan coast, was small, about fifteen by ten miles. In the morning haze it had the prosaically pretty look of an overrated resort. The sight of the island evoked little enthusiasm from either Hal or Vic. "Well," Hal said flatly. "We found another one."

"Yop," Vic said, taking over at the wheel. "East Jockstrap, sure enough."

Hal rammed a cigarette into the corner of his mouth, struck a match on the deck, and cupped his hands about the flame. "Hey, Yoke," he called down the open hatch. "We'd better get the sails down."

Yvor came up on deck, red-eyed and sleepy, and the crew set about dropping the sails. Their casual technique would have made a Sunday yachtsman's bones curl, but it seemed to work better than most. No voices were raised. No tempers lost. Hal and Yvor stood on either side of the mizzen and each seized a halyard.

"Ready?" asked Hal to Yvor, who was on the lee side.

"Yop."

"Vang free?"

"Yop."

There was a pause as the gaff swung down horizontally. Art silently began to fold the sail as it came down.

"Too damn fast," Yvor muttered.

"Okay, okay." Hal eased up slightly.

There was another pause. "Duck," Hal said. The gaff was swinging, and then the sail was down. Art shoved the boom lift forward and finished folding the sail.

Yvor stretched and yawned. "Which one shall we take in next?"

"Genny, I guess."

I smiled to myself, because I finally knew what the Genny meant. It was the general term aboard for the Genoa jib, which I thought was a beautiful name for a sail.

"Wait until I finish my weed." Hal took a long, last drag from the cigarette and then flipped it overboard and went up forward. I watched them standing precariously on the bowsprit hauling down the Genny. We sailed inside the breakwater, spotted a buoy and moored to it. The whole operation had taken less than twenty minutes.

"Pretty efficient," I said.

"Well," Hal said, "it ought to be. It's around our hundred and twenty-fifth anchorage. The first couple of times we tried it we screamed like Sea Scouts on their first day out. Now we don't say much. We don't have to. We could do it in our sleep almost." He shrugged deprecatingly. "We're unsalty as hell. Did you ever see any other yachtsmen who looked like us?" I allowed that I hadn't.

All four of them were in their usual morning attire or lack of it, and all four were smudged and smeared with grease and dirt—even Art, who had foregone his usual clean-up and shave to work on the engine.

Now that we were at rest I asked what would happen next and why didn't we make ourselves presentable and row ashore. The buoy we were moored to was about twenty-five yards from the beach, and I was curious to find out what lay beyond the quiet esplanade and tidy row of white plaster houses.

"We can't go ashore," Art said. "We have to wait for the port authority and the customs and general pratique. They'll be along shortly. Have no fear. This is your Cook Day anyway. So get going. We're not going to spend money getting breakfast on the beach. And don't make too much mess in the galley. Try to keep it looking fairly decent."

I had completely forgotten that was my Day, my day not only to cook but to clean and do all the odd chores that befell the cook, who, being excused from watches, was supposed to compensate for this idleness. The four men seemed to dread their Cook Days. But apart from the odd jobs which I might be required to do, I didn't think that the cooking end of things would be too difficult. I went below to the galley with naïve self-confidence. Instead of stacking the crockery and slapping down the cutlery tray, I set the table—a glass, a plate, a cup, a fork, knife and spoon for each place. The plates and cups were covered with a thin film of grease, so that fingerprints showed up on the slick surface. Only Art ever took the trouble to heat up a pan of salt water and make use of a detergent in the washing-up process. The cutlery was also oily to the touch—Hal had said that this cut down on the rust— but, even so, there was rust along the edges of the knife blades, and rust on the fork tines. I carefully chose the least rusty of the utensils and then began on the centerboards. Pepper shaker and salt tin. The remains of last night's evaporated milk. There wasn't enough. The sugar jar. Empty. The jar of Australian preserves. The tin of margarine. It smelled rancid and I shivered with distaste as I plopped it down at the far end of the table and went off to get a new tin of milk and refill the sugar jar.

The sugar was in a tin barrel in a small storeroom that was a wild farrago of shoe bags, sail bags, painting equipment, Polynesian paddles and other bulky souvenirs. The milk, in a white tin with a cow's head on it, was in the chow bunker, a shelf-lined cubbyhole opposite the storeroom. Having fetched milk and sugar, I turned on the valve of the Primus stove, poured in some alcohol to prime the wick, turned off the valve and pumped the burner. Several times the draft from the overhead skylight extinguished the flame, but after a number of tries, and using the breadboard as a shield, I managed to get the stove going and succeeded in brewing quite tolerable coffee.

While the coffee was bubbling, I went back to the chow bunker and returned with the last of the papayas and the last loaf of Singapore bread. I cut the papayas into rather jagged sixths and sliced the bread into uneven slices, climbed up on top of the bar so that I could reach the basket of eggs on the galley shelf beneath the skylight, climbed down again, replaced the coffeepot with a frying pan into which I put a tablespoonful of bacon grease, and then, because we had had fried eggs the morning before, I decided to make eggs-in-the-nest. While the eggs fried, I brushed the crumbs from the breadboard and laid the remaining circles of bread aside to be fed to Scupper later.

"Chow," I fluted wearily up the skylight. "Chow."

"Finally," Art said.

"Look how fancy-shmancy," Vic commented, surveying the table.

Hal glanced at the eggs. "Ah, goodies," he said appreciatively.

Yvor poured himself a cup of coffee and laced it liberally with milk and sugar. "Too strong," he muttered, but drank it down just the same.

Kippy sat in enforced silence and munched happily on the papaya.

"Good chow, kiddy. You get a greenie button for effort." I beamed at Vic, and the others agreed that I hadn't done as badly as they thought I would. When breakfast was finished, I cleared the table, washed the dishes and put them and the provisions away.

While I swept the deck of the lounge and surreptitiously brushed the sweepings under the mat, Art removed the table centerboards and covered the table with the jaguar skin, which was reserved for use at port only. I sponged off the yellow-leatherette couch covers, and still the customs officials hadn't arrived. We all trooped up on deck and took hurried bucket baths and then I went below to the chartroom to change.

I was surprised to find that it was only a quarter to seven. I felt as if I had been up for hours. My hair was sticky with salt and smelled like Scupper's fur, but when it was brushed into a chignon it didn't look too bad. My clothes were a little wrinkled and smelled faintly tarry and moldy, but after I had put on my make-up and finished dressing, I felt I looked good, all things considered. It is surprising how your personality changes with your clothes. Going up the ladder, I was cautious to hold my skirt away from the rungs so that it wouldn't get spotted with grease, and with equal discretion I picked my way down to the lounge.

Vic whistled and assumed an expression of surprise. "What do you know," he greeted me. "You're a girl!" Vic's face looked thin and unfamiliar without the customary stubble, and the others also looked peculiarly clean and spruce. Our timing was excellent, because almost as if by given signal the customs launch chugged alongside, and four officials came aboard. After a brief survey of ship's papers and passports, off they went. Arrival seemed so much simpler on the *California*. No long wait. No opening and closing of luggage. No lengthy examination of documents. No fluster.

When the officials had gone, Art brought out more papers and spread them on the table. "Let's get organized. Let's see," he said, riffling through the papers. "The 'Must Buy' List." He studied it carefully. "Well, we're all right on enamel and paint and varnish. We got those in Singapore. Diesel oil, okay. Lube oil, okay. At least it will last until Ceylon. Gasoline we need. Ditto kerosene." He paused. "Now, food. We're stocked up on staples, but we'll need some more canned fruit and meat if you can find any. Dog biscuits we need. Evaporated milk, too. I'll take care of the fresh stuff when the time comes. Spices . . . "

"We need rosemary and cinnamon," Vic cut in.

"All right. You get them. That's it. Do we need to take on water?"

Hal shook his head. "It'll last."

"Well, that's that. All set?" Art moved on to the next list. I had never realized the mechanics involved in the process of living aboard before, nor the infinite details concerned.

"The 'Must Do' List," Art said. He began on a recital that seemed endless. "Check standing rigging. Check fenders. Check lights and generator. Check all lines. Check Genny sheets. Check mast coat on main. Check topsail lines. Check fore and mizzen halyards. Pump bilges. Square away engine room. Serve stays'l block. Patch Genny. Fix zinc collar on Main. Paint pin rails. Straighten port main spreader. Replace jib tie-downs. Re-serve leather on mizzen gaff bucket. Make new flag staff. Reweave bow basket. Patch Main. Paint exhaust pipe. Serve on starboard Genny sheet block. Replace flag halyards." Each of the boys scribbled down notes on the work which each of them would take on.

"But you've just left Singapore," I said wonderingly. "I thought you had everything all squared away there. Why do you have to work now?"

"This is nothing." Art dismissed both lists airily. "We always check everything when we get to port. The rest of the stuff is just little odds and ends we didn't get time to do in Singapore."

"Little odds and ends!" Hal mimicked Art. "That damn bow basket to reweave is no little odd and end. It'll take half a day's work."

"Well, you could have done it in Singapore. One day out and a line gives. I told you it would."

Hal shrugged his acceptance of Art's mildly self-righteous rebuke. Vic tilted the barrel he was sitting on backward so that his head rested on the base of the mainmast. "Well," he asked me in a rather fractious tone, "what did you think we did all day—sit on our milk-white asses? Hell, kiddy, we work damn hard. You ought to see us sweating it out when we have to paint the hull or burn off the paint on the decks or scrape off all those jolly little barnacles that take a fancy to us. Sure, we'll go ashore and give the girlies a treat and have a look around and maybe pick up some gee-gaws if we've got one nickel to rub up against another after everything is bought, and sure we'll have a merry time, but it's not all honey and jam by a long shot. Take it from your old Uncle Vic that what you've just heard Art read out is only a clue to what we'll be doing three ports from now." He glanced over his shoulder at the sea clock. "Let's have a look at the town," he said.

The boys collected their pandanus hats which had been woven in Tahiti and which were banded with seashells, rammed them rakishly on the backs of their heads, and up we went on deck.

Hal jumped into the dinghy and held out his hand to help me. I handed him my shoes and, using the porthole as a step, slid into the dinghy, perched in the stern, and drew my toes up out of the bilge that sloshed around the floorboards. The other three boys and Kippy got in, and we rowed off, leaving Scupper barking plaintively.

CHAPTER SEVEN

Penang and the Ritual of Thaipusam

THE EURASIAN HOTEL MANAGER lifted a suety face oozing perspiration. "Yes?" he said inquiringly.

I said that I wanted a room with a bath. No, not for five, just for myself and my son.

Hal followed me up the broad teakwood stairway to the second floor. "We don't want you to get gypped," he said. "And," he added, with a rare smile, "as long as we're going to take baths here, we have a sort of personal interest in your welfare."

After the chart room, the room I was given looked enormous. A three-bladed fan was suspended from the high ceiling, and there were louvered shutters at the balcony window through which the sun spilled like rich yellow cream over the tiled mosaic floor. The bathroom was antique but clean, with the inevitable gecko perched on top of the watercloset. "This is fine," Hal said, stripping off his shirt and turning on the bath. "I'll be through in fifteen minutes. Be a hero and order me an ice-cold Tiger beer."

I went back to the lobby where the other boys were lounging in wicker chairs about a wicker table ringed with beer bottles. Kippy was perched on a stool by the bar, having already conned someone into buying him an orangeade.

"A *besar* [big] orangeade, Mummy, not a *kitchie* [little] one," he said, greeting me triumphantly.

The pink-skinned men in white bush jackets sitting hunched over the bar laughed appreciatively and went on talking about what was happening in Kuala Lumpur and in the highlands of Malaya, breaking off every once in a while to call out "Boy, boy, *boeroe, boeroe* [hurry, hurry]" to sweating dark-skinned stewards.

Vic eyed the men at the bar with faint contempt. "Kuala Lumpur might as well be on Mars," he said. "You'd never think that only a couple of miles away the British are having a wing-ding battle with guerrillas, would you?"

"No, you sure wouldn't," Art agreed. "This looks like the quietest place we've hit so far. No chance of getting any wild adventure pictures here."

And so it seemed. By tacit agreement neutral territory, rest camp and holiday resort for both the British police force and the Communist bandits they were fighting on the Malayan mainland, the island of Penang was a quiet tropical backwater with an air of placid lethargy. Around the suburbs of Georgetown, where the hotel was located, there was an orderly, stylized prettiness. Sealing-wax palms and tamarinds bordered the road, and bougainvillaea wreathed the white-plaster, red-roofed bungalows which were set in formal gardens of cannas and etiolated zinnias. Toward the town, clusters of poorer houses were screened from the road by leafy shade trees, so that if you didn't look too closely all you were able to see was rich green foliage and lush rolling hills beyond.

Georgetown was a pocket-sized edition of Singapore. The main street was fronted by much solid bank architecture of a Greco-Victorian style, and every third house was an export-import company, every fourth, an agency for cars or steamships. Signs were lettered with the decorative complexities of Chinese, the fastidious sweep of Malay, and some few with the black-barred stylishness of Hindustani, but in general English was retained as the medium of advertising prestige. Indian tailors boasted "Finest Gent's and Lady's Clothing"; a pharmacist claimed "AN AMAZING CURE, EYES AND PILES"; and the hoardings were plastered with posters showing a smiling, elderly Chinese and a young matron proudly pointing him out to her son, saying, "Your honored and revered grandfather has such strong white teeth because he uses Gibbs Denti-frice."

There were a few tea gardens, restaurants and dance halls, a number of Chinese and Indian curio shops selling scrimshaw sou-venirs, an amusement park guarded by papier-mâché chow dogs, a market bazaar and a diversity of religious establishments for the polyglot Malay, Indian, Chinese and European population. There were several shrines dedicated to Kali, the black-bodied Hindu goddess of life, death and destruction; a mosque that I, as a non-believer, was forbidden to enter; and a hundred temples, façades encrusted with fish, and flowers, dragons and phoenixes, testifying to Buddhist piety.

Going sight-seeing with me bored Kippy—he complained that I always dawdled about too long—and he preferred to remain in the hotel with the other guests who sat in heat-stricken stasis about the lobby, desultorily waving palm-leaf fans and agreeably disposed to buying quarts of orangeade for a six-year-old boy who spoke know-ingly about television, New York, and a mother who was traveling with four men and a dog on the most beautiful schooner in the world. Though he was willing to forego expeditions with me, Kippy hated to miss anything the crew saw, so on the few occasions the crew and I went sightseeing together, Kippy loped after Hal, who would stride briskly through a temple and then sit in the courtyard reading *Astounding Science Fiction* while he waited for us to catch up. Or he would trail after Art, who was recording the voyage of the *California* on ciné film and who was hardly ever without two cameras and a light meter. Or he would skip along at Vic's side as eager as Vic to ferret out the adventure that might be around the next corner, or the next or the next. But Kippy seldom tagged behind Yvor, because Yvor's plans were sudden and unpre-meditated, and when you wanted him he was usually somewhere else.

And so I, for the most part, went my own way. The heat affected me with a drowsy, mental numbness and there were hours when my world was confined to what I could see through the window while lying beneath the cooling draft of the propeller fan. The window was burglar-proofed with diamonds of iron mesh and was regularly flown through by cicadas and turquoise butterflies with black markings. Beyond, there was a view of casuarinas, feathery and trembling, and a grove of coconut palms in which rhesus monkeys performed acrobatic tricks the whole day long. After the monsoon rains of the afternoon were over, I usually drifted into the golden outside blare to wait for a bicycle rickshaw to pedal up to the veranda and pedal me away along a lane walled with frangipani to the Esplanade between the parklike town square and the sea. The square was sprinkled with canopied food stalls where cooks in dirty aprons fanned the charcoal fires beneath shallow iron pots and dished out the *specialités de la maison*—skewered *kebabs* of meat and fish, steamed dumplings stuffed with peanuts, meat and vegetable curries burning with chilies, and balls of shaved ice flavored with rose sirup. I would walk about among the stalls, breathe in the odor of fried cakes and the heady jasmine scent of the Malay women, price the fruit, and perhaps buy peppermint candies which smelled like Christmas. Round the sides of the market square, children sailed nutshell boats in the stinking monsoon drains. Below, on the beach, other children swam and played about the *California's* dinghy, which was pulled ashore high on the sand. Sometimes I would climb the low walls of the Esplanade, jump down upon the scummed, wet sand, walk over to the dinghy and examine the oarlocks or remove a clump of seaweed from the bow, just to show I had a proprietary interest in the dinghy and the three-masted schooner that rested tranquilly out at sea propped between sky and water in a patch of silvery shadows.

It so happened that we were in Penang for Thaipusam, the annual Tamil or Southern Indian penitential festival commemorating the birth of Subramaniam, the son of Siva and Parvathi. From the rubber plantations and the tin mines of Malaya, Indian laborers by the thousand flocked to Penang to expiate the sin of receiving over and above their rightful share of happiness during the past year. The recovery from an illness, the birth of a healthy child, a successful harvest, the conception of a child from a womb that had not previously been fruitful—whatever the blessing, the Tamils came to do penance. Preceding the festival, which took place in the Hindu month of Thai when the moon was full and the star of Pusam was in ascendance, was a ten-day preparatory ritual during which the pious abstained from all sensual pleasures and cleansed their souls with prayer and their bodies with no less than three baths a day.

On Thaipusam day those taking part in the Penitential March were scheduled to assemble at the Dato Kramat Temple from six o'clock on in the morning. Having been informed at the local constabulary that I would be permitted to attend the ceremonies, I was in a bicycle rickshaw on my way to the temple by seven. Kippy had gone off earlier with Vic. The road was already beginning to fill with a crowd dressed in holiday attire, the men sprucely nondescript, the women in their best and brightest sarongs and saris. A little boy holding a live duck in one hand, a live hen in the other, was trudging past the hotel. I told the driver to stop and lift him into the rickshaw, for he was so small and the birds so large. He rode with me until we reached the roadside shrine of Ganesa, which was a stage point on the main route to the Dato Kramat Temple. The shrine was a house of flowers in which Ganesa, a god of good fortune, was enthroned, his brass human body and benign old elephant's head garlanded with tinseled wreaths of creamy jasmine and lotus buds. The crowd thickened, and by the time I reached the temple I was in the midst of a milling mob.

Inside the temple the air was dense with the sound of voices. The smell of jasmine, joss and human bodies was almost overpowering. The brilliance of the sun had temporarily blinded me, and, feeling dazed and queasy, I passively allowed myself to be jostled about. The outlines of the temple were misted over with smoke, but its general appearance was that of a great gray barn with a wide central hall opening onto chambers on either side. The ceiling bulged with Oriental cherubim and seraphim painted in carnival colors and illuminated by hundreds of candlelit globes. All around me the sound of voices echoed and throbbed.

Suddenly there was a piercing shriek, followed by another and another in an offbeat rhythmic cadence. Almost before I knew what was happening, a figure rushed at me, a metal cage with legs, barbed all over with long quills like some demonic porcupine. It darted straight at me, then swerved and dashed out the door. It was a sight that filled me with purest terror, and I would have run from the temple had there been the least chance of escape, but the crowd had closed ranks again. Stepping backward, I lurched against a Chinese woman, lost my balance and would have fallen if she hadn't caught my arm and helped me up. "It's all right," she said in English. "It's all right." There was another burst of screams and something else rushed past us.

"Was that a real person?" I asked incredulously.

"Of course," the Chinese lady said. She pointed to a man wearing nothing but a yellow dhoti diapered about his loins. "See," she said. "Here comes another one eager to torture himself. I come every year to this. I'd never miss it. Come. Don't you want to watch?"

I didn't know if I did or not, but I squeezed behind her through the crowd to an antechamber where a votary was prostrated before a six-headed gilded image of Subramaniam. He chanted a loud rhythmic prayer and then moved along to another room where a priest guided him to a stool and motioned to him to be seated.

The Chinese lady and I stood alien and apart, surrounded by dark Tamil faces. The room was an eerie tableau such as I never believed existed outside the writings of Dante or the grotesqueries of Hogarth. Ringed by championing groups of friends and relatives, there were a score or more Tamil penitents, men, women and even children in various stages of flesh-pierced torture. One man had his tongue skewered to his lips, and another spike as long as a knitting needle driven through both his cheeks. A child, smaller than Kippy, had dozens of bangled needles punched through his upper arm. An elderly woman sat in a corner, saliva dangling in viscous threads from the corners of her lips, which were pierced through by hooked barbs.

The chamber was oyster-colored with the smoke of incense. The sound of rapidly beating drums and the shrill of flutes coming from another room was a convulsive undertone beneath the shouted invocations of the penitents and their followers. The penitent whom we had followed sat calmly, his retinue grouped behind him in a semicircle. Two temple attendants stepped forward and hoisted a huge iron cage above his head. They rested the base on his shoulders for a moment before they let the cage slide down to settle at his waist. A crude harness of straps was then cinched tightly

around the man's body so that he was girdled from head to groin
with arched and perforated iron bands.

"What's the cage for?" I asked.

"That's a *kavadi*," the Chinese lady said. "Wait and see what
they do next." She smacked that "next" as though it were a delicious grain of rice.

An acolyte stood by, holding a brass platter heaped with a pyra-
mid of slender, sharp-pointed lances tipped at their blunt ends with
pennants. The priest selected a lance with a crimson pennant, thrust
the point into a green lime proffered by another attendant, ran
the point through one of the holes in the *kavadi* frame and then
stabbed the lance into the flesh of the penitent.

The victim looked surprised but said nothing. The attendant
dipped his fingers into a brass bowl of sacred ash and daubed the
flesh where the lance now quivered. The group behind the penitent
raised their hands in prayer and sang out *"Vel! Vel!"* A *vel*, the
Chinese lady explained chattily, was the name of the lance Subramaniam had used to kill his enemies, and the reason the priest
dipped the lance into the lime before he stabbed the votary stemmed
from the ancient legend that Subramaniam dipped his weapons
into lime juice "to cool their anger lest he destroy the forces of
good as he wrought destruction upon his enemies."

The priest selected another lance and drove the point into the
lime, through the frame, and again into the man's flesh, this time
just above the left breast. Once more ashes were smeared on the
wound. The priest picked up a third lance.

"Of course these ancient legends are all very well," the Chinese
lady said in a low voice. "But our peasants often use lime as an
antiseptic and ashes to stop a cut from bleeding. Perhaps, however,
the healing properties of lime and ash are overrated. Perhaps it is
all a matter of faith. Who knows?" She shrugged her pretty sateen-
covered shoulders.

Again and again the red, yellow and blue pennants fluttered as
the lances were plunged into the devotee's body, the priest adjusting the lances so that they fanned symmetrically at a meticulously
exact angle, each lance spaced evenly from the next. The weight
of the *kavadi* was borne in part by shoulder supports, but it still
pressed with sufficient force upon the lances to make the furrowed

skin crawl and pulse like worms whenever the *kavadi* was moved. Not all of the perforations in the iron frame had been filled, but there must have been at least a hundred lances pincushioning the man's back and chest. The perfunctory shouts of his band of followers swelled to frenzied howls. The Chinese lady began to laugh at the crudities of this monstrous performance, her laughter as manifestly incongruous as I had thought the amusement of the picnicking trippers had been before the murals of torment at the Tiger Balm gardens in Hong Kong.

Presently a wooden platform was secured to the top of the *kavadi* and on it a miniature shrine was placed, a magnificent affair of peacock feathers and white jasmine, with a tall image of Ganesa standing in the center. The priest twined a ceremonial garland about the *kavadi*, an attendant flung a handful of powdered saffron over the penitent's body and then the penitent leaped up and whirled around the antechamber. His followers ran after him, shrieking *"Vel! Vel!"* Whirling and stamping, they toured the temple the traditional three times and then dashed out the door to join the other votaries in the Penitential March.

More pentitential candidates surrounded by their delegations filed into the chamber, and the piercing and puncturing, skewering and chanting continued in counterpoint with the pounding drums and screaming flutes. Several men covered their torsos with fishhooks and attached limes and coconuts to the barbs.

The Chinese lady was still chuckling as I left the chamber of ritual torture and retreated to the altar room where worshipers were writhing before a jewel-studded statue of Subramaniam. A large urn, filled with the year's supply of burned-out joss, partially blocked the single entrance to this innermost shrine, and as I was edging my way past a priest flung a handful of the ash at a penitent whirling toward the exit. The ash caught me full in the face, stinging my eyes and making me sneeze apoplectically. A woman stopped to sponge me off with a rag soaked in lime juice with which she had been swabbing one of the sweating votaries.

Stumbling against the tide and the surge of the crowd, I forced my way out. After the semidarkness of the temple, the sunlight and the endless variegation of color of the crowd's mass composition were stunning. Along the three-mile line of march the festival cottons and silks of saris streamed in a vivid, jewel-like course as far as I could see. The temple disgorged devotee after devotee to join the dipping and spinning, reeling and shrieking parade of penitents stampeding up the road toward the temple on the hill which was their final destination. In keeping with the convention that the way must be cleansed for the devotees of Subramaniam, water trucks had been commissioned to drive up and down the processional lane sluicing down the pavement.

I walked along slowly, following the procession until I came to the Ganesa shrine. Here the chanting of *"Vel! Vel!"* was intensified as the penitents swayed and writhed in lurching pirouettes of obeisance to the image. As each penitent halted before the shrine, a priest hurled a coconut onto the ground. I stepped out of the way of the flying shell shards and spattering coconut milk and sat down for a moment to rest beneath the shade of a palm tree. A Tamil priest was also sitting there. He was sipping a bottle of cream soda through a straw and eating an oily curry puff. I asked him about the significance of the coconuts. He removed a scalded fly feebly palpitating on the edge of the curry puff, set his bottle of cream soda on the grass, and clasped his hands about his knees. "You see," he said. "We think of our God as Light enclosed in the darkness of our bodies. He is wrapped in the blackness of our sins, just as the milk is encased in the shell of the coconut. Break the shell and deliver yourself of sin, and there is Light, there is God."

A few minutes later I watched him pelting coconuts into the road, and I got up and walked on. The midafternoon sun poured down, but as the hill temple came in sight, the penitents reeled and whirled with renewed vigor. Swept along with the teeming mass of onlookers, I reached the base of the hill, which was clotted with gaudy bazaars, teahouses and an amusement fair, all newly erected for the occasion. I walked past an open-air altar heaped with broken coconuts and started up the rough stone staircase winding to the hill's summit. Since each penitent was pledged to donate a certain amount of money to charity, beggars were wedged three deep along the stairs, flourishing their deformities and gathering their tribute in their cupped hands. Most of them were blind, leprous and rotting with disease, and it was difficult to imagine them as creatures who loved, thought and begot children.

At last I reached the top of the hill and looked below at the stillness of heat-paralyzed palms and the wriggling serpent of people coiling up the slope. Penitents domed with *kavadis* raced by, causing a rippling tremor in the crowd as they passed. Having gained the summit, they were chivvied by their followers into an exhibition of frenetic vitality. On and on the votaries came, saving, with an Oriental sense of showmanship, the most grisly spectacles for the last. In the late afternoon they drew lotus-filled wagons up the hill, and flower-decked floats, and gilded coaches harnessed with barbs tugging at their flesh with every step. Long after nightfall the procession continued, the *kavadis* and carriages flickering with candles and kerosene lights and gleaming like pewter in the white light of the full moon.

I watched a penitent bearing a colossal *kavadi* enter the temple and approach the altar to receive a final blessing. Then, squatting in the only open space available, he had his trappings removed. The priest jerked out the barbs and lances and spikes with ruthless haste, and where the dark punctures were, attendants smeared a gritty solution of lime juice and ashes. Miraculously, not a drop of blood oozed from any of the wounds. The penitent exchanged his sweat-stained yellow dhoti for a fresh white one, shouldered his *kavadi* shrine, which only he was permitted to carry, walked down the hill to take a ceremonial bath, his entourage trooping behind him bearing his disassembled *kavadi* cage. Then, refreshed from his bath, cleansed and sinless, he and his cohorts joined the merry-making crowd in the bazaar and stood in line for a turn on the ferris wheel.

CHAPTER EIGHT

Voyage to the Nicobars

WHEN THE CREW decided to leave Penang, a farewell party was held aboard the *California*, with the focal point of activity established in the lounge, where Art acted as bartender, mixing stengahs like an old colonial hand. Several English and Eurasian girls came aboard, and I observed with some smugness that they were incapable of climbing from the dinghy to the deck without help. They expressed shrill amazement at the "teeny little boat." I noticed one girl holding Hal's hand and begging him to write to her when we arrived in Ceylon. Another girl with auburn hair and a long, full body kissed Vic exuberantly every few minutes. There was a lot of rapid conversation and loud laughter, but finally the party subsided and the last guests left, the crew taking turns ferrying them ashore. It was well after midnight before the lounge was tidied up and the glasses washed and put away in the cabinet.

The engine refused to work, so we left the harbor in the early morning under sail and headed up the Malacca Straits. It had been four hundred miles from Singapore to Penang, and we had thirteen hundred and twenty miles to go before we arrived in Ceylon. "If the winds are right," Vic said, "we'll stop off at the Nicobars en route. *Sailing Directions* says the islands are pretty much unsurveyed and that the Nicobarese aren't dangerous to foreigners." I had never heard of the Nicobar Islands, and sailing there sounded like the most sublime of romanticisms. But to the crew, who had seen many dozens of atolls in the South Pacific, the Nicobars were

just another stop, just another tropical island group. No one shared
my enthusiastic excitement except Kippy, who hoped he might see
a cannibal.

"Look, lady, we've hardly left Penang, so don't get hopped up
about islands we may not even reach," Hal said, giving me a re-
proving look. "Women," he muttered disgustedly, "Yak, yak, yak,
all the time."

"Yes, for heaven's sake," Art said. "You may fall overboard before
we get there."

"If you do, do it in the daytime," Yvor said. "Our night flares
have all gone to pot."

I grinned at them and continued to sit on the gunwale cap,
dabbing the water with my feet.

"Watch out a barracuda doesn't get your toe," Yvor said. "Look,"
he added. "We're in good fishing water now. Let's get out the
fishing gear and try our luck."

The rest of the morning I spent separating fishhooks, leaders,
jigs and lines from a tangle of chaotic disorder. Kippy pricked his
thumb experimentally with a fishhook. "It hurts," he said, in a
tone of surprise.

"Well, what did you expect?"

"I was just trying to do what they did at Thaipusam," he said
indignantly. "Why didn't it hurt them?"

"Bright kid," Vic said. "Why doesn't he ever ask something you
can answer?"

"Well, why didn't a fishhook hurt them?" Kippy persisted.

"I don't know," I answered. "I really don't."

Yvor spotted in the water a jellyfish shaped like a badminton
shuttlecock. It streamed away before we could get a good look at
it. "Damn," Yvor said. "I hope there'll be more. I think that was
a medusa of Obelia. I couldn't see the manubrium, though, so I'm
not really sure." This was the sort of teasing fragment Yvor often
tossed our way.

He came from what he affectionately spoke of as an "education-
happy" family. His uncle was a distinguished poet, his father was
a writer, and his mother a well-known doctor of psychology. Before
he took off on the *California*, Yvor had completed a major in both
chemistry and zoology, and had taken a rather bizarre assortment of

extra courses, including a year of Mandarin, in which he had been one of two European students. The rest of the class had been Chinese. "I sure took a bruising," he had said. "But I passed the course."

Yvor was the linguist of the crew, and also the expert on scientific esoterica. He could make any topic attractive and engaging—even fish. Fish have no eyelids. A flounder has migrating eyes. The lamprey is the vampire of the ichthyological world.

Yvor's slow, soft voice rolled on, enumerating related curiosities. I listened intently, my legs swung over the side, the green water rushing and swirling about my ankles. A bamboo rod covered with barnacles drifted by, and then a green lotus shoot and dark clusters of sea weed. A broad band of tawny water lay ahead, a ribboning path across the Straits. Yvor cast a critical eye over the expanse of sea and sky. "Junction of currents," he explained to me. "Good feeding grounds for fish."

We were almost abreast of the muddy current when a myriad of filmy jellyfish streamed past the hull. They were beautiful things, delicately colored—lemony, lavender deepening to purple, pale rose, aquamarine—some like fragile bladders of Venetian blown glass, some like the pinky-fawn undersides of toadstools with pearly streamers. Yvor pointed out the deadly, exquisite Portuguese men-of-war, their pulsating bodies flowing away in a profusion of crimson tentacles. It was impossible to believe that their soft-textured, quivering fragility could almost sting a man to death.

Suddenly there was a roll of thunder. "Squall coming up!" Vic shouted.

Art came up on deck with a box of Dreft in his hand. "Ah, bath time," he said, and, going forward where he was partially concealed by the foresail, he stripped off his *pareu* and knotted it on the life line so that it wouldn't be blown overboard. All at once the rain sheeted down, and I scrambled into the wheelhouse.

"We're making no progress," Vic said, grumbling. "The squall's going to blow us off course, and the damn engine doesn't work. We should have junked the engine long ago if we'd had the dough to replace it." He stared moodily out at the sea. "Here," he said. "Take the wheel a minute." He went forward and savagely retrimmed the mizzen and the foresails. He was soaking wet when he returned.

I offered to get him a jacket.

"That's silly stuff," he said, but I hurried down to the chartroom and brought him back a heavy canvas parka. Vic slipped it on and began to talk to me in the tone he usually reserved for the crew, a tone not overlaid with the facetious tolerance with which he habitually addressed Kippy and me.

He related a number of yarns about the voyage and pictured himself in the role of a two-fisted, hard-bitten, rough and tough character who found the world much to his liking. Vic's ideal image of a man was a superior being at least six feet tall, weighing no less than two hundred pounds. That he didn't measure up to these standards was a source of constant personal chagrin. Sometimes he magnified his shortcomings by referring to himself as "just a skinny little runt." Sometimes he said defensively, "I'm no iron man like How Dog, but I'm pretty handy in a bar fight." But he never was resigned to the skimpy girth and stature in which he had been imprisoned.

I told him I was sure that if he had been the physical giant he wished he were he never would have got around to doing all the things he had. "It's just a matter of psychology," I said. "If you'd been Hal's size, you wouldn't have had to prove to anyone how tough you were. Everyone would have taken it for granted, and you'd probably have ended up in an advertising office." Vic snorted derisively at my pronouncement. Among the many dogmatic opinions he held, a man behind a desk was only a half man, and as for psychology, it was pure buncombe. He was always uneasy when the conversation turned to personalities and human motivations, for he felt that real men didn't concern themselves with such things, that, ideally, men only dealt with action—the wilder and more heroic the better. He alluded to his college days—he had been on the wrestling team and an expert tumbler on the trampoline net. He gave an account of a summer when he had been a logger in Puget Sound and another summer when he had hitchhiked across country, stopping along the way to climb mountains and shoot rapids in a cataract boat. He had been a stowaway in a cargo boat and had jumped ship at Juneau to work in a placer gold mine. Ever since he had floated leaves in mud puddles, he had wanted to sail around the world.

Once started on a flow of reminiscence, there was no stopping him. He told a series of anecdotes about girls and fights and outraged duennas. In Panama, there had been two young Navy nurses —"It was about then," Vic said, with a sidelong glance at me, "that we realized there would always be certain rewards coming the way of four good-looking bachelors on their way around the world."

"You don't need to go into the lurid details," I said.

"Why, what do you mean?" Vic protested with a great show of heavy sportiveness. "What's the matter, kiddy? You sour because I haven't chased you up the mast yet?"

"You can't," I reminded him. "Remember the deal. I don't chase you. You don't chase me."

"Ah, so." Vic nodded with exaggerated solemnity and then veered off on a subject dear to his heart—The Girl He Planned to Marry. His opinions concerning his future bride were as dogmatic as his opinions on psychology and the Male Ideal. "I want a wife who's beautiful, talented and a virgin. And she's got to be ten years younger than I am so that when I'm forty she'll still look good. She's got to cook well . . ."

"And be a good mother," I added, turning my head so he wouldn't see my smile.

"That's right," he agreed with naïve enthusiasm. "And I'll find her too." He paused to give this matter some private thought, and for a while we both sat there, comfortably sheltered from the squall which was dying out.

"Tell me more about the trip," I said after a bit. "What happened when you finally left Panama?"

Vic yawned loudly. "Take months to tell you. I'm off watch now, anyway. You can shoot the breeze with Hal when he comes up. Take over until he gets here."

But when Hal jackknifed himself into the wheelhouse, he was in an uncommunicative mood, and I went down to the lounge where Yvor was preparing dinner.

The squall had blown over, and Kippy had fallen asleep, his head pillowed on his arms on the hatch coaming.

"Don't you think he'll fall?" I asked Yvor.

Yvor wiped off the top of the bar where the rain had leaked. The ledge of the skylight was scalloped with drops of water. Yvor swiped at them wearily with a dirty dishrag. "No, Kip won't fall," he said. "He's all right."

"Ever hear of Missoul?" Yvor asked.

I shook my head.

He opened a can of string beans. "It's a little island off the tip of New Guinea, and a training center for witch doctors," he said. "All sorts of strange things go on. A German couple migrated there to start a coconut plantation, and eight months later the man was dead and his wife was stark, staring mad. She kept seeing human heads in the palms where coconuts should have been, and although she never saw another woman on the island she was plagued with the sound of female voices all the time. Lots of other people went there and were never heard of again. We tried to go there, but it was way off course, so we didn't." He stopped to scrape a bunch of carrots.

"I'd sure like to see the place," he said after a little while. "When the trip's over, maybe I'll head out this way again." He pumped a dented tin pot full of sea water and put the carrots on to boil. "Hey, did I ever show you the bird of paradise I picked up in New Guinea?" Yvor shared my passion for the acquisition of odd curios.

"No," I said. "Show me."

He went back to the storeroom and pried open the lid of a wooden crate. He picked out a tissue-paper-wrapped parcel. "There," he said, carefully unwrapping the bird of paradise. "Isn't that a beauty?" He waited for me to gaze at the dried carcass and plumage with wonderment and to praise it warmly before he disclosed the rest of his treasure trove—black-lipped pearl shells from the Tuamotus and silky gold-lipped pearl shells from Banda; a boar's-tusk bracelet capped in silver from the New Hebrides; a gold Colombian *guaca*, a little serving figure supposed to work for the dead in the underworld; a chamois pouch filled with pearls from the Northern Cooks; a silver bowl from Bangkok and a carved tiger's tooth from Northern Siam; *batik* and two Balinese wood carvings; a ten-legged *kava* bowl from Samoa.

"The bowls used to have seven legs," Yvor said. "But for some reason the price of the bowls became dependent on the number of legs, at a standard price of fifty cents a leg. Now the Samoans make them with as many as fifteen or twenty legs." Yvor smiled lingeringly over the bowl. I came to the last layer in the box: two spare Tahitian *pareus* and a Fijian *tapa* cloth. Abstracted with envy, I helped him repack the crate.

"I'll take this all home with me from Ceylon," Yvor murmured. "Got to go home then. The Navy wants me."

I knew that he didn't want to go back. None of us discussed his leaving, and Yvor kept his feelings to himself. When we returned to the lounge I said that it didn't seem right that after three and a half years aboard he had to leave before the voyage was completed.

"It doesn't seem right to the Navy that I stay here." Yvor's voice was suddenly rough. "Well, it's no use brooding about it. Let's have a little light in here. It's too damn dark." He filled and lighted the kerosene lamp and forced a smile. "There. That's more cheerful. Go wake up Art and tell Vic chow's on. I'll relieve Hal after I've eaten."

After supper we left the sultry humidity of the lounge and went up on deck to cool off. The sea glittered with phosphorescence, and as the schooner cut through a school of fish they spurted into hundreds of shimmering aquatic rockets and went spinning through the water like weaving fireworks. Vic patted me paternally on the back. "Go hit the sack, kiddy. Don't forget you're back at sea and you've got a watch to keep tonight."

Having caught on to the knack of steering, I loved keeping watch, particularly at night. The *California* creaked companionably, and on such a night as this, when the wind was gentle and steady, there was only the sibilance of the sea and the schooner's answering *eeek-aawk, eeek-aawk* to listen to. I was beginning to "learn" the stars, and from the collective mass I was now able to distinguish individuals, each with its particular virtue. I was familiar with some of the red stars, old and cooling, and with some of the hot, young blue stars. The Pleiades were comfortably middle-aged and the Hyades were older. When Vic or Yvor took a star fix in the early evening, it pleased me that I could pick out the stars as quickly as they could—at least Canopus, Sirius, Pollux, Procyon and Capella.

The stars faded out and the horizon paled in the East, light sweeping across the sky until the glowing white circle of the moon was only a ring of white smoke against the clouds. The sun rose, and with startling swiftness, the sea, the sky and the schooner were bathed in the clear, fresh radiance of morning. I heard a tide rip off in the distance, the sound like that of a shell held close to the ear, and for about half an hour I had trouble holding the schooner to her course as the waves slapped and splashed against her. Then she steadied, and a school of flying fish skimmed across the water on the port side and Scupper barked and howled in a frenzy of frustration.

Art came up on deck and began to work on the dinghy. He sanded it down and scraped off the old varnish, before it was time for him to begin getting breakfast ready.

I looked forward to Art's Cook Day because he was by far the best cook aboard. He always managed to serve food that made everyone else's attempts look amateurish. With ease and dexterity he baked bread and turned out pineapple upside-down cakes and delicious meat loaves and shepherd's pies, an accomplishment that was magical considering the limitations of the galley. I complimented him on the breakfast waffles. "Cooking's a cinch in this weather," he said matter-of-factly. "But wait until it gets rough."

I ventured to say that I'd like to be in a storm, that it would be exciting.

"Don't be crazy," Hal said.

"Typical dumb feminine remark," Vic said. "Only a dame would say something as nutty as that."

Feminine was an adjective the crew used in the derogatory sense. I had a hard time adjusting to a situation in which my being a girl was generally regarded as a liability and at best as an inconvenience to be put up with and ignored whenever possible.

I had been forewarned that my being aboard would effect no change in the crew's routine and habits, and I discovered that they meant pretty much what they had said. They announced themselves before coming down to the chartroom if they thought I might be dressing or undressing, but after they had miscalculated once or twice, I took the precaution of sleeping with most of my clothes on. As a concession to me they sometimes wore *pareus* when they took bucket baths, or else partly screened themselves from view behind a sail. They grumbled about these trials of enforced modesty, and I was querulous at times about my lack of privacy but, all things considered, our living arrangements worked out smoothly.

I knew my limitations as a sailing companion as well as they did. I knew nothing about engines, electricity, carpentry or mechanics. I wasn't strong enough to haul up a sail, pump the bilge or help raise or drop anchor.

However, I worked as hard as I could at my bit of the cleaning, cooking and watch-keeping. The crew, who made a fierce pretense of being harsh taskmasters, demanded my best efforts, although they never required me to do more than my share. They were scrupulously fair, and if I washed the dishes for Vic one night, he would take over an hour of my watch the next day.

On the afternoon of the second day out of Penang, Hal clambered out of the engine room and announced dismally that the engine had a cracked oil pump and was beyond repair—at least until the ship got to Ceylon. "Dear sweet Jesus, more expense." Hal slumped gloomily on the hatch. I tried to cheer him up by offering to wipe the grease off his back.

"Go ahead," Hal said, sighing. "I could do with a little tender, loving care at this point." He looked exhausted. It was fiery hot on deck, but in the engine room it was worse. I sponged cleansing cream over his back, smudging the grease but not removing it.

"That feels good," Hal said drowsily. "But it sure as hell is inefficient. If you want to get the grease off, use the deck brush and salt-water soap." I scrubbed his back until it was ruddled with red marks. Then I lighted a cigarette and watched the fish line secured to the stern ripple behind us. I reached out and tugged it experimentally, but it pulled easily in my hand. I let the wet line slip back into the water.

"No fish yet," Hal said. "Sure wish we would hook a tuna. I'm sick of corned-beef hash." He had changed from a pair of torn and filthy dungarees to a pair of white shorts with a Siamese label stitched on the outside of the rear back pocket.

Taking a cigarette from my tin of Abdullah Imperials, Hal struck a match on the deck. The match flared and fizzled, dropping a molten bit of the spent head onto his bare foot. "Lousy gook matches," he said, striking another match. *Gook* was a term much in use aboard, a vague disparaging classifier not so much of race as of character. Anything foreign which didn't work was automatically labeled gook. Anything outside the United States which didn't come up to par was referred to as gook. All foreign dock hands, shopkeepers, laborers and rickshaw boys were gooks.

"I'm sick of gooks," Hal said suddenly with resentment. "I'm tired of the food and I'm tired of the haggling and I'm tired of the language barriers." He sighed hugely. "You know what I would like right now? Beefsteak. Rare. Corn on the cob and baked Idaho potatoes. Lemon meringue pie. Ice-cold beer. And someone who could talk intelligently about theories. A good physicist, for instance."

He smiled as he audited these pleasant thoughts, and elaborated further as the dream of another life matured in his mind. "I'd like to hunt again, and drive a sexy car. I'd like to get back to engineering and exercise my mind again. When I was twenty I was an assistant physics instructor. But I couldn't do it now. Too out of touch." His voice dropped to a murmur. He was talking more to himself than to me. "I'd like to make enough money to live comfortably. Don't care if I get married or not."

"But think how lonely you'd be," I interposed softly.

He looked at me strangely. "Isn't everyone lonely?"

I let the question, which was more of a statement than a question, go unanswered. "What else do you want?" I asked. It was the first time I had succeeded in thawing Hal out a little from his masking screen of restraint. For once I felt I had caught him off guard, and, half ashamed of taking advantage of such a moment and half curious, I repeated my question. "What else do you want?"

"Nothing," he answered deliberately. "I don't want anything, because you get hurt if you want anything. Either you're deprived of what you want or else, having got what you want, you're afraid you're going to lose it, or sometimes you feel that what you have isn't enough and you make yourself miserable trying to get more. I don't care what it is. Money. Adventure. Power. Prestige. Love. It's all the same. Me, I'd like to not want anything. I'd like to be detached from everything and live in comfortable solitude."

"That sounds depressing."

"Not to me."

"Why'd you come on the trip?"

"I don't know. I guess I couldn't think of anything better to do. Strangely enough, no matter what I say, I still couldn't. Funny thing is I look at each port we're coming to and can only think of all the work that's got to be done, and yet, when I look back, all I can think of is how good the trip's been. I never even feel I'm traveling. The *Cal's* our home. She moves and we're on it, that's all. I think about it sometimes at night when I'm on watch. Hell, who knows what it's all about anyway?" He got up abruptly. "I don't know what pleasure people derive from baring their souls to anyone who'll listen. Everyone talks too much. Everyone's indentured to the sound of his own voice. Don't try to probe me any more. I don't like it. What good does it do? You tell me what you think. I tell you what I think. And nothing either of us has to say will really make any difference." He towered above me and, like a thunderclap, went away.

The third day out we sailed from the Malacca Straits into the Andaman Sea, which was kingfisher blue in the morning, gray and somber in the afternoon when another squall hit. Since the arrival in Penang had lopped off two thirds of my Cook Day, I volunteered to help Vic in the galley. It was hard work, quite unlike cooking in calm weather. In a light sea a saucepan could be put on top of the bar, or the Primus stove could be placed on the counter of the sink, or a kettle set on the Diesel stove with the expectation that they would stay put for a few minutes. But not so in rough weather.

Using the Primus stove was out of the question, unless you clutched a leg of the stove in one hand and steadied whatever was cooking on top with the other. In a heavy sea, when you had all you could do to keep your own balance, this was a feat no one had ever been known to perform successfully. In rough weather all cooking was therefore done on the Diesel stove.

The stove had a checkerboard of iron strips across its top, providing three squares—room enough for three pots, or two pots and one flat pan, or two pots and a kettle. Since these squared-off areas varied unpredictably in temperature, the pots had constantly to be shifted from space to space to avoid burning or undercooking. In the best of circumstances water took half an hour to come to a boil, and a simple meal that might have taken twenty minutes to prepare in an ordinary kitchen on shore required two hours or more on the *Cal.*

Pots and pans turned into demons; wedged on the stove they clashed and rattled together, wouldn't stay still, wouldn't stay in place, boiling over malevolently or simmering sullenly, slopping their contents over the edge of the stove in blistering spatters. Imprisoned in the sink cabinet, they battered resentfully at the door with a furious banging, sometimes with such force that the door flew open, hurtling utensils all over the lounge. The crockery in the cabinet above jiggled and jounced, and in the small stores cabinet spices spilled out of containers and caps worked themselves loose, liquid vanilla seeping into packaged baking soda, ketchup oozing into tea bags, vinegar dripping into the lidless tin of Blue Band margarine.

"It takes the heart right out of you," said Vic, glumly understating the situation.

"Well, it can't get much worse."

"Oh, this isn't so bad," Vic said to me. "This is just ordinary-brand hell. We often can't cook at all. Eat everything cold out of cans. This is really nothing." Leaning against the direction of the rolling hull at a thirty-degree angle, he lurched cockily up on deck and dropped potatoes down the skylight for me to catch as they tumbled off the skylight shelf. Back in the galley again, he hacked the potatoes into bits, mixed them with condensed milk, seasoning and flour, and wedged the pot into the oven. "Scalloped potatoes. Done." He grinned at me triumphantly. "See? Nothing to it at all."

I made some tinned-corn fritters, rescued them when the soup boiled over into the frying pan, and set about concocting a stew. Perspiration streamed down my face, coursed down my arms, pooled at my wrists and elbows, and dripped steadily.

"Real nice steam room for free. You'd pay two bucks for the privilege in the U.S.," Vic said, smiling. "Maybe it'll rain and cool off some." His optimism never deserted him. He would grumble

about conditions and circumstances with a fine, steady flow of im-
aginative expletives, but the moment anyone else complained, Vic,
with a dramatically pained look of surprise, would say, "What are
you moaning and bellyaching about? Don't let a little thing like that
get you down."

So when the rain came and water sheeted down on the deck, spurt-
ling through the skylight and trickling through the hatch, I waited
for Vic to say, "See, kiddy. Now it'll be cooler." Having said exactly
that, he listened attentively to the hiss of the water past the hull.
"Wind's freshened some," he said. "Bet that's a Force Five."

Being at sea for so long had developed in all of the crew an extraordinary sea sense. When they were below deck they knew from
the feel of the craft whether we were on the right course or not; an
imperceptible change in the rhythmic creaking would send one of
them racing above to retrim the sails. On one afternoon watch when
I was off course ten degrees, Yvor, who had been napping in the
yo-yo room, roared up to me to pay attention, and when he awoke
he swore he never recalled doing so.

"That's a Force Five, all right," Vic repeated, with reference to the
Beaufort Scale, which identifies wind strengths by numbers. (Five
corresponded to a stiff breeze.)

A stiff breeze seemed a highly inadequate description for the
frightful pitching and rolling that was going on, but, feigning indifference, I helped Vic wedge and block the crockery on the table
for lunch.

No one talked much at lunch. It was effort enough to eat without spilling the food. I started to clear the table and stack the
plates. "Don't stack the plates, kiddy," Vic said. "If you stack them
it just means two sides to clean."

"Lazy," Art said jeeringly.

"Well, wipe them off anyway. It's my Cook Day tomorrow." Hal
yawned and announced that if no one minded he was going to rack
out with a good book if anyone could recommend one he hadn't
read.

"Toynbee's *Study of History*," Yvor suggested.

Hal shook his head. "Don't feel like it."

"What about Huxley?"

"Doesn't excite me."

Vic interrupted. "Who is this Huxley anyway? What's his racket, philosophically speaking?"

"Here we go again. Another forum," Art said, sighing. "If you'd just *read* the book, Vic, instead of asking Yoke about it, you'd be much better off."

"Yoke knows what I'd like. I don't want to waste time reading something I'm not interested in."

"Okay, okay. Don't get huffy," Art said quickly.

Hal reached out and plucked a book from the rack, glanced at the title, shrugged, and went up for his turn on the wheel, leaving Yvor and Vic huddled over the table.

Vic's early background had not fitted him to the role of an "intellectual." In the early part of the trip, faced with the alternative of being left out of Hal's and Yvor's discussions or acquiring enough know-how to take part in them, he had chosen the latter course and had attacked Culture with unremitting energy. Discarding chronological outlines and systematic study as being preposterously boring, he circumvented tedium by reading snatches of Schopenhauer one day and Plato and Bertrand Russell the next. As he came upon references to books unfamiliar to him, he scribbled down a notation in his "Must Read" list. He was not at all awed by the wise men of the world. He spoke of Socrates as "a crafty old bird" and Nietzsche as "a hard-headed old son of a gun."

Vic listened patiently to Yvor. "Well," he said, "Huxley doesn't sound like such of a much, but I'll give him a whirl." Leaving Vic to flip through the pages of *Point Counter Point*, I went off to keep my afternoon watch.

"West by north," Hal said, grunting. "You're late." As I took over the wheel, he reached for a rusty harmonica and began to play a sweet and sorrowful little tune, the name of which he said he had forgotten. The crew had a repertoire of songs which they knew how to play solo or in harmony, Hal on the harmonica, Yvor on the guitar and Vic on the cocolele, a ukulele made out of coconut shells. The favorite song, which was rendered over and over again, was a missionary hymn:

> Way out on the desolate billow
> The sailor sails the sea,

> Alone with the night and the tempest
> Where countless dangers be.

The chorus:

> Yet never alone is the Christian
> Who lives by faith and by prayer,
> For God is a friend unfailing
> And God is everywhere.

Hal played the first verse and chorus on the harmonica and then carried on with the rest of the repertory: "Oh, My Pretty Quadroon," "Beautiful, Beautiful Brown Eyes," "You Are My Sunshine," "My Father Was a Drunkard," "Isa Lei," "I Was Seated One Day in a Gilded Cafe," "The Streets of Laredo" and "Tune X," the song he had first played. At my request, he cheerfully ran through the songs a second time and then, putting aside his harmonica, he abstracted himself into himself and said nothing for the rest of the watch. Scupper snortled sleepily at his feet, and at intervals Hal would reach over and pat him as if he entrusted to him the brooding sentiments for which he had no human confidant.

At the hottest point in the afternoon the rain slacked off, drizzled for a while and then ceased abruptly. The California's sails winged out, white and graceful, and, pitching and rolling, she sailed with the wind through the sapphire sea. Hooking my arm around the mast, I stretched out on the chart-room hatch and watched a majestic man-of-war bird circling high in the sky.

When I squinted at the sun, prisms floated before my eyes, and when I shut my eyes, my eyelids were black screens scrolled with crimson and gold spinning with sparks. I narrowed and closed my eyes, experimenting with different effects. Suddenly Kippy shrieked that there was a fish on the jig line.

"It's a marlin!" Vic shouted rapturously and galloped from the deck to the lounge and back to the deck again with the movie camera, Art close on his heels swinging a Rolleiflex in one hand and a Leica in the other. I bolted down into the chartroom for my own Rolleiflex. Yvor blocked the wheel, and all of us crowded together on the stern.

The line over the stern was taut and quivering. Hal and Yvor commenced to haul it in hand over hand. The line was unbelievably heavy, and the muscles and vertebrae and shoulder blades pulled white against the dark tan of their backs. The marlin arched from the water and plunged, only to leap again and again.

"Jesus, what a monster," Hal murmured. The line slackened momentarily and he found time to add, "Better get that thousand bucks' worth of camera gear into action. No one's ever going to believe us if you don't." He gripped the line with renewed strength as the marlin gave a sudden lurch and pulled away. Then it leaped again, a shining iridescent blue, its huge body churning through the water, leaping and twisting. Slowly it came in on a circle toward the boat; it was plunging in panic, rising high out of the water. Hal and Yvor tugged it closer and closer until I could see the disks of its eyes and the gleaming length of its sword. Yvor slipped the gaff hook under the fish's head and wrenched it up sharply so that the hook clawed through and caught in the fish's gills. Instantly there was a gush of blood, and the water all around reddened. The great fish, with its head pierced through, thrashed and hurled itself against the stern.

"Here—" Hal shoved the line at Art—"take it." He came back seconds later with a shotgun. "This is not very sporting," he said, sighting along the barrel and taking aim, "but we'll never be able to hoist it up with the gaff if it's going to keep on fighting." He leveled the gun at the struggling marlin and fired. Blood showered over the transom and spattered on the deck. In an agony of death the great marlin gave a final leap, splintering the gaff, the battered flesh around its jaws tearing as it ripped itself loose from the line and fell back floundering in the water. Heaving spasmodically, it drifted away from the boat, and then, with a last feeble roll, it sank.

Dumfounded, the crew watched it disappear. Vic swore in anguish. Hal groaned. Yvor sank down on the deck and put his head in his hands with a look of despair. Art slumped sadly over the gear box.

"Maybe you'll get another," I said timidly.

"Never," Yvor answered despondently. "Never another like that one."

For the next few hours the crew moped about, mourning the loss of the marlin. "It's all my fault," Yvor said over and over again. "I should have known the gaff wouldn't hold."

"Only hope the pictures turn out," Art intoned dully.

Hal, in a pall of gloom, sequestered himself in the fo'c'sle with a volume of the works of Charles Fort. Reading was not only a tonic regimen for Hal but also provided him with an all-embracing nepenthe.

The following morning Vic announced that he had worked out our position and that we should, if all went well, come to anchor at the Nicobar Islands early the next day.

So we really were going to the Nicobars after all. I was so preoccupied with this entrancing thought that, having scrubbed the deck thoroughly in the morning, I absent-mindedly scrubbed it over again in the afternoon.

CHAPTER NINE

The Nicobar Islands on the Magic Side of Time

THE SCHOONER'S LIBRARY yielded little information about the Nicobars. *Sailing Directions* mentioned that this group of nineteen islands, located in the Andaman Sea off the northwestern tip of Sumatra, had been used by the Japanese during World War II as an out-of-the-way submarine base; warned all craft to be on the lookout for uncharted wreckage in the area; and said nothing else about the islands except that they came under the control of the Indian Government, that the climate was unhealthy for Europeans and that the fresh-water supply was bad.

Professor Lips, in *The Savage Hits Back,* referred to the Nicobarese natives as an animistic tribe of Malay origin and made note of the curious fact that they often used drawings and carved wooden figures of white men to frighten away thieves, ghosts and evil spirits.

From Yvor's ornithology text, I learned that the Nicobar Islands were a habitat of *Collocalia nidifica,* the species of swift famed for its edible nests, which were esteemed in Hong Kong as the choicest of delicacies.

This was all I could find about the Nicobars, and in a way I was glad, strangely pleased to be coming to a place so little contained in any frame of reference.

Vic and Yvor hovered over a dog-eared chart and laid out a

course to Nancowry Harbor. The harbor, a deep lagoon embraced by the islands of Nancowry and Camorta, was only accessible through a shallow sliver of a pass on the east and by a slightly deeper sliver of a pass on the west. *Sailing Directions* warned that both entrances were hazardous.

"Huh," Vic scoffed. "We've been through worse than that." With a stubby pencil, he drew a firm line marking our course through the western pass.

At dawn, when I was on watch, I looked over the quiescent stretch of the Andaman Sea and saw on the horizon the filmy, unsubstantial image of landfall. Settled over with the peace that comes from gliding forward into a meditating world of waveless calm, I watched the tiny thickening of the horizon grow into a violet smudge. Later in the day sounds would fuse, but now each sound was distinct: the sibilance of the sea; the schooner's creaking; the clicking of Scupper's toenails as he made his way purposefully toward the bow to perform his morning functions to the right of the anchor chain; and the alarm clock on the wheelhouse ledge that defied conventional onomatopoeia and went brink-brunk, brink-brunk.

The level space of water between us and the violet shadow of Nancowry and Camorta shook with the gold of the sun. Space all about, and the islands now coming closer, darkening, expanding to a long, low mound of jungly vegetation, with the palms so closely crushed together that no one tree was outlined, the whole a solid palisade of dark, quivering foliage. Finally, unexpectedly, the pass appeared between the islands. We sailed cautiously through the narrow breach, the jungly headlands seeming to slide back together behind us, cutting off all sight of the sea. On either side, the islands' massive palm forests sloped down to a beach of lime-white sand dotted with beehive huts hunched beneath the clotted plumage of silvery thatch. The lagoon curved out and round again, the water turquoise where it lapped over coral reefs and sapphire where the coral ended.

"It's beautiful," I said.

"Beautiful, hell," Art retorted. "That's coral and it's a bastard to anchor in."

We sailed toward a sheltered cove rimmed by Champin Village

the main settlement on Nancowry Island. Crowned with the arching plumes of areca and coconut palms, the village took on shape, the sun catching and blazing on a shed roofed with galvanized iron, the shaggy huts set high on stilts clustering all about.

I leaned against the wheelhouse and stared at the village, my consciousness flowing out to the alien huts and the palms beyond. It was a moment which filled me with a kind of ecstasy, and I find I return to it time and time again in memory.

We anchored. The sails were dropped, the boom lifts were pushed into place, and the anchor chain was clankingly paid out through the hawsepipe. While I was helping to fold the stiff canvas sails, I saw that a crowd of natives had lined up on the beach, all of them solemnly shading their eyes to look at us. A group of coppery-colored men in scarlet-tailed loin cloths detached themselves from the crowd, shoved a high-prowed outrigger into the water and paddled out to us. Standing up in the outrigger's tapering prow, which was painted with a black telesmatic eye, they caught hold of our gunwale cap to steady themselves as they came alongside.

"Gooks," Hal muttered, as the natives stared at us and began to babble excitedly.

"Boy, they sound just like you, Hadley," Art said. "Why don't you try talking to them?"

Trying what little Malay I knew, I had already done just that, with no response other than wide grins exposing blackened teeth and gums stained crimson from betel-chewing.

"Save your breath, Hadley, and watch the expert," Yvor said, flourishing a box of stick tobacco left over from Polynesian trading days. "I'm going to have a go at cornering the coconut market."

When he had finished bartering, there was a hill of green coconuts on the deck. With a long-bladed knife Yvor whacked off the top of one of them and gave it to me to drink. It was the first coconut I had ever drunk. The sweet-tasting liquid reached coolingly inside me and I sat on deck drinking it slowly. My eyes ambled over the shore where my feet wanted to, exploring the cluster of thatched huts with the jagged frieze of villagers standing in front and the little chickens and thin pigs darting around them. The natives in the outrigger cast off, and almost at once another outrigger pulled alongside bearing a barefooted, khaki-clad, portly Indian civil serv-

ant with gray hair and features oddly similar to those of Ezio
Pinza. A stethoscope hung around his neck and he carried a furled
black umbrella as though it were a scepter.

"I am the government doctor and port official," he said in hesitant English as he climbed aboard. "Are any of you diseased?"

He plugged the stethoscope tubes into his ears and gravely listened to the sound of our hearts, inspected our health certificates,
shuffled and reshuffled the ship's papers, and finally, sitting down
on one of the barrel seats in the lounge, inquired if we had a drop
of whisky on board. The heat, he said, had given him a tickling
thirst. His manner was glazed with a Victorian punctilio which
was strangely accented by the singsong diphthongs of his speech. He
tossed down two neat jiggerfuls of whisky, rewarded us with a
dazzling smile and suggested that we go ashore and pay our respects
to the Queen. Yes, yes, there was a Queen, the Ranee Islon, and it
was customary for all strangers upon their arrival to have an
audience with her. He hinted delicately that the Ranee Islon, like
himself, was not above a wee nip now and then, and that she
might appreciate an offering of this sort.

"We're low on liquor," Art said pointedly. It was decided that
a tin of Spam and a canister of cocoa would be acceptable as gifts
to royalty.

The doctor cleared his throat and turned upon me an uncertain,
appeasing regard from large brown eyes with yellowish whites.
"You have the honor to be the first European lady to set foot on
the shores of Nancowry," he said. "I believe," he continued, glancing at my halter and shorts and then glancing away again, "I believe that it would perhaps be fitting to change to more formal
attire before honoring the Queen with your presence."

I changed to a skirt and blouse, the crew put on their pandanus
hats banded with Tahitian shells, and Kippy put on shoes and a
clean shirt. The doctor summoned his outrigger by raising his
umbrella and waving it in the air; and we set out for our royal
visit.

The doctor pointed to five poles festooned with tufts of palm
leaves which stood in the water a little way from the beach. "Those
are scare-devils to frighten away the twin fiends of the monsoon,"

he said. "I do not believe in such things. I am Hindu myself," he pronounced loftily.

When we landed on the beach, the soft murmur of the villagers' voices hushed. Every eye turned to stare at us. "Do not be timid," the doctor said. "The people are friendly here. They are just curious about you. Many have never seen a white face before."

As we walked up the beach and along the edge of the jungle, the natives remained at a respectful distance. Chickens, dogs and pigs fled at our approach, squawking, yapping and squealing. From the stilt-raised huts on either side, faces peered down, watching us go by.

"Please to wait here," the doctor said, stopping before a round hut bigger than the rest and roofed with a woven dome of thatch. He mounted a ladder and disappeared inside. The wooden lintel of the doorway was impressed with a red-stained hand print, a talisman to guard the dwelling against the evil eye. A few minutes later the doctor's head reappeared. "Now you may enter," he said.

Up the ladder we all went, Kippy and I leading the way, and the doctor ushered us into the royal sitting room, which hardly seemed large enough to hold us all. The room was circular, and equipped with a window, a table, two wooden chairs and a bench. The woven wall matting was plastered and painted blue around the lower half and separated from the white-painted upper half by a broad orange stripe. The Queen entered from another chamber in the back. Correctly imperturbable, she greeted us with the calm dignity of her station and motioned us to be seated. She then sat down on one of the wooden chairs, smoothed her flower-printed sarong over her knees, adjusted the safety pins fastening her red blouse and smilingly surveyed us over the tops of spectacles from which both lenses were missing.

She was a plump and pleasant-looking woman. Age had narrowed her mouth and eyes and somewhat spread her nose, and her cinnamon-colored skin, like the jacket of a baked apple, wrinkled loosely over flesh that was no longer firm. Since she spoke only Tamil and Nicobarese, the doctor acted as interpreter. At the Queen's suggestion, he produced a gilt-clasped, leather-bound guest register, discolored and peeling with age. The entries dated back to 1870, and most of them had been made by captains of sailing whalers and trading schooners who had been driven by typhoons to seek refuge in the landlocked shelter of Nancowry Harbor. We signed the register and, having neatly blotted our signatures, presented the Queen with the Spam, the cocoa and a silk scarf saying "I Love You" in six languages which I had thought to bring along. I don't think the doctor thought much of the scarf, but Ranee Islon seemed pleased. Then Princess Laxshmi, the Queen's daughter, and Laxshmi's daughter, Mochan, glided in.

Princess Laxshmi was a handsome woman with an air of distinction. Her gray-black hair was pulled back smoothly into a knot at the nape of her neck, and her features were arresting in their delicacy. Mochan, shy and round with adolescence and a little awkward in a mauve crepe-de-Chine sari, handed us each coconuts to drink and carefully decanted mine into a cloudy jelly glass.

Since Easterners are not obsessed with the notion of keeping up a sustained conversation, little was said, but for our entertainment photographs were passed around showing Laxshmi and Mochan at the amusement park in Madras, where they had gone for a vacation several years before. When our smiles began to stiffen and Kippy began to fidget, Mochan brought out a wind-up gramophone, and after she had played several scratched and warping Indian records, the doctor said that it was in order for us to leave.

Laxshmi filled Art's pandanus hat to its brim with bantam-sized hen's eggs. She and Mochan smiled good-by, and the Queen cheerfully exposed two rows of blackened and stumpy teeth.

We spent what was left of the afternoon visiting the trading store. The store, stocked with such necessities as salt, matches, yard-long bars of soap and bolts of cloth, was a branch of a Madrasi firm that annually sent out a dozen or so clerks to run the establishment and to handle the export of copra and betel nuts which an itinerant trading schooner collected every month.

Since the trading schooner was due the next morning, villagers were already at work stacking sacks of copra and betel in the clearing in front of the trading store, while the clerks from Madras stood in the shade of the veranda directing them. The clerks offered us weak, heavily sugared tea which made my stomach feel hot and sleepy. To a man, they said that they found the islands dull and monotonous and couldn't wait until the time came for them to be returned to India. "There is nothing here to do but work," they said, sighing wearily as they lighted the Coleman lanterns in their quarters and closed up the store for the night.

Early the next morning the *Mahmoodia,* the monthly trading schooner, two-masted, square-sailed and disheveled, anchored close to the *California.* For the rest of the day, natives, with their long-ended loincloths wagging behind them like scarlet tails, transferred the sacks of copra stacked inside the stockaded clearing of the trading store to the schooner's hold.

After watching the proceedings for some time, I paddled the *California's* outrigger over to the white, starfish-dotted beach, where I found all sorts of shells as I wandered along—ruffled white tridacnas, some the size of a small ashtray, others as large as a giant bird bath; creamy spider shells with splayed white fingers; dark and speckled cowries with a golden sheen; white shells, pink shells, gray shells. The clerks at the trading store gave me a wooden box, and I walked along the beach, picking up shells and putting them into it. I was followed by a flock of native children who would scatter whenever I glanced behind me and scamper like sandpipers to hide behind the talipot palms by the trampled path that edged the jungle.

Beneath the sun's nearly vertical rays, the sand was parched and bleached with heat, the clear water along the curving littoral a brilliant blue-green. Farther along, there were the rusted remains of a Japanese landing craft and a submarine. A pig squealed as it rooted in the palms, and from the jungle came the monotonous piping of parakeets. Behind me the voices of the copra carriers were muted with distance.

I waited for the children to come closer. They bunched together and watched me with brow-dark eyes. I smiled and waved and they looked at each other uncertainly. Presently, a girl, whose adolescent breasts threatened to burst from the prison of her safety-pinned chemise, edged forward. When she was within a few yards of me, she stopped and held out a cowry shell. It was the gesture of Psyche offering a sop to Cerberus. I placed the cowry on top of my other shells and gave her the only thing I had with me that I thought she might like—a blue hair ribbon, which she immediately tied around her waist. From then on, she followed me about like a solicitous shadow. A transient missionary had baptized her Sophia and had taught her the meaning of "yes," "what" and "no," and this knowledge equipped her to become my interpreter. She combed the beach for shells to add to my collection—none but the perfect ones would do, the ones with the sharpest steeples, the ones fresh from the cove, with their lustrous patina unimpaired—and she brought me black-beaked nautiluses and the white-gold cowries which were so hard to find.

She led me from one thatched hut to another until we had made the rounds of all thirty-one, a guided tour that took several days, for each stop required a formal ritual of greeting and an exchange of cigarettes for drinking coconuts. The villagers were a gentle, friendly lot, and if they weren't a particularly handsome people, they were obviously healthy and cheerfully disposed to spinning out their lives in an isolated state of grace.

Their arrangements for living were of the simplest. Few huts were furnished with more than sleeping mats, coconut calabashes and earthenware pots, a tin trunk and a lamp. Each family owned an outrigger, a dog and a small flock of chickens and pigs that roamed the village in a noisy foraging company during the day and dutifully assembled at nightfall beneath their respective huts.

Sophia took me to the village carpenter, who carved for me one of the demonifuges which I had read about, a top-hatted wooden figure with nautilus-shell eyes and one arm raised in a gesture of power. Sitting on the ladder of a hut with a pet parakeet swinging on its perch beside me, I watched the carpenter whittling. Beneath me, at the foot of the ladder, a rusted gasoline drum left over from the days of the Japanese occupation and a bird-bath-sized tridacna shell served as rain-catchers. The sun's rays slanting through the canopy of palms dappled the settlement with light, and under this chiaroscuro everything was washed in a soft haze. Parakeets piped and chittered in the jungle; the water whispered over the white beach. In the great quietness of the afternoon the air seemed weighted with a stillness which human voices never quite pene-trated—it was as though the voices were an illusion. Sometimes the whole village seemed to be an illusion. It was the first time since my childhood that I had been able to sit for hours doing nothing and not feel guilty about it.

For once I felt I had enough time between the rising of the sun and the setting of it to do as I pleased, enough time to sit mindlessly gazing at the pattern made by the smooth, burnished leaves of the talipot palms against the sky, enough time to wander along the beach picking up shells and feeling the hot, sugary sands scrunching between my toes, enough time with Kippy to search for starfish and make stones skip across the water until our wrists ached, and to hunt lizards and lungfish. Then, having found them, we would watch until they were hidden from sight in a crevice, when, according to the rules of our game, we could go on until we found another one and start all over. And when the shore was explored, there was time enough to explore the bay in the *California's* outrigger, which the crew had picked up in Samoa.

The water was as clear as glass, and in the deep places troutsized trigger fish looked like minnows as they swam up and over the knobbly, branching arms of red-purple coral. In the shallow places the coral lightened to creamy white, carpeting the bay with a lobed and lacelike web which rose higher and higher as I skimmed toward the far shore until it massed before me in a long, jagged reef, beyond which the water rippled onto a shell-strewn beach.

The afternoon of our last day in the Nicobars I invited Ranee Islon, Laxshmi, Mochan and Sophia to a farewell get-together on the *California*. They filed into the lounge and, encouraged by gestures and smiles from me, seated themselves in a row on the couch. Sophia, evidently intimidated by the presence of royalty, bowed her glossy black head and could hardly be persuaded to raise her eyes. The party began to flag before it had even started.

I passed around tea and slices of a chocolate cake Art had baked, and brought out the schooner's photograph album. From time to time the crew sauntered in, looked over the situation and left. Time wore on, and at last the Queen rose with dignity, adjusted her spectacles and, in her wake, the entourage trooped on deck. The royal outrigger was summoned from the shore, and when it came alongside, the oarsman handed up two baskets, which Ranee Islon presented to me. One was filled with taros and papayas, the other with clumps of pink and lavender coral, sea-wet and glowing.

In the center, half hidden, were two tortoise-shell combs which Sophia indicated with shy pride were a special gift from her.

We hoisted sail early the next morning, the doctor, the clerks and the villagers lining up along the beach to wave good-by. The Queen, wearing a crimson sarong, was prominent in the foreground and one of the most vigorous of the wavers. Our sails were sheeted out, and soon Nancowry faded and blurred on the horizon. The last swift which was keeping us company wheeled in the sky and disappeared. The sun blazed down on the crates of shells that I had lashed to the shrouds, and the coral smelled as it died and began to lose its color.

CHAPTER TEN

Voyage to Ceylon

EARLY THAT NIGHT I was wakened by the discordant, clanging clatter of the sheet-blocks. The schooner was heeled so far over that my bunk felt as if it were at a ninety-degree angle with the sea, a notion which seemed only slightly exaggerated once I had turned on the light. The chart room was a shambles. Everything movable had shifted from starboard to port in a frightful jumble of papers and charts and books. "What's happening?" I shouted up through the binnacle hole.

Hal's voice returned, faint above the clanging and keening of the schooner. "We've just hit one hell of a squall, that's what's happening, lady!"

Amazingly, Kippy was still asleep. I pulled the poncho over him to keep off the water that was leaking through the overhead. And then, bundling myself into somebody's leather jacket that came down to my knees, I tugged the hatch open.

It was raining, and the wind was chill and harsh. The sea rushed past the hull in turbulent mounds glimmering with phosphorescence. There was a ghostly spurt of light as a freak wave dashed against the shrouds and broke over the deck in a gleaming track. Slipping and stumbling, I made my way along the deck and crawled into the wheelhouse. It was fuggy with the wet-dog smell of Scupper and the fumes of Hal's pipe. Hunched over the pale glow of the binnacle light, Hal looked tense and grim. Vic, Art and Yvor were shouting to each other through the wind-shriek as they ran down the mainsail and the Genny. Through the patch Hal kept rubbing on the misty window of the wheelhouse, I could see the undulating ranges of water racing alongside and swirling across the gunwales on my left. A mountain of water soared behind the stern, subsided and rose again, vanishing and re-forming with swift and ominous repetition. The sea hissed and roared and, strangely, above all the clamor, I could hear the shrill cheeping of sea birds—a mournful, lonely sound.

Art often said of me that I knew too little about the sea to be frightened by it, and it was quite true. The threat of danger intensified my sense of adventure, and for a few hours I felt elated, an adventurous stranger to myself, and then, shiveringly, I hugged the leather jacket about me and swore at the wind and the water which swept through the lacings of the wheelhouse's canvas sides and pooled on the cushion I was sitting on.

A little after three in the morning the worst of the squall blew over, and Vic crumpled wearily into the seat beside me. "Boy," he said. "I haven't felt such a wind since Christ was a cowboy. Must have been hitting fifty knots for a while back there. Must have been at least a Force Ten while it lasted."

For once Hal didn't question Vic's pronouncement. He had fallen into a preoccupied silence, his pipe dangling from his lips, and only by the way he kept both hands gripped on the wheel did he indicate that anything unusual had happened.

The squall ushered in a series of lesser squalls which approached with tedious regularity about two every afternoon for the next four days, broke with gusts of wind and an angry downpouring of rain, and then went away again just before suppertime. In the calm, candent mornings, mattresses, pillows and clothes were spread on deck and knotted to the life lines to dry, but as they dried only to get wet again in the afternoon, the schooner was overhung with a strong odor of mold, distinctly noticeable for a day or two and then becoming less and less evident as we became accustomed to it.

Following a west by southwest course across the Bay of Bengal, we made some headway toward Ceylon, but not nearly enough to satisfy Vic, who was highly impatient with such a slow passage. Secretly, I was pleased that the passage was slow, since it was the final lap of the voyage, and I hoped that the nine hundred miles from the Nicobars to Colombo would last as long as possible. In spite of the dank discomfort of the afternoon squalls, the mornings and nights remained infinitely pleasurable.

In a world where there was nothing but the sea, the sky and the schooner, the introduction of anything new took on significance, the appearance of anything unexpected became An Event. In these terms, the mornings were eventful, as almost every morning was accompanied by the manifestations of some new natural phenomenon. We were followed for a while by a trio of tropical birds with sweeping, three-plumed tails. Splendid and white, the birds swooped about us in easy, dashing flight, vanishing as suddenly as they had appeared before any of us ever found out what they were.

Once a waterspout materialized on the horizon; it poked through the distant haze like the trunk of some celestial elephant. It was visible for some time before the inside part of it paled, and then the sharp outline on either side gradually became fuzzy and blurred into nothingness.

The day after the appearance of the waterspout, the trailing line fastened to an eye bolt on the stern tautened, and we pulled aboard a skip-jack tuna weighing about thirty pounds. It was silvery and plump, with flaring fins, its appearance as maudlin and cherubic as a Disney cartoon creation. Landed on deck, its colors shimmered and then waned, dimming like a rainbow in the sun. Yvor butchered it expertly, and Art supervised the cooking of it, all the way from choice fillets to the inevitable chowder.

The day of the tuna was also the day of the flying squid. I was in the wheelhouse when I heard a rustling behind me as though leaves were being twirled in an autumn wind. Looking aft, I saw a column of small oblong things rising straight out of the sea. Spurting upward to a height of perhaps ten feet, they described a perfect parabola and landed a few seconds later in soft thuds about my feet. The creatures were about six inches long, reddish, with feathery tentacles at one end and parachutelike membranes at the other. They were capable of exhaling a spurt of water with remarkable force. Kippy quickly recognized their possibilities as water pistols, and with his face heavy with concentration, he pressed the torso of one squid after another, shooting water at Scupper. Yvor showed Kippy how to dip the squid into a bucket of water so that they could obligingly recharge themselves, and this diversion kept Kippy wide-eyed and shrieking with pleasure until he happened to squeeze one poor creature too vigorously and a protesting jet of dark, viscous fluid was discharged over the wheelhouse tarpaulin. Art, surveying the mess, coldly put an end to any further experimenting, and the excitement died down as quickly as it had begun.

There was a day which was, as Hal said, hotter than a bandit's pistol, and none of us felt like doing much. Earlier in the morning Vic had dared me to climb up to the yardarm.

"How's it up there, kiddy?" Vic shouted.

"Fine," I replied glibly, and then looked below at the yawning deck, an easy two-story drop. I became a terrified idiot, and the crew howled and hooted with laughter.

But now the subject had palled, and Vic was sitting on the hatch, poring over Bertrand Russell and alternately soaking his feet in a solution of Lysol and daubing them with tincture of merthiolate in an attempted hurry-up cure of athlete's foot. Art was trying to get a good picture of Scupper "singing" while Hal played the harmonica. Yvor was lying on his stomach, his elbows resting on the gunwales, and was indolently trapping jellyfish with my string shopping bag, which he had attached to the gaff hook. Suddenly, some twenty yards away, the arching, glossy back of a blue whale slowly rose above the water. As a fine white mist appeared above its head, there was a huge sound, like the noise of steam siffling from a locomotive. Almost instantly we were enveloped with the heated, fetid odor of the whale's breath. In all the world there is nothing quite like the halitosis of a whale.

The whale was easily as long as the schooner. Set in its huge, vaulted bulk was an eye the size of a dinner plate. For a moment the eye stared at us. Then, with a low sucking sound, its flukes at right angles with the water, the whale submerged and swam directly beneath the hull of the *California*.

"Well, call me Ishmael," Yvor said. "Who does he think he is? Moby Dick?"

"If that brute gets the notion to breach, we're in one hell of a tight spot. I kid you not," Vic said.

We all regarded the whale with tense interest. It seemed an eternity before the whale glided away and broke water some distance beyond.

"I guess we're not going to be capsized this time," Vic said, and went back to soaking his feet in Lysol.

Apart from these appearances of natural phenomena and the cyclic occurrence of Cook Days, there was little to distinguish one day from another. In between boat-keeping chores, we talked, read and drank quarts of coffee. The crew weren't much for writing letters, but I was obsessed with the delight of using the *California's* schooner-silhouetted stationery and preposterously worldly envelopes marked AIR MAIL in French, Arabic, Chinese and English, and I wrote to everyone I knew. I also spent a good deal of time working on the magazine article that had been my original ticket to board the schooner. Every night after supper I would get out my typewriter and a folder of notes and diagrams and begin to question the crew, until one of them would yawn and stretch and say, "Time for beddy-by, Hadley. It's time the rest of us hit the sack."

I felt that I had hardly had any sleep at all when I heard Vic say, "Okay, you can't sleep forever." He shook my shoulder. "Come on, now. Up. You're on watch." Slow with drowsiness, I pushed myself out of the bunk and followed him up the ladder.

It was cooler on deck. The Bay of Bengal, phosphoric and flashing, as if imprisoning millions of sub-aquatic fireflies, showered the bowsprit with brilliance and infolded the hull with sparkling froth. The schooner sailed smoothly forward, streaming radiance. There was a rhythmic creaking as the bowsprit rose and fell with majestic monotony. I lingered for a moment and then climbed into the wheelhouse and settled myself on the narrow seat ledge opposite Vic. We exchanged companionable grunts. I squinted sleepily at the binnacle. "Due southwest?"

"Due southwest. No strain. Easy steering," he said, and yawned noisily. "I'm going to catch me some shut-eye. She's all yours."

After he went below, I checked the compass once more and, bracing one of the wheel spokes against my left knee, I leaned back and looked at the sky, wondering which star I would choose to steer by. Arcturus, obviously, a veritable giant among stars, pendent now over the yardarm, the brightest of golden orange drops. I remembered how, when we had first started out, I had spent the watch sitting and staring at the dim glow of the binnacle, hardly taking my eyes off the compass card. Now I had learned how to steer by the stars, which was a different matter entirely. The schooner seemed to rest motionless, and I had the illusion that I was no longer her helmsman. Instead, I felt that I was controlling the course of the stars. A gentle pull of the wheel toward me, and Boötes the Herdsman marched off toward the north, taking Arcturus with him. Faint little Virgo sidled closer, hardly noticeable except for Spica, her only jewel. When I eased the wheel back and pushed it two spokes away from me, Virgo skittered off with the Herdsman in full chase, and Alcaid soared above the mast at the tip of the handle of the Big Dipper. Mizar followed, and even tiny Alcor was visible. Then the sails started flapping and the blocks rattled angrily on the travelers. I brought Arcturus quickly back into place.

The dawn watch. It was one of those chance rewards of travel, a magic moment, untranslatable from its time and place, a moment which lives on perpetually, with all its colors made fast. Just then there was no sign of dawn. The masts were still black against the luminous darkness of the sky, the sails gray in the starlight. There was a thrilling flush of wind against my skin. I listened to the chorus of rustlings and creakings and whisperings, the clicks and bangs of loose and swaying things below. Lazily, I stretched my right leg forward, keeping my other leg against the wheel, and with my foot I maneuvered the small alarm clock on the ledge of the flag locker around so that I could see what time it was. Six-ten. A little less than two hours to go. The sun should rise around six-thirty. It was rising later every day. We gained an hour because it did. If you were east of Greenwich, your time was later than Greenwich time. West of Greenwich, earlier. Something like that, anyway. Hal had explained it to me three times with diagrams and had thrown in a lot of miscellaneous information about parallels of latitude and longitude, but I still didn't understand it. "God, women are dumb goofs," Hal had said. If I did nothing else aboard, at least I served as a constant reaffirmation of male superiority.

Lighting a cigarette that was musty with mold and keeping an eye on Arcturus, I contemplated on the wonder that I was aboard. It was a situation that called to mind all the clichés of the escapologist, all the fictive fancies about tropical islands, tropical nights and languorous kisses in the moonlight. Life aboard the *California* transcended the stuff of all the movies I had sat through, all the books I had ever read. It was an experience filled with satisfaction and beauty, the memory of which I knew would serve me as a sanctuary for the rest of my life. Realizing this, it was hard not to think too much about the days as they happened. Like pulling a flower apart to examine its petals, it was a mistake to try to be aware of and to profit by every second. I had schooled myself to resist this temptation so that even now, with Ceylon only a few days away, I relaxed carelessly, as though there would never be an end to the voyage.

Although I was sure that in the minds of the crew, who really knew what they were about, much of my activity on board had the quality of a little girl playing house, I had the feeling that the boat was the one place in the world where I truly belonged, the one place where I had the least need of an exterior self to make conversation and put on a show for other people. There was another world, another way of living, and all sorts of urgent and important things which didn't matter. They existed somewhere past the horizon, hints of a past life, seen but shapeless, images and sensibilities which had ghosted away the day we had sailed from Singapore. The *California* was the only world I recognized.

On land there was such an infinite variety of people and things over which my consciousness could flow, but now all my consciousness and senses were suddenly confined and focused on the minute area of a schooner whose over-all length was sixty-three feet, and whose beam at her widest point was only fourteen feet—a universe that I could walk around in seconds. It was as if I had disconnected my emotions from a lawn sprinkler and had hooked them up to a fire hose. I looked at a ring bolt the way I used to look at a mountain. I anthropomorphized practically everything aboard, cherishing the sails as though they were babies and making tentative overtures of friendship to the stove. I felt about the schooner and the crew in a way I supposed I could never feel about anything or anyone else.

As for the crew, aboard the schooner each one could qualify as a great man. Perhaps in another environment which called for different facets of personality and character, they might lose the quality which made them great. But aboard the boat they were secure in their heroic roles and they kept me in a state of decent humility.

What a change, I thought, from New York. I looked down at my toes, and although I couldn't see them clearly, they felt dirty, and I thought about all the shoes, all those rows of polished discomfort I had left behind me in New York. All the clothes. That giant closetful, a small part of which was included in the trunk that was probably waiting for me now in Ceylon. It was odd to reflect on the turn events had taken. The closetful of demanding elegance had given way to a trunkful of practicality, and the trunkful had been replaced by a ridiculously small locker, a little less than a foot square, in which my entire collection of boat clothes was stuffed—things with legs and sleeves and a hole to put my head through. It seemed to me that there was a direct ratio between the size of my wardrobe and the quantity of my problems. Clothes and problems —I had so few now of either. There was a kind of poetic justice about the fact that the only girdle I had brought with me, a symbol of uncomfortable deception if ever there was one, was now wrapped around a leaking pipe in the engine room.

When Art came on deck to relieve me of the watch, the wind had died down, and he scowled as he took over the wheel. "We should've been in Colombo by now," he said sullenly. "Well, go down for breakfast. Beans and dog food are now being served."

Because of the calms and the alternate headwinds we had run into, the voyage was taking longer than the crew had anticipated. Our provisions were almost finished, and it was the fourth day that our diet had been restricted to corn meal, beans and an Australian brand of corned-beef hash which originally had been bought for Scupper. Our main source of anxiety, though, was that the water supply might give out. Ever since we had left the Nicobars, the water had become increasingly orange with rust, a sure sign that the tanks were almost empty. Just how much water was left was anyone's guess, so we rationed the water on a don't-take-a-drink-unless-you-absolutely-have-to basis, and hoped for the best.

Water still trickled thinly out of the pump the day we sailed into the harbor of Colombo. It was a clear, bright day, and we sailed past the breakwater under full sail. We came into the wind, and as the sails began to flap, the schooner fell back on the wind, the sails were dropped and the anchor was set. Then we all went below to wait for the immigration and customs officials to come aboard.

As I glanced through the ship's papers which had been laid out in advance on the lounge table, I saw that I was listed in the crew manifest not as cook but as seaman.

"We figured you deserved a promotion, kiddy," Vic said, giving me a good-natured clout across my shoulder blades that made my head judder.

In Colombo, Yvor booked passage on a Norwegian freighter which was sailing for America later that week. His imminent departure for renewed military service cast the crew into a gloomy mood of despondence. On the afternoon Yvor was to leave, I took a water taxi out to the freighter, where I found him lying on the bunk in a carpeted, chintz-curtained cabin.

"It doesn't look much like the *Cal,* does it?" he said wryly, his china-blue eyes looking out dully over the cabin.

I've forgotten whatever it was I said to be comforting, and whatever it was he said in reply. I can only remember that there seemed to be a great many things I wanted to say and didn't.

Presently, a man beating a gong walked past in the corridor and called loudly that all visitors must go ashore. Yvor and I talked as fast as we could. Suddenly, Yvor bent down and rummaged through a cardboard carton that was stacked beneath the porthole with his guitar and the rest of his luggage.

"Here," he said, giving me the tiger's tooth from Chiengmai and two black-lipped pearl shells from the Tuamotus. "I meant to give them to you before. Something for you to remember me by."

The man beating the gong walked past the door again, calling out more loudly, more urgently, for all visitors to go ashore.

"Well, I guess you'd better go," Yvor said. "Drop me a line if you have a chance."

"Yes," I said, and awkwardly reached up to kiss his cheek.

I took a water taxi back to the *California,* and when I went down to the lounge, I found Hal, Vic and Art quietly and seriously drinking what was left of a fifth of gin.

"We're drinking a toast to Yoke," Vic said.

"It's a crying shame," Hal said. He shrugged. "Well, what can you do? The Navy is the Navy."

Art poured another round of drinks.

A few days later the *California* sailed for Aden, the Red Sea and the Mediterranean. "Well, lady," Hal said, "it's been nice knowing you, but I suppose it's time to say good-by."

My mouth twitched, my nose tickled and my eyes slowly filled with tears. I felt it happen, and they all saw my brimming eyes.

"Hey, kiddy, it's not so bad as all that," Vic said. "If you're going to be in Beirut in five months' time, why don't you meet us there?"

"I'll be on the dock when you arrive," I said. "Cross my heart." Beirut? I didn't even know where it was, but I'd be there.

I couldn't believe that the *California* had gone. The next morning I hired a rickshaw and told the rickshaw boy to take me to the dock area. The boy jogged on naked feet (the skin of his feet like rough gray bark) to a gate which was called Bagdad for no reason that I could ascertain. There he left me to argue with a guard whether or not I should be allowed through. I needed a pass that I didn't have. Possibly, five rupees slipped discreetly in the guard's palm would have done the trick, but somehow I could never bring myself to bribe anyone. I was sure I would make a mess of it. Fortunately, the guard was sufficiently confused by my credentials and explanations to let me pass.

I hailed a water taxi, a dilapidated dinghy with a canopied top. The oarsman, as soon as I was settled in the boat, asked me for an American cigarette and was manifestly disappointed when he discovered that I was smoking a local brand that came in a tin labeled Peacock and which cost two rupees a hundred.

We nosed past Maldivian buggalas with galleon transoms and twin-hulled catamarans and came to where the *California* had been anchored the day before. In her place was a squat, rust-streaked freighter. There was no doubt about it, the *California* had really gone. I gazed at the freighter silently with a sadness and loneliness I don't ever remember feeling before.

CHAPTER ELEVEN

Ceylon

I HAD BEEN INVITED to stay in Ceylon with a young American couple whom I hardly knew—it was one of those "friends of friends" arrangements. They lived near Maharagama, some ten miles out of Colombo proper. The village of Maharagama was squalid and sour-smelling, but the home of my hosts, whom I shall call Peter and Betty Howard, was agreeably luxurious, with furniture brought from America, an ebony piano and copper bowls filled with frangipani set about in spacious surroundings. The guestroom was on the first floor and opened onto a broad colonnaded patio. With all the jalousies closed, the room was soothingly cool and shadowy, but Peter and Betty were quick to draw my attention to all its Eastern drawbacks: the substitution of a teak armoire for a built-in closet; the necessity of the cloud of mosquito netting above the beds; the outside wiring of the electrical system, which sometimes worked and sometimes didn't. Betty said she couldn't see for the life of her why the Singhalese couldn't learn to fix the wiring inside the walls in a civilized fashion, and Peter said, well, we all had to remember that things are different in the East and that we just had to put up with the differences.

Both Peter and Betty found it hard to conceal their exasperation with the "differences." What irritated them most were the minor inconveniences and precautions imposed on them by the climate and living conditions. You could never get rid of the insects no matter what you did, Betty said. The local busses were too dirty to

167

travel on; the merchants off the main street too unreliable to deal with. Peter warned me that if I didn't lock up my jewelry and cash the servants would steal it. Betty, who apparently was haunted by bacteriological bugaboos and tropical bogeymen, warned me that if I walked about barefoot I'd get hookworm; if I went about without a hat I'd get sunstroke; if I didn't take diodoquin regularly I'd get dysentery, and if I didn't tuck the mosquito netting firmly beneath the mattress I'd get bitten by horrible insects.

"I don't think I can stand another year here," Betty said.

"Poor darling," Peter said to her, putting his arm around her waist. "You're an angel to put up with everything. Let's pray that I get a better post next year."

Nonetheless, for all their "putting up," I thought the Howards lived very well. In America, Peter's salary might have entitled them to a small suburban two-bedroomed house or apartment and the services of a cleaning woman once a week. In Ceylon, where the cost of living was low and the rate of dollar exchange favorable, the Howards could live on a far grander scale. They had rented a large house with ample grounds and they had a staff of servants to maintain both, so that neither Peter nor Betty ever had to lift a finger.

Heading their roster of servants was Chilliah, who supervised the work of the other servants, attended to the menus and the marketing and doubled as a butler and valet. Then there was the amah, who took complete charge of the Howard's year-old son and who also acted as a lady's maid for Betty. There was a cook boy and a kitchen maid. These four were considered part of the household and they slept in. There were, in addition, the *dhoby*, or washerman, who came daily to pick up and deliver the laundry; the *syce*, who took care of the car and performed odd jobs of chauffeuring; the gardener and two helpers; and the charwoman.

Betty complained that none of the staff was any good, that unless she "kept at" them constantly, nothing was ever done. Chilliah, she said, mismanaged the accounts terribly, and if she didn't look over the chits scrupulously, he would have stolen her blind. The customary practice of receiving a commission on all purchases—the traditional right of servants in the East—was one thing, Betty declared, which really drove her out of her mind.

"It's ridiculous," she said. "No matter *what* I paid Chilliah, he would still see to it that he swindled me out of five dollars every month. I'm sure it's not the money that matters to him so much as the feeling he's putting something over on me, and it drives me crazy."

I liked Chilliah. He was a frail autumn leaf of a man who from time to time expressed the hope that he would lead a happier life in his next reincarnation. He sprayed my room sedulously with insecticide and kept the wick of the lamp trimmed and its chamber filled with kerosene. Although I tried to discourage him, he insisted on dressing and undressing Kippy, whom he referred to as "the little master." He attended Kippy's needs with slavish devotion and even wove garlands of jasmine for him, stringing the flowers with the same precision and care with which he arranged my clothes in the armoire and polished my jewelry until it was winking bright. In short, Chilliah saw that my life, like that of the Howards', was one of easy indulgence. It was hard to believe that the other world of Colombo was only ten miles away.

As I walked along the main streets of Colombo, which have such respectable names as Prince, York, Chatham, Church, I found that a certain sense of familiarity with the East had sharpened my perceptions to a point where I no longer felt that I was a spectator of a mass of Asiatic countenances, all looking curiously alike. People had resolved into types again—their way of life implicit in their features in a hard to define but recognizable trade-mark. Students, shopkeepers and merchants were as easy to spot as their Western counterparts. Of course, as in any other cosmopolitan city, some of the passers-by escaped classification, their lack of distinction accidental or perhaps cultivated for a purpose. I liked to think that they were foreign agents, but most likely they were merely the reflection of played-out genes. But whoever they were, whatever they did, like the Eurasian bank tellers and the prosperous Chinese compradors, the Afghanistan moneylenders and the Singhalese businessmen in their ankle-length sarongs and Palm Beach jackets, sea trade and money were the magnets that had attracted them to Colombo. Colombo is a port of call and a city of transients—nobody's home, but a great many people's business.

The port area was dominated by the Grand Oriental Hotel, its ceilings whirling with fan blades. In the lobby, provocative half-caste maidens loitered about and flashed meaningful glances at the sailors of six continents. Through the lobby doors you could see the landing jetty and the long sequences of little shops selling ebony elephants with plastic tusks and boxes made from porcupine quills and crows whittled out of carabao horn.

From the docks, the streets coiled back with their tattered super-cargo of houses, and there the Pettah was, the bazaar, the air full of flies and brick-red dust. The food stalls were beaded with flies and plagued with madly cawing crows that would swoop down and make off with a titbit the moment a merchant relaxed his watch. Trundle carts dispensed soft drinks, artificially flavored and tinted a dyspeptic green or a poisonous pink, which the vendor ladled from an enamel basin for a penny a dipperful. The dust-tormented lanes swarmed with high-wheeled bullock carts, busses with quiver-ing bodies, rickshaws, bicycles and cars with anguished horns. The traffic stopped for no one, and portly Buddhist priests with up-raised umbrellas were forced to scamper out of the way just as nimbly as the rest of the pedestrians.

Added to the street noises, to the crows' cawing and dogs' bark-ing, was the din of gramophones harshly needling American jazz and the whining quarter tones of a thousand Chinese and Indian love songs. Beneath the hubbub and clamor the sound of human voices ebbed and flowed like the sound of the sea. All of life was carried on in full public view and hearing. Each house, with its open doors and unshuttered windows, was a peep show for anyone who cared to peer at the occupants as they ate, slept, worked, lived, copulated and died.

Only the astrologers operated in secret on a street called Silver-smith.

I found my way there, through the warren of the Pettah, and entered the shack of K. V. Amerasekera. As I stepped through the tilting doorway, Mr. Amerasekera came forward to meet me. He was a sad, earnest little man with a crescent-shaped comb of tor-toise shell on top of his head, indicating that he was a member of the upper castes. (Combs were unsuitable for the lower castes, who carried bundles on their heads.)

A Tamil, sitting in the corner and sipping a mug of palm toddy, got up, walked into the street, and came back with a stool for me to sit on. Exchanging compliments, Mr. Amerasekera and I slowly worked up to the matter of his fee. When we had agreed upon the sum of three rupees, he fanned himself vigorously with a lollipop-shaped fan and ushered me through a narrow dark tunnel that connected the front room with a small cave in the back, three of whose walls were earth and whose floor was of tamped earth. Candles flickered on a small shrine of Ganesa. In one corner was a tin trunk painted all over with tongue-pink roses, and on the walls were framed photographs of Joseph Stalin and Nicolai Lenin, a monochrome of Gautama Buddha, and a photograph of Queen Elizabeth worked in oppressive pastel tints and adorned with a faded wreath of lotus and jasmine. Otherwise, the room was bare.

Since I could tell Mr. Amerasekera neither the minute nor the hour of my birth, he said he couldn't possibly cast my horoscope. Although the opacity of cataract made it difficult to judge the expression in his eyes, I imagined that he was looking at me with pity and contempt, for even the poorest peasant knows the exact time of his birth and from childhood onward lives by the immutable laws of his horoscope. Mr. Amerasekera expressed astonishment that I had been able to live so long without the help of celestial guidance and said that the only thing he could do to help me was to predict my future.

He opened the trunk with the roses on it and took out a handful of white cowry shells, some bright blue beads, two moonstones, a wooden board painted with occult signs and a pointed stick. With the stick he traced the outline of my right hand on the earth floor. Following the direction in which my fingers slanted, he placed the beads on the board. He scattered the shells and the moonstones about the beads and shifted them rapidly to form various patterns. Each pattern determined a prediction.

I squatted on the floor, brushed the ants off my feet and watched Mr. Amerasekera's spidery fingers shuffling the beads and the shells and the opals, the light from the candles throwing leaping black shadows on the board and projecting Mr. Amerasekera's tortoise shell comb onto the opposite wall so that it looked as if he were crowned with an octopus. I was so caught up in a sensation of mysticism that even the banalities of my future—a lengthy voyage, a serious illness, an unforeseen event—assumed the importance of

Great Truths. Suddenly, Mr. Amerasekera swept the shells and beads and opals back into the trunk and announced that he had told me my three rupees' worth.

Once out in the narrow lane, with the frowsty-smelling room and the guttering candles behind me, I felt ashamed for having been touched at all by Mr. Amerasekera's performance. It was as if I had found myself crying at a second-rate movie, and with the uncomfortable feeling that I had been emotionally tricked, I made my way back toward the Fort.

It was after six. The bats were flitting overhead and the metal shutters were beginning to rattle down over the shop fronts. The Hindu temple in Sea Street took the last rays of waning light on its writhing sculpture. The gem merchants were still standing outside their dingy boutiques soliciting trade in three languages: "What kind stones Mem like to buy? Nice tourmalines, very cheap." A stream of dusty cars passed by carrying civil servants home to their bowered bungalows in the Cinnamon Gardens. A fuzzy-haired child sat in the doorway of a tenement house and sucked the milk from a trepanned green coconut.

Suddenly there was an eerie piping of flutes and a melancholy *din-din-din* of cymbals as a Chinese funeral procession came down the mauve street. Behind a shuffling band of flute players and cymbalists, the pallbearers jerked along a crimson and gold hearse. The widow of the deceased was clutching its hind bumper and howling like a wounded dog. Behind her trailed the professional mourners, wailing fiercely and taking turns towing the bannered funeral cart with its wreaths of wilting flowers. The procession lurched and moaned up the street, with a band of children following after, screaming like seagulls in the wake of a ship.

I passed the alley from which the procession had come. The funeral cart had shed broken bits of fern and flowers at the entrance of the Death House on the corner where the dead man had apparently gone to die. To the poorest of the Chinese poor there is no worse fate than to die in the streets, then to be picked up by the municipal refuse truck and to be dumped into the city's burial pit. When a Chinese coolie feels that his end is near, he goes to a Death House. There, for a small fee, he is allowed to wait in peace for death. He is given food and opium for the last days of his life, and a funeral with professional mourners when he dies.

I turned into the alley and was at once enveloped in its pocketed smell of stale urine and the chokingly sweet fumes of opium. I stood for a moment in the doorway of the Death House looking in. The dark hall was crammed with hundreds of wooden benches on which the old and the pestilence-stricken lay waiting for death, their withered bodies suppurating with sores and smeared with blood, vomit and feces. Those not lying on the benches smoked opium and moved fretfully about, their features made savage by the shadows thrown up by the shuddering light of candles stuck in the earthen floor. The mutterings and the whimpering of the inmates were pierced by a sudden sharp shriek, the sound quivering like a knife in the air. A woman leaped up to caper in a lunatic dance. I was sickened by the putrescent odor of rotting flesh, opium and excreta that sluiced over me in stinking gusts. The sight of such human misery made me aghast, and all my feelings overflowed into revulsion and terror.

Ratnapura, the City of Gems, lies southwest of Colombo, five and a half hours away by train. I decided to go there with Kippy and buy a few star sapphires for a twentieth of what they would cost me in New York. The train for Ratnapura left Colombo at four in the morning. At that hour, the feebly lighted station was carpeted with the confusion of sleeping and waking forms bedded down on the platform, heaped about with the indispensable Oriental appurtenances of travel: tin trunks, bulging string bags, wicker baskets of provisions and hens with cord-bound legs.

A Eurasian couple, a little island of gentility, sat stiffly on one of the few available wooden benches. At their feet a Tamil laborer and his family, stirring vaguely like an ant hill, were sprawled. The father, struggling on the edge of consciousness, rubbed his eyes and scratched his crotch. His wife lay at his side, her lips blood-red with betel, her long black braids disheveled, her soiled white sari mussily wrinkled. A baby was stretched like a puppy at her feet, its fingers curled around a half-eaten mango.

The train was about to arrive, and as the stationmaster bawled out the announcement, the grumbling hum of voices changed to a brisk staccato while the travelers scrambled to their feet and readied their belongings. When the train pulled in, there was much shouting and running to and fro and a wild dash for the third-class coaches. A porter tugging at my sleeve and urging me to hurry hustled Kippy and me into a first-class compartment and told us to lock the doors. It was soon obvious why. Since the train was comprised of compartments with no connecting corridor, ticket inspection was eliminated, and the third-class passengers who had failed to get seats rushed to the first-class compartments, where they would be sure of getting a ride to the next station. When the train started, several men clung to the door and the window ledges of our compartment. While I was fumbling with the lock to let them in, the train picked up speed and the men jumped off. I was surprised to see them turn and wave good-naturedly.

The compartment was small, but it had the luxury of a tiny lavatory and an overhead fan. The train clickety-clacked leisurely along past the city limits and headed south on a track that was thickly bordered on either side with palms, their fronds and feathery panaches somberly elegant in the fading moonlight.

As the sun rose, we came into plantations of cinnamon trees that smelled sensually sweet, and on into a monotonous regimentation of tea bushes that smelled aromatic but quite unlike tea.

We stopped at several stations neatly planted with cannas and yellow crotons, and with a water-filled oil drum out in front labeled in Tamil, Singhalese and English that it was for drinking purposes only. No one paid any attention to these notices, and the barrels were always ringed with a crowd of people scooping up the water with tin dippers to wash themselves and their clothes and to rinse the chewed twigs they used for toothbrushes. At each station a vendor of betel chews or *pans,* as they are called, struck a little gong to advertise his wares. The rich carry their *pans* in special boxes, the poor generally carry their spare *pans* tucked in their turbans. There are expensive *pans* and cheap ones, but the basic ingredients remain the same: betel-nut shavings, powdered shell lime, turmeric or cardomom, the whole encased in a vine leaf. Having read somewhere a translation of a Sanskrit poem that said a betel *pan* contains thirteen qualities unsurpassed even in Paradise, I bought a *pan* and thought it tasted too awful for words.

The train ambled placidly along, puffing asthmatically up the gentle hills, rattling through the valleys, and came at last to Ratnapura. Everyone rushed to the station restaurant, a board lean-to attached like an ell to the station shed and sheltering no more than half-a-dozen tables covered with oilcloth. The proprietor wandered out from the curtained chamber in the rear, where the cooking was done and, having wiped his hands on his sarong—which was all he was wearing—spat on the floor, shouted at the pye dogs fighting outside and asked what we wanted.

Flies swirled over the saffron-tinted curry puffs that Kippy ordered. The button-sized yolk was quite lost in the boiled egg that I ordered. Fat black crows bounced about the dirty floor scavenging our crumbs. I asked where there was a place we could stay. The proprietor cranked the handle of the station telephone, shouted into the mouthpiece, and reported that there was a vacancy at the government rest house. We drove there in the one taxi in town, a large Brougham automobile of ancient vintage, whimsically called a quickshaw.

The only other occupants of the rest house were two Indians, traveling salesmen for Peacock cigarettes. The food was standard country fare. Our dinner that night consisted of tepid mutton curry submerged in coconut oil, side dishes of plantain, jack fruit and rice, and a wedge of papaya served with a flourish by a red-sashed Tamil waiter in a white suit and a plastic bow tie. (Dried egg, of course, on the tines of the forks.) Afterward, coffee was brought to the lounge accompanied by a pitcher of boiled milk with a wrinkled piece of scum floating on top and a bowlful of rough gray sugar crystals that I had to stir the ants out of.

The lavatory on our floor was a disinfectant-smelling cubicle furnished with a wooden-seated pail and a bucket filled with sawdust. But our bedroom was large and high-ceilinged, everything white and fresh and perfumed with the fragrance of the champak tree in the courtyard below. The windows were without screens, so that at night the darkness of the room was streaked by the sulphur-yellow flares of fire beetles. Kippy and I went to sleep listening to the nocturnal chorale of cicadas, owls and tree frogs, and we were wakened by the retching brays of a donkey and the trilling descant of bulbuls and golden orioles coming to life in the champak tree.

The town of Ratnapura had one main street of hard-packed red earth, rutted with the wheel tracks of bullock carts, pitted with pot holes, and lined on either side with one-storied, open-fronted shops and dwellings, their doors and windows covered with bamboo blinds to keep out the sun. The mazing side streets were soft and muddied by the monsoon rains and piled high with decaying middens and urine-soaked refuse. The heat and the smell of open drains hung over the city like a pall. Wherever I went I was accosted by wheedling-voiced men importuning me to buy precious stones at bargain prices. They followed me down the streets like frenzied magicians, pulling topazes out of their turbans and rubies out of their pockets.

In the afternoon of our second day in Ratnapura, Kippy and I were caught umbrellaless in a monsoon rainfall that came flinging down in sheets of water. We took shelter in the boutique of a Mohammedan lapidary by the name of Ismail. Mr. Ismail was seated at a rickety pigeonholed desk shuffling through his accounts and smoking a thin black cheroot stuck into the mouth of a dragon-shaped ivory holder. He instantly sent a boy out into the rain to fetch us chairs and glasses of a sticky chemical-cherry mixture covered with circles of bead-weighted muslin to keep out the wasps and the flies. He was a man of middle age with coarse, curly gray hair, a dark, pock-marked complexion and protruding, almost batrachian eyes. His white duck trousers held a knife-edge crease, and a fountain pen and pencil set were clipped to the breast pocket of his white shirt.

"Americans," he said dreamily. "I am so pleased to meet Americans. I am a great admirer of your cinema." He gestured to one wall covered with photographs and sepia magazine illustrations of Hollywood movie stars. Allowing his English to fall word by earnest word, he exclaimed over the wonders of America. He held the unshakable belief that all Americans were rich and that life in the United States was lived on a scale of cinematic extravagance. As he spoke, he clasped and unclasped his hands emotionally. His hands were like a woman's, thin and fragile, with oval nails impeccably manicured and varnished with transparent pale pink polish.

After some little talk about America, we got down to the pleasant ritual of looking at the jewels Mr. Ismail had for sale. He seated

me before a green baize-covered table out of the way of an assistant
who was polishing a sapphire against a lapidary wheel. He switched
on an overhead light, opened the door of a standing safe and removed several trays filled with small square paper packets fastened
with elastic bands. The elastic bands were snapped off, and the
heavy parchment wrapping, with much rich crackling, undone.
Each packet revealed a linen square with its four corners tied in
a knot. Mr. Ismail unknotted the linen squares and spread them
before me in order of the value of the stones which they contained,
the smaller, more common gems first—satiny moonstones, greeny-
yellow cat's eyes, garnets, cinnamon stones and rose spinels. Then
a choice lot of tourmalines, topazes, aquamarines, chatoyant opals
and glittering zircons. Mr. Ismail pinched up stone after stone with
his jeweler's tweezers and held the gems up to the light, counter-
poising them against minuscule weights on a balance scale. His face
was shuttered from expression, his voice cooing the prices.

Then he swept the lesser stones aside and laid before me an assortment of star sapphires and pigeon-blood rubies, the light quivering in their mounded depths, the most exquisite stones I had ever
seen. I should like to have the two largest and most beautiful of the
sapphires, I thought, the ones of the deepest violet-blue with the
brightest of six-rayed stars, but of course they were too expensive,
and I had to make a compromise. The smaller ones. *Those.* I
flicked two from the pile. How much were those? Mr. Ismail ex-
truded a purplish wet lip and pulled at it thoughtfully. "For you,
six hundred rupees only."

We bargained, and at last, in the hollow, despairing tone of a
bassoon playing in the upper register, Mr. Ismail consented to let
me have them for two hundred rupees. He implied that he had
lost on the transaction, but I knew very well that he had not.

The rain stopped, a brilliant rainbow arched the sky, and the
peanut and *pappadum* vendors scurried back to their usual place
beneath the branches of a huge silk-cotton tree. Mr. Ismail said
that it had been a pleasure to meet me, and perhaps if it wouldn't
be too much trouble would I send him some autographed pictures
of film stars from America. With the rather grating, exaggerated
solicitude for the merest of acquaintances, a trait peculiar to many
Mohammedan shopkeepers, Mr. Ismail pressed upon me a handful

of cards to various friends of his in Colombo whom he said I might enjoy meeting. I thanked him and tucked the cards away in my purse.

It was only after I got back to Maharagama that I discovered that one of the cards Mr. Ismail had given me was addressed to a Buddhist priest, or *bhikku*, named Kassypa.

"I'd like to see Bhikku Kassypa, please," I said to the manservant. He opened the screen door of the monastery and led me to a reception hall where two other visitors were waiting. We eyed each other covertly, like patients in a doctor's waiting room. They had left their shoes by the door. I hadn't and I stood there holding mine awkwardly. Two priests came in, and the visitors jackknifed to the floor in respectful obeisance. They followed the priests through the doorway, and then I was left quite alone. On the whitewashed walls between the grilled windows were hung illuminated texts of the Noble Eightfold Path, the Four Noble Truths and the Three Signs of Being. There were pictures in mirror frames of Siddhartha Gautama, the most recent Buddha, in cross-legged attitudes.

A priest in an orange toga opened the door and looked inquiringly at me.

"Bhikku Kassypa?"

He tilted his head in the Singhalese motion of affirmation. When I gave him Mr. Ismail's letter, he smiled.

"That scoundrel," he said in a tone of affection. "That old rogue. So he still remembers me, does he? He used to make my rings and cuff links. How is he keeping? Come, let us talk in my little room."

But this is ridiculous, I thought, thoroughly taken aback. Kassypa had none of the remote, sacerdotal solemnity I had expected. I had imagined him as being utterly different—Singhalese, to begin with, and not Eurasian as he was. By some quirk of nature, he had been given one of those ancient Greek faces of which you see sculptures in libraries—a large head, deeply beveled nose, strong chin and gently curving mouth. In his orange toga, he looked more like a kindly monarch than a monk.

As I followed him down cool corridors, he introduced me to several Singhalese monks wearing horn-rimmed spectacles and to a

German Jew who had come from Munich to Colombo fifteen years before and who, with his shaven head and moist, gray, oystery skin, seemed in his toga like a man who had chosen an ill-becoming costume for a masquerade party and felt uncomfortable in it.

Kassypa preceded me into a small rectangular cell. It was severe and plain, furnished with a desk, a stool, a chair and a wooden bed frame with tape webbing across it. In English that was a rippling flow of the idiom of the late nineteenth century, he told me that he had been a member of the monastery for five years. Before that, he had been a surgeon. He had been married, he had two sons. He had been a rich man, he had traveled. He followed my gaze to a begging bowl resting on top of a stack of books in a corner. He had been happier in this room, he said, than he had ever been anywhere else. I asked him what he did all day.

"Since I donned the ascetic garb and forsook earthly possessions," he replied, "I have striven to lead a Holy Life. Specifically, I read, translate Pali manuscripts and meditate."

In following the precepts of the Holy Life, Kassypa had virtually abstracted himself from the world, to concentrate on his spiritual progress and a development of self-perfection which meant the extinction of his ego. He denied himself even the simple pleasures of having flowers in his room and of listening to the music of Bach and Beethoven which formerly he had so enjoyed.

"Forgive me, Bhikku Kassypa," I said, "but surely a few flowers and a little music can't be evil?"

Kassypa's curving lips flickered in a smile. "Little Sister, and I call you Little Sister because are we not all born again and again and therefore related? Little Sister, music and flowers are not in themselves harmful, but they are to be compared to an ulcer on a gentleman's leg. The gentleman has an ulcer on his leg. He enjoys putting poultices on it. He fans it to make it cooler. Then the doctor comes and cures it. Is it not much better that way? Buddhism is like the doctor, and you become no longer the servant but the master of the five senses and of the sixth sense of your mind."

He noticed a large cockroach on the floor and, rising from his chair, stooped and gently picked it up. "Careful, little fellow, you may get into trouble," he admonished, setting it down gently on the window sill. The possible reincarnation of some poor soul who had accumulated too much evil *karma* or adverse merit in previous existences, somewhat dazed by its rescue, remained for a moment motionless on the ledge, and then scuttled through the grille.

I saw Kassypa several times after that, and the day I left Ceylon, just before the Howards drove me to the airport to catch the plane for India, a messenger delivered to me a letter from him. "Dear Little Sister," he had written. "Live in *mittra* [loving kindness]. You may be young in your present incarnation, but you are old in *sansara*." I didn't know what *sansara* meant, but it sounded nice. "We may not meet again in this life, but I'm sure that we shall in lives to come."

CHAPTER TWELVE

Bombay

THE PLANE LIFTED AND SOARED and Ceylon became small and map-
like below. Kippy rested *Hugo's Hindustani Simplified* on the
buckle of his seat belt and intoned the cardinal numbers softly:
Ek, do, tin, char, panch, chau, sat, atch, nau, das. The sound of
the words pleased him and he said them over and over again.

After a while the stewardess announced through the loud-speaker
that we were flying over India. I leaned across Kippy to peer out
the window and saw a slanting panorama of dust-green hills and
plains that were scribbled with gun-metal rivers and sand-colored
roads. I stared down, cherishing the view because it was my first
glimpse of India, the place beyond all other places in the world I
wanted to see. India—what magic and glittering bewilderment was
contained in that word! Everything I had ever read about it evoked
longing and amazement. I saw India through an enchanted, dreamlike web, its images slipping from the grasp of my imagination as
they whirled around in my mind—images that I expected, like
fragments of colored glass in a kaleidoscope, to come together in a
wonderful pattern the moment the plane touched down.

Yet when the plane descended, the air terminal was the same as
any other, bleak and bustling, with leatherette settees and standing
ashtrays that smelled of stale smoke. And the hotel, with its lovely
name of Taj Mahal and its exterior whipped into a frenzy of domes
and curly cornices and crenelations, was disappointingly prosaic
in its gilt and plush interior.

It was too hot to think of unpacking. I switched on the overhead propeller fan, and its three blades rotated noisily, causing everything in the room to vibrate. Kippy straddled the long Dutch Wife bolster on his bed and trotted his tongue against the roof of his mouth. "Bang, bang," he shouted, making pistols of his hands. "Bang, bang. Another tiger bites the dust! *Ek* tigers, *do* tigers, *tin* tigers!"

There was a knock. I opened the door and saw a woman in a white sari standing outside. Slender and tall, with copper-gold skin and blue-black hair drawn into a bun at the nape of her neck, she was as graceful as a young tree.

"Mem, I am Lucy," she said. "I speak English. I am an *ayah*." She held out a bundle of soiled and torn envelopes. "Please, Mem, you read my chits. Very nice things the other Mems I worked for are having to say."

"When can you start?" I asked.

"Now, Mem," she said.

Lucy unpacked the trunks and summoned the *dhoby* to do the necessary pressing and washing. She annihilated several beetles in the armoire and flushed their carcasses down the water closet. Lucy ran a bath for me, and as I was lying in it with my feet floating, she suddenly appeared and knelt at my side. "I'll do your back," she said. I don't know anything that ever embarrassed me more, unless it was the time I stood before the mirror in my first evening dress and said, experimenting with different inflections, "What a beautiful, beautiful, sophisticated woman you are," and my mother came in and heard me.

"No, *please*, I can do my back myself," I protested.

Lucy stared at me. "But all my ladies liked the way I scrubbed their backs," she said, picking up the soap and sliding it across my shoulder blades. She worked the soap gently up my neck and around my ears.

"All my ladies liked the way I scrubbed their backs," Lucy repeated, more firmly this time, and went on with the tender perfection of fulfilling her task.

When both of us had been given baths, Kippy and I descended to the candlelit Rendezvous Room for dinner. On the buffet was a swan carved in ice, with a wreath of red roses around its neck.

Myself at Malacañan Palace in Manila

Myself on an outrigger canoe in the
Nicobar Islands

Fishing junks and sampans, Causeway Bay, Hong Kong

The *California* en route from the Nicobars to Ceylon

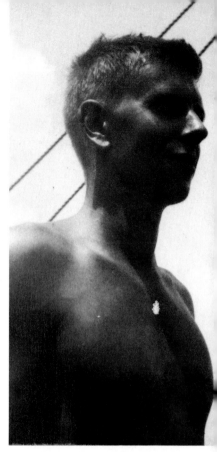

Hal

Yvor

Scupper

Vic

Art

Vic rowing out at dusk to the *California,*
Penang Straits

Thaipusam Festival: devotee in
process of ritual, penitential
torture, Penang

Mohammedans at prayer-time.
Mosque of St. Nicholas where the
Lusigan Kings were crowned kings
of Jerusalem.

Opium addict, male, twenty-four years old, heating up opium "pill" over spirit lamp

A traffic hazard in Bombay. (A sacred cow.)

Street barber, Bombay, India

Shepherd and goat flock, Hyderabad Province, India

Hill Marias dancing, Rakhikhol,
near Chindwara, India

Village well, Madhya Pradesh Province, India

Coming into Colombo, Vic at the bow

Fisherman beaching catamaran at the end of the day

My struggles with breadmaking

Kippy checking on merchandise of sidewalk
bazaar, Karachi, Pakistan

Masked women of
Dubai
on the
Persian Gulf

Kippy and the Queen of the Nicobars, Champin Village,
Nancowry Island, the Nicobars. Inside the Queen's house.

Stone sculpture of
seated Buddha.
Ajanta Caves. India.

Bedouin sheik, Lebanon

Syrian manservant

Merchant smoking nargile and
waiting for his tea to cool,
Damascus

A corner of the souk in Damascus

Makran father and son,
Persian Gulf—aboard the *Dwarka*

Supper at sea. Left to right: Yvor, Hal, myself,
Art and Kippy in the foreground.

There were whole fishes, glazed, with their scales squiggled on with tinted cream cheese. Kippy wanted to touch them to see if they were real. I hadn't seen such food since I had left New York. A waiter whipped zabaglione to a froth in a copper bowl. Butter spurted in golden rivulets from *poulets à la Kiev*. Lobsters and steaks sizzled on steaming platters. *Crêpes Suzette* and baked Alaskas were haloed in blue flame. Our waiter, apologizing profusely, said that we must limit ourselves to only four courses because there was a food shortage.

I didn't realize until I read the morning paper that he had been referring to a terrible and widespread famine in the south of India.

On our way out of the hotel that morning for our first look at Bombay, I stopped to admire the glass-windowed showcases packed with jewelry and saris that could be purchased in the hotel's shopping arcade. As a concession to Western influence, there were "new-look" saris made of chiffon and georgette with sequin and beaded decorations. But the traditional saris were the ones I coveted, the gossamery, glinting gauzes from Benares, the rich, heavy silks from Madras with a sheen to them like a butterfly wing, sprinkled with gold medallions, and with magnificent *pallaus,* or borders of gold embroidery, worked in the time-honored Lotus, Peacock and Mango designs.

"I must have one," I said.

"Too dear," Lucy said. "I know a *sariwalla* who will make you a better price."

I left the showcases reluctantly, and we walked down the marble corridors lined with potted palms, past the beauty parlors where dog-eared copies of *Vogue* were piled beside manicurists' tables, past the coffee shop that advertised mango milk shakes. Lucy nodded to the other ayahs and made disparaging asides to me about their mistresses and their charges.

"Her mem has no more credit in the shops. . . . Her mem is a chee-chee [Anglo-Indian]. . . . Her mem has a bad temper. . . ."

With a few sharp words Lucy dismissed the crowd of beggars that swarmed about us as we left the hotel. There was one I felt particularly sorry for, a man with a red turban and no arms. I gave him a handful of annas. Lucy looked impatient and cross. "You shouldn't, Mem," she said. "His mother cut off his arms when he was a baby just so he could have an easy profession."

The central section of Bombay, the area about the hotel, had been conceived by British architects who knew well how to impart a sense of dignity and grandeur. The streets were broad and embraced much bronze and marble statuary. An army of coolies was at work removing dust and bird droppings from the solemn images of British viceroys and Indian baronets knighted for their services to the Empire. Queen Victoria kept a watchful stone eye on the Telegraph Office and King George V and Edward VII flanked the entranceway to the Prince of Wales Museum. The municipal and civic buildings had been constructed in the same extraordinary style as the Taj Mahal Hotel. Architectural follies, combining every known form of dome and spire, they were uniformly lofty, imperious and charmingly overdone, like a child's idea of Oriental palaces. The extravagant buildings, the shade trees, the oval street parks in use for cricket practice, the tea shops and the haberdasheries were all such an attempt to keep the East at bay that it was hard to believe that the British were no longer in control.

There was a fleeting sense of order, and then we came to Hornby Road, a commercial junction of East and West. Along sidewalks roofed over with high colonnades, the crowds swept along, and my eyes strained at the mass of color and sought relief in the patches of white and black. Faces daubed with caste marks swam up to meet my eyes and then passed on. Kippy had ascertained the significance of caste marks from Lucy, and when a man came along with a sort of trident outlined in red and white on his forehead, Kippy pointed him out to me. In a voice that shrilled above the clamor all around, he identified him as a man who believed in Vishnu. "Oh, dear," I said. "Oh, dear, please be quiet. Not so loud."

"Vishnu, Vishnu, Vishnu," Kippy cried out, making a song of it. "Vishnu, Vishnu, Vishnu."

I looked about anxiously. A few people smiled, but no one seemed to pay much attention to this thin, Christopher Robin-like child prancing along at the side of his ayah trilling out over and over again the name of one of the sacred gods of the Hindu Trin-

ity. I hated to think what would have happened had he walked
down Fifth Avenue chanting "Jesus! Jesus!" at the top of his lungs
at eleven o'clock in the morning.

The crowd surged and eddied and swept around us. There were
holy men who wore long citron-colored robes and necklaces of seeds,
and there were roving eccentrics in harlequin capes and ragged
electric-blue mantles. There were peasant women with vivid saris
hiked up above their calves, and elderly women who went without
blouses. They were old-fashioned, Lucy said; long ago it had not
been proper for women to cover their breasts.

Indians seem to have a passion for personal adornment. Coolies
who couldn't afford bracelets and earrings, or such imported luxuries as steel watches and monogrammed rings of rolled gold, tucked
jasmine behind their ears and in the waistbands of their dhotis.
I was fascinated by the sight of the peasant women, their necks
weighted with silver collars and belled necklaces, their long, straight
toes clasped around with the bright lozenges of toe rings, their
forearms covered from wrist to elbow with massive bracelets of
carved silver. Hand-wrought earrings as big as babies' fists dangled
from their ear lobes. Often little gems studded their nostrils, and
their septa were pierced with nose rings. Their saris glowed in the
sun like panes of stained glass. Their silver ornaments flashed and
gleamed. The whole effect was marvelously splendid.

"Why don't you wear jewelry like that, Lucy?" Kippy asked.

Lucy registered surprise, then laughed merrily at the suggestion.
Touching her own tiny gold earrings, she declared that she would
rather have them than all the silver stuff put together. Later I
discovered that Lucy's feelings reflected those of the "white-sari"
girls whose rank she aspired to. Like thousands of shop assistants
and typists, denied by their social position the handsome adornment of the poor and prohibited economically from the fabulous
jewels of the rich, Lucy proudly wore her thin little wristwatch and
inexpensive glass bangles as a badge of gentility. Poor Lucy, I
couldn't resist shocking her by buying an enormous peasant's bracelet for myself.

The sun arrowed down from a sky as clear and blue as Bristol
glass. It was terribly hot. I followed Lucy from Hornby Road

through a warren of twisting side streets where there was no clear dividing line between living quarters and the street. Children used the gutters as latrines and their parents squatted on the pavement gossiping, grooming themselves and eating things that were rolled up in palm leaves.

We jostled our way through a mass of people. I supposed it couldn't be helped, but it seemed to me that I was forever in back of or in front of someone who was clearing his throat, spitting out gouts of betel juice, or blowing his nose with his fingers—a nasty habit that Indians performed with the utmost vigor and flourish. I sucked on a lemon drop, for I had found them an unfailing antidote for queasiness.

There was a premonitory change in the atmosphere, a quickening of tempo, an increased volume of sound. Then we fell from the side street as though we had been leaning against a door that had suddenly swung open, letting us stumble directly into the heart of the bazaar's prodigious hubbub. The clamor and animation into which we had been precipitated were far more intense than anything I had ever experienced before. I hesitated, in a moment of consternation, as a panicky, childish desire for escape welled in me. The memory of still Sunday afternoons in Connecticut, where everything was prim, clean and certain, suddenly became very dear. For an instant my mind swerved away into half-formed thoughts of friends and grape arbors wet and fresh with rain and long drives on roads arched with maples. Then these thoughts were squeezed from my consciousness as the bazaar poured into my eyes and saturated my senses.

The press of people was so thick that it was almost impossible to move freely, and, holding onto Kippy, bumping into Lucy, aimless, purposeful, now darting ahead to take advantage of an open place in the crowd, now slowing to a standstill, stopping, looking, I tried to take in everything at once: the crowds and the confusion, the array of things to taste and smell and look at, the costumed people with waving arms and flying fingers engaged in the eternal game of buying and selling. Circus, fair, side show, carnival, theater—all put together in a fantastic pandemonium.

Impression after impression merged into ever-changing patterns of wonder and astonishment. How beautiful the Indian faces were, the shining, dark, oval eyes, the fine bone structure, the classic mouths, with the upper lip a thin and perfect bow and the lower lip full and sensual. There were dark-haired Christs at every turn, and men with the sad eyes of early Donatello saints and faces reminiscent of Rouaults, dark and angular. There was an epicene quality about the men, conferred, perhaps, by the prevailing under-fed thinness combined with a racial delicacy of build, and accentuated by a remarkable emotionality, the voluble, gesticulating emotionalism of the southern Mediterranean peoples played in a high, falsetto key, punctuated with giggles and sometimes with tears. The women floated through the traffic like butterflies. The men, on the other hand, leaped and darted, tentatively jumping forward and back in the path of the onrushing motorcars, cyclists and oxcarts. Rickety gharries hurtled past, driven by whip-cracking turbaned charioteers.

A small herd of oxen, cows and bullocks ambled about, the deified cattle, the famous "sacred" cows of India, many garlanded with yellow flowers and blue beads, others with elaborately scalloped ears. A cyclist—I supposed him to be an office worker or a bank clerk—was pedaling along, his Gandhi cap perched over his right eye. I noticed him because he was close by and singing "Yankee Doodle." A pye dog ran out into the street, and in order to avoid hitting it, the man swung his bicycle violently to the left and collided with a rangy bull that was munching on some refuse in the gutter. The bicycle wheel grazed the animal's hind leg, and the impact of the collision sent the cyclist and his machine toppling onto the sidewalk. Jumping up, the man retrieved his cap, and, flinging his arms about the neck of the bull, he covered its pink-scarred face with kisses. Then he hurried to a woman selling dry grass that one could buy for a few pice as an offering to the sacred cows. He returned with an armful of fodder, which he offered to the bull handful by handful until the last straws feathered out in wisping mustaches from either side of its mouth. He gave the bull a final embrace, gently rubbing its scalloped ears, stroking the horns, which had been painted and were now a faded blue, straightening the blue beads and the silver bells hung about its neck. Then, picking up his bicycle, he dusted it off with his white shirt and rode away.

My nose was an inadequate filter for the bazaar smells. I felt as though I were inhaling odors with the whole of my being—the strong yellow smell of urine and sweat, like the acrid smell of a caged lion, the smell of sulphuric spices, a musty smell, a burned smell, a smoky smell, copra, onions, jasmine, the city smell of oil and gasoline and the wet, unpleasant smell of garbage.

A man ran past, swaying under a long pole from which hung two panniers filled with gleaming purple mangosteens. Men pushed along smeary, glass-walled carts filled with curry samosas and tiers of red chilies and brandished long spikes speared with chapatties, a sort of fried wheat cake like a tortilla. A sickening, greasy smell poured out of a vegetarian eating house where dusty coolies heaped pale chunks of dripping brinjals onto chapatties coated with curds and ghee. In one hole-in-the-wall establishment a glossy red display case of Coca-Cola had been set up on a zinc-topped table, with greasy tumblers and muddy brown chunks of ice supplied by courtesy of the enterprising storekeeper. The Indians had none of the Chinese artistry with food. The food stalls and carts, like the eating places, were embellished with pictures of Gandhi and assorted deities of the Hindu pantheon thumbtacked to garlands of tinsel and flowers, but the food was displayed without imagination. I could feel something inside me lift and turn, and my mouth was suddenly hot and tight as I looked at the welter of grayish, triangular pastries islanded in pools of ghee and dead flies; the trayfuls of Bombay duck the color of dried blood; and the nauseous concoctions of boiled milk and oil that looked like babies' vomit.

A woman, with one eye grayed over with trachoma, her dark face lacquered with sweat, dispensed pulse and dhal in newspaper cones, and behind her someone had painted on the betel-blotched wall, "Don't Make Urine Here." Near by a man had gone to sleep in an empty grain basket, his legs hanging limply over the side, his head slumped on his chest.

Somewhere a drum was thumping, suggesting that a temple was near by, but I couldn't see where. The jabbering syncopation of metallic-stringed lutes sourly spiraled through the air.

All along the way, walls and buildings were papered with signs

printed in English, with sub-headings in Hindu and Urdu, advertising American cowboy films and Asiatic epics:

MAA, WHICH WILL STUN YOU WITH ITS NATURALNESS,

AAN, SON OF THE SOIL VS. SON OF ROYALTY. A SPECTACULAR
SAGA OF THE PEOPLE'S AWAKENING, DIRECTED BY MEHBOOB,

RATNADEEP, THE CRAZE OF ALL BOMBAY FAMILIES. CRITICS
AND COMMONERS APPLAUD IT. HER LOVE, HER FAITH, WERE MORE
POWERFUL THAN ATOM BOMB.

Beneath a poster which read "Sunday Is Paludrine Day—Protect
Your Household against Malaria! Make Sure You, Your Family
and Your Servants Take One Tablet of Paludrine after a Meal
Every Sunday!" an herbalist, employing several newspaper-covered
orange crates for a counter, had set up shop. There were cough
cures and fever remedies in high-necked, cork-stoppered bottles; a
large selection of human and animal teeth in tin trays; packets of
powdered gold and silver leaf, and other mixtures highly recommended as aphrodisiacs; and putty-colored animal fetuses pickled
in cloudy mixtures.

Near by, an itinerant barber and a professional ear cleaner offered their services; despite their barbarous medieval equipment,
they were doing a brisk trade.

After a while, the bazaar effected a personality change in me. I
could feel myself a child again as I cast aside prejudices about food
and cleanliness. All exclamations, I poked about the stalls, nibbled
on salted banana chips and bought a brass teapot, an ivory spoon, a
black wool braid tied with silver bells (a device that many Indian
girls used to supplement their plaits), a box of metallic caste marks
that one could paste on like beauty spots, a silver-belled toe ring—
all objects with so temporary a charm that afterward I was cha-
grined at having bought them. But there it was—I had neither a
sense of selectivity nor of time in the bazaar.

At noon merchants rolled down bamboo chicks over their doors
and windows, and the street vendors lay down on the pavement
beside their goods and went to sleep. During the following two-hour
lull we retired to a café where Lucy was called upon to explain
over and over again that we were not Angrezi (English) but Umri-

cans. Mouths were rounded and lips pursed at this, and someone
gave Kippy a sugary, yellow sweetmeat cooked in a circlet called
a *jalebie.*

The café owner, a bearded man wearing a tweed jacket over his
soiled dhoti, beamed on us, and mostly for the benefit of the other
customers, I felt, peppered us with questions: Did we like Bombay?
How did India compare with Umrica? Where were we from in
Umrica? Was it true that everyone was rich in Umrica? I was never
very good at answering the questions of strangers. Conscious of
being an American, I wanted to make a good impression, and somehow my smile became nervous and overbright, my manner arch and
my enthusiasm absurdly exaggerated. Really, I thought, the whole
thing was as awkward and as embarrassing as having a violinist
serenade you while you're eating. I tried to will him to go away,
but he stood there at the edge of the table smiling and scratching
his crotch, translating my responses to a curious crowd. I listened
as he spoke. There was nothing melodious or rhythmic about Hindi.
The combination of sounds was as harsh and ugly as Brooklynese.
Ai . . . kie . . . hai . . . nay . . . wuh . . . tumhurry . . . hom,
he seemed to be saying.

The afternoon was white-hot. Whenever we entered the darkness
of a boutique, there would be a great fuss to bring Kippy and me
a tepid "cold drink." The proprietor would flutter about me solic-
itously, his hands darting like brown bats among the shelves to
find the "something smart," the "something too nice," to show me.
Almost every shopkeeper could speak a little English in a clipped,
singsong accent, and my entrance was inevitably the cue for a
volley of twittering phrases of inquiry and flattery. Compulsively
confiding, the shopkeepers told me how many children they had,
how bad business was, and often where they had gone to school.
Some of them, as proof of an education that seemed to have been
a meaningless competition with clerkhood as a prize, pulled cards
from their wallets that read:

KRISHNA MEHTA, ATTENDED UNIVERSITY OF BOMBAY.

FAILED FRESHMAN YEAR

or

M. NANUBHAI, ATTENDED UNIVERSITY OF MADRAS.

FAILED B.A.

Late in the afternoon we returned to the Taj, where armies of coolies, engaged in washing the floor, were dreamily skating up and down the marble-chilled corridors on large wet rags.

For a while at least I wanted Bombay all for myself. I met few people except those whose business it was to be about—the shop-keepers, the hotel porters and waiters, the bearers that flirted slyly with Lucy outside the door, and the merchants of the bazaar. I went to the bazaar every day, and Hindustani, which at first had sounded absurd, presently began to be sprinkled with random words that jumped out of their alien context in italics of recognition and then seemed to repeat themselves with magic frequency.

There was a leisurely pattern to the days. Lucy busily occupied herself with Kippy and me. Now I felt less tense and embarrassed when she brushed my hair, and sometimes even experienced dubi-ous enjoyment when she scrubbed my back with a loofah that shed black seeds in the tub. Lucy was always about, unobtrusive, but there, like the gecko lazing on the molding. In the morning, as I squinted with sleep, my eyelids wet with perspiration, the first thing I would see would be Lucy skimming across the shadow-striped room, emptying ashtrays and gathering up clothes. At night, she would sit out of sight behind the door, but I would hear the tiny sounds of sewing, the snap of the thread, the snip of the scissors.

Every three days Lucy sorted the dirty clothes and wrote out a list for the *dhoby*. Lucy was proud that she could read and write, and the writing of the list for the *dhoby* was a task performed with ceremony. Lucy would smooth out a piece of the sleazy, brown wrapping paper that parcels from the better shops came in, and then she would dip the hotel's stick pen into the inkwell. After tapping the nib against the bottom several times and holding up the pen to let the drops of ink splash back into the inkwell, she would begin to write. With the sound of the pen's slow, circular scratch forming the large, childlike letters, the *ssst* of a crossed *t*, the confident whisk of a downstroke, the account was made out— so many sikats, pijmas, boddys, pattycots, draws, sirtys. After a few days' practice, I could translate this intelligibly into a list of skirts, pajamas, bodices (a euphemism for brassières), petticoats, Kippy's underpants and shirts.

The *dhoby* came and went on spidery legs, bringing back the laundry, taking it away to wash and pound and dry on the flight of concrete steps that circled the harbor. The *durzee,* or tailor, came regularly for a while. Squatting on the floor, his mouth full of pins, he ripped and sewed and measured until he had made a dress for me out of a sari. I had bought two saris, one of iridescent blue silk with a superb *pallau* of gold embroidery, the other of deep reddish-purple. Lucy showed me how to knot the length of material about my waist, how to pleat and fold and drape, but she couldn't show me how to walk, for I discovered that to wear a sari one had to have the carriage of the Indian women, the gliding, floating movements. On me, the sari didn't flutter; it bunched in unflattering fullness about my hips and waist. I reluctantly folded the purple-red sari in tissue paper and laid it away in my trunk, and had the blue one made into a dress.

Sometimes in the evenings I would walk along Marine Drive to Chowpatty, a stretch of beach punctuated with the blaze of little flapping fires from food vendors' braziers. At night Bombay was a dazzling spectacle, throbbing, golden, flashing with light, the headlights of cars streaking like comets along Marine Drive, the revolving finger of the lighthouse on Malabar Point probing the blue-black sky and the comb of stars. With the sand scrunching in my shoes, I would climb to the street, where the pavement was corrugated with the sleeping forms of a huge company of people lying on rags and worn coir matting. They stirred, snored, mumbled and cried out. Every sneeze, every cough, every splash of spit, was the occasion for an invocation to the Infinite Spirit. They lay there twisted in sleep, huddled together, and I would run past them, strangely frightened, the tit-tat, tit-tat, tit-tat of my footsteps racketing in my ears.

Once I woke at dawn and, looking down from the balcony, saw the assemblage of the sleeping poor and wondered why at night they seemed so formidable. The gray light showed them as amorphous mounds, drained of color; it was impossible to tell where rags left off and skin began. A policeman came along, swinging his stick against their naked feet, and within seconds there was a scrambling, scuffling commotion, a wave of coughs and grunts, a rolling up of mats, and the figures dispersed. When the policeman had gone away, two old men crept back and lay down again beneath the monumental arches of the Gateway to India, where they remained for the rest of the day.

There was a section of town that I stumbled on from time to time, never quite knowing how I had found my way there—where the Hindus who had been driven out of Pakistan during the Moslem-Hindu riots lived in a wretched encampment of improvised tents pitched against the sides of decaying tenements in a jungle of tortuous alleys, crumbling walls and brooding shadows. Some of the "tents" were no more than jute sacks flung over packing boxes; others were rusted sheets of iron pieced together.

Smoke from the hundreds of charcoal cooking braziers hung in a motionless layer overhead. Flies crawled in shimmering ribbons over heaps of refuse. Naked children with sore eyes and runny noses swarmed about me crying for baksheesh. Here the human plant had bloomed too often and the puny seedlings had blurred features and lackluster skin. Women with pocked faces sat in the sun picking lice from each other's heads. A man, his head shaved except for a thin black lock tufting from the center of his scalp, would often be squatting beneath a ragged black umbrella and shifting with catatonic gestures two grains of pulse back and forth in the dust. The children pelted him with pebbles, but he never looked up. Back and forth he moved the grains, over and over and over again. In this scene of appalling squalor, there was a woman whose presence was quite inexplicable. Taller than the other women, she was slim-waisted, with delicately rounded wine-jar hips. Her wrists and ankles were cuffed with broad silver bands, and her sari was of some faded, flower-soft shade. Her wheat-colored face had the same poetical quality, the same features, as the face of an Ajanta princess—long, winged eyebrows over long, translucent, almond-shaped eyes, faintly flaring nostrils, a rather melancholy mouth with a full underlip. I thought at first that she couldn't belong there, that she must be a stranger or a visitor. Yet every time I walked past the dreadful camp, there she was, an anonymous part of that singular, assertive beauty of India's which occurs so fre-

quently in the midst of poverty and dirt—a beauty that was sudden
and startling and which I was never quite prepared for.

Bombay was neither a visually nor emotionally restful city. The
city itself was embroidered in piercing colors, the subtle and smoky
grays and brick reds of its buildings eclipsed by the blazing tones
of saris and turbans and flowers and fruit and by the flash of brass
and silver. At the end of a day I felt emotionally bruised, buffeted
by astonishment, excitement and distress. I loved Bombay, but a
mild malarial attack heightened my feeling that it was preposterously too much: too hot, too many people, too many colors, too
many contrasts. I often longed for the relief of watching ordinary
people dressed in ordinary clothes doing ordinary things.

CHAPTER THIRTEEN

We Don't All Live in Grass Huts

I MET DOSOO F. KARAKA in the offices of the *Current,* a weekly news-paper of which he was owner, publisher and editor. Mr. Karaka, who was obviously accustomed to interviewing people, ably dis-pensed with the empty formalities of introduction and asked me a number of quick and pointed questions. I knew I was being "drawn out" and resented it a bit, but once started, there was no holding back. I told him about my life in New York, about Kippy, about the *California* and about my impressions of India.

"You don't think you're slumming with us colored folk?" he asked blandly.

It was one of those questions, like Do-you-believe-in-Heaven, that embarrassed me horribly. So much was implicit in its answer, but my reply seemed to please him.

"That's nice," he said. "Very nice. One never knows about Americans." He took a cigarette from a gold case and lighted it with a gold lighter. His hands were small and graceful, and he held them and moved them to advantage, the way a woman who knows she has a good profile arranges herself accordingly. Suddenly he leaned forward across his glass-topped desk. "You know, I once was going to marry an American girl, but her family objected," he said. "They said I was colored. Do I look like a buck nigger to you?"

I looked at his square face intently. "No," I said. "Not at all."

Slowly he exhaled the smoke from his cigarette. "No," he said, "I don't believe I do either. It was all most shattering to the ego. But then Oxford hardly prepared me for America. At Oxford I was the President of the Oxford Union." He paused. "You know what the Oxford Union is, don't you?" He looked at me expectantly.

"Yes," I said. I saw that my lie hadn't been very convincing because a momentary flicker of irritation flitted across his face.

"It's an extremely high honor to be the President of the Oxford Union," he said. "It's almost unheard of for an Indian to be elected." He attempted to sound casual, but his eyes gave him away—they glowed with self-satisfaction.

He asked more questions. What did I want to see in India other than sacred cows, sensational poverty and the Taj Mahal? Whom did I want to see apart from snake-charmers, fakirs and people doing the rope trick?

"There are some civilized Indians, you know. We don't all live in grass huts." He laughed rather stagily. "That's my cable address, however. Grass hut. Get the point? Grass hut. If I told a New Yorker that I lived in a flat every bit as well furnished and equipped as the average Park Avenue duplex he wouldn't believe me. Everyone *knows* that Indians live in daub and wattle lean-tos."

He adjusted his impeccably knotted tie. "Your mother is Scottish? Any titles in the family? What year did you make your debut in New York?"

"Why?" I asked warily.

"Snob appeal. I want to do a story on you. People go for the upper-crust outlook. Are you in Debrett? Social Register? That's fine, that should go over excellently." He scribbled notes on a yellow scratch pad. Then, pushing the pad aside, he asked if I didn't want to stay in his apartment rather than at the Taj.

"Oh, for God's sake, don't look like that," he exclaimed. "I'm not making a pass at you. You're not my type. I like them older and less breathless. I just thought you might as well save your money, and the flat is large enough for you and the ayah and your child, so why not? I'm sure my fiancée won't mind in the least."

He pressed a buzzer on his desk, and then, as the door opened, he stood up to introduce me. "My fiancée, Pita Roberts."

She was English, attractive, and I liked her at once. Mr. Karaka explained to her that he had invited Kippy, Lucy and me to stay at his flat.

"But that's a wonderful idea," she said. "Though nobody will quite know what to make of it, will they?" She turned to Mr. Karaka. "Dosoo, darling, what do you think people will say?"

"Darling, really," Mr. Karaka said with measured patience.

"Dosoo never minds what people say. He's really a remarkable man," Miss Roberts said to me, smiling. "Come early tomorrow morning and then you won't have to pay for another day at the hotel."

Kippy and I moved into Mr. Karaka's flat and we stayed there for six weeks.

Dosoo Karaka was eclectic, brilliant, emphatic and voluble. He was the son of a gentle, conservative and rich Parsi family. The pictures he conjured up of his childhood were delicate vignettes of well-bred Parsi faces, lawn parties, sashed and turbaned servants bearing heavy Edwardian silver tea trays in a sumptuous world. As an extension of his role in such a background, Dosoo made a point of conveying the impression that he had carried off his distinctions and honors at Oxford with the careless good humor consonant with the conduct of one of gentle birth and good breeding.

Yet you could not know him long without running across a vein of buccaneering toughness, a quality on which he rather prided himself and which was reflected by tangible symbols all over his apartment—crumpled citations stuffed into dusty albums stacked untidily on the bottom shelf of the bookcase; a dilapidated trench coat hanging on one of the back hooks in the coat closet; and in the storeroom a square black trunk with *D. F. Karaka, War Correspondent* stenciled on it in white letters. Lucy used the lid of the trunk as an ironing board.

In his early days as a journalist, he had followed Gandhi on a tour from village to village. He had greatly admired Gandhi's intensive struggle for Indian freedom, but he had drawn the line at wearing a white cap as an emblem of his sympathy to the Nationalist cause. "*Que voulez-vous?* D. F. Karaka in a white soldier cap? Not jolly likely."

I remember one morning when Dosoo unlocked the heavy teak

doors of his armoire and showed me, in the manner of a bride
trotting out her trousseau, his good clothes, the things he wore in
London and in Paris and in New York: the tweed coats, nicely
shabby, some with chamois elbow patches; the gray flannel "bags"
and the gray flannel business suits; the tasteful array of dark suits
and light suits and above on the shelf the boxed Homburgs and
straws to go with them; the tails and the dinner jackets and the
thick black Chesterfield with the black velvet collar; the Italian
silk ties and the handmade shoes. He unbuttoned the buttons on
some of the jacket sleeves to show me that there was nothing de-
ceptive about the workmanship. He rubbed the fabrics appreciatively between his aristocratic fingers, and for a moment the Oriental passion for finery overcame his attitude of English reserve as
he paid homage to his wardrobe.

He fastened the doors together, opened them again to push back
the sleeve of his Oxford blazer, and then turned the key in the
lock. He dropped the key into a Florentine leather box on his
bureau where the sun glinted on silver-backed brushes and crystal
bottles filled with Molyneux perfume with which he scented his
monogrammed handkerchiefs.

I wondered over Dosoo and his little affectations. He was, as his
fiancée had said, a remarkable man. Three years before, he had
started the *Current*, run it with a handful of assistants, written three
quarters of it, and operated it at a profit. The newspaper had become a gusty and going concern, a jaunty, tabloid-sized weekly
which boasted "less than 1,000,000 circulation" and which had "God
Save the Motherland" for a motto. It was known for its exposés of
scandal and corruption in the government, its anti-communist policy and its scathing editorials against prohibition in Bombay. Dosoo
abominated prohibition. It was all very well for Hindus and Mos-
lems whose religion banned the consumption of liquor, he said
testily, but he was a Parsi and a civilized man who preferred a more
interesting beverage than sweet lime juice. An inhabitant of Bombay could obtain a small amount of liquor each month on the
presentation of a doctor's certificate stating that as a confirmed
alcoholic he must have liquor for the preservation of his well-being,
and tourists and foreigners were provided with liquor rations. Consequently, a thriving bootleg market had sprung up and Dosoo

contended that all of his friends had been forced to perjure themselves for the sake of enjoying the privilege of a decent brandy after
dinner. However, prohibition remained in effect, and Dosoo took
savage pleasure in announcing in the *Current* the State Treasury's
loss of every last rupee of revenue.

Every line in the *Current* bore Dosoo's firm mental fingerprints.
It was a lively periodical, spitefully humorous, bright and swagger-
ing, and you could count on at least one tantrum in every issue. It
preferred its politicians and statesmen to wear custom-made suits
instead of dhotis or achkans. It favored the European bow or hand-
shake to the Indian namazkar, a greeting performed by inclining
your head and steepling your palms. It ridiculed the custom of
presenting and wearing tinsel and flower garlands on "occasions"
that ran the gamut from a birthday to a departure on an overnight
train trip. It was sardonic about the brand of English generally
spoken in India. Dosoo made a point of publishing letters to the
editor in which Indian English was reproduced in all its stilted and
archaic flavor. The following letter was in answer to an editorial
inviting correspondence about the promotion of cleanliness:

> Take, for instance, the home. We are very, very particular to see that
> the home is kept neat and clean and if we have occasion to clear our
> throat or clear our nose we do it outside the window—not in the home.
> No, sir, out of the window and on the public road, but definitely not in
> the home.
> But let us take up the not uncommon habit of spitting betel onto public
> habitations, and sometimes, even on the public themselves. If these multi-
> tudinous and incarnadine splashes of this most unfortunately fast-dyeing
> liquid were landed in the allotted spittoons (of which, however, we find
> so few), I think our land would less resemble the wreck of a bloody
> revolution.
> Then comes the never-absent menace of cow dung. If cows were dis-
> possessed of their badly used privilege (which I need not mention) and
> cared for in proper enclosures, I think, not only would they enjoy life
> but also would we be benefited by tons of milk and, the tourist by roads
> safer to walk on and better to speak of.

Glancing through the paper, I was always intrigued with the
novelty of Indian names. Were there really such people as Miss
Me-Too Kumwalla, Miss Corset Rao, Sir Jamsetji Jeejeebhoy, Mr.
Gool Nath and Miss Leila Rajagopalachari? Lucy said that Leila
was a common name in India and that it meant "one night." I was

to grow very tired of hearing people tell me I had a Hindustani name and that it meant "one night," but when Lucy told me for the first time, I was pleased. I had never thought my name meant anything at all.

In the course of his career, Dosoo had written fourteen books that included political commentaries on India, a slight obloquy on New York, an autobiography, and a pasquinade of Bombay society. Writing, for Dosoo, was a life passion. Not for him the reconsidering, pruning, shaping, rearranging of manuscripts. He wrote as he talked, volubly and with a marvelous facility. He considered any year a failure during which he had not published a book of some sort. At the time I was staying with him, he embarked on his fifteenth book, this one about Nehru and titled *The Lotus Eater from Kashmir.*

Submerged in his job and in his writing, Dosoo had no time for outside interests or hobbies. The only form of exercise he took was breathing lessons with a yogi, with whom he closeted himself in his air-cooled bedroom for an hour once a week. Ordinarily, Dosoo expressed a dim view of Oriental mysticism, but the yogi, he said, was wonderful. "You should try the exercises; they're very good for you. You look rather rundown," he said to me.

The next time the yogi came, Dosoo summoned Kippy and me to his bedroom. I shivered in the air-conditioning's humid chill. The yogi, who had laid aside his black umbrella and divested himself of his collarless transparent shirt, smiled at us with a Mickey Mouse smile. Looking like an aging vaudeville tumbler, he sat back on his heels and in a high-pitched voice said that he would demonstrate a few simple exercises in *asana* and *pranayama.*

Before he had finished explaining that *asana* was the muscular discipline of the body, he had flipped both feet behind his neck, and in rapid succession interlaced his arms and legs in carrick bends and clove hitches. His virtuosity was startling but, like all things freakish, a little horrid. Kippy stared at him raptly. When the yogi had unraveled himself and was once again squatting on his heels, smiling complacently, Kippy begged him to do it all over again.

"You try, little boy," said the yogi.

Kippy obligingly placed both feet behind his neck. Dosoo and the yogi both said, "Well," and looked surprised.

A twinge of irritation crossed the yogi's face. "Children are very supple," he said. "Now I shall demonstrate *pranayama*, or regulation of the breath."

He closed his right nostril with his middle finger and inhaled deeply through his left nostril. Then, closing his left nostril and unstoppering his right nostril, he exhaled the air he had just inhaled. He did this several times. "Excellent for the sinuses," he said. We all tried this. I promptly felt faint. The yogi, with a superior saintly expression, continued to inhale and exhale.

Having effected a final exhalation, the yogi said, "So. May I ask you carefully to observe my body." We focused our eyes on his glabrous, dark torso. The muscles of his stomach writhed like a nest of snakes. After the serpent wriggling had subsided, the yogi made his stomach turn and roll on itself in a succession of sinuous convolutions. When he had finished his demonstration, he embraced us with the triumphant smile of one who knows he has done something supremely difficult and done it well.

The next half hour was devoted to a "practice" period, during which we huffed and puffed and twitched in an attempt to command the muscles of *our* stomachs. Both Dosoo and Kippy had stripped off their shirts. I sat protectively swathed in a faded blue T-shirt, contracting and dilating my muscles dutifully. The fluttering sensation made me feel a little sick, and after a while I stopped altogether and just made little grimaces as though I were still exercising. Kippy and Dosoo managed to obtain dramatic and convulsive ripples of which both of them seemed very proud.

After the yogi had left, Dosoo flopped on the bed. "Good Lord, what a workout!" he said in a tone of exaggerated weariness. He shouted for Makahn.

Immediately an answering "Sahib" floated back. The soft sound of running footsteps, a tap at the door, and Makahn appeared, a bronze-skinned, gray-eyed Gujerati, haloed with a deep red, platter-shaped turban.

"Sahib?" he asked inquiringly, lingering over the two syllables as though he savored the sound.

Dosoo kicked off his sandals and waved one bare foot in the air. "My feet," he said. To me he said, "Makahn massages feet delightfully. It's most restful to have one's toes cracked." He sensuously nuzzled the pillow until it conformed to the shape of his head. "I do love to have my feet rubbed," he said, letting his foot fall into Makahn's cupped hands. "Ah," Dosoo murmured, and "Oh," he sighed sumptuously as the tiny hush-a-hush-a-hush sound of Makahn's ministrations began.

"That's one thing about England," Dosoo said. "You'd never get a servant like Makahn." He lowered his lids slowly over the lazy dark eyes which betrayed his Persian ancestry. "Rub that ankle more, Makahn. That side. That's right." As though telepathy existed between us, Dosoo knew what I had been thinking. "Pretty picture, isn't it? The perfect tableau of the lord and his vassal. And won't you just miss it, though, when you go back to America." He grunted comfortably. "The little toe, rub the little toe, Makahn. That's the way."

No, I thought, much as I loved comfort, I would never miss the attentions of an Indian servant. I was ready to admit that I would rather have a servant than not, but there was a certain obsequiousness about Indian servants which cut across the grain of something fundamental in my nature. Their subservience was so relentless that it was difficult to think of them as paid domestic labor, free to come and go as they chose. Had they behaved in a superficially toadying manner, had they been mere lickspittles, I could have disliked them and that would have been the whole of it. But the nature of their servility was slavish and self-abasing, not so much dislikable as it was oppressively embarrassing and, consequently, exceedingly trying.

"My dear, don't give it a thought," Dosoo had said. "Slavishness is a convention of the servant profession here." But whether or not it was a traditional manner of comportment, I found Makahn's unfailing reverence disconcerting, and I could never quite adjust to Lucy's relationship to me. There was no use in remonstrating that, like having a bath, there were many things I preferred to do for myself, for Lucy would look at me with eyes drained of understanding and say, "But it isn't Mem's *place* to do such things." Instead of feeling that I was liberating Lucy from humiliating tasks, I would feel that I was not fulfilling the role of the *pukka* Mem, the proper Mem Lucy expected.

The imprimatur of a *pukka* Mem, with all its Kiplingesque connotations, did not appeal to me, but, as it is generally beyond my power to resist playing up to whatever people expect of me, I weakened and in no time at all Lucy had established a series of intimate tyrannies. She insisted on holding out my dress for me to step into. She would drop to her knees to wipe a speck of dust from my shoes. If I were wearing sandals, she would run her thumbnail beneath the rim of my toenails to be sure that they were spotlessly clean.

Once, in the bazaar, while I was taking notes, a drop of ink spattered from my pen onto my skirt. Lucy seized my skirt, balled the stained part into her fist and popped it into her mouth. She sucked and chewed on the material. "Don't, Lucy," I kept saying in an agony of embarrassment. "Ah, Lucy, please don't. The *dhoby* will wash it. Please, Lucy." But she shook her head and kept on chewing and sucking and spitting out the ink until only a wet spot remained.

On the way home I bought her a suède American handbag. Although she was delighted with it, as it was the sort her beloved white-sari class usually carried, I felt that nothing I could do would settle the score between us. The more I thought about the ink-stain incident, the more it bothered me. "Why did you do that, Lucy?" I asked. "I wouldn't even do it for Kippy. You know I don't *expect* you to do things like that." Lucy shrugged and assumed the Mona Lisa smile that Indian women can put on with such perfection. Was it, I asked, searching in my mind for some logical reason for such behavior, an act of merit that would better her chances of advancement in her next reincarnation? That was always to be hoped, Lucy said politely.

Then, without looking at me, as if she had wanted to say it for a long time, because her tone conveyed the decisive clarity of a thought well seasoned by repetition, she said, "Mem is an Umrican Memsahib. I am only an ayah. I do not at all times understand Mem, and Mem does not at all times understand me. It is all too much for understanding." She gestured, swinging her thin arm toward me, then swinging her arm away to encompass the crowd.

And there you had it, I thought, the whole spirit of India. What Lucy did, what the saffron-smeared sadhu on the corner did, what Dosoo did, was not quite understandable. Nothing really was. That was why India was so seductive; almost everything exceeded the grasp of my mind and my senses. Things casually opened themselves for inspection, revealing a quality, an aspect, a tendency, but behind each there lay something more, unrevealed. The more I learned, the more complicated that knowledge became, each stage of understanding illuminating another but never explaining it.

This is not the place to try to write of such things, for as I come to write of mystic exhalations that struck me at the time, I find they have vanished and are as impossible to reconstruct as the scene of a dream. As I explore my memory, perversely I can recollect incidents of a completely different quality where my lack of understanding of some of the complexities of India resulted in gross and sometimes ridiculous misunderstandings. The time, for instance, when Dosoo appeared at breakfast wearing the white Parsi costume and headdress, a black patent-leather hat shaped like a cow's hoof, which he had set well forward on his head. Since I had never seen Dosoo in any but Western clothes, nor ever heard him say anything that wasn't derogatory about other forms of clothing, I was stupefied.

"I know," Dosoo said, before my thoughts had hardly formulated. "Don't say it. I am going to a memorial service for my mother at the Tower."

Impulsively, in a gesture of sympathy, I put my hand on his. He jerked his hand away. "Don't touch me," he said sharply. "I'm clean." He must have seen my expression, for he added more temperately, "A matter of religion, you know. Ritually speaking, you're not clean."

"Oh," I said, somewhat mollified. "Toast?" I swung the little silver rack toward him.

"I can't eat breakfast," he said.

"Matter of religion?"

"Yes," Dosoo said stiffly.

"Oh," I said, reaching out to help myself to another poached egg.

"Good God!" Dosoo exclaimed angrily. "You're the most insensitive person I've ever seen. Here I am, going to a service for my mother and you sit there and don't have the decency to stop eating. Really!"

"I'm sorry," I said. "Please forgive me."

"You, of all people, to be so thoughtless," he said, looking at me reproachfully. His tone, I noticed with relief, sounded more theatrical than resentful, but I still thought it necessary to make amends by asking if I could come with him.

"If you wish," he said. Congratulating myself on my diplomacy, I allowed him to get his own back by telling me pointedly not to brush against him in the elevator and by directing me, as though I were a servant, to sit in the back seat.

Apparently satisfied that I had been properly punished for my insensitivity, Dosoo looked at me through the driver's mirror. "D'you know anything about our Parsi religion?" he asked.

"A little," I said.

"Well, you should know a lot, considering that Christian ideals are a direct outgrowth of Zoroastrianism."

I had the good sense to say nothing, and Dosoo, with an unfamiliar humility that was touching, told me about his mother's funeral. He explained that in death all Parsis were the same—no elaborate caskets, no impressive corteges. The corpse, rich or poor, is placed naked on a litter and covered only with a sheet. Members of the family and priests carry the litter to the Tower of Silence. Then the priests carry the body inside and lay it in the open amphitheater.

The horrible thought visited me that the corpse was then picked clean by vultures.

Intuitively defensive, Dosoo quickly said, "To my way of thinking, it is far better to have one's bones picked clean by vultures than by worms."

When we arrived at the Tower grounds, he parked near the gate and told me to wait in the car. "This is as far as you can come," he said. "And, for my sake, I wish you'd cover your head with something. This is sacred property, after all." He hurried up the path to the Tower, which was partially hidden from sight by dark cypresses.

I put a handkerchief on my head and waited for Dosoo to return. Near at hand, a congress of crows had settled in the branches of a golden mohur tree. Their hoarse cries seemed to be amplified by the heat. High in the sky, the vultures wheeled and circled. A small boy walked past swinging a cicada on a string.

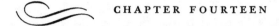

CHAPTER FOURTEEN

The Root of Life

ON ONE OF THOSE perfect clear and hot Indian days, I set out with
Kippy to explore the caves of Elephanta. Along the quay near the
Gateway of India we obtained a small motor launch and the services of a boatman to take us out to the island of Elephanta, which
lay some seven miles distant between the peninsula of Bombay and
the mainland. The launch was old, badly in need of bailing, and
it was coated all about with a skin of salt, dirt and oil. The boatman searched the folds of his dhoti for a length of twine with
which to start the engine and, finding none, he borrowed the string
from the package containing our lunch of sandwiches and mangoes.

From the water, the island appeared to be nothing but a mass of
foliage, the usual tumbling, chaotic greenery of tropical vegetation.
A row of concrete stepping stones extended through a mangrove
swamp from the shore. It was here that we landed. The shore path
that led to the cave temples was bounded on either side by towering
banyans whose branches arched overhead and whose roots writhed
above the ground like the tentacles of some monstrous octopus. The
air resounded with the chattering of gray leaf monkeys and myna
birds, the bland warbling of bulbuls and the metallic clamor of
parrots and crows. There was the frequent shimmering flash of a
kingfisher through the leaves and the orange flutter of butterflies
in the scrub. We reached the top of the rise where the path broad-
ened into a walk railed with iron and flanked with picnic benches.
At the far end of the path, an evil-smelling iron pavilion served as

a lavatory. Rounding a corner, we came suddenly on the caves. The cave temples, arguably dated at the eighth or ninth century, are considered to be the last great achievement of architectural sculpture in western India.

Hollowed out of solid stone, the temple proper, dedicated to Siva, is a pillared hall, with rows of columns "supporting" the rocky hillock overhead. Set off in recesses of darkness are tableaux in rock devoted to significant aspects of Siva Mahadeva.

The carvings loomed out of darkness—tender, lyrical, terrible, the light slipping and sliding over them in such a way that they seemed imbued with a life that was more than life, a life distilled into eternity. Out of seemingly unlimited darkness, the figures emerged —the magnificent Saivite Trinity, with Siva Mahadeva the center of the three heads. Mahesa, his wife and mother-force, to his right. Aghora Bhairava, the cobra-clutching Destroyer crowned with skulls, to his left. The face of the Supreme Siva was contemplative and impassive; the sensual, full lower lip seemed butter-soft even though carved in stone. Ranged about, the subsidiary tableaux emerged— figures from the dream kingdom of the past, blocked in with masses of shadow: Siva and his swaying, full-hipped consort, Parvathi; Siva as Nataraja, the cosmic dancer, and the strong illusion that music whispered about him, an illusion similar to that which the deaf must have of music felt but not heard; Siva, the Androgyne, with his sacred bull; Vishnu poised on Garuda; eight-armed Bhairava; and Ravanna, the demon-king of Ceylon, with ten heads and twenty arms. The grotto was alive with demons and majesty.

Bats clung in clusters to the ribbed, cushion-shaped capitals of the columns and swooped about the statuary niches like ghostly swallows. A troupe of Indian picnickers burst into the cave's damp stillness, eating bananas and shouting *coo-ee* to hear the echoes bouncing back at them.

We moved outside to a sunlit courtyard and a smaller temple that was guarded by stone lions. Around the temple portico a mass of wild bees had clotted in a quivering triangle. Other swarms had settled on the face of the rocky hillside out of which the temples had been hewn. Seen from a short distance, they could have been the shining black drip of a subterranean lava flow. It was only when you came closer that you could hear the humming of them.

Attached to the courtyard temple was a niche set aside as an altar for the Siva *lingam,* an ithyphallic stone about three feet tall which stood on a pedestal. The *lingam* is one of the emblems of the widespread Saivite sect. Saivites wore *lingam* replicas, sheathed in silver tubes, about their necks and wrists. *Lingams* decorated the graves of Brahmin *sannyasis* or ascetics. There were *lingam* shrines along the roadside and throughout the bazaars.

According to one of the innumerable legends concerning the *lingam,* Brahma went one day to visit Siva and surprised him in the act of intercourse with his consort. Siva, blinded with passion, not recognizing Brahma, continued his pleasures, and Brahma retired in a fury. When Siva recovered his senses somewhat, both he and his consort died of grief and shame in the same position in which they had been found unaware.

Siva's last words have been recorded as follows: "My shame has killed me; but it has given me new life, and a new shape, which is that of the *lingam.* Yes, the *lingam* is I myself, and I ordain that men shall offer to it henceforth their sacrifices and their worship. . . . I am the Supreme Being and so is my *lingam.* To render to it the honors due to a god is an action of the highest merit. . . . Those who make images of it with earth or cow dung . . . shall be rewarded; those who make it in stone shall receive seven times more reward and shall never behold the Prince of Darkness; those who make it in silver shall receive seven times more reward than the last named; and those who make it in gold shall be seven times more meritorious still. Let my priests go and teach these truths to men, and compel them to embrace the worship of my *lingam.* The *lingam* is Siva himself; it is white; it has three eyes and five faces; it is arrayed in a tiger's skin. It existed before the world, and it is the origin and the beginning of all beings. It disperses our terrors and our fears, and grants us the object of all our desires."

The *lingam* at Elephanta looked like half of an upended watermelon. It was identified properly in Hindi and in Urdu, but a note of prudery had prevented the English identification from being any more specific than "Eastern Shrine."

It is a typically Indian phenomenon that the phallic symbol of the *lingam* should occur as the basic talisman of the country, and that there should be temples which are sculptural encyclopedias of sexual postures. Although there is in India little of the moral nudism prevalent in such erotic utopias as Siam and French Oceania—public demonstration of affection, for instance, is considered shocking; kissing scenes in the cinema and theater are forbidden; only the most Westernized men and women walk side by side in the street and would never think of holding hands in public; no one would dream of defacing a wall with pornographic drawings and scribbled obscenities—there surely can be no other country where the sexual act and sexual symbol figure more importantly in art, tradition, religion, mythology and daily life.

Sex in India is regarded at once as the root of life and as a ceremonial ritual, and the sexual provender which lay at hand was astonishing in its abundance and variety. From any Ayurvedic firm of chemists, you could obtain ointments guaranteed to induce "lusty and electric tremors," pills guaranteed to "enslave a woman's heart" and sirups guaranteed to "infuse young men with the vigor of an elephant." Herbalists in the bazaar offered aphrodisiacs concocted of honey, pepper, licorice and herbs, and rejuvenating tonics made of powdered camel bone and dried sparrow's eggs.

Since it came as the most natural thing in the world to an Indian to give serious attention to the sexual act and to all its subtle refinements, it was not unnatural that there should be in existence the *Kama-Sutra,* an exhaustive study of *kama,* or sensual pleasure. Originally compiled in the fourth century during the hedonistic age of the Imperial Guptas and enjoying a notoriety which no other Sanskrit work can equal, the *Kama-Sutra,* translated into three languages, was a stock item on the shelves of all Bombay booksellers.

Apart from several informative chapters concerning the art of courtesans and the behavior of their paramours, the *Kama-Sutra* deals with subjects that range from the technique of approaching another man's wife to miscellaneous recipes for aphrodisiacs and methods for increasing the size of the *membrum virilis.* The bulk of the book, however, is given over to detailed instructions in lovemaking, a unique particularization of such esoterica as the art of scratching love patterns with the nails, the art of erotic biting and the art of erotic articulation as a consequence of rapture. Besides eight different kinds of murmurs, one is enjoined to make seven interjectory sounds:

(1) Resembling the nasal sound *hing*
(2) Resembling the rumbling sound *hong*
(3) Moaning or weeping
(4) Forceful breathing
(5) Tongue and dental clicking sounds
(6) Other exclamations denoting excess pleasure, such as "Oh, mother!"
(7) Cooing in imitation of the love cries of the pigeon, the cuckoo, the turtledove, the cockatoo, the hummingbird, the snipe, the wild goose and the quail.

Vatsyayana, to whom the authorship of the *Kama-Sutra* is accredited, was presumably an ardent amateur ornithologist and zoologist, for most of his similes and metaphors are drawn from animal life. The most striking of these is, perhaps, his classification of men into the three categories of Rabbit, Bull and Horse, and of women into the corollary groups of Doe, Mare and She-Elephant.

Possibly some of the more bizarre aphrodisiacs recommended by Vatsyayana were no longer in use. I doubted that many people would take the trouble to procure "the eye of a peacock that has not shed its plume and that of a heat-maddened wolf" and enclose them in a gold case to be worn on the right arm. But many of the simpler remedies and tonics were sold in the bazaar, and in Chindwara, a little village in the Central provinces, I came across artificial brass *membra,* tallying exactly with their description in the *Kama-Sutra,* for sale in the jewelry section of the bazaar. Fashioned in an assortment of shapes and sizes, some were embossed with raised, rough nodules, some had little wheels and metal petals, some had latticed tips, others were smooth. At first, not recognizing them for what they were and supposing them to be cosmetic jars or cooking utensils of some sort, I bought several. "Aren't they nice?" I asked my week-end hostess in all innocence. "Whatever are they for?"

When my hostess, an American girl who had married an Indian, told me, I was dumfounded. "The coolies around here wear them," she said. "And because they *will* insist on perforating themselves so they can fasten the contraptions on better, a lot of the poor things die of septicemia." She held one of the brass *membra* up to the light and examined it. "Maybe you could use it for a cocktail jigger," she said gravely.

CHAPTER FIFTEEN

Portraits

I HAVE FORGOTTEN where or when it was that I first met Mulk Raj Anand; it was simply as if I had always known him. A man of abundant creative force and humanity, he looked like an elderly and mischievous cherub. His gray hair waved round his large head like the curls of a statue. He had the brown-bright, affectionate eyes of a child, and a child's energy and impatience with formalities. The breadth of his intellectual curiosity was astounding. I suppose that he knew more than anyone in India about Indian art and the perplexities of Indian sociological custom. In the thirty novels which he had written about Indian life—he planned to write a hundred—he had captured the facts and flavor of the country and set them down in a style of writing that was at once graceful and vigorous. Mulk was a truly good man who loved life, accepted it and still remained an idealist.

When Dosoo left for Alexandria on a business trip, Mulk invited Kippy, Lucy and me to stay at his winter house in Colaba. He had a summer house in Khandala, whose furniture he had painted a brilliant crimson, the "life color," he called it, the color of arterial blood, the raw vital color he associated with his peasant origins. Mulk loved red things, the stabs of scarlet hibiscus in his garden, the fiery vermilion of a Mahratta woman's cotton sari, the soft brick reds of a Keyt painting. He was extremely fond of a pair of poppy-colored trousers which he would wear on every possible outing, along with a floppy white golf cap that he had bought in Paris which gave him the appearance of a plump, angelic *apache*.

It was in this garb that he led me puffing and blowing up the steep bluffs of the Western Ghats to the rock-cut sanctuaries of Bhaja and Karla. These early Buddhist temples carved from gray rock, with their fluted columns, impressive stupas and rich sculpturing, were more austere than the temple at Elephanta, but they shared the same compelling beauty, the same quality of timelessness. Two thousand years had done little more than mellow and weather their vaulted halls, and there, high up in the hills, with the plains below taking on the subdued pinky-violet tones, wash by wash, of the rapidly westering sun, the silent dark loveliness of the caves forced itself like a knife blade into our consciousness, separating thought from contemplation.

"Was there ever a country," Mulk said wonderingly, "of such real suffering, of such bellyache, and of such beauty?"

Through Mulk's house passed an endless succession of visitors. When Lucy and Kippy and I returned from our excursions in town, I was never sure whom I would find in the shade-dappled living room—an elderly poetess with a rich-cream voice or a pretty young thing whose kum-kum dot (the red dot, or *tika*, which Hindu women place in the center of their foreheads as an indication that they are not widows) would be filled in with the newest shade of Elizabeth Arden lipstick. An Irish journalist who had once tutored the present King of Siam would come for lunch, a meditating millionaire from Darjeeling who was an amateur botanist would drop in for afternoon coffee. Mulk sat in a large wing chair listening to them all—exiguous playwrights, consular officials, dancers and actresses—as he knocked out the dottle of his pipe into a ceremonial brass *yoni*, the female counterpart of a *lingam*, which he used for an ashtray.

Unlike the majority of Indian men I met, Mulk was easygoing and casual. Once past his ever-open front door, you stumbled over stacks of magazines, boxes of manuscript, unframed canvases that he had never got round to hanging, wooden carvings, prayer wheels from Tibet and suitcases he was storing for friends.

I protested to Mulk about the state of his kitchen—dirty pots, the wallboard behind the stove vermiculated with congealed grease, the old-fashioned meat safe covered with cobwebby fluff. Yes, Mulk replied absently, it was a disgrace, and he went on reading the galley proofs of his latest novel. As long as the coffee was hot, and his papers, books and typewriter left undisturbed, it was of little consequence to Mulk what Daniel, the houseboy, did or did not do.

Daniel was an empty-faced, bandy-legged Tamil who wore a seed necklace of the kind known as *rudrakshas*, or "tears of Siva," and a perpetually grease-stained pair of shorts. It was his job to keep the house clean and to do what little cooking there was to be done, but usually he put aside his work with detachment and went off to flirt with the ayah next door.

Although Mulk apologized for him, saying that he wasn't really a servant but a *hamal* (boy of all work), I decided that a stand of some sort should be made. "Look, Daniel," I said one morning after breakfast, "the kitchen is filthy. If you don't keep it cleaner we're all going to get sick." Daniel smiled blandly, blew his nose with his fingers, and continued to mince the meat for the *samosas*. For my own satisfaction, I spent the morning scrubbing the kitchen walls, the stove, the icebox, the meat safe and the floor.

When I had finished, I still felt ambitious. "Now," I said to Daniel, "let's do the living-room floor. You bring a pail of water and some soap, and if we do it together, we can get it done before dinner." Daniel, who had fled the kitchen while I was washing it, looked at me incredulously and murmured about other very important work that he must get done.

No, I said, with a good deal of determination, he was going to help me scrub the living-room floor. Having waited for him to gather together the soap, the brush and the pail, I began to shift the furniture. The living-room floor was of tile, and I told Daniel to start with the middle tiles and work outward to the corners and doors. Daniel hung back apprehensively. "I can't scrub the floor," he said sullenly.

"And why not?" I asked, making an effort to control my temper. "If I can scrub the floor, why can't you?"

Daniel backed away from me toward the door. "I can't scrub the floor," he repeated stubbornly. "It's not my work."

From the safety of the doorway, he fired his parting shot. "Mem can scrub the floor because she is an Umrican and has no caste. But I am a *Sudra* [the lowest of the Hindu castes] and I am above such work." He turned and pounded up the back stairs.

Mulk, who had overheard the last of this exchange, roared at him, "Begone, you mother-raping rogue, or I'll break your head for you!" And then he laughed—a loud, rich sound of the sort you seldom hear in the East, where hearty laughter as an emotional expression seems to have been bred out by thousands of years of civilization. Mulk's shoulders shook and the tears came to his eyes. "Poor innocent Leila, doing battle with the main currents of Indian tradition. Even an American can't teach an Indian peasant new tricks in an afternoon," he said chokingly, between great gulps of laughter.

I met Dilip at one of Mulk's supper parties. He was a young architect, the son of one of India's leading statesmen. Educated in America, he had been graduated with highest honors from the Massachusetts Institute of Technology. I had heard that he was an excellent amateur sculptor, and I asked him how he had become interested in sculpture. "Mostly because I'm a Saivite Brahmin," he said, and went on to explain rather diffidently that one of the practices of the Saivite sect was to make a daily offering to Siva's *lingam*, some families prefering, as an act of further reverence, to mold the model of the *lingam* themselves. His family belonged to the latter group, and every morning after breakfast, he said, the servants placed before each member of the family a tray with a lump of clay on it with which to fashion a *lingam* image. These representations would be garlanded with jasmine and anointed with sacramental milk, honey and ghee, after which formality they would be removed by the servants and deposited among the roots of a banyan tree near the kitchen entrance.

"Father always considered the pile of little clay images at the foot of the tree terribly unsightly, but Mother thought it would be blasphemous to throw them out with the rest of the household trash. Every few months Father would pay the sweeper to haul them all away, and Mother would always pretend not to notice." Dilip smiled indulgently. "And so," he said, "by daily practice, I became quite expert in the sculpture of a limited portion of the anatomy and decided to branch out, as it were, and then, well, there you are, that's the whole story, really."

Dilip had great respect for his family, but he was not above telling droll stories about them, so that when I met them, I felt somewhat embarrassed by my knowledge of so many of the family intimacies. When his father invited me to share his nostalgia for Washington, D. C., and Georgetown, where he had lived when he had been resident ambassador, my thoughts kept returning to Dilip's anecdote about how furious his mother had been when his father had returned from America without his Brahminical cord.

Between the ages of five to nine, Dilip had told me, all Brahmin children are presented in an elaborate investiture ceremony with a thin cotton cord that is looped around the left shoulder and falls to the right hip. The cord is woven of three strands of cotton—after marriage the number of strands is increased to nine—and the cotton gathered, carded and spun by persons only of the Brahmin caste to avoid the possibility of its being defiled by the hands of lesser castes.

"There is a huge to-do about the triple cord," Dilip said. "And, naturally, one is never supposed to remove it."

I am one of those people who always want to know all the practical details, and I asked what happened in case the cord wore out or snapped.

"Oh, it's a deadly performance," Dilip said. "The Brahmin priest has to come to the house and recite *mantras* and fiddle about with sacrifices and finally he weaves a new cord for you. Anyway," he continued, "to get back to Father. He was always taking baths and he hated the feeling of the wet cord, so he got in the habit of taking it off and hanging it on a peg in the bathroom, unbeknown, of course, to Mother, who would have been horrified. It was inevitable that he should lose it one day, and he did, at the Mayflower Hotel. He never wore one again, a fact that has always galled Mother. Mother is awfully old-fashioned about religion. Father maintains the formalities mostly because he feels he should and, in his position, he can't afford not to since religion is the driving force of the country. As for me—" he gave a slight shrug—"I keep my own counsel and am careful to observe all the traditions whenever I stay with the family."

In Old Delhi there was a man named Ram Lal who owned a shop in Chandni Chauk, the Street of Silversmiths, where you buy silver by the weight—so much a *tola* for unworked silver, so much a *tola* for worked silver. Ram Lal was a big man with comb-runneled blue-black hair, a U-shaped nose, a terrible garlic breath, a Parker pen in his shirt pocket and a son in America. Three younger children, like scrawny bantam chicks, played about the counter of his cubbyhole shop.

At whatever hour I passed by, it was always the same. "You are taking tea? You are having a cold drink? Susheila," Ram Lal would call out to his wife, "bring the tea!" His son was a clerk in America, a good son, always sending home money. See, Ram Lal would say beamingly, this is his photograph, these are the post cards he sends. Susheila would appear with the tea in two cups on a brass tray. Sometimes there would be a sticky cake, or a milky sweet flavored with rose water or a dish of chapatties and chilies. Ram Lal and I would exchange cigarettes, and I would gaze at the silver things through the thick dusty glass of the showcase. Indian silver jewelry is marvelous stuff, weighty but not chunky, fine but not finicking, its inherent traditional artistry neither staled nor dulled by Western influence.

"See what I am having for you today," Ram Lal said, and with quick, delicately articulated movements, he plucked an exquisite bracelet, a ring pyramiding with sea-green stones and a pair of belled earrings out of the hodgepodge of a display cabinet. The earrings? I tried not to sound as if my heart were set on having them.

Ram Lal dropped the earrings on to the pan of a balance scale, and slowly and carefully piled the little coin weights on the other pan until the pans balanced.

"For you, four *tolas*."

Although the price was less than I had expected, I shook my head. "No!" I exclaimed, feigning surprise.

"Two rupees less. No? How much you want to pay?" Ram Lal grinned, exposing two gold-capped teeth. His demeanor was at once arch, coy and deceptively placating, the opening gambit of the bargaining ritual. It was a ritual I had grown fond of—the gentle reproaches, the suave sarcasms, the indignation, the mock departure evoking a summons to return to an offer of a lower price. No more equity existed in my bargaining with Ram Lal than there did in Kippy's playing chess with Mulk, but to make the game more sporting, just as Mulk pretended to Kippy, so Ram Lal pretended an equality of skill with me. It was not a matter of *winning*, but rather a matter of seeing how close I could come to it, and when the earrings were finally wrapped in newspaper and looped to my finger by a knotted string, I felt I had come closer than usual, for Ram Lal didn't offer me the customary lagniappe, the little gift bonus of the merchant who has profited generously from his client.

I had been given a letter of introduction to Indira Gandhi and I had been instructed to telephone her when I arrived in Delhi. "She'll probably invite you for tea," I was told, "and then you might meet her father informally, which is by far the best way." As her father was the Prime Minister, Jawaharlal Nehru, the arrangement sounded like a most preposterous presumption on my part. The accessibility of Eastern celebrities always came as something of a shock to me, but I doubted that in this case all was as simple as it had been made out. I was so certain that a lot more would be involved than a telephone call that, having called the Prime Minister's residence and given my name and reason for calling, I was stunned when I was put straight through to Mrs. Gandhi.

"Mrs. Hadley? Of course, Mrs. N—— wrote to me that you were going to be in India for some while. Would you be able to come to tea tomorrow?"

"Why, yes," I said. "I'd love to." And then I wondered what I should wear, and what I should do and what I should say if Nehru did happen to be there. The thought of meeting a prime minister terrified me. I laid this thought aside, and by three the next afternoon the thought was still laid aside, like the fresh white gloves lying on the bed. I looked at myself in the speckled, cloudy mirror that was nailed to the inside of the armoire door. My feet, swollen with heat, felt pinched, but I looked the way I wanted to look, and I began to feel optimistic about the afternoon.

"To the Residency," I said to the taxicab driver. I wound up the windows so that my hair wouldn't blow. The driver fanned himself languidly with a fan made of three peacock feathers mounted on a stick, thumped the horn with the heel of his hand at all the oxcarts and pedestrians along the way, and twice he dismounted to kick the tires, presumably to reassure himself that they were on straight.

When we reached the tall grilled gates of the Residency, two turbaned sentries punctiliously presented arms. A guard asked me my name and checked it off on a list of names attached to a clipboard. Another guard peered inside the taxi and inspected the rear compartment. The driver's name and his license number were written down and a ticket stuck on the windshield behind the windshield wiper. Another guard shouted something that sounded like Ho! Ho!, the sentries presented arms again, the gates were swung open, and we crunched solemnly and slowly up the graveled driveway.

The lawns were splendidly green and stamped at tasteful intervals with trim ranks of cosmos, salvias and crotons. The taxicab driver braked to a halt beneath a concrete portico. An attendant came forward, assisted me as I stepped from the taxi, smartly flung open the doors of the Residency and escorted me into a vestibule-office where again my name was checked off against the master list of visitors for the day.

After Mrs. Gandhi had been notified by telephone of my arrival, I was conducted upstairs by a secretary, the first fat Indian woman I had seen, her hippopotamuslike bulk quivering beneath her flimsy cotton mull tunic and pajamas. Resting on the great yoke of her shoulders, her face was like that of a sentimental Buddha, tender, wise, and androgynous. Up the blue-carpeted stairs we went, she in front, treading incredibly lightly, and I following behind, pausing to glance at a framed photograph of Winston Churchill.

I was ushered into a small sitting room, and I was relieved to see that Nehru was not there. Mrs. Gandhi came forward, introduced me to the other guest, a cousin of hers, she said, and the three of us sank back into heavy, deep and not too comfortable club chairs.

Mrs. Gandhi's cousin had pale, satiny, honey-colored skin and clear gray eyes outlined and elongated with kohl. She patted her shiny black hair, although there was not a hair out of place, and extended her gentle, pleasant talk to include me. They had been talking about wedding dresses, she said, before I had arrived. Hers had been of the traditional rose-scarlet silk, and her mother-in-law had given her a glorious set of ruby jewelry to wear with it. It was almost as nice, she added, as Indira's jewelry, only Indira would never wear hers. Did I find the heat unbearable? Had I seen Indira's children on the lawn? Such sweet little boys they were, so clever. Wasn't Indira incredible, the way she managed to be her father's official hostess, his helper and secretary, as well as running the Residency?

Indira Gandhi had the same handsome, chiseled features as her father, the tortured eyes, the aristocratic bearing and presence of a Kashmiri Brahmin. Yes, she said, there was much to do, an immense amount. Her father came home exhausted every day. He was late today. She had expected him to join us. Did I like India? Was I going to Kashmir? No? That was a shame. Kashmir was the most beautiful place in the world. She spoke of the exalted Kashmir scenery, the forests and the waterfalls. There sounded in her voice for the first time an undertone of emotion. Her conversation until then had been perfunctory and social and I had felt that her mind was elsewhere.

With the arrival of tea and sweet biscuits, the talk about Kashmir was diverted and the conversation redirected by the cousin to the subject of shoes. She admired mine and said that American shoes, next to Italian shoes, were the nicest in the world, but that high heels combined with saris looked awful and you simply *had* to wear sandals if you were going to wear saris. It was a fallacy, she said, that women's feet spread in sandals. Indira Gandhi lifted the hem of her sari and glanced at her feet while we both bent over to examine them. They were exquisitely thin, the skin stretched tightly, almost translucently over the bones and the bare blue vein trees. Her toenails were unblemished and smooth, glossily pink like the inside lip of a seashell.

I felt that I should pose an interesting question that would lead to an animated discussion. This was an exceptional opportunity to hear something intimate and possibly previously unrevealed about Nehru's personal life that only his daughter could disclose. Everyone knew how close Indira Gandhi was to her father. Surely there was something I could ask her that would "draw her out" about her life or that of her father. But I could think of nothing to say at all, and sat there drinking my tea and listening, in a trance of frustration, to the soft voice of the cousin and the clipped responses of Mrs. Gandhi, whose sons, Sanjaya and Rajiv, suddenly appeared in the doorway. They came in and shook hands as directed. Sanjaya was eating a mango, Rajiv a banana. They were nice children, long-legged and with velvety eyes. Having excused themselves politely, they darted out the door.

As I was about to leave, Mrs. Gandhi clasped my hand in a strong, firm grip. She said she was sorry that I hadn't met her father and that perhaps I would like to visit her in the morning. She was sitting for a sculptress. Would it be possible to do her the favor of picking up the sculptress at her flat and coming by with her around ten? Yes, I said, that would be fine. I had just reached the landing when I saw the Prime Minister at the foot of the stairs, starting to come up. I stood where I was, uncertain as to what I should do. He saw me and smiled, a warm and friendly smile, but he said nothing until he reached the landing.

I said, "How do you do," and he said, "How do you do," and shook my hand. "You are . . . ?"

"Mrs. Hadley," I said.

"Ah, yes," he said, pretending to recognize me. I believe we were both rather startled by the encounter. "Thank you very much for coming." I replied that it was indeed an honor to have been asked. He bowed his head and folded his hands in a namazkar. Following his example, I made a namazkar, and he went upstairs and I went downstairs to the vestibule-office. The secretary with the sentimental Buddha's face telephoned for a taxicab.

Nehru had looked just as I had thought he would. His voice had been soft, his accent pleasantly Oxford. His image took shape in my mind: the tired look that had thinned away as he smiled, the grave and gentle face, the patrician aura and the wilting tea rose in the middle buttonhole of his loose white kurta, over which he had worn a dove-gray waistcoat. I felt a flush of physical regret, a kind of inward blush, for all the things I might have said and hadn't.

The next morning I met the sculptress at her flat. She was an English woman in her thirties, blowsy and cosmopolitan in the way of one who has knocked shabbily around the world. She smelled faintly of perspiration and rubber, like an old corset. Her hair had gone an odd greeny-yellow color and fell in a frizzled flourish to her shoulders. Her lipstick had run into her skin so that her mouth was fringed all around with minute capillaries of purplish-red. Beneath the penciled arches of her eyebrows, her eyes, large, brown and moist, gazed at me pertly and appraisingly. "Hello, love," she said.

Competently executed bronze samples of her sculpture were scattered about her studio room—on the mantel top, on the bureau, on the floor. An unfinished wet clay head, swathed in cheese-cloth, was propped on a board bridging the bathtub. Pointing to it with a forefinger poking above a thick cube of topaz, she said she wasn't going to do any more work on it until her client paid her.

Her manner and tone were so like that of a Cockney music-hall actress that I couldn't help asking her if she had ever been "on the stage." "Why, yes, love, before I took up sculpting," she said. "How'd you guess? You should've seen me." She sat astride a chair back and struck a *grande-dame* pose. Then she scrambled to her feet and pirouetted over to the bureau. She rummaged in a drawer filled with shoes done up in gray stockinette reticules and brought out a book of clippings.

The pages of yellowing newspaper paragraphs, with the paste showing through in ridges, were mnemonics which made her go off excitedly into recollections of the success of her Australian and South African tours. Her voice ranged on, as she remembered the cabarets of Melbourne and Jo'burg and "Kipe" Town. One pink shoulder strap hung down her back and the other was pinned in front to the boned bodice of her Paisley print sun dress, which pinched the inner corners of her upper arms into little lumps of sallow, wrinkled flesh. She closed the album, giving it an affectionate pat, and then began to talk of her "sculpting business."

The head of Indira she was working on (she stressed the first-name relationship), the head of *Indira,* she reiterated, was certain to be one of her best works. "My," she said, glancing at the clock on the mantel, "we'd better get a move on. Indira will be mad if we're late."

We left her unaired room with its overflowing ashtrays and ancient red velvet portieres, and taxied to the Residency, where the formalities of the day before were repeated.

We went upstairs to a room on the same floor as the sitting room where I had had tea. This room, which I had not seen before, served as a storeroom for unwanted furniture, a sewing room, an auxiliary playroom for the children—a room, in short, where it didn't matter if ink spilled or clay got ground into the rusty dark-blue carpet. In the center of the room, resting on a tripodal stand, was a veiled sculpture. The sculptress unfurled the wrapping of dampened cheesecloth.

"There," she said. "What do you think of it?"

It was not a bust at all. It was a half-head, the face chopped off beneath the nose. "Novel," the sculptress pronounced authoritatively. "Artistic. It's the spitting image of her, isn't it?"

It was, I thought, one of the worst pieces of sculpture I had ever seen. "Does Mrs. Gandhi like it?" I asked, restrained by politeness from saying anything else.

"Indira adores it," the sculptress said.

I looked again at the beaky-nosed, bulging-eyed semi-head, and I could see it only as a malicious travesty without any particular artistic merit. I watched Indira Gandhi's face closely when she came in, but I could detect in her expression no clue as to whether she was really pleased or not with the sculpture. She sat down on a couch to pose. She was wearing a white *choli* (a type of short-sleeved, high-necked, tight-fitting blouse) and a white sari printed with an all-over pattern of flowers, pagodas, and Chinese teapots with curly spouts. Except for a gold locket on a chain, she wore no jewelry. Her quality, as I was aware of it, was simplicity and an intense purposefulness of dedication to her father. Here was some-one who acted as an agent rather than as an individual, a disciplined being, not an emotional one, and unquestionably one of India's most influential women.

I felt a curious resentment against the music-hally little sculptress for not portraying her with more dignity, and I wondered why Mrs. Gandhi had called in such an unsympathetic, alien artist to "do" her. I watched Mrs. Gandhi sitting on the couch, and the sculptress with her greeny-yellow hair falling over her face as she whittled and dug at the clay. She had taken off her topaz ring and laid it on the floor. The tableau depressed and embarrassed me. I hoped that the half-head would never gain the permanency of a bronze casting, but I never had the satisfaction of knowing what happened to it.

CHAPTER SIXTEEN

Monument to an Empress, Fatehpur Sikri, and the Fever of the Wind

I LEFT KIPPY BEHIND for a few weeks with American friends in Bombay and set off alone for Delhi, the capital city of India. Delhi was really two cities, New Delhi and Old Delhi. In New Delhi so much of the color of the East had been bleached out by the strong British Colonial disinfecting agents of unimaginative order and maiden-aunt tidiness that even after several years of independence, the city retained the starchy, respectable gloss of a small English town. A few miles away, the sprawling village of Old Delhi was like another province. Bounded by rose-gray walls that the great Shah Jehan had built three centuries before by the tawny, sacred waters of the Jumna River, the alleys of Old Delhi fissured through time-stained, crumbling buildings, and promontories of dirt heaped up in the rushing turbulence of its channel-like streets. I stayed there at a small inn where pigeons nested in the transom of my door, and hot water, smelling of wood smoke, was delivered to me in a bucket every morning and every night.

It was my plan to make the hundred-and-twenty-five-mile excursion from Delhi to Agra to see the Taj Mahal, with a side trip to

Akbar's long-deserted, royal city of Fatehpur Sikri. By a stroke of good fortune, Jehangir, the older brother of an Indian girl I had met, had business dealings in Agra and offered to drive me there and back.

We were to leave for Agra in the afternoon, and about half an hour before we started, the *lun*, a scorching westerly wind, swept over Delhi, filling the air with flying particles of dust and sand, obscuring the town in a dusty, ocherous haze. For a moment the sun shone through the haze like the reflection of a gold coin in a basin of soapy water; then it melted and was gone, and the ceiling and walls of the visible world crushed together with a suffocating, gritty yellow closeness. When the *lun* blew up, Jehangir was in a café filling the thermos bottles and buying sandwiches. I had forgotten my camera and had gone to fetch it. By the time I was two thirds of the way back to the café, I could hardly see more than a few yards ahead of me. The blizzard of sand whipped and whirled about me in hot, stinging blasts. People lurched along the sidewalk and were thrown against each other by the wind. Cars with pale, groping fingers of light inched through the streets. The sand burned against my eyes and lips.

"Oh, Lord," Jehangir exclaimed, as I came into the café. He sprang from the table at which he was sitting, and the chaotic flurry that Indians manage with such consummate skill began. Hot towels were brought to wash my face and arms. Tea, slopping in its saucer, was rushed to the table. Jehangir and the waiters and the people at the surrounding tables dithered around me, embarrassingly sympathetic about the sand storm and my having been in it. No one paid any notice to the Indians who stumbled with noisy relief into the café. It was I, the foreigner, the Umrican, who was the focus of attention.

"I hope you don't get a fever," Jehangir said, looking anxiously at me. Ah, yes, murmured the people standing about, the *lun* brings the fever. Someone suggested that mangoes were an excellent remedy for *lun* fever, and a wicker basket filled with mangoes was brought to the table.

"Eat them, eat them," Jehangir pressed me.

"But I feel fine. I'm not sick," I protested. "I don't want to eat a mango now." This was not quite true. I did feel like eating one, but certainly not in an Indian café where there were no forks. Like corn-on-the-cob, there is no graceful way to eat a mango in your fingers. I felt a ridiculous diffidence, rooted in an equally ridiculous vanity, about eating a mango with everyone staring at me while shreds of fruit clung to my teeth and juice trickled down my chin, as it was bound to do. I felt enough of a gazing-stock as it was.

"Eat, eat," Jehangir persisted.

"No," I said, feebly temporizing. "I'll eat them in the car."

"Do you still want to go to Agra?" Jehangir asked in astonishment.

"Well, yes. Why not?"

Had I not been too distressed by the *lun?* No? Weren't American women amazing? He looked to the surrounding crowd for affirmation, and now they all nodded good-naturedly and offered advice as to the best routes for going. It pleased me that I understood a little of what was said in Urdu, a language that had been so short a time ago synonomous with the incomprehensible. There was a great fuss when we rose to leave—the Indians love partings more, I think, than they do arrivals. Wrapping wet towels about our faces, Jehangir and I ran to the car, with a whirlwind of sand eddying about us.

Guided by the fuzzy feelers of our headlights, we crept out of town through a shadowy sulphurous world. In the respectable darkness of the car, I ate two of the warm, soft mangoes. Jehangir smoked Turkish cigarettes, which, not completely stubbed out, smoldered in the ashtray. The heat, the stuffiness of the closed car, the compound of the rose-and-turpentine odor of the mangoes and the heavy, sweetish smell of the cigarettes drugged me into a stupor. The sound of the sand grinding against the windshield and windows sounded like the crackling of the snapping shrimp that used to lie against the hull of the *California* when she was in port, and for a while I fancied I was back aboard. Those days aboard the schooner! I thought about them a lot.

Later I awoke to feel the fresh wind blowing across my face. We had driven past the storm, and Jehangir had rolled down the windows. I looked out on a plain that was silvery in the moonlight. We passed a camel caravan, and the cameleers floated by like white shadows. Then the broken level of the town of Agra—gray buildings, overhanging balconies, the ghastly brilliance of lanterns and a sheet of paper like a live thing dancing over the tattered row of pavement sleepers. A murmuring of the town, a sense of restless sleep, the rattle of our car very loud as we jolted over cobbled streets, and then into open country again. The chorus of frogs and crickets, the whiz and click of flying beetles hitting the windshield, sounded distinctly over the hum of the motor.

"How much farther?" I asked. "How many more minutes before we see the Taj?"

Jehangir yawned. Soon, soon, he said. He turned the car off onto a rutted dirt road, drove for a few more minutes and then came to a stop beneath towering sandstone walls. "Here we are," he said, jumping out of the car and stretching, lacing his fingers above his head. He came around to the other side of the car to help me, but I was already out and looking about. Over the tangled dark trees, rising above the walls some distance away, I could see the tips of the minarets and the dome of the Taj Mahal, lustrous and white, high against the night sky.

"Oh, dear," Jehangir said, checking his watch. "It's way past midnight and I don't know if we can get in. One really should see the Taj at night; it's the only time. Where is that idiot watchman?" There was no sign of anyone around.

"*Chaukidar!*" Jehangir bellowed, hammering his fists against the padlocked wooden door hinged across the entrance of the great gatehouse to the Taj gardens. "*Chaukidar! Chaukidar!*" But no watchman appeared. Jehangir kicked the doorway. "You must see it in the moonlight," he kept saying.

"But I can see a little. The dome. The minarets," I said, and since they in themselves looked magical, I was content. The air was clear and fresh, as though it had just been created; a breeze blew off the River Jumna—a damp, mossy, river smell that was sharp and clean. It was a beautiful night; everything was luminous and defined in the dark registers of the night spectrum—the trees with sleek, mouse-colored bodies and black, velvety wings, the glistening gray grass, the gray-mauve of the sandstone walls, the deep, dark blue of the sky.

"*Chaukidar! Chaukidar!*" Jehangir shouted for the last time, and came around to the side of the wall where I was looking up at the minarets and the dome. "Fool of a watchman isn't there," he grumbled. I suggested that we look for another entrance, or perhaps a foothold in the walls so that we might climb up, look over, and see the Taj drenched in moonlight.

To walk about on such a night was like recalling some long-forgotten past, some mystic, ancestral affinity with the moon. Suddenly filled with a child's crazy excitement, I ran down the narrow foot path to the edge of the Jumna. There it was sandy and marshy. Rising fish made hollow, plopping noises and a water snake oozed off a rock in the water. Across the lapping river were the ruins of the Black Palace that had been built to rival the Taj and had never been completed. Beyond the ruins was a flat, quick-silvered, misty plain. From the back of the Taj Mahal I could see the minarets quite clearly and the singing beauty of the dome with its curlicue spire lucent in the moonlight.

"Look out, look out!" Jehangir rushed up to me and caught me by the arm. "This place is alive with snakes and crocodiles. Look. See? There's one," he said, pointing to a mound in the river. "Watch," he said, flinging a stone. The mound submerged.

But I felt reckless and invulnerable to either snakes or crocodiles, and raced ahead along the path, breathing in the night odors and the moonlight, splashing through wet places and dislodging stones that fell *chunk* into the water. Nowhere was there entrance or foothold in the solid, inward-sloping walls. The dawn was advancing, suffusing the sky with light when I went back to the car. I brushed my hair and sponged my face with the dusty, damp towels. Jehangir and I shared the last of the mangoes, he cutting his into neat segments with his gold penknike, and I not caring, holding the sticky pit in my hands and sucking it hungrily.

The dawn breeze stirred the fiery-edged cumulus clouds banked overhead, sighed through the palm plumes that gleamed as if they had been oiled, and ruffled the banyans and the plane trees so that their leaves glinted like little mirrors. The crows and sparrows went berserk with the coming light, and as the band of white widened in the sky, tiny-headed doves with bluish-pink breasts flew down to peck and scurry across the shadow-freckled ground. The sky was curdled from corner to corner with coral and fuchsia clouds. Then, with a surge of light, the wistful minor key of dawn gave way to the major cadence of the morning. The day cicadas took over, the active hum of their friction sweeping aside the melancholy chirping of their night fellows.

The *chaukidar* sauntered up the path in curling-toed slippers. He rubbed his eyes and noisily cleared his throat. Jehangir scowled at him. "Idiot good-for-nothing," he muttered, and then, changing his tone, he addressed the watchman in the patronizingly coaxing manner of a father trying to ease a toy away from a child.

"You'll let us in now, won't you?"

The watchman smiled stupidly, and shook his head from side to side.

"Is that yes or no?" I asked Jehangir. The two gestures in the East resembled each other so closely that I was never sure which was which.

"It's *no*," Jehangir said curtly, "and I'll no *him* all right." He sputtered peevishly in Urdu at the watchman. He waved a five-rupee note at him and received in reply a shrug and a smiling grimace of betel-stained teeth. "Whoever heard of an incorruptible watchman?" Jehangir demanded angrily. "It's the bloody limit, that's what it is." Since the car had no running board, he opened the car door and sat on the floor, resting his foot on the ground.

The *chaukidar* squatted outside the locked gatehouse and stared at us with his black eyes; he idly passed his ring of keys from one hand to the other, slapping the keys against his knobby knees. "The cheek of the bloody beggar," Jehangir said furiously. "I suppose he thinks he's just going to make us sit here until eight o'clock."

We sat and waited. I watched two wasps picking their way over a dried tump of goat droppings and the mud-brown lizards flickering in and out of crevices in the sandstone wall. Jehangir prowled around restlessly. He raised the hood of the car and tinkered with the motor. With the characteristic disaffection which exists between Indians and engines, he fiddled with the fan belt and then, insinuating a stick into the throat of the carburetor, he made a series of savage, jabbing motions, to what purpose I, and I'm sure he, was not certain.

At last, at eight o'clock, when a soft, golden light spread across the land, the *chaukidar* rose to his feet and inserted a key in the lock. The dark, splintery door embossed with brass creaked as he pushed it back. Since he left the far door unopened, the Taj Mahal was still not visible. The interior of the chambered gatehouse— an impressive building in itself—was somber and chilly. The ox-blood red sandstone walls were inscribed with the calligraphic traceries of Koranic texts inlaid with white marble that glimmered eerily in the half-light. I wanted to climb the spiraling stairway to the top balcony, but I was deterred by a host of bats that rushed into wild commotion at my approach.

"Chaukidar!" thundered Jehangir. "Open the door to the garden!"

"Ayee," said the *chaukidar,* very surprised. Of course! He had forgotten to undo the other door! He bustled in with the key, unlocked the door, and with a thrust of his bony shoulder, opened it wide. There was the Taj Mahal, with its elegant minarets and exquisite dome. Pearly. Serene. Perfect.

Over three hundred years before, Shah Jahan had employed twenty thousand workmen to build a tomb for his beloved Empress, Mumtaz Mahal, "Exalted of the Palace," who had died in childbirth after bearing him her fourteenth child. He had desired that her tomb be an expression of the miracle of their love and a fitting monument to his grief, and surely his wish had been fulfilled.

Perhaps somewhere a more beautiful building existed, but it was difficult to believe. What I had imagined would be a shining white marble mausoleum of lovely proportions had none of the stolidity of its photographs. Like the dream castles illustrated by Edmund Dulac in fairytale books, it appeared to float in the mist that rose from the river beyond it. It shimmered. It glowed. It had the magical property of not looking man-made. Its marble walls had the tender radiance of seashells, petals and moonlit snow. At close range, the pearly fragility of its walls took on substance and bloomed with jeweled flowers carved with infinite delicacy from carnelian, jasper, turquoise, onyx and agate. I passed my hands over the lacework of pierced marble and everywhere I walked I was filled with self-consciousness by the tranquil beauty and silence which radiated about me.

Well on in the morning, Jehangir drove back to Agra, left me at Laurie's Hotel, and went off to attend to his business meeting. Laurie's was the fashionable stopping place of Agra; it was a dreary place, dark and hot, with a handful of elderly guests sitting on the veranda fanning themselves and signing chits for drinks. Of the two rooms vacant, Jehangir had been given, and naturally took, the choicer, the larger and the shadier. (Only in America does that comfortable deferential treatment of women seem to exist.) I slept the remainder of the morning on a lumpy mattress in a stifling room, awoke when the brass gong rang for tiffin, and fell asleep again.

In the early afternoon, we drove the twenty-mile distance to Fatehpur Sikri, a city at Sikri built by Akbar, the grandfather of Shah Jahan, as a thank-offering for the birth of his sons. Later, after he had successfully defended Ahmadabad, Akbar named the city Fatehpur Sikri, or Sikri, the City of Victory. Later still, he had moved his court from Fatehpur Sikri to Lahore, and ever since then the city had been deserted.

From the time I had first heard of the city, it had been, like Khatmandu, Lhasa, Petra and Istanbul, one of the cities in the world which had captured my imagination, and I was determined to see it in my lifetime. Like Petra, Fatehpur Sikri was alluded to as deserted and rose red, adjectives that conjured up mysterious and lovely imagery.

Fatehpur Sikri was not disappointing. Akbar, a contemporary of Queen Elizabeth I of England, and one of the most noble of all monarchs in history, had spared none of his genius for creativity in its conception and planning. Its deep-rose sandstone walls encompassed a glorious mosque and a splendid palace, a magnificent triumphal arch, an exultant blaze of marble pavilions and a beautiful, terrible, brooding desolation. In the Hall of Private Audience, there was a carved column of red sandstone with a huge goblet-shaped capital of stone from which radiated four marble balconies. Here Akbar had been enthroned, surrounded by his ministers of state and his courtiers, and noblemen had looked admiringly upward, the favored, I imagined, standing just about where I did, directly beneath the throne.

Walking beneath the cusped arches of colonnaded galleries, Jehangir and I made a circuit of the central courtyard, wandered on to admire a system of sumptuous marble baths, and came to a circular stone well plunged deeply into the ground. A film of slime, the color of verdigris flecked with gold, patinated the top of the water. Through the brilliance of the film, three young Indian boys were diving. Vital and exultant, flashing their male nakedness in the sun, they laughed when they saw me looking at them, and scrambled up to higher and higher places in the crumbling sandstone rock from which to leap.

Jehangir, festooned with cameras, podgy, rumpled and out of breath, hurried up the path. "My," he said, looking hard at the young boys, "look at those beggars in the filthy water. Watch 'em scramble." He flung a handful of annas into the well and grinned as the boys dived for the little square and scalloped coins. I felt a rasp of irritation and started back toward the mosque.

"Tired?" Jehangir asked.

"Yes," I said, falsely confirming his impression. But when I returned to the white marble pavilion, I realized I was tired—terribly tired, not just from lack of sleep but from a sort of progressive exhaustion that had become more and more noticeable in the last month. The symptoms of vague malaise and ready fatigue didn't worry me particularly, since they could have been due to so many causes—a poor diet of anemic meat and overcooked vegetables, occasional malarial attacks, overexertion, the heat—but as I reached the pavilion, I was a bit alarmed by a feeling of weakness in my back and legs. It was as if my bones were deliquescing. I sat down in the sheltering interior of the tomb of Selim Chisti, and then, seeing that no one was about, I lay down on the floor of the outer corridor that bounded the inner chamber and the tomb itself. I felt with relief the coolness of the marble seeping into me.

Outside, the sun diffused itself over everything with a pale, honey-gold hue, its beams lying like a glittering crust on the richly ornamented corbel brackets and stalactitic capitals. Inside, needles of light fell through the creamy, fragile screens of pierced marble in gold and violet shadows. There was no sound at all except fly buzz and the distant whir of Jehangir's ciné-camera.

Jehangir seemed surprised to find me in the tomb. "What? Still here?" he exclaimed. "But there's a lot more to see." So we set out again to look at ruined cloisters and the elaborately decorated quarters of an unknown Mogul queen; at marble paving stones laid out to form an immense pachisi board on which slave girls were once moved as pieces; at carvings and faded frescoes; at bastions and balustrades; at stables and waterworks with fallen coping stones; at gardens long overgrown; at latticed stone and enameled tile; at the red sandstone walls cutting sharply against a sunset sky.

Because I was so tired, Jehangir postponed our return to Delhi until the following morning, and we started back a little after dawn. It was market day; from the villages the Indians were coming to Agra with their supplies and produce. Jehangir skillfully negotiated the increasing impedimenta of donkeys ambling under twin nets of clay pots and bundles of dried dung, ox wagons heaped with crated chickens, bicyclists with pannier baskets, and camel caravans all moving in the opposite direction toward the town.

Divested of their dimming zoo-ness, lifted from their context of jostling children and peanut shells, the camels looked most extraordinary. Like strange, tall beasts emerged from the recesses of a medieval artist's whimsical imagination, they swayed down the road in a knock-kneed, rolling trot, their divided, horny hoofs making deep pockmarks in the rust-red dust, their sadly supercilious, equine heads waggling on their serpentine necks.

Often they were hitched to vehicles of a peculiar shape, as if a stagecoach had been crossed with a gondola. I felt I must photograph these even though Jehangir said that they were as common as trailers were in America. Getting out of the car and stationing myself at the side of the road, I managed to get quite a few good pictures of a camel train coming toward us. Jehangir called out to the head cameleer, who was perched on a footstool-like saddle between the humps of the lead animal, to halt the animals and the vehicles so that I could photograph them at my leisure. I shrank from such a highhanded order—asking anyone to pose for a photograph never failed to embarrass me—but the cameleer, far from being offended, was amiable and co-operative.

When the women of the caravan crawled out from under the tarpaulins of their wheeled gondolas and crowded about me to see what I was doing, the cameleer gestured them away until I was finished photographing. He guided his camel this way and that so that I could take advantage of the different effects of light and shade I wanted. The camel stood there, batting its wiry eyelashes over its mournful, rebuking eyes and twitching its faded pelt of mummy-brown fur, which, when I touched it, felt rough and gritty, like a worn stair carpet.

Having deprived the caravan of half an hour of its traveling time, I thought the least I could do would be to give the head cameleer a few rupees, but no, he said, he couldn't accept money for nothing.

I asked Jehangir to tell him that if it hadn't been for his help I would have had great trouble in getting the photographs I had.

No, no, the cameleer asseverated. He had done nothing.

"He doesn't want to be tipped. These peasants are damn proud," Jehangir sang out in English from the car. "Tell him you want to buy some of his ruddy camel's milk. He'll overcharge you shamefully and then the pair of you will be happy."

The Indian personality demands a special diplomatic approach of its own. Just as Jehangir had predicted, the cameleer sold me a gourd of milk and overcharged me with beaming geniality. The milk was lukewarm and faintly rancid, and when I put it to my nose, it had a sour, leathery, camel smell. Both Jehangir and the cameleer went off into fits of laughter at the face I made.

Several high-wheeled wagons drawn by curving-horned, caramel-colored oxen passed us. Then we drove on along the dusty road that trailed across the arid, gaunt intensity of the landscape, the somber, squatting earth spreading for miles and miles. Peacocks rustled before us in a blaze of blue-green pyrotechnics. Troops of black-faced monkeys frequently appeared ahead, scattering with a bravura display of acrobatics when we were almost upon them and leaping into the dusty-leaved peepul trees shading the road.

We reached Delhi in the early afternoon. The city was sweltering, sunk in an aftermath of exhaustion from the *lun* storm. The air was harsh with dust, and white with the glare of the sun. When Jehangir left me at the inn, I felt a bit headachy and tired, and as I climbed the steep, dark stairs to the second-floor balcony which led to my room, I began to feel weaker and weaker. I suppose I must have collapsed on the landing and been carried to my room; at any rate, I can only remember lying on the bed and hearing the pigeons cooing in the transom and a great many faceless forms standing around me. Then there was a dark face above mine and a man's voice saying, "Drink this,"; only it sounded like "Trink dis," and I drank something sweet that left a bitter taste.

Although I was covered with ice wrapped in burlap, I had the curious sensation that I was getting lighter and hotter, until I seemed to be floating in a sea of heat. I remember isolated moments when the sweet stuff with the bitter aftertaste was poured into my mouth and a voice said "Trink dis"; when a woman with a silver nose ring rubbed ashes on my forehead; when a lamp shone on my face. I thought it was an hour or so later, but it was actually twenty-six hours afterward that I connected sounds and sensations into meaningful circumstances. An old woman with hennaed hair and a silver nose ring was sitting by my bed brushing my hair. Head on, her black button eyes peering out of wrinkled flesh and the long, thin line of her mouth gave her the look of a turtle wearing a clown's wig.

A dark man, squatting on the floor, was there also.

"Who are you?" I asked, trying to sit up and strangely surprised to find that I couldn't.

He was, he said, a doctor, an Ayurvedic specialist. I recognized his voice as the one that had said "Trink dis." "You were having the *lun* fever, the fever of the wind," he said.

"Who are you?" I asked the woman who was brushing my hair.

"She is not esspeaking the English language," the doctor said. "She is a nurse and a qualified midwife and veterinarian."

He removed a plug of newspaper from the neck of a rectangular glass bottle and held the bottle to my lips. "Trink dis," he said.

"What is it?"

"Fever medicine."

I drank some of it, and then asked what it was made of.

"Ah," the doctor said, smiling, "it is essecret of the trade." Later he wrote me a prescription for it, and I learned from a chemist that it was a mixture of herbs and cows' urine.

The hotel manager and a lady missionary who was in the room three doors down came in to visit me. The missionary lady brought me a religious calendar and a small bottle of cologne. The manager brought me a wreath of jasmine and tinsel and the bill for the services of the doctor and the henna-haired, turtle-faced nurse.

"Dear child, you had a very bad heatstroke. Your fever was a hundred and seven degrees for over four hours before it began to drop," the missionary lady told me. "You were very, very close to death."

This thought was impossible to take in all at once and called for a great deal more reflection than I felt up to, but the superficial details fascinated me.

"Was I really?" I asked.

"Yes. I even called the American Consulate," she said.

"And what did they say?" I pressed.

"Well, let me see," the missionary lady said, frowning slightly. "It was a woman who answered, and first she asked if I was positive you were an American. And I said, Oh, my, yes, I knew you were. And then she asked me what your passport number was, and I asked the manager to show me the registry book—which he kindly did—and I took the number from that because I didn't want to go through your things. I gave the woman at the Consulate the number and she said, Oh, dear, she didn't know what to do, but she would call a doctor and to call her back if you did die and she would do what she could. But the American doctor was away on vacation, so the hotel manager called in a friend of his. Rest assured, my dear child," she added cheerfully, "if you had passed on, I would have done everything in my power to see that all the proper arrangements would have been made."

I thanked God that that hadn't been necessary, and as soon as I was able, I flew back to Bombay.

CHAPTER SEVENTEEN

Ellora and Ajanta

MULK RAJ ANAND made arrangements for me to go to Ellora and Ajanta with Dilip and a young English girl who was in India on an art scholarship. Kippy preferred to stay behind in Bombay with the American family who had looked after him while I had been in Delhi. The morning that Dilip, the English girl and I left on our trip, Kippy was in a state of wild excitement. Where he had placed two baby teeth beneath his pillow, the Good Fairies had left four rupees, and what was more, he had finally succeeded in catching an earwig. Indian insects had the peculiar fascination of being large-scale models of insects anywhere else, and Kippy sedulously collected beetles and spiders that barely could be squeezed into the cigarette box containers he provided for them. When we made our conventional dawn start, Kippy was standing in the driveway, wearing a sola topee and a T-shirt printed with an anthropomorphized airplane, waving good-by to us and triumphantly flourishing the cigarette box with the overgrown earwig inside.

Once we had issued from Bombay city and crossed over from Salsette Island to the mainland, we drove northwest along the Deccan plateau toward stark, naked hills of volcanic rock eroded into fanciful castles overlooking treeless plains and villages of blind-looking, mud-walled huts. We drove through a village where a woman whose ears were perforated with a spiral of silver rings was grinding wheat between two millstones that she rotated with a wooden handle. A potter near by was squatting before his wheel with a honeycomb of round, red pots before him drying in the sun. As his hands played over the wet clay, the clay taking on form and the wheel's turning sending black shadows leaping hypnotically in the ferruginous dust, the potter sang, his voice filling the village with its sour changes of tone and key. Overhead the vultures circled and hovered. Women looking superb in risky combinations of orange, scarlet and magenta swayed out of a grove of teak trees, the sun glinting on their well-wet copper jugs and on the massive silver nose rings that kissed their lips, the colors of their saris bright and flashing, dominating the landscape.

The plains spread wide between the hills, somber and dusty, cultivated squares and oblongs of scratchily furrowed land alternating with stretches of withered savanna. A speck of crimson glowed in the distance, sharp against the cocoa-colored road. We overtook a peasant woman with a great bundle of kindling on her head. We passed a young boy playing a flute, his head shaved to guard against ringworm. On we went to Nasik, which rose from the banks of the Godavari, the sacred sister river of the Ganges.

The banks of the river were pleated with stone steps crowded with bathers and with clothes spread out to dry. In the background were the bubble domes and the fretted spires of temples and shrines. We bought a bunch of bananas from a truncated beggar on a trolley and then drove on to Manmad, where we stopped at the train junction for breakfast. From Manmad, it was not far across the border of Hyderabad State to Daulatabad. It was searing hot. The sunlight had drugged the countryside into somnolent accidie. A peasant was plowing dry furrows into the ungiving plain. An old man had subsided on a charpoy beneath a tree with yellow blossoms, and here he lay with the tube of a hubble-bubble pipe laxly held in his mouth. Farther on, a man led a team of white oxen in ever-narrowing circles over a patch of harvested wheat while two women with saris pulled above their knees winnowed and cleansed the grain by throwing it into the air with a scoop basket. The limitless panorama of the country stretched away, exact in its perspectives—camel's-thorn, furze and a thin wood of long-podded tamarinds in the foreground, a dust-dry plain in the middleground, and, in the distance, fawn-colored hills as dry and scaly as the lizards which flicked across the road.

A granite cone butting through the sere plain was topped by a thirteenth-century fort. Usually an indefatigable sight-seer, I was perfectly content to sit in the car and watch its bastions and towers pass from sight. The road branched off here for Ellora, but as Dilip thought it better to see Ajanta first, we continued on toward Aurungabad, stopping briefly at the semi-deserted city of Khuldabad on the way.

Khuldabad was surrounded by battlemented stone walls built by Aurungzeb, the son of Shah Jahan and the last of the great Mogul emperors. The town contained his tomb, an unpretentious sepulchre that he had self-righteously stipulated be paid for out of the proceeds of the sale of caps which he himself had quilted. The Nizam of Hyderabad, however, had built a pretty screen of pierced marble about the tomb. The sanctuary, which included not only Aurungzeb's tomb but also several other cloisters and outbuildings, was shaded by immense peepul trees, so that the courtyard was brindled with light and leafily hemmed in like a child's secret hiding place. A spry old *chaukidar* showed us all the wonders and relics: a saint's tomb with doors inlaid with silver; a small locked chamber built into an angle of the courtyard wall which contained a robe of Mohammed's; a shrine that contained hairs from the beard of the Prophet which yearly increased in number; and the remarkable treasure of a tree on which money grew. Every year, the *chaukidar* assured us solemnly, when the moon was full in a certain holy month, the tree sprouted buds of the finest silver, and these buds were broken up by the priests and sold for the maintenance of the shrine.

"Moslem balderdash," Dilip commented, with a Hindu Brahmin's superiority.

Mimosa trees, trembling in the wind, had carpeted the street with little balls of greenish-yellow fur, and we set off again along the historic thoroughfare to Aurungabad over which the Aryans, Pathans and Moguls had passed on their way to the conquest of southern India. There were few travelers on the road now: a girl child (it was impossible to tell how old she was, for Indian children look so small and grave) wearing a red and yellow *choli* embroidered with circular bits of mirror (the effect more like flashes of mica than mirror, really) walking up the road munching on a long stick of sugar cane; an old woman resting beneath a tree, her head drawn beneath the mantling end piece of her sari as a bird draws its head under a wing; a goatherd with his flock.

We stopped for the night in Aurungabad at a government-owned rest house. We sat for a while in the lounge listening to American records of the thirties being played on a juke box by three Indian sewing-machine salesmen, then ate a tasteless European-style dinner and went to bed. A scorpion, like a black baby lobster, surveyed me grimly from the bathroom floor, and there was a hole in the mosquito netting through which troops of mosquitoes found their way, but otherwise the night was uneventful.

At dawn I was awakened by the ragged chorusing of wild parrots and by the English girl thumping on the door telling me to hurry to get dressed because Dilip wanted to drive in the comparative cool of the early morning.

We drove northwest along a road that was sporadically fringed with banyans and acacias, peepul and neem trees, with clouds of dust puffing and swirling behind us. It was forlorn and barren country. The road twisted and climbed through the scorched, nude Indhyari hills, then dropped down to a level, ocher plain, only to rise to another eminence. Dilip whisked the car around the road edges with what he called his American-style precision. The English girl and I were yipping with anxiety.

We stopped near a hill that looked like all the other hills, and Dilip announced that we had arrived at Ajanta. We left the car and as we walked around a curve in the path, there was a tired little pavilion that looked exactly like a Parisian *pissotière* minus the posters, but it turned out to be a rain shelter for picnickers. There were no picnickers, and it was apparent that we were the only visitors.

We walked along the narrow path until it ended abruptly at a flight of iron-railed concrete steps ascending an almost perpendicular hill. Thin stalks of grass leaked through cracks in the concrete, and the steps scaled into a withered wilderness of parched grass and naked outcrops of gray-brown rocks. The early morning sky was already pallid with heat. We climbed the steep hillside, and below, through the gorge, the Baghora River wriggled like a weary cobra.

All at once—above a crescent-shaped sweep of arched and pillared halls cut deeply into an escarpment—I saw the cave temples, dark cavities in an amphitheater of shadeless, tawny hills.

There was the momentary but annoying intrusion of an iron turnstile, and the appearance of a *chaukidar* guide eager to sell dusty packets of post cards and to rent for five rupees a battery lamp to illuminate the caves and for another five rupees to provide his services as an escort. Dilip, with his acquired American efficiency and the lofty peremptory tone that upper-class Indians employ with cheeky servants, brushed aside these importunings, brandished two flashlights he had foresightedly brought with him, paid the entrance fees, produced a slip of consent from the Director of Archaeology in Hyderabad allowing us to photograph the caves should we wish to, and led the way through the turnstile.

Ajanta means "a place unknown in the world," and I suppose it was almost that when Buddhist monks first started to hew the temples out of the rock two centuries before the birth of Christ. Between then and the seventh century, twenty-nine temples were carved from the rock face, frescoes painted on the temple walls, the life of Gautama Buddha recorded in sculptured tableaux, and domed *stupas* housing Buddhist relics erected. Then, in the late seventh century, when Buddhism disappeared from India, the monks vanished mysteriously from the valley sanctuary, and Ajanta was forgotten, overgrown and lost to the outside world for more than a thousand years, until the caves were discovered in 1819 by members of a British hunting party.

As I went from cave to cave, my flashlight sliding slowly over statues and paintings, faces and figures rounded enchantingly and were filled with life. That afternoon, just before sunset, the sun's rays slanting through the caves performed the same Pygmalian miracle. It was astonishing then to see how each figure, sculptured or painted, had been placed to receive this enlivening glow. There is a legend that once, long ago, the gods and goddesses, jaded with the monotony of celestial pleasures, received permission from Indra, the King of Heaven, to descend to earth for a night of enjoyment on the condition that if they did not return before the cock's first crow, they would be shut out of Heaven forever. They chose

Ajanta as the site for their revelry and enjoyed themselves so thoroughly that they forgot their time limit. The cock crowed twice, and they were transformed into paintings and statues.

The fragmented world of Ajanta and the characters which peopled it assembled in ravishing images. There were portraits of rajas and their retinues, soldiers flourishing curved swords, hunters, mendicants, musicians, cowherds, archers, servants, winged angels and children. There were delightful studies of animals—white geese, horses, tigers, river snakes, panthers, owls and glorious elephants, brilliantly canopied and roped with jewels. There were kings and princes. But of all the figures, the Ajanta women were the loveliest —inordinately sensual yet innocent creatures, with high, rounded breasts, tiny hand-span waists and long, graceful limbs. Almond-shaped eyes glanced modestly from bright and beautiful faces, and just as I thought that I had found the most beautiful face, there was always another to match it.

Possibly there was one princess a little more lovely than all the rest. She was leaning languidly against a pillar, her left leg drawn up behind her, her lips and the soles of her delicate feet stained with crimson dye. Champak flowers and ripening buds were woven with jewels in her dark hair, which rippled in ringlets onto her shoulders. A necklace of pearls and sapphires lay between her breasts and, half-smiling, she looked down at a handful of crushed flowers whose petals had fallen about her feet. She was radiant in all the wonder of her beauty and youth, and above her shining, dark head the rock bees buzzed ominously whenever anyone approached.

We left Ajanta and returned to the rest house at Aurungabad. The next day we drove back through Khuldabad, past the ruins of the Daulatabad Fort and then branched off on the unfrequented, dusty track to Ellora. Ellora, a colossal theological and architectural enterprise, was conceived more than a millennium ago. Its magnificence was created by the Hindus, the Buddhists and the Jains. Its central temple, Kailasa, built to symbolize the abode of Siva, was sculptured from the base of a mountain and was embraced on three sides by the towering gray basalt rock face out of which it had been cut. Thirty-four outer temples encircle Kailasa like a nimbus. The vast whole is deserted, mysterious, bewildering in its congeries of galleries, porticoes, pagodas, pavilions, colonnades, cloisters, chambers and friezes.

As I walked into the courtyard, my heart seemed to clutch and fold in on itself, and like a Lilliputian suddenly thrust into a Brobdingnagian world, I felt shaken and awed. I looked back at Dilip and the English girl, who had diminished to tininess beside a soaring tower resting on a frieze of immense elephants. The courtyard was flooded with blinding Indian sunlight, and I followed Dilip and the English girl into the shadows of a curving gallery where the light shivered over an assemblage of great, gray Brahmanical gods—Indra, Indrani, Siva, Parvathi, Durga, Ganesa and Kali.

The English girl had taken out a notebook and was making sketches. Dilip peered at his light meter and adjusted the stops on his Leica. "I think f-two-eight at forty will do it," he said. I went on walking, going from harsh sunlight to somber chambers where streaks of light outlined Buddhist sculpture and Hindu architecture so beautiful that I longed to become a part of it and was filled with a sense of dispossession at the thought of returning to a conventional world.

"It's incredible," the English girl said. "There isn't a piece of movable sculpture here. Everything's carved in the mountain."

"It's fabulous, isn't it?" Dilip asked.

"Yes," I said, but when I tried to formulate in words what I felt, the words lost their sincerity and emerged as flat and mechanical as the phrases in the REMARKS column of a guest book the *chaukidar* produced for us to sign hours later.

From the guest book, it appeared that relatively few people came to Ellora and, of those who did, most came from the neighboring part of India. "Did you like it?" the *chaukidar* asked, with an imbecile grin.

Yes, we all said. "Yes, is a nice place," he said ponderously. Probably, if we had said, no, we didn't like it, he would have replied in the same tone, "Yes, is a bad place."

We returned to the car and drove to Manmad, my thoughts ribboning back to Ellora all the way. We reached Manmad at midnight, and of course there was no hotel. Only the largest of Indian cities have hotels. The only accommodation was a state-owned *dak* bungalow which provided neither bedding nor linen, but it was that or nothing.

Dilip drove up to an unlighted building. "I'm sure this is it," he said, knocking on the door.

At length the manager appeared, an elderly Anglo-Indian dressed in a brown woolen bathrobe with innumerable stains down the front of it. Yes, there were rooms, he said, and we were lucky to have them without writing for reservations. He led the way down a grubby, yellow passage. "There," he said sullenly, pointing out our rooms.

After I had shut the door, I could hear Dilip attacking the manager in the corridor. How dirty, how badly kept everything was, how unlike other *dak* bungalows, and the manager's sulky, shrill replies.

The room was miserable. The smudged, peeling plaster walls bore witness to the bloody deaths of countless flies and mosquitoes. The mosquito netting hung in soiled wisps about a charpoy covered with tape webbing. Bits of fluff stuck to the splinters and the protruding nails in the floor, and a hairpin and two white buttons were embedded in the crack of the door sill. The gray sail of the punkah fan suspended from the ceiling was motionless.

I was surprised in the morning when I awoke stiff and uncomfortable from lying on the charpoy and noticed the fan flapping slowly to and fro. I saw that its guide rope, which had been coiled in the corner during the night, had now been drawn through a hole behind the washstand. Peering out the latticed window, I saw the *punkah-walla* lying stretched out on the grass pulling the guide rope back and forth with the toes of his left foot, which he supported on his right knee. His feet, scurfy with dried skin, looked like chickens' feet, dry and thin. He lay there on the dried grass, his dingy dhoti bunched up around his waist, his hands every once in a while moving torpidly to brush off clinging horseflies. Tirelessly and rhythmically, he drew the rope toward him and let it slide back again through his toes.

The languid pendulumlike movement of the punkah heralded a morning of stupefying heat, but on the return trip to Bombay, relinquishing myself to the remembered pleasure of Ellora and

Ajanta, I managed, for the most part, to forget the heat in the breathless sweep and swing of loveliness acutely recalled.

The time had come for me to move on, for I wanted to be in Beirut when the *California* came into port. I booked passage for Kippy and myself aboard the *Dwarka,* which was sailing within a week up the Persian Gulf to Basra. From Basra I planned to go to Bagdad, and from Bagdad to Beirut.

I should have liked to have left India calmly, to have left realizing that I was going. Instead, I left in a flurry, conscience-stricken that I had forgotten to say good-by to at least four people, struck with last-minute doubts about the number of visas I needed, wondering where I had put my passport, Kippy's vitamin pills and a small bronze carving of Siva and Parvathi that Mulk had given me.

Lucy wept, saying between snuffles how much she would miss Kippy and me, at the same time putting in a bid for an extra-large farewell baksheesh by extolling her own virtues—"I never stole from you, Mem. I never wore your dresses. I only slept a little in the afternoon. I never overcharged you. I never hit the *baba* . . ."

Kippy interrupted indignantly. "I'm no baby, Lucy," he said, striking a pose with his arms akimbo and his feet planted wide apart. This brought on a fresh outburst from Lucy, who declared that he *was* a baby, "her little *baba,*" and she would miss him so that her heart would never be the same.

At the pier all was confusion. Where had the porter gone with our luggage? Where was my typewriter? Where were we to go for customs and health inspection? And then more confusion when we found the health inspector, because my small-pox vaccination had been of the modern cosmetic variety and had left no scar. In vain I showed the International Health Certificate bearing the data relative to the vaccination—the date, the doctor, the type of serum used.

"But where is the mark? You must have a scar," the inspector said stubbornly.

And if I had no scar, what then? I would have to be vaccinated before I sailed, the inspector said. In desperation, I pointed to a paling mosquito bite. "There's the scar," I said.

"Ah, yes," the inspector said, nodding. "Fine, fine," he said, waving me on to the passport officials, who stamped my passport and sent me on my way.

All this took place in a pier shed so crowded that Kippy and I could hardly move. The surging, excited urgency of bewildered travelers; the scraping yells and tears and leave-taking sentimentality; the bumping, shoving mass of porters balancing chicken crates and tin trunks on their heads; the monumental tangle of officials and passengers and onlookers—from this chaotic emulsion we were finally ejected and catapulted up the gangway just in time to hear the gong sounding for all visitors to go ashore.

I waited for the shuddering blast of the ship's whistle and was startled when it came. Bells jangled in the wheelhouse, and the mates shouted down to the dock hands to clear the lines from the bollards. Quivering frantically, the *Dwarka* eased away from the dock and nosed out into the Arabian Sea.

CHAPTER EIGHTEEN

The Oman-Trucial Coast

THE *Dwarka* was a tropic merchant tramp, bare and stubby, with a pervasive odor of grease, mold, copra and brass polish. She was white—not a cool pallor, but a blistering, crackled, rust-stained white, a white that was hot, bleached, blinding and mercifully bit off by darkness the moment I closed the door to the deck and went below through intestinal alleyways to our cabin.

Kippy and I had been assigned a three-berth cabin opposite the galley. It was a stifling cubicle furnished with a frayed strip of green carpeting, scarred mahogany bunks, a wicker chair and a narrow, standing wardrobe that contained a tumble of orange life jackets and an empty gin bottle. There was a chipped enamel basin with a mirrored medicine cabinet above it. A fixture on the bulkhead to one side of the basin held a water carafe with bubble-coated sides. On the other side were framed directions for lifeboat drill. There was a wall fan, and that was all, or almost all, for the steaming, sickish exhalation that poured out of the galley, and which we were committed to breathe for the whole of the journey, was as much a part of the cabin's furnishings as anything else.

The claimant of the third bunk was a young Hindu girl from Travancore on her way to a nursing position in the General Hospital at Kuweit. She had a virgin moon face and a diamond screwed through a hole in her right nostril. She was terrified to move from the cabin. It was the first time she had been away from home. As soon as the boat began to move she curled up on the bunk and lay there, silent, miserable, motionless. Very shortly afterward another young Hindu girl from Travancore crept into our stateroom. She was a friend of the first, and also traveling to Kuweit. Mute and frightened she sat on the edge of her friend's bunk. I administered aspirins and dramamine. But it was no use. They were both sick. One in the basin. One on the tin windscoop fixed to the porthole. Then they lay down together pale and expressionless, thin arms and plump pigtails entwined, the yellow of one sari lapping over the pink folds of the other. For the remainder of the voyage they scarcely moved from the bunk. At all times of the day they were there, alternately dozing, braiding each other's hair, throwing up or eating. The *vichywalla* from below decks who cooked for the lascars prepared their meals for them. This vegetarian cuisine, delivered on a Damascened brass tray, was repetitious and repellent to look at—brass bowls brimming with oily spinach leaves, curds, chilies, lentils, boiled pulse, and stacks of ghee-soaked chapattis.

The food dished up in the dark little dining saloon with its rough-ironed linen and greasy cruet stands was little better. Dinner, the first night out, led off with a viscous cabbage soup. This was followed by a gobbet of fish afloat in a glutinous white sauce, a charred meat cutlet and an unidentifiable lumpy pudding—fare that set the standard for the rest of the meals.

All was to change as passengers seethed aboard at later ports, but in the beginning the ship felt empty and sounded empty, the way an auditorium does after the crowd has gone. The barefooted lascars, the handful of British officers, and the subdued huddle of deck passengers gathered beneath a tarpaulin on the poop deck all made themselves as inconspicuous as possible. There were, besides the Travancore girls, Kippy and myself, only three other cabin passengers—a salesman from Delhi with a soapy smile, and two Seventh-Day Adventist ladies traveling to the Holy Land on a pilgrimage excursion. The salesman represented the *Islamic Review,* a monthly magazine, and the official organ of the Woking Muslim Mission and Literary Trust. He also represented a curio house. Shortly after he had introduced himself he offered me a certified correct copy of the Koran printed on a foolscap sheet folded into a tube container with a magnifying glass attached, a charming Moslem memento, he declared, at a bargain price. The missionary ladies were very sweet to Kippy and me, and they gave us quantities of religious pictures.

After I had unpacked our things, I settled Kippy in his bunk with his collection of bottle caps and labels that he was indisposed to part with, placed on top of the medicine cabinet the bronze statue of Siva and Parvathi that Mulk had given me and peeled the most recent labels from the suitcases for Kippy's collection—he particularly liked the ones featuring a muscular Britannia armed with a trident and shield and a lion at her side, the lion resting its paw on the top of a globe covered, for some unknown reason, with a red doily. Then I went out on deck. The moon was gold and gibbous, the water dark and dancing with light. I felt I could reach out and touch the Big Dipper and the bright outlines of Cassiopeia. The ship had begun to roll gently. When I returned to the cabin I found Siva and Parvathi gliding with dignity back and forth across the top of the medicine cabinet.

And so the *Dwarka* proceeded, sailing past the Cutch, bisecting the Tropic of Cancer and on past the multi-mawed terminus of the Indus. At Karachi we paused for a day to take on and discharge cargo. We went down the shaky iron steps of the gangway onto the pier, where green parrots and mongooses were offered for sale. I found it hard to resist buying a mongoose. I liked their sharp, feral faces. But to travel about with a caged mongoose would be difficult, and with that purchase forfeited we taxied into Karachi.

What I saw of the town was very ugly. Prospecting the streets and bazaar area, I found nothing that I hadn't seen before on a much larger, finer, grander scale in Delhi and Bombay, nothing but monumental tawdriness, and merchants endlessly masticating betel. Bluebottle flies. Dust. New nationalist offices temporarily housed in Quonset huts. Sewing machines sluggishly treadled in open-fronted cubicles. American cars and oxen vying for the right of way on manure-mounded streets. With Kippy trotting ahead (nothing ever tired *him*), we went up one street and down another, and another and another. Then suddenly there was the harbor, a cool sapphire blue, and the wings and whiteness of gulls and sails. Down at the quay side, we sat on the rough, sun-warmed wharf and dangled our legs over the side. The harbor was full of ships—chunky little tramp steamers; a single, elegant cargo-cum-passenger liner; a Maldivian *buggala*, richly carved with a tier of stern windows; double-ended *booms* with built-up stern and bow stems; and from all the small ports of the Yemen and the Hadramaut, from Madagascar, Zanzibar, Mombasa and Aden, the *dhows*, their commerce and appearance almost unaltered from Biblical times. All about were small craft, with patched lateen sails, bows raked forward, skimming along at dragonfly speed, swift and audacious.

When we returned to the *Dwarka* she was nearly ready to pull out and hooting for all she was worth. We were swept aboard with hundreds of deck passengers bound for Pasni, a small Pakistan port, a day away. The deck passengers were mainly from Makran, the southwest division of Baluchistan, and they were wonderful to behold. The women, with turquoise nose rings caressing their curved upper lips, wore neither sari nor Punjabi dress, but, instead, the Baluchi shirt, an ankle-length tunic encrusted with embroidery and dyed scarlet, the story went, so they would be less likely to be an accidental target in the incessant feuding that went on in the Afghanistan-Baluchistan-Pakistan area. They and their menfolk also wore *salwars* wrinkling around the ankles. Everyone wore masses of silver jewelry. Flinging down their strips of carpet, they spread their bundles and crates and tins and trunks on deck. A few set up makeshift tents. Goats were tethered to the railing. Mats unrolled. Cook pots brought out. By nightfall all was a chaos of camaraderie, but by morning the passengers rose like phoenixes from a nest of mango peelings and litter and, miraculously fresh and cheerful, their ankle bracelets tinkling, they surged off on the *booms* from Pasni that came alongside.

The *Dwarka* thumped across the mouth of the Gulf of Oman, which was streaked silver with flying fish. Clouds, presaging the southwest monsoon, billowed overhead. A school of porpoises frisked about the hull, and gulls with creaking cries of gluttony wheeled above the gaudy garbage the *vichywalla* hurled over the stern. On deck, the brass fittings sparkled in the sun. The *Dwarka's* hot white flesh was crosshatched with rust stains, and in places the woodwork was splintered from dryness, but the brass was tended to lovingly, polished daily by the lascars to gleaming perfection. A turbaned deck passenger had crept to a shady corner near the dining saloon and was busily sewing a rent in his *salwar*. The water reached out smoothly to knead the rocky hills on the horizon. On and on, and now the uplooming craggy hills and frowning capes and fastnesses were close and eyed with caves, dark, mysterious, watching.

As though a wet sponge had been drawn across its multicolored, sensual filigree, the Orient vanished and was superseded by the severe pattern of the Arab world. The barren rocks slid away and parted to form a pass to 'the wicked little cove of Muscat, the cove gripped fiercely on three sides by great, bruise-colored cliffs mounted with the grim vigilance of Martello towers. The Sultan's castle, the fortressed donjon-keep, the town crouching at the water's edge, bristled with sunshine and piracy, calling forth all the dark echoes of the past when more slave trading, more freebooting, more smuggling, more gunrunning, were carried on in the Gulf than on any other waterway in the world, with Muscat the most formidable of all the piratical strongholds. Muscat still retained its formidable appearance and many of its old practices—carried on in secret, to be sure, but still operative. It was rumored at the time to be doing a brisk trade in false passports and pretty Caucasian girls.

As we sailed into the harbor a swarm of canoes raced out to meet us, elongated lollipop paddles beating the water into white froth, the craft skimming along like otters after prey. Flocked about us, the oarsmen were transformed into eager, shouting vendors of pearl shell, prickling starfish, conch shells with orangey-pink insides, point-lace fans of coral and tarry packets of dates. Faces tilted up to us, their Bantu and Somali features proclaiming their slave origin. Plaited rush trading baskets were attached to coir lines, and the lines flung up, to be caught by the passengers pressed against the rail. Rubbed all over with the railing's powdery white paint and rust, Kippy bargained wildly, impatiently hauling up a basket, examining the shells with the greatest of care, selecting one, discarding another, smiling, frowning with indecision, estimating the cost, counting the coins into the basket and then sending the basket jingling and scudding downward.

The first mate strolled by, stopped to toss a few annas into the water, leaned over the railing to watch the men dive for them, remarked that the divers were clever bastards, and after considerable haggling, bought a large conch shell which he said he was going to electrify and make into a lamp.

A lighter lumbered out from the silent, burning shore, and with much commotion, cargo was loaded and unloaded, the passengers for Muscat herded down the gangway, and the passengers for northern ports jostled aboard. There were no women passengers. The newcomers were mostly traders from Sur and Muscat with lean faces, tough, sharp features and fierce eyes. They filed up the gangway, many bearded and carrying amber prayer beads and sticks in their hard, sunburned hands. Over their heads they wore bobble-fringed *kefiyehs* held in place with black head ropes; each of them had cinched his flowing white robe with a dagger-stuck belt, the daggers sheathed in silver, J-shaped scabbards.

I wanted to go ashore, but since all visitors' permits had been canceled because of a suspected attempt on the Sultan's life, there was nothing to do but gaze wishfully at Muscat from the deck of the *Dwarka*.

Muscat, lying on a sulphurous crescent of land, was a small, sun-baked assemblage of flat-roofed buildings imprisoned between the uprearing, rocky hills. Save for a few white figures near the water's edge and the Union Jack limply hanging on a staff above the British Residency, there was no sign of movement or life in the town at all. Remote and withdrawn, Muscat had retreated into its lair like some nocturnal creature and was intent on keeping all of its secrets to itself.

The lighter wallowed away. The canoes were paddled shoreward. Swinging slowly about, the *Dwarka* moved out of the cove and back once more into the Gulf of Oman. The sky flickered with venomous tongues of lightning, and a southerly blast of wind blew up a heavy sea. The Travancore girls moaned more loudly than ever on their bunk, and the Arab traders retired from a deck that was slippery with spray to the dining saloon to recite their prayers. In spite of the drunken roll of the ship, they knelt, prostrate, heads toward Mecca, to chant the prescribed *suras*. They prayed again at nightfall and at dawn and at midday and at midafternoon and again at sunset—five times in all. In between prayers they fingered their amber prayer beads, and because it was the month of Ramadan, from sun-up to sundown they neither smoked, nor ate, nor drank. They were an austere company of men, given to much harsh expostulation among themselves, and yet pleasant enough traveling companions. They delighted in telling me discursive legends about my name-sake, Leila, and her lover Majnoun, now taking their places in the heavens as Sirius and Betelgeuse, and they entertained Kippy with dramatic tales about helpful jinn and wicked *giaours*—that Kippy could also be classified as a *giaour* seemed not to occur either to storyteller or listener.

The monsoon winds blew over, and the *Dwarka* steamed ahead in fine weather past the salt-heaped island of Hormuz and the narrow Hormuz straits, and then ran down along the Trucial Oman coast toward the desert sheikdom of Dubai. The sun had just risen when we moored in the lee of the harbor curve of Dubai. The fretwork of the town, its minarets and mud walls and watchtower, rose like a mirage from the scimitarlike sweep of the littoral, with the pale sand of the desert stretching away on either side in sunbleached levels to the horizon. The third mate, who doubled as purser, announced that no one could go ashore other than five of the Arab traders who had been "cleared."

And what about me? I asked. Could I go?

"Certainly not," he said. But why? It was against the ship's policy to assume such a responsibility, he said—the vague arglebargle of a man who doesn't really know the reason but can't bear not to know—and he asked wearily why I wanted to go when there was nothing to see, nothing to do. Take his word for it, he'd been up and down the Persian Gulf for ten years and there was nothing, absolutely nothing, worth while in these little ports. His ideas were, of course, not my ideas, and the moment I saw the launch come bobbing out for the chosen five, I asked the traders to smuggle me aboard. Willingly they would render such a simple service, they said, and with their natural passion for intrigue of any sort, they had, before the launch wheezed alongside, outfitted me in one of their long white *abbayahs,* with a checkered red *kefiyeh* and black *aghal* for my head. Kippy? All too simple. They would shield him from view with their robes.

Everything went according to plan. One of the traders, Sherif, engaged the attention of the sailor on watch while I hurried down the iron gangway into the sheltering cockpit of the launch. Then, with Kippy concealed in their midst, the five traders swept down the gangway, and with Kippy still invisible, they leaped aboard. The launch spurted off with a roar.

Sherif and the four other traders politely waved aside my thanks.

"We did it with pleasure."

"It is not worth mentioning."

"To serve you is an honor," Sherif said, letting his orange prayer beads click and slip through his right hand. "We are obliged for your company." They returned to chatting with each other in Arabic; it was a thick, guttural speech which gave the impression that every throat clearing was a word. After a while, Sherif, the evident spokesman of the group, asked me whether I would consider it amiss if, as I was not meeting anyone in Dubai, he should escort Kippy and me for the day. "It would be better," he said, before I could answer. "There is only one European lady in town, a so very old doctor with a wooden leg. Only one European lady. You, so young, alone . . ." He paused delicately. The implications were such that they hardly needed to be stressed.

"Thank you," said I. What could be better? How thoughtful. How kind.

"A pleasure, I assure you," he replied. "That is," he added in a fatalistic aside, "if God permits us to arrive in safety."

The other traders murmured ceremoniously, "Please God let us arrive well." There was something mesmeric about these formalities of speech. I found myself reshaping my own casual phrases into more elaborate rhetoric—how far we are still from the land, how fortunate that the sea is so tranquil—that sort of thing.

The throbbing engines of the launch were cut off. We glided into the inlet between the breakwater and the quay; the water, agitated by our arrival, wavering back to glassy smoothness almost immediately, supporting and reflecting a myriad of boats—the familiar square-sterned *dhows;* lovely, driftwood-colored boats, nail-studded, with long and slender hulls and rounded bowsprits; canoes; and boat-shaped bundles of reeds hollowed out like birds' nests. We tied up to an iron ring at the crumbling landing stage near a steep-staired watchtower.

The landing stage was enclosed in a cavern of concrete with a rounded archway that led out to a gray sand street flecked with rind and refuse, a sinuous passageway flanked by windowless walls of mud and screened from the light of the sky by a canopy of wooden gutters overhead. Out of necessity we walked in a single file along this alley. Rapidly twisting and turning, we met no one until the alley unexpectedly debouched into the *souk,* which was unlike any other market place I had ever seen. It was mud-walled and shadowy beneath a wattle thatch—a cool, smoky mole burrow with a blinding bright square at the far end where it tunneled through to an open courtyard. There was a charred, burned-meat, roses-after-rain smell, a general hubbub of noise, and again the feeling, which I never got used to in the East, of unreality, of a *tableau vivant* to amuse the senses and the mind.

Shallow cubicles, cut into one of the lateral walls, served as shop booths. Their shuttered doors, instead of being flush with the level of the sand street, were a yard above it, broaching a long, wooden ledge on which the merchants squatted, everything in their dark dispensaries within arm's reach. An enterprising baker had used his cubicle for an oven and was shoveling large, flat pads of dough into its fiery maw, pulling them out again and spearing the baked *khubz* like quoits on a pole. Near him, in the aura of scalding heat, a public scribe sat sideways in a chair carefully inscribing Arabic calligraphy onto rough yellow paper with a ball-point pen.

The opposite wall had been partitioned off into open-fronted chambers, divided one from the other by wattle screens. Here the ironmonger, the butcher, the copper and brass smiths, the cabinet-maker with a display of nail-studded chests, and the chandlers had set up trade. Next to the brass smith was a clothier's stall with the only English sign in the *souk:* "DIAMOND TAILORS, Gent's Outfitter, Cutter and Dressmaker." Street sellers were stationed in front of most of the stalls and cubicles, sellers of camel bells and tomatoes and cheese and water pipes and dusty grapes and onions and tubs of dates. Frail-legged, creamy-furred donkeys twinkled by, laden with goatskin water bags.

The people who moved about were like shadows, tipped here and there with soft light. A crowd moved forward to embrace and welcome Sherif and the four traders. One by one they came—men in long white robes and quilted skullcaps; men wearing European oddments; men with sashed gowns of striped silk, their heads shawled with ball-fringed, cambric *kefiyehs;* men with rectangular black and gold *aghals;* Hadjis, who had completed their pilgrimage to Mecca, with white-topped tarbooshes; a man with a falcon chained to his wrist; another with a splendid vermilion cape; several trailing the elegance of gold-embroidered black camel's-hair cloaks. They were men with strong, sharp faces, their eyes rimmed with kohl, or antimony, against the desert sun. All of them carried rifles, and since no enemy tribes or camel thieves appeared for them to shoot at, they spent the day intermittently firing at invisible targets in the clouds, with every high-flying eagle or kite receiving an ear-splitting, gun-cracking salute.

The four traders departed with fervent cries of *Allah ysallmak* (God keep you), and Sherif proposed that I accompany him while he attended to a few business transactions. Leading Kippy by the hand, he strode ahead into one of the open-fronted chambers, the shop of a saddler named Wahed that was crowded with harnesses and bridles and saddles smelling faintly of the excrement in which they had been tanned, and decorated with turquoise beads to avert the malediction of the Evil Eye.

Wahed accorded us the most gracious of salutations and brought out two goatskin hassocks for Kippy and me to sit on while he examined the pearls that Sherif had brought him. Sherif undid a chamois pouch and gently spilled the pearls onto a brass tray. Wahed glanced at them. He turned to me. "It is regrettable that the Gulf no longer produces the fine pearls that it used to," he said. Sherif smiled amicably and toyed with his amber beads. I could see that this, like all Eastern transactions, was going to be an unhurried affair.

Because it was Ramadan, an offering of coffee and sweetmeats was out of the question, but Wahed was not the man to worry about a ritual restraint on smoking. He clapped his hands, summoning a yellow-gowned servant, who hurried off to fetch a box of Egyptian cigarettes. Wahed glanced at the pearls and pushed a pinkish one to one side. Sherif said something to him in Arabic, and Wahed picked the pink pearl up, examined it and replaced it with the others. The servant returned with cigarettes that were rolled in black paper. He was followed by a squarely built man, an Arabic Henry VIII, who left a saddle girth to be repaired. As he gave the girth to Wahed, I noticed that his right hand had been severed at the wrist. Kippy also observed this.

"Excuse me," he said. "What happened to his hand?"

"The which hand?" asked Wahed.

"*His* hand, sir." Kippy pointed in the direction the squarely built man had gone.

Wahed walked over to Kippy and dramatically unsheathed his *sikeen* from its silver scabbard. "Feel it," he said to Kippy. "Like a razor, yes?" Kippy nodded. Wahed rubbed the curved blade between his fingers. "It is a good rule. Anyone sees gold and picks him up the police-soldiers say, 'Which hand you pick him up with, hey? Right hand? So . . .'" In a fearful pantomime, he swung the *sikeen* through the air with a vicious, chopping gesture. "See? No more right hand for the thief. Right hand is finished. It is a good rule." Smiling broadly, he moved a camel saddle away from the brass tray and, sitting down with his gold-embroidered cloak swirling about him, gave the pearls his full attention.

Sherif cheerfully concluded his business with Wahed. I asked if it would be possible for me to visit the lady doctor with the wooden leg who had spent fifty of her seventy years in Dubai, but, no, I was out of luck, for she had left only the day before to visit friends in Basra. Two of the three other Europeans who lived in Dubai were also away, the banker on home leave to England, the geologist out in the desert. The third European, the shipping agent, was already aboard the *Dwarka,* and I undoubtedly would see him on my return there that evening. "What's he like?" I asked Wahed.

"He has a toilet that flushes. Imported," Wahed replied. "Real pipes."

Sherif and Wahed bade each other farewell with exuberant melancholy, and I followed Sherif into the street. Seeing no women about, I presumed that they were all tucked away in a harem, but Sherif said no, this was not the case, that although there were women confined to the *harim* (he stressed the Arabic pronunciation—*hareem*), there were also others who gathered daily in another part of the *souk* reserved mostly for women but also accessible to men.

"The women do not have naked faces, of course, like in Europe," Sherif remarked. I was aware that my naked face was the subject of great interest and I felt the insistent stare of many eyes upon me, but on turning around I merely saw an averted face or head suddenly withdrawn into a cubicle. I walked with Sherif the brief distance to the end of the main *souk* and through the bright square of light into an open courtyard. And there were the women. Masked with black-ridged nose pieces and flaps that left only their eyes exposed, mantled in black, they looked like the malefic spirits of darkness. Horrifying personifications of bat women and vampires, creatures from *Walpurgisnacht,* shrilling with curiosity—it was no use for Sherif to tell me that they were only harmless women—I felt as uneasy as a mouse in a company of hawks.

Outside of the little *souk* area Dubai closed down, contracted again into a sandy labyrinth of paths pinched between thick mud

walls. Occasionally, from an open postern let into the panel of a
nail-studded door, there seeped small sounds of life from a hidden
inner court—a baby wailing, someone singing—but every sound was
muted and far off until the ambit of the quay was reached. Then,
with the unexpectedness of a blast of wind, there was the harbor,
and the glare of sun on sand and water. I stopped to watch some
men weighing lumps of rough salt on a wooden scale, and some
others treating the hull of a hauled out *boom* with camel fat and
lime against the ravages of warm-water borers.

Sherif made inquiries at the palace, but the Sheik had gone on
an outing in his jeep. His Buick, the only real passenger car for
miles around, was on display outside the palace, a balconied stucco
building with teak traceries filling in the windows.

The day spun out. Sherif had disposed of the last of his pearls
just as the sun was beginning to slip down into the Gulf. "Come,"
said Sherif. "We shall go to the house of my cousin Selim."

Kippy had eaten a handful of dates, two bananas, an apple and
a chocolate bar since we had started out that morning, but I, in an
effort at politeness and self-adaptation, had fallen into the scheme
of Ramadan and eaten nothing. Feeling virtuous, faintly irritable
and excessively hungry, I followed Sherif down a maze of dark alleyways and up a wooden ladder to the roof-top level of the town,
across narrow plank bridges spanning wattle roofing, over inexplicable ridges and hummocks, down steps, up steps, jumping from
one roof top to another, never quite sure that I was not going to
crash into the street below. Sherif seemed to float above every
obstacle, and Kippy looked like a miniature cat burglar. We leaped
down at last onto a balcony where Sherif's cousin Selim was waiting
for us. Selim courteously touched his palm to mine (Arabs hate
shaking hands) and said, *"Baytee, baytak* [my home is your home]."

The darkness had come quickly. On the roofs about us and in
the courtyards and streets below the firefly flashing of lanterns began. The desert air, tonic and distilled, was freshened with a sea
breeze, and from the tops of the lime-plaster minarets the muezzins
arrowed their voices through the darkness—*la ilaha ill-'llah: Mu-
hammadun rasulu-'llah* (No God but Allah: Mohammed is the
messenger of Allah). At the first cry Sherif and Selim and the household servants fell to their knees, their foreheads pressed against the

balcony floor. As they murmuringly intoned the prayers, their bodies and arms rose and fell with the ritualistic monotony of waves gently breaking on a beach. They stopped abruptly. The voices of the muezzins trembled away. The youngest of the male servants brought out a black-grained sliver of Lifebuoy soap and an earthen pitcher. Following the lead of my hosts, I held out my hands, then my feet, to be wet and rinsed. There was no need for a towel. The water evaporated from my skin almost instantly.

Selim, a nephew of the Sheik's, was a young man with the violent good looks of Arabic nobility. From time to time I glimpsed both of his wives hiding behind the portieres and peering at me with glittering kohl-rimmed eyes. As it was considered unseemly for them to join us, only the four of us, Selim, Sherif, Kippy and I, retired from the fly-buzzing balcony to the reception room of Selim's apartments. It was a small room with whitewashed plaster walls, an exquisite Tabriz carpet on the floor, leather and fur cushions to sit on, a Zanzibar chest and, in one corner, a huge, white refrigerator, purring on power supplied from a specially imported generator. Next to an American car, the refrigerator seemed to the Eastern world to be a crowning symbol of power, prestige and wealth, an object worthy of the most prominent position in the household. Selim had thought fit to use it as a repository for a revolver, a tin of shoe polish and two saucepans full of yoghurt.

Selim spoke no English and I no Arabic, and as few remarks appeared to be of sufficient worth to surmount the inhibitions of translation, the attempt at general conversation soon bogged down —which was all to the good because I didn't feel like talking. I flinched at the intrusion of the experimental, awkward politenesses, the whither and why and of what questions that were so out of place in this room now illuminated with the light of candles glowing in pierced brass lanterns. Rosewater and sunflower seeds were served, and then dinner was brought. As I sat on a leather cushion eating roasted lamb, rice and *khubz* sweetened with wild honey, listening to the guttural Arabic of Selim and Sherif, it was all a highly romantic and exotic picnic. As a final piquant touch, thick, sweet, sirupy coffee was decanted from a toucan-billed brass coffeepot into minute pottery cups. After we had finished coffee Selim prepared a nargile.

With the candlelight projecting scintillant patterns on its brass bowl and stem, the nargile, an apparatus for smoking tobacco that bore out nicely the Eastern penchant for complicating simple matters, bumbled and bubbled voluptuously as Selim drew deep draughts of water-filtered smoke through the blue plastic smoking tubes that were coiled about him. Responding to encouraging smiles and gestures from Selim, I tried a few experimental puffs, which made me feel giddy. Kippy had fallen asleep looking more like Christopher Robin than ever. Tailor-fashion, Selim, Sherif and I sat around the nargile in that contemplative semi-silence of people who have eaten too much and are drowsily resisting sleep. When the time came to start back to the ship, Selim and Sherif embraced each other dramatically. Selim and I exchanged calling cards, furbished by Sherif with neatly penciled translations, and then off we went again across the roof tops, Sherif carrying Kippy on his back.

We were ferried back to the *Dwarka* on the same launch on which we had set out. There was considerable excitement when we reached the *Dwarka*, as the rumor had been circulated that Kippy and I had been abducted by Arab brigands. Neither the Captain nor his official myrmidons had been quite willing to accept the fact that I should have disobeyed their orders so flagrantly.

"My dear young lady, I said *positively* no visitors ashore. Arab traders only," the Captain shouted down to the launch, and after the iron gangway had been let down and we had climbed up, he berated me in angry little gasps. There were several repetitive phrases—"mucking Arabs," "den of thieves," "murder, and a fate that was worse," "not a place for a white woman"—and frequent asides to Kippy such as "You poor little tyke."

"I had a good time," Kippy said sleepily. The Captain smoldered and ground his jaws in the style of the white sahib and finally tromped off to the bridge.

I sought out the ship's agent and asked him if it were really true that he owned the solitary *toilette* in Dubai. Although the Gallicism was admittedly strained in its archness, the shipping agent caught on right away to what I meant and said, Lord, yes, it was true, and a bloody awful time he'd had of it with everyone visiting him just to hear it flush. Unfortunately, I could detain him no longer as a raconteur, for the ship's whistle blew, signaling our imminent departure.

CHAPTER NINETEEN

The Road to Beirut

THE *Dwarka* turned into the muddy Shatt-Al-Arab River and headed for Basra. There was land on either side—the land of Ur and Chaldea, of Sumer and Akkad, a land that had cradled civilization and witnessed the luxuries and the licentiousness of Babylonia and Assyria. Out of the detritus of memory I scooped up names and let them sift again through my mind—Hammurabi, Nebuchadnezzar, Tiglathpileser, Assurbanipal, those kings and conquerors with crisp, curled beards and cruel faces.

The date palms, with dark fronds fanning from squat orange trunks, rolled by, and then, far away, there was Basra, the Bassorah of the Arabian Nights, with smokestacks now instead of domed palaces. Tranquillity left off, vanished in the rush of passengers to the rail side, the boarding of the pilot, the distraction of readying luggage and passports for examination, the exchanging of rupees and annas for dinars and fils. Transformed by arrival from sanctuary to restraint, the *Dwarka* was now to be hurried from, to be left with no more regret than a streetcar or subway.

On the wharf, all was a tempestuous tohu-bohu—the echoing, muddled complexity of the Customs Shed; the company of gabbling officials with their stamps and forms and pieces of chalk; the minnowlike darting of the ragged, turbaned porters and the rattling of their trundle carts across the cobblestoned pier; street-corner loafers rushing forward to offer their services as dragomen; taxi drivers popping out over the sides of their cabs, wheedling and beckoning, pounding and squeezing their hooters to attract attention, and the porters gibbering and scrapping with them and me over tips and commissions. With a clutch of nostalgia, I remembered the peaceful arrivals of the *California*.

Kippy and I were crammed at last into the hot and smelly interior of a taxi. Where did we intend to go? I didn't know. An exploratory excursion about town and suburbs yielded nothing evocative of the glories of Cyrus and Sennacherib, nor any intimation of the mysteries of the great god Marduk, or of the passionate Ishtar, or of the moon god Sin. The impetus to linger in Basra to see the tomb of Sindbad, the famous emissary of Harun al-Rashid, was gone. I decided to leave at once for Bagdad, and back we headed the way we had come—along dusty roads bordered with carob and fig trees, past neat stucco houses with tiled roofs, past the primness of gardens and clubs, and through the shabby gray town with its gowned and veiled population and the smell of corn roasting on charcoal braziers.

I arrived at the station in time to claim a compartment on the night train to Bagdad. The man at the counter was vastly amused by the vocal horrors of my foreign speech. It was not, as I had thought, *Bag'-dad*, but *Bogdodt'*. The train had neither dining nor sleeping facilities. To offset this inconvenience I had to buy tickets for pillows, blankets and sandwiches. The compartment was tiny and stuffy, no larger than a china closet. Kippy lay down on one of the faded green plush seats and braced his head against one arm rest and his feet against the other. He ate a ham sandwich and placed the crusts on the window sill. He made a spit bubble which he transferred carefully from his lips to the ball of his thumb, and for some time he amused himself by pinching his first finger and thumb together and then ever so slowly apart to see just how long a spit thread he could make. I munched my sandwich and wondered why eating on a train should be the sticky and dirty process that it always was. At sunset the train started to rock and sway northward over the sandy plain toward Bagdad.

I had loosely imagined Bagdad, from its description in the *Arabian Nights*, as a sunlit city crowned with golden domes and minarets, a city of frankincense and myrrh and *oudhs* softly strummed, a city of cooling fountains where gardens flowered with figs and pomegranates. I was confronted instead by a city coated with the sickly film of dust, dreariness and dilapidation. The town was infected by the gimcrack and the tawdry. In the *souks*, the East and the West combined and emulsified in pallid squalor. The tin roofs were rusty colanders through which the sun's rays sieved harshly over the squatting, slack-jawed merchants and their catchpenny wares—the paste and plastic ornaments in toadstool colors, the nargiles spreading their tasseled plastic tubes octopuslike about them, the scrubby prayer rugs, the cheap bolts of cloth, the toiletries and patent medicines, the celluloid toys aligned on boil-pink shelves—a scrappy, hideous fantasia. In the streets, camels, disconnected from romance, plodded alongside rattling trams. Donkeys were tethered behind Buicks. The gilded domes and mirrored minarets of the Kadhimein Mosque were obscured by lines of flapping laundry. The main hotel, with the lovely name of Semiramis, was listless and seedy, with peeling plaster and cracked tiles. I sat on the banks of the yellowy-brown Tigris where the water buffaloes came down to drink and the ragged packmen walked past carrying their merchandise on basketwork trays balanced on their heads, and I watched the fishermen drifting by and the twiggy, bowl-like coracles in which the boatmen sat like broody hens. I went to the museums, where my fancy was momentarily taken with the whimsicality of the Assyrian sculptors, who had required that the four legs of an animal statue be visible from every viewpoint. As an extra leg was needed to maintain this illusion, all Assyrian animals gave the appearance of being five-legged mutants.

I walked about the town, hoping to assimilate the city, hoping to find somewhere a quality, an impartation, however wispy, of Saladin or Scheherazade or the splendors of the time of Harun al-Rashid. I wished that I could sense something historically romantic. The Abbasid Palace was floridly and unconvincingly restored; a vaulted caravansary, now housing an art collection, was equipped with iron turnstiles and the sustained distraction of belligerent horseflies; a street vendor sold orange pop by the only city gate remaining of medieval Bagdad—and so it went. There was always something that curtained off the past.

I was eager to continue westward to Beirut, where I hoped that the *California* would be waiting. I found it difficult to explain to myself my enthrallment with the schooner and its crew. Perhaps I saw the *California* as an expression of liberation, as a romantic ideal that, in a businesslike, brisk, utilitarian age, could still be translated into reality. Perhaps it was because on the schooner there was always the sense of living so dramatically within the moment that everything else was forgotten. I really wasn't sure why I felt the way I did about the *California*. All I knew was that I felt irresistibly drawn to see her again, to board her and to sail away. It didn't matter where. All having gone according to plan, she should be mooring in the harbor of Beirut within a few days. I wanted to be there when she arrived.

The Nairn Motor Transport ran a service from Bagdad across the Syrian desert to Damascus, and from Damascus on to Beirut, a trip that was estimated to take eighteen hours. In all hot countries there is a respected convention that as much as possible of a journey be covered in the coolest hours. The intent is intelligent, but in practice it is abominable. Either you lie awake all night waiting to get up at dawn or you travel by night unable either to sleep or to see anything much of the countryside. The Nairn bus left at sunset. From every mosque came the shrill cry of the muezzin's call to prayer, magnified to siren sound by loud-speakers. The bus appeared to be the size of a subway car, and the seating arrangements had been made to accommodate the maximum number of passengers. This had been achieved simply by fitting the seats so closely together that one's knees were cupped by the plush of the seat in front. The driver informed us in Arabic, English and French that there was a bathrooom to the rear of the bus, that there was a limited supply of Coca-Cola on hand, that if anyone were foolish enough to open the windows the dust would come in and the air-conditioned air ("Hair-conditioned hair," he pronounced fastidiously) would escape. And off we rushed through the evening.

Busses, like trains, place a stamp of homogeneity on travelers' faces. As I looked about at the men, they all seemed dreadfully alike—Westernized suitings topped by mushroom-cap faces. There were half a dozen or so heavily veiled women whose draperies dripped over the plush seats and puddled onto the floor. There were, in the seats directly in front and behind me, four Greek cabaret *artistes,* with pale, translucent skin and bandanna-covered, bobby-pinned hair. Plain black bandanna and polka-dotted green in front; red bandanna and pink chiffon bandanna behind. Black pinched Kippy's cheeks affectionately, and Green offered him chocolates and squares of *baclava* oozing with honey and ground pistachio nuts.

For the first ten or twenty miles out of Bagdad we were in flat, between-the-rivers land, the road edged with dust-filmed palms and stunted tamarisk. By nightfall we had reached the village of Fallujah on the banks of the Euphrates. We made a brief stop, and all the passengers got out to buy food—dates, packaged biscuits and hardboiled eggs with furry, greenish yolks. The air was hot and gritty and all about was the throbbing singing of cicadas. The bus was watered and fueled, and its tractorlike tires were inspected and thumped. A bevy of runny-nosed children demanding *baksheesh* was driven back again into the shadows by cries of *Allah ya'tik* (God give you something, not I). The passengers returned to the bus, where the harshly lighted interior purpled the lipstick of the *artistes* and prematurely aged every face. Then the bus lumbered forward across a bridge, past the grimy, riparian thicket of palms and scrub, and into the Syrian desert.

It was hard to tell by the lights from the bus whether the road was hard-packed earth or dust-covered macadam. It was a narrow road. There was no other traffic. The bus took us rushing through the moonlit desert, the land running past us in softly curving hills of dun-colored earth where nothing grew. The hillocks were ridged and rippled by the wind, their rise and dip broken occasionally by the outline of a ruined wall shrouded with sand, or by the silhouette of a camel herd slowly lolloping toward the horizon. A gazelle, frightened by the flare of the headlights, raced ahead of us, streaked to one side and was gone. Then for a long time there was nothing but the moonlit hollows and hills. The interior lights of the bus were dimmed, and most of the passengers subsided in a restless sleep. I tried to sleep but couldn't. I looked out on the desert and its desolation. Generally, travel stirred my consciousness, animated new thoughts and old memories, but the desert absorbed my feelings and gave nothing back. As I watched the sun rise and the road ahead liquefy in a glassy mirage, I could only think how tired

I was and how nice it would be to take a hot bath and to lie down between cool sheets.

We stopped at a sun-baked, fiercely hot outpost on the Syrian border. A guard wearing a kepi and looking like a member of the French Foreign Legion examined our passports, and again all the passengers got out of the bus to get something to eat. Outside the small garrison was a mud-walled café with a white Persian cat sitting in the window; for some reason the presence of the cat emphasized the terrible desolation all around. The Greek *artiste* with the green polka-dot bandanna picked up the cat and, standing beside the guard, she posed for a photograph taken by the *artiste* wearing the pink bandanna. After her picture had been taken, the guard and the *artiste* with the camera helped to brush the white cat hairs from her black jersey blouse. We continued on our way toward Damascus. The monochromatic landscape was relieved by the infrequent appearance of a Bedouin encampment of black camel's-hair tents, seemingly deserted, as the Bedouins were not the sort of people to relinquish their privacy to wave at the bus from Bagdad.

The bus was flooded with the inescapable glare of the sun. As we neared Damascus, the sun-smitten hills became stubbled over with spiky grass and coarse scrub. The road widened. Fields of wheat and barley sprang up. There was the silvery green of olive trees and the darker green of poplars and cypresses. Apricots hung bright and golden in forests of apricot trees. Blessed by the benevolent waters of the Barada River, orchards of figs and pomegranates flourished, and there were groves of walnut and almond. We came into Damascus, one of the oldest cities of the world, the heart of the ancient caravan routes, which had, from the time of Abraham, been invaded, besieged and conquered.

When we pulled into the terminus to pick up additional passengers, I decided, on impulse, to spend the afternoon and night in Damascus and to take another bus for Beirut in the morning.

Kippy and I climbed from the bus in the state of stupefaction a long motor journey induces. I felt shrunken and unsteady, as if I had just dismounted from a horse. Kippy said that he was thirsty, and we bought some iced rose water from a vendor of cold drinks who dispensed his wares from a curving silver urn strapped to his

back. I checked our luggage at the terminus, and then Kippy and
I just walked around.

Damascus was an odd distillation of the old and the new, the
East and the West. An electric trolley clanged to a stop to wait for
a camel with a washbasin tied between its humps to cross the track.
The Biblical "street called Straight" was spanned by telegraph
wires. A man in a red flowerpot fez sat in an eggshell-colored convertible twiddling the dials of a dashboard radio, and a public
storyteller across the sidewalk raised his voice to be heard over the
metallic burst of a whining hillbilly song.

Heedless of the Westernized quarter of town, with its plastic-
chaired cafés and bank buildings with revolving doors, I walked
with Kippy from the bright hotness of the Boulevard de la Victoire
into the labyrinthine twilight of the *souks,* where the defections of
the East were hardly noticeable, for they were lost in the supremacy
of things Arabic, lost in the glitter of Damascened brass, lost among
local brocades and carpets from Samarkand and Bukhara, and buried beneath a mountain of camel chests and furniture inlaid with
mother-of-pearl. After the vast tempestuous bazaars of the Orient,
with their blinding brilliance of clashing colors, their ear-piercing
clamor and their numbing smells, the *souks* seemed strangely still
and quiet. There were no more lunatic caperings, no more inexplicable shrieks, and there was a great falling off in the number of
people about. A man accidentally touched my bare arm and apologized profusely for this infraction of etiquette. I saw a child cuffed
for relieving himself in the street, something I couldn't imagine
happening in India.

Women, bundled up in veils and cloaks, appeared neuter and
nunlike. The tumultuous sensual undercurrent of the Orient had,
like water in the desert, gone underground and though perhaps it
bubbled up behind courtyard walls, in public places it kept out of
sight. The symbol of fertility had changed from a phallus to a fish;
herbalists no longer displayed aphrodisiacs but attended to more
cunning and bizarre sirups to insure pleasant dreams and dark,
troublesome ones, and potions to cause painless deaths and agonizing ones, and powders to sprinkle as a curse upon the threshold of
an enemy.

The market lanes and alleys were covered over with corrugated tin so pierced and rusted that the light sieved through the roofing in tenuous shafts, dappling the dust. Shallow booths on either side of the narrow thoroughfare brimmed with exotic merchandise, each *souk* given over to the display of a particular type of product. In the perfume *souk*, I called on a man named Sayed in the hope that he would be able to duplicate my favorite scent—Patou's *Joy*. He could not, but he compounded an acceptable substitute. It was not quite the same, a little sweeter, a little stronger, a scent so powerfully evocative that even now, sniffing the last few drops, I feel—exactly as though I had just experienced it—the lumpiness of the low leather pouf on which I sat while he essayed a trial mixture, and I see with a rush of clarity the dark cubicle lined with jars and bottles of extracts—jasmine, tuberose, bitter orange, carnation, geranium and verbena. With hands that were welted with veins and freckled with yellowish brown patches, his old vagabond's face heavy with concentration, he siphoned up drops of this and that and stirred them together. When he had finished, he offered me the conventional titbit of refreshment, a finjan of coffee and some *majnoun*, a confection made of henbane, poppy seeds and candied hashish that had the texture of a gumdrop and a horehound taste and, so far as I could tell, no narcotic effect whatsoever, although, to be on the safe side, I wouldn't let Kippy have any.

Having paid twenty piastres for the perfume, Kippy and I wandered on past the shoemakers' *souk*, where heelless red and yellow slippers sprouted from the stalls with the prodigality of fungi growing from the cracks and corners of a cellar, past the spice *souk*, redolent with cinnamon and cloves, and past the jewelers' *souk*, garlanded with dangling earrings and the enameled needlepoint elegance of Isfahan miniatures. Here I bought a necklace of amber beads linked with ambergris pressed into fragrant, deep-brown coins.   ,

The vein of the main street of the *souk* carried us on to the heart and soul of Damascus, the Ommayad Mosque, which was surrounded by tall plaster walls. As we stepped over the high door sill of the gateway, we were intercepted by a dragoman who offered us his services and scuff slippers of brown paper so that we would not have to walk about barefoot.

We followed him down arcades of black and white striped keyhole arches ("Very old," he said. "Like pianos," Kippy said.), took a long look at mosaics and domes as white as beaten egg, paid the dragoman a few piastres and left.

The sun set, the voices of the muezzins slanted from the minarets across the city, and the streets became dark and silent and secretive, all life having been shut off behind massive walls of mud and stone. Arabic domestic life seemed as guarded as Indian domesticity had been public. A chink of light showing beneath a paneled door inlaid with brass bosses hinted at an inner world we could only glimpse as a door would swing open to receive a member of the household. It would close again swiftly, having revealed for a moment a lantern-lit fountain and a slender fruit tree.

Above the walls, jutting latticed moucharabies cut off all but a thread-thin line of stars. Our footsteps made no sound on the soft-tarred lanes. Robed passers-by drifted like moths about us. Like black giants, Kippy and I swam before ourselves in an occasional lantern's pool of light before we disappeared again into the darkness.

The next day after breakfast we boarded the bus for Beirut. Kippy sat on my lap so that he could see better, but after a while he leaned his head on my shoulder and fell asleep.

The morning was clear and blue. There was a radiance about the countryside, and up we went, up the road that crossed the slopes of the Anti-Lebanon mountains, the hills green and striped with stone terraces. A shepherd—in black breeches which were tight-fitting from ankle to knee, and from knee to waist pleated and full as a schoolgirl's gym bloomers—herded a flock of sheep out of our way. We slowed down again for a brace of donkeys led by a peasant who was wearing a felt hat shaped like an inverted U and brimmed by a ball-fringed black woolen kerchief. He had a thin face and eyes like pale ovals of aquamarine. His nose was long, with a stubby tip, and his gingery mustache looked like the comic, clip-on kind. As far as his features went, he could have been a Minnesota farm hand or a workingman from an English shire. Most of the mountain peasants we passed were fair, with no external trace of their Arabic or Levantine lineage. They were big-boned people, the men generally lean, the women stocky. Perhaps, after all, it was true, that romantic allegation I was to hear later from time to time, that the mountain peasants were descendants of the Crusader armies.

We stopped at the Syrian-Lebanese frontier. No one had to pay duty on anything, but there were many forms to be filled out and stamped by perspiring, fly-slapping gendarmes. Questions were asked, and exclamations made in English and French and Arabic. Patently entranced by their country's emblem, a cedar tree, the Lebanese had reproduced it with the enthusiastic repetition of a child given a rubber stamp to play with. The cedar-tree motif, at once Japanese and Christmasy in feeling, appeared on the national flag that waved above the roof of the customhouse, and it appeared on the official seals, excise stamps, labels, stickers, tourist information pamphlets and the shoulder patches of the officials' uniforms.

After a little while the white wooden barriers across the road were lifted, and we were allowed to set off again. We climbed farther up the hills; there was a sense of space all around. The peasants working in far-off fields were curiously distinct, their black and brown costumes vivid against the landscape. A few gray and white stone farmhouses in between the checkerboard of gray stone walls dividing tilled land from pasturage, and then we dropped down onto the Bekaa plain, where I wanted to run my hand over the rich, dark chocolate-colored earth. After the rusty and dry-clay soils of the tropics, I had forgotten how black earth could look.

Fields, filled with the fresh, green shoots of young crops, were interspersed with grasslands dotted with grazing goats and sheep. We passed a Bedouin encampment, and I caught sight of a henna-haired woman weaving something on a primitive loom. Then, having crossed the plain, we began to ascend the Lebanon mountains, the driver keeping one hand on the horn as we sped through scrubbed and polished villages of white stone houses capped with glinting red-tiled roofs. How few people there seemed to be. How un-Eastern Lebanon appeared. The villages that went roving up the slopes of the foothills tumbled into indescribably pleasant valleys where chocolatey fields sprouted greenness, and barrel-fat sheep grazed over rich pasture land. The view was magnificent when we reached the crest of the range. The steep gorges were filled with white mist, the valleys were threaded with a river's mirrored strip, and the roads were splendid and bordered with low walls of cut stone. We drove along the crest, then coasted down the winding road to the hill resorts and the summery gaiety of their swimming pools and casinos and open-air cafés.

Now that we were nearing Beirut, the driver jauntily held the steering wheel with two fingers and used his other hand to bleat the horn and wave reassuringly at the pedestrians who scattered before us. It was now well on in the morning, the sun was golden through the umbrella pines, and we went pelting along down a road that looped and twisted on the rim of a precipice. We came up onto a little rise, and suddenly there beneath us was Beirut, bright and white, and the glorious, glistening harbor. Was the *California* there? Even if she were diminished by distance to fingernail size, I was sure I would recognize her. I felt my breath catch as I searched the harbor. But I couldn't see her. Then the harbor slid behind a ridge, darted back into sight and hid again, like a child playing hide-and-go-seek.

With the mountains now behind us, we raced for Beirut. When we arrived at the bus terminus, I rushed to a pay telephone and called the maritime office, asking for the number first in Arabic and then in French with the savagely clear enunciation one uses for the foreign ear. The operator repeated the number in English, and I felt queerly humiliated and nettled at being caught out.

No, the maritime office said, they had had no communication from or about the *California*. I called the office of the port authorities. They had received no request for clearance of any craft answering to the description of the *California*. I called the American Legation to see if I had received any letters from the crew. The mail clerk patiently read the return addresses on the mail that I had received, but there was nothing from the schooner. At least, I thought, the *California* hadn't come and gone without us—a consolation cold as charity. There was nothing to do now but wait for her to arrive.

CHAPTER TWENTY

Land of Milk and Honey

I HAD GIVEN almost no thought at all to Beirut. It had been the point of reunion with the *California,* nothing more. I knew no one. I had no idea how long I should have to stay, nor where. I telephoned from the bus terminus for a taxi, and when it arrived, I asked the driver if he could recommend a nice, inexpensive place for me to stay.

"Okay, sure," he said, circling his thumb and first finger together and waggling his other three fingers in a gesture of reassurance. He was a young man with thick curly hair, brown eyes, a large nose bending to a moist red mouth, and the rapid speech and enterprising demeanor of an American teenager—mannerisms no doubt purposely cultivated because he was, like most Lebanese, violently pro-American. He squirmed with delight at hearing from Kippy that we came from New York. He turned in his seat to get a better look at us. "Gee," he exclaimed, "New York. I'm going to go there when I make enough money. I'm going to be what you are calling the big-shot."

He asked me if I knew his uncle, who also lived in New York. "His name is Lofti Hitti, and he sells rugs on Madison Avenue."

He looked disappointed when I said no, but he added cheerfully that he guessed it was a big city.

He deposited me at a *pension,* where I was greeted by Monsieur *le concierge,* a neat old man, a bit shaky when he walked, and Madame, his wife, nimble, plump and pink-cheeked. A porter in an apron of blue-striped mattress ticking, who looked as gray as a

gravestone and far too old to be lifting trunks, laid aside his morning paper and carried our luggage up a spiraling marble staircase
to a room which was scrupulously clean and old-fashioned, with
curlicue brass beds and wallpaper of faded wreathes of posies. I
opened the shuttered windows and stepped out on a balcony overlooking the violet blue-green of the Mediterranean. The palm trees
lining the promenade directly beneath us cast shadows like black
ostrich feathers on the pavement.

Madame pit-patted through the doorway, her onyx crucifix with
its silver Christ swinging like a pendulum across her pillowy bosom.
"Vous devez avoir faim," she said, all bustling affection, and soon
Kippy and I were busily buttering hot, flaky *croissants* and spreading them with strawberry jam. There was coffee spooned over with
whipped cream for me and hot chocolate with cinnamon for Kippy.
There was a plate of homemade puff pastry, Napoleons and *mille-
feuilles.* There was a wicker basket filled with apricots and cherries.
There was a tossed green salad, and a plate of juicy, rare roast
beef. Kippy and I ate like Somerset Maugham's three fat ladies of
Antibes, with the same sort of silent, serious greed—rapidly, intently, ecstatically.

"Where there's fresh whipped cream," I said to Kippy, "there
must be fresh rich milk, and I could drink a quart of it, ice cold."

"Me too," said Kippy, "and orange juice, and I'd like some real
ice cream with real chocolate sauce and waffles with maple sirup
and chocolate cake that's chocolate through and through . . ."

To our surprise, we found what we wanted two blocks away from
the *pension,* at a place called Albert's Snack Bar, where the re-
frigerated show cases were filled with clove-dotted Virginia hams
and Philadelphia cream cheese. In the stuffy little kitchen in the
rear two chefs followed directions set down by Fannie Farmer's
Boston School of Cookery, and on the wall by the stove were pinned
side to side a framed text from the Koran and a recipe for angel
cake torn from the *Ladies' Home Journal.*

It was like going from one world to another, passing through
still another on the way, to walk from the *pension* to Albert's.
Everything was very French at the *pension*—the *pension* itself, with
its faded, nostalgic charm; Monsieur *le concierge* sitting in his armchair sipping coffee or Armagnac; Madame knitting a sweater for

one of her nine grandchildren or going over the accounts, murmuring *Tiens!* and *Zut!* Then we would walk down the steps that Madame insisted be washed daily and onto the street, where Kippy would begin to hop over the feathery shadows of the palms.

In front of the stationery shop, dispensing delicately its woodshavings smell, two men with white muslin *kefiyehs* and black *aghals* often would be sitting facing each other on rickety chairs, moving the Coca-Cola bottle tops they used for counters back and forth on a *tric-trac* board balanced upon their knees. The street photographer was at the corner, a *sola topee* casting a black domino of shadow over his wrinkled face. His dilapidated camera was wound round with string on which were clipped with clothes pegs the sepia prints he snapped of passers-by.

Then there was a block to be covered with diffidence and deflection, an area of commercial hotels that provided the attraction for a derelict group of loiterers and hawkers—a scattering of figures tilted against shop fronts waiting to whistle at and comment on every girl who went by; shabby-capped men who rushed to open taxi doors; men who peddled fountain pens, women, pocket watches; a man who sold roasted chestnuts and another who sold spiky sea urchins slimy with gray mucus; and the money-changer, softly demanding travelers' checks, dollars, dinars, rupees, drachmas, francs, lire—any currency at all—to be converted into Lebanese pounds and piastres. He had the odd, stiff-legged gait of a heavily diapered child just learning to walk, and his roving eyes would seek me out. "Dollars," he would say, coming toward me smelling of bad beer. "You have dollars? I buy dollars. Good exchange."

"No, no," I would say, hurrying by and turning up the almost empty side street to Albert's, where the curtains on the glass doors were starched and white and tied in the middle with white bows, and where, inside, Albert's favorite record, "The Red, White and Blue Polka," inevitably would be playing.

Daily, from Albert's, I telephoned the port authorities to inquire about the whereabouts of the *California*. Every day the answer was the same: No word. *Rien.*

I cabled for funds—a grandiose word for such a little amount—and waited. The days went by and there was no sign of the *California*. Like palms in the wind, everything seemed to incline toward her arrival. When Kippy and I set off in a taxicab for the beach, I would look out over the clear, diamonded sea and search for the *California*. Each time I saw a sailing schooner I would feel a grip and clutch of excitement which would melt away, leaving a bruise of disappointment when the schooner turned out to be a fishing vessel. It was a relief, in a negative sense, to sight nothing but the usual harbor craft, the pretty little boats with triangular sails and the trim launches; then there was no expectation, and I would push the thought of the schooner to the periphery of my mind. On arriving at the beach club, I would subside into its simple routine. Fetching a key from the clubhouse desk for a numbered cubicle, undressing, showering, changing into a bathing suit, leaving the gritty chill of concrete floors to walk over sand that felt hot beneath my feet. Lying on the sand, with the sun flowing over me, I would take refuge in the world of the beach, the sun and the sea. I would sink as smoothly into its sandy, salty warmth as a child slips into a protective world of sleep.

There was a restaurant set well back on the beach where you could buy the most delicious fruit imaginable—peaches and grapes and nectarines—and I remember the pleasure of eating chilled sweet peaches, my bathing suit wetly cool against me.

By my feet Kippy was building a moated sand castle bannered with seaweed. "What are you eating, Mummy?" he asked.

"Lotus," I said.

"Oh," he said, looking at me a shade distrustfully, and then he went swiveling off into the sea, his skin as brown and shiny as the pebbles washed up by the waves.

On the strength of an insertion by the American Legation in the newspaper announcing my arrival, the director of the Lebanese Tourist Bureau invited me to his office. My various credentials styled me importantly as a journalist, and the director was eager that my impressions of Lebanon should be favorable.

"So far you are thrilled by the marvels our little country has to offer?" he inquired anxiously.

Yes, I said. Everything had been most pleasant.

And what had I seen? Well, I had to admit, not very much.

But that was terrible, that wouldn't do at all, the director re-

monstrated, shaking his head. He rapped out a command to his
secretary, who clicked out of the office and came back a few minutes
later with an enormous man in a khaki uniform who was introduced
by the director as Colonel Halim, Chief of Police. The colonel
acknowledged my presence with an august bow.

"The colonel shall be your guide. He shall show you our beautiful country as it should be seen," the director said. "No, no," he
exclaimed, waving aside my protestations. "It is no trouble, I assure you. Are you not a journalist? Are you not eager to see our
country? Then, it's all settled."

Nothing I could say without sounding rude or ungrateful could
unsettle the situation, and the leisurely routine of the beach was
canceled in favor of a sight-seeing tour that proceeded inexorably
as the colonel chauffeured Kippy and me with joyous, methodical
industry about Lebanon.

The colonel was a massive man who cast off all presentiments of
doubt and anxiety from his thick, square shoulders. His curving,
beaky nose, thin mouth and gray eyes were so composed as to give
an exaggerated, hawklike appearance to his face, which, like the
head of an Egyptian animal god, seemed to have no relationship to
his bearlike body. He was a man of sentiment rather than emotion,
the sort of person to whom fogs and flowers and sunsets are always
significant, and although he could, on occasion, bawl with rage or
be needlessly vehement over something quite trifling, he was for
the most part sumptuously happy, a man of immense good will and
hearty camaraderie. As we embarked each day on the "little pro-
gram" he had arranged, he hunched down over the wheel to enjoy
the scenery as if it were a particularly delicious meal set before him.

His knowledge of English was as sparse as mine was of Arabic,
and therefore we conversed in French. The colonel's brand of
French was flavored with Oriental richness, adjectivally scented with
the linguistic perfume of tuberoses and orange blossoms. Lebanon
was *"une terre divine, pleine de beautés et de merveilles."* And in
a land where rocks and stones abounded, he solemnly asserted that
*"chaque pierre arrête le voyageur passif, reveille des souvenirs,
libère des songes, évoque enfin un passe prodigieux de conquêtes,
de légendes, de beauté et de gloire."*

Sometimes the wonders and the glory defied articulation, and he would burst into a tune from *Carmen* or *Faust* which he delivered in a roaring, *la-la-la*-ing baritone. If the road map were handy he used this as a baton; if not, he pounded out the rhythm on the top of the dashboard with his fist.

We drove northward along the coastal road from Beirut to Djounieh; to Byblos, to Chekka, to Tripoli and down to Ehden, Bcharre and the Cedars; to Afka, to Harissa, to Broumana, to Aley, to Bhamdoun, to Ain Sofar, to Dhour Choueir, to Beit-Mery, and to Zahlé; we crossed the Bekaa plain to the ruins of Baalbek; we drove south to Beit-ed-dine and to Djezzine and along the coast to Sidon and to Tyre.

At the dead, melancholy city of Tyre, I kicked along the beach looking for the purple murex shells from which Tyrian purple had come, and, finding none, I watched fishermen spreading their cork-floated seines on the sand.

At Château de Beaufort, a fortressed castle occupied by Saladin and the Crusaders, I sat beneath tawny walls slitted for arrow shooting and gazed across at the snowy summit of Mount Hermon.

At Djezzine, the colonel bought Kippy one of the local specialties —a knife with an enamel handle fashioned in the shape of a bird, and beneath a grape arbor by a waterfall Kippy played mumblety-peg, the colonel ate a confection of honey, nuts, cream, sirup and pastry, and I ate black olives and cheese.

Racing up to the snow-dusted peaks of mountains and then coasting down corkscrew slopes into rolling hills planted with fruit orchards and olive groves, we traced a meteoric course over the countryside. We drove through desert plains and past icy water-falls, going from one extreme to another in less than a day, the landscape laid down as unevenly as Lebanon's historical palimpsest.

The beautiful sliver of Lebanon lay between Europe and Asia like a compass needle with affinities for any direction, belonging to nowhere, having belonged to so many—to the Phoenicians, the Babylonians, the Assyrians, the Hittites, the Persians, the Greeks, the Romans, the Turks, the Crusaders, the Moguls, the French— seesawing finally in self-government between Christian and Moslem control, a form of administration that was not a simple duality of power but a battle for power by a multiplicity of sects. Maronites and Protestants, Syrian and Greek and Armenian Catholics on the

Christian side, and on the Moslem side warring factions of Druses, Sunnis, Shiahs and Metoiles and those who enjoyed an intermediate existence between.

The colonel cared nothing for political complexities, and, faced with the landscape's pastoral serenity, the glorious mountains and the tidy utopia of a countryside unblemished by poverty, he sang exuberantly and foundered himself with the fresh fruit juice—apple, plum and grape—that he pressed and bottled on his farm.

As Chief of Police, the colonel, like royalty, never went out for dinner anywhere: he Made an Appearance. To be escorted by him to the various *boîtes*, to Ciro's, to Domino's, to Le Corsaire, to the Kitkat, was to be greeted with unctuous ceremony by the head-waiter and, while the orchestra executed a welcoming fanfaronade, to proceed to the one table that was somehow apart from all the others. If, as it often happened, a score of patrons were penned in by the velvet ropes at the entrance waiting for a table, the occasion would be sweetened, and good humor would emanate from the colonel like a cloud of steam as the waiters ostentatiously disengaged the napkins from their starchy bishop's miter folds. While the waiters scurried about us like waltzing mice proffering butter-balls and ice water, the colonel would settle back and recite to me his favorite verses of Lamartine, or we would talk about Lebanon, the only subject that we both seemed to have in common. He was so at pains to be helpful to me, so benevolent, that I felt ashamed of myself for being so weary of his company. As the evening wore on, I would catch myself in more and more frequent yawns, which I would convert into increasingly falser and brighter smiles. The thin second hand of the colonel's wristwatch would swing about the dial, giving the illusion that time was passing. But there was no time. There was only space—space filled with the hearty, benevolent colonel.

At last a letter came from Hal. When the secretary at the legation handed me the envelope with Hal's writing on it, I suddenly didn't want to open it. Suppose they had changed their minds and weren't coming to Beirut? What then? I ripped the letter open, skimmed through it first and then read it over slowly. It was a depressing letter. Six days out of Aden they had run into a sandstorm. The

California's rigging and masts had been sprung. Sand filtering into the engine had "really screwed it up." Sails and equipment were in poor condition. The crew were "flat broke after shelling out for repairs in Port Sudan." They were sailing that night for Port Said. "Cross your fingers that we make it. We're expecting headwinds all the way. So long. Hal."

The letter had been written ten days before. I immediately cabled the American and British consulates in Port Said. Had the *California* arrived? If not, was there any word of her? The replies came back in the negative. No word of the *California* since she left Sudan.

For a week I lived a suspended existence. I was muddled, worried, apprehensive, jittery, attending to the mechanics of living without noticing, and then news came from the British Consulate that the *California* had arrived safely in Port Said, and a letter from Vic came saying that the Sphinx was peachy; that a friend of Art's, a provisional crew member, was aboard; that they would arrive in Beirut soon—"but don't hold your breath."

We shall prepare a good welcome for the little boat, the colonel said. He loved projects, and he outdid himself over the arrival plans for the *California.* He had a special Lebanese flag made—it would never do for the schooner to be without one. He arranged things so that when the Coast Guard lookout sighted the *California,* the port captain's office would be notified and the pilot boat dispatched instantly to escort her into the harbor. He even arranged for the customary harbor fees to be waived.

Everything turned out as he had planned. When the *California* arrived, and the colonel telephoned me, I was in the bathtub. By the time I reached the quay, the schooner was moored, the Lebanese flag was fluttering from her main shroud, and the colonel had already arranged for haul-out facilities, the use of a darkroom for Art, and the services of a veterinarian for Scupper, who was badly in need of a pedicure.

I was in a frenzy of happiness. Kippy and I leaped aboard the dear, familiar *Cal.* Laughing and crying and talking all at once, I hugged and kissed the crew. The great occasion had finally arrived. I was a bit stunned. The filtering lens of nostalgia had served to enlarge the image of the schooner I had carried with me ever since Ceylon. Now, in the frail, lucid regard of the Levantine morning, she looked so *little*. Like a beautiful woman seen in childhood and then seen again years later, she seemed to have shrunk, with every discoloration, every blemish of age, startlingly apparent. Her slender hull was scratched and her paint had gone dingy. Rust trickled from her portholes, and in the lounge the overhead was coated with oil and dust. But the impress of magic was indelible. I felt a marvelous elation to ɔe on board again, an extravagant excitement.

"Oh," I said, hugging Hal, my head just about reaching his shirt pocket, "I'm so glad to see you—and Vic." Vic swung Kippy in the air and, making a loud smacking noise that nearly deafened me, kissed me on the ear. "And Art. Don't look so apprehensive, Arturo. I shan't get lipstick on you," but I did, of course. It was strange not to see Yvor. I kept waiting for him to appear, the way you half expect someone you're thinking about to come in the door, to come suddenly around a corner. I knew it couldn't happen, but I thought how nice it would be if it did.

The provisional crew member was named George. He and Art had grown up together. At Art's suggestion, George had drifted down from Germany, where he had been studying dead languages, to Aden, where he had been signed on tentatively as a member of the crew for the last leg of the voyage. He was tall and slim, with crew-cut yellow hair and a face as round as a pocket watch. He was dressed in British tropic regimentals: white, short-sleeved bush shirt with four buttoned pockets, white drill shorts, white ribbed stockings cuffed below the knee, white buckskin shoes. He was talking to the colonel in French and emitting little neighing laughs at the colonel's remarks.

"Hi," I said to George, regarding him warily, daring him to horn in on the reunion I wanted all to myself. "*Bonjour,*" I said to the colonel.

The colonel was perspiring, and his face had taken on the shiny pinkness of one freshly emerged from a Turkish bath. "*Bonjour, la belle Leila et le petit Keepy,*" he boomed. "*Quelle joyeuse réception, n'est-ce-pas? J'emmène ce chien, quel noble animal, chez le vétérinaire pour lui faire couper les ongles des pattes. Vos désirs sont mes ordres.*" He bowed to us all.

"*Permettez-moi,*" George said, helping him off the boat. "But my dear," he said to me as soon as the colonel was out of earshot, "*quel drôle de type!*"

"Hey, Hadley," Vic called up from the lounge, "quit yakking with George. Come have a cup of joe." George followed me below. In the general hum of conversation, I was glad, I'm afraid, to see that George was somewhat left out. Sitting on a yellow-cushioned barrel, my sandals falling away from my heels, I listened rapturously to a wild farrago of anecdotes about sandstorms, reefs, pub-crawling Navy types and the girls in the Cairo Embassy.

"The passage was a nightmare," Art said.

"We almost didn't make it to port," Vic said, with the swagger in his voice of one who has had a close shave and lived to tell the tale.

"Oh, God, Hadley, you didn't *really* try to have a search party sent out for us, did you? What do you think we are? Sunday yachtsmen?" Hal asked, with the amused incredulity of a male at female vagaries.

"I went with Mummy to the British Consulate," Kippy said, "and she asked and asked the man to send out a search party, but the man said no, he couldn't, and Mummy cried and everyone got very upset."

"I'll bet they did," Vic said. "Hadley, you're really nuts. But thanks, anyway."

Last night's coffee was reheated, and over many cups of coffee and packs of Egyptian cigarettes rolled in black paper with gold tips we talked and talked, volubly, discursively, compulsively, as if we were never going to get a chance to talk with each other again. The cigarette smoke that had been a wavering, wraithlike band across the cabin spread, and through the enveloping haze I looked up from time to time to see George sitting on the couch opposite us and gazing on with the sort of expression you see at cocktail parties—a fixed grimace of interest which denotes only boredom. After a while he gave up all pretense of listening and read *Les Fleurs du mal* instead.

It was noon before Vic said, "Let's shove." We crowded into a dockside taxi—Kippy, Vic and I on the jump seats, Hal, George and

Art behind us. "Please," George snapped at Hal, "you're crushing my coat."

"Sorry," Hal said, with terrible politeness.

George proceeded to be indefatigably Gallic with the taxi driver, asking him how things marched in Beirut and how far was it to Baalbek and the Cedars.

"You've seen Baalbek, of course?" George asked me.

"Oh, yes," I said. "I spent almost a day there poking about the ruins."

"How was the peripteral octastyle of the Temple of Jupiter? What were the patterns on the capital—egg-and-tooth or rose-and-acanthus?"

He had scored, and as I made some ignorant, bumbling reply, his smile was unmistakably triumphant.

The crew picked up their mail at the American Legation and then we drove on to my *pension* so that they and George could have baths. Madame glanced up from her knitting, and her eyebrows arched like circumflex accents as she watched me leading the four men up the marble staircase.

"*Bonjour,*" I called out gaily. "*Le bateau est arrivé!*" For of course I had told her all about the schooner.

"*Quelle chance!*" Madame waved her plump, red hand. "*Amusez-vous bien, Madame.*"

"Delightful, the French spirit," George murmured. "Her mind is obviously running to orgies. Mrs. H., if you ever let on we're just here for baths, your reputation is ruined." He stopped suddenly, straddling the top stair and the landing. "I've had the most wonderful idea," he said. "Let's have a feast. I saw a splendid cheese in the shop on the corner. And there must be a wine shop somewhere." He glanced at his wrist watch. "The stores won't be shut, will they? It's not one yet." He cocked his head and looked at me anxiously.

"No, the stores'll still be open, and the wine shop is—well, you just go out the door here and turn right and it's about halfway up the block, or you can go to the one that's next to the stationery store across the street. I don't know which is better." I shrugged my shoulders lightly, a little annoyed that the "feast" had been George's idea and not mine.

"Ah," he said, and went off gaily, tippety-tappeting down the stairs.

With Kippy sitting beside me turning the pages of a book of riddles, I lay on the quilted, moss-green chaise by the window, my hands behind my head, listening to the sounds of the sea, watching the three men get half undressed, then, one after the other, slouch off, hands thrust in trouser pockets, to shave and bathe, coming back again looking incredibly clean and tanned, running their hands through their hair to get the wet out of it, padding about the room trailing damp footprints, putting on their shirts, slipping on their sandals and shoes with lazy male grace. I felt a melting warmth, the *tendresse* of one just beginning to get drunk, the feeling that everyone and everything around me was dear and good and obscurely touching, a feeling that was almost always operative where the crew and the *California* were concerned.

"What goes up and down at the same time?" Kippy asked.

"A piston rod," Art said.

"No," Kippy said, bursting with the pleasure of knowing something that Art didn't.

"The yo-yo room," Vic said.

"No," Kippy said, absolutely ecstatic with the success of his riddle.

"A staircase," Hal said.

"Yes. How did you guess?"

"Easy," Hal said.

"Oh," said Kippy, looking so downhearted that no one but Hal had the heart to guess any more of the riddles correctly.

George returned with the cheese, a Provolone—it was like a little pumpkin done up in a string cage—and two bottles of wine. The wine was raw and warm and the color of melted rubies, and George pronounced it "quite dreadful" after the first sip. "I should have bought some Châteauneuf du Pape," he said ruefully. "The new house of the Pope. It's a ridiculous name for a wine, isn't it?"

"Come again?" Vic had picked up a hairpin from the bureau and was cleaning his nails with it. Now he looked up at George with an expression of exaggerated bewilderment.

George shook his head. "It's nothing, Willie. I keep forgetting you don't speak French." His tone was tinged, ever so faintly, with patronage.

"Oh." Vic looked vaguely aggrieved. "Well, you'll have to teach me to *parlez-vous* one of these days because when we get to Paris I don't want the girlies to think I'm just a dumb oaf." He smiled good-naturedly and went on placidly cleaning his nails.

Vic was not to be patronized and, unlike me, he was too sure of himself ever to *feel* patronized. Later on in the afternoon when George said, "Of course you know Couperin's 'Pièces de Clavecin' . . ." I nodded my head in false affirmation, feeling that if I didn't know I *should* know, but Vic said bluntly, "Well, I *don't* know. What are they? Who the hell's Cooperwhatsit?"

George had a peculiar way of speaking: his sentences came in little clutches of italics, in little pounces, with now and again a word like *gracious* or *splendid* that he hung onto, vocally hugging it. "But it's simply too *splendid*," he would say, swooping down on *splendid* and giving it a big squeeze before he threw it into the air. He was a tireless conversationalist, his tenor voice effortlessly spinning out gossamery anecdotes and daintily malicious cosmopolitan gossip. As he talked, he roamed the room, his hands performing a variety of gestures. He paused to lean against the posy-papered wall in a stance suggesting pensive elegance, his chin resting on his bony knuckles, his left elbow cupped in his right hand. He looked at me. "Do you ever wear your hair long?" He asked. And before I could answer, he said, "You should. You could get away with it. It's too Degas-ish the way you have it."

"I don't know," I said self-consciously, but not without interest. "Bangs. Chignon at the back. I like it this way. My hair's down to my waist. I couldn't possibly wear it long."

"Gracious, I didn't know it was *that* long. Let me see." He looked at me expectantly.

I shrugged, smiled, and said it was too much bother to undo my hair and put it up again. But no, he urged. Please. I must. Impatiently, and feeling rather foolish, I pulled the hairpins out. "There," I said, shaking my hair free.

"It's splendid!" he said fervently. "What fun!" And then, almost before I was aware of what was happening, he had taken the comb from the bureau and was redoing my hair. Ignoring my flurried protests, he quickly arranged a coiffure invisible to me and, turning to Hal, asked him what he thought of it. Hal, lying on the bed, not so much quiet as inert, raised his head a trifle from the pillow. "It looks okay. Why don't you wear it like that, Hadley? It looks. nice."

Examining myself in the mirror, I had to admit that the changed hair-do was becoming.

"You see, it's right." George looked over my shoulder at my reflected image. "Essentially, you're an exotic creature."

And so, for a few days, at George's suggestion, I wore "mad combinations": Chinese brocade with embroidered gold Punjabi shoes; a Siamese stole over a batik dress; Indian toe rings on the beach. But my initial pleasure and excitement with the novelty of my transformation quickly changed to impatience with the effort necessary to sustain it, particularly since the toe rings had given me blisters. I went back to being my unexotic self and, in blue jeans and sweatshirt, busied myself with the *California*.

Hauled out, the *California* sat on the ways, propped up with timbers, while we ministered to her. We scrubbed her down from stem to stern with stiff-bristled brushes, caulked her seams and filled up the holes in her hull with cement. We burned and scraped off her old paint and applied new.

Vic prophesied that with luck the engine might hold up until Malta.

"That is, if we don't use it," Hal said.

"How come you're always so cheery, How Dog?" Vic asked in a halfhearted attempt at sarcasm, and without waiting for a reply, he returned to the engine room.

George meticulously coiled and braided line into circular mats. which he laid before the hatches so that no one would track dirt below. Kippy polished brass, and Scupper lay in the shade licking his paws and snapping at flies.

"You don't really mind if I come with you across the Mediterranean?" I had asked Hal.

"It's okay with me. Ask Vic," he had said.

"It's okay with me. Same rules apply as they did before," Vic had said.

"It's okay with me if it's all right with Vic and Hal," Art had said.

And so I was to sail again aboard the *California,* but this time without Kippy. Kippy had to return to America. I didn't want him to go, but his father and his father's family and my family, anticipating accidents and illnesses that had never happened, had implored me for months to send Kippy home. Now their letters and cablegrams had become insistent—I must think of what was best for Kippy; I mustn't be selfish; he had been out of the country longer than it had been initially agreed; he should lead a routine and settled life; he had to go to school; it was much too risky for him to travel on the *California;* he must come home. I gave in and filled out forms and affidavits. I was not really aware of their significance; I only knew, really knew, when a consular clerk drew a scratchy X across Kippy's face in our passport and gave Kippy a new passport of his own.

We were to sail on Thursday for the island of Cyprus, and on Wednesday morning Kippy left for New York. I cried as I packed his things. He brought me a box of Kleenex and a scrap basket and sat beside me with his toes crossed, asking me riddles I couldn't answer. I wondered why it was that Kippy could memorize riddles with such ease, could remember how to count to ten in six languages, could recall the names of people I had forgotten, and yet never remembered to tuck in his shirt or to comb his hair.

He was thin and brown and freckled. His hair was bleached almost white by the sun and his eyes were large and gray-green. There was a hole in his right sneaker where his toe showed through. At seven, he was self-absorbed, independent and candid. Nothing ever seemed to bother him. He was not shy with strangers, not hesitant about eating foreign food, wonder-stricken neither by customs nor places. Because he accepted rather than judged situations and people, he seldom made "bright" or cute remarks, but at the same time, he rarely made awkward ones. Unobtrusive, he had always been ready to be helpful, to be comforting, and I knew I would miss him terribly. I never worried any more about whether or not I was a "good" mother. There seemed to be no reason to: I was happy with Kippy, he was happy with me.

When I cried again at the airport, he said that I should please try not to for it would make *him* cry. When I asked him if he would miss me, he said no, he wouldn't, because he would remember me. And when I watched him climb up the ramp with a lady passenger who had promised to look after him until he was met at La Guardia by his grandparents, and I saw the plane take off and dwindle into a speck of silver, I felt a terrible tugging hollow in my stomach and a great sadness.

That afternoon I packed up all my belongings and transferred them from the *pension* to the schooner. Early Thursday morning I went with Art to the market to buy fresh provisions and to change my Lebanese money into Cyprus sterling. Hal bought the store provisions. Vic secured the necessary clearance papers. George bought the ice for the old-fashioned icebox Art had bought in the Cairo Mousky. The colonel composed a poem for me in honor of the occasion, of which the first verse was:

> *Ainsi tu vas partir sur ce petit bateau,*
> *Tu emportes sûrement quelques bons souvenirs.*
> *Mais tu laisses derrière toi quelqu'un qui va souffrir,*
> *Ton départ est pour lui un grand coup de couteau.*

George pronounced the rhyming of *bateau* and *couteau* inspired, and at two o'clock we hauled up the sails and sailed from the harbor anchorage into the Mediterranean.

CHAPTER TWENTY-ONE

Northeast to Cyprus

THE SKY WAS TUFTED with high, fair-weather clouds, and as I watched the waves running up to us and then dropping behind I experienced the supreme content that I am convinced can only come from traveling in a small boat on an open sea. I was I. The wind that filled the sails blew on Me and not on something looking out of a body. As a child, when I had anthropomorphized everything, I had peeled the bark from twigs and envied them their clean, unencumbered freshness, and now I felt the same way. I went below to make some coffee.

It was the first time since Ceylon that I had made coffee aboard and, settling myself in the galley corner, I savored all the ritual of remembrance. Navy mugs and saucers of thick white china from the cabinet; spoons from the yellow plastic cutlery box; percolator from the cupboard under the sink; coffee from the tin on the porthole ledge; castor sugar in a glass apothecary jar and a sticky tin of condensed milk with two triangular punctures on top to be placed between the fiddle boards on the table so that they wouldn't topple over. I pumped fresh water into the pot, and then reached into the cabinet for the bottle of methyl alcohol to light the Primus stove, but my fingers grasped air and not the long neck of the familiar bottle. I bent down to look for the bottle.

"It's in the other cabinet," Hal said. "George's tidied everything up."

I jerked open the door of the other cabinet. Oil tins, cleaning fluid, and bottles of aspirin stood in parade formation, short bottles in front, tall bottles in the rear. The bottle containing the methyl alcohol was in the back row. I had to lift it out slowly and at a precise angle to avoid knocking over the other bottles, and in the process of unstoppering it, I spilled a few drops of alcohol onto the counter.

"Please, dear, be careful. I just varnished that counter," George said.

Realizing that George was watching every move I made so rattled me that I took what seemed to be ages before the coffee was ready. I felt wildly irritated with George, and, jittering with suppressed annoyance, I took a mug of coffee up to Vic, who was on watch. I climbed into the wheelhouse and, stretching myself out on the cushioned ledge, announced that George had got on my nerves.

"Please, Hal, you're crushing my coat," Vic mimicked. It was a remark of George's which had flabbergasted him. Shaking his head in disbelief, he repeated the words slowly. "Now what kind of a guy makes a crack like that?" Vic began, and then stopped abruptly, as if he thought better of continuing. "Look, kiddy," he said, "you've got to get along. The boat comes first. We can't have any crew troubles." He smiled at me ruefully. I was longing to say what I felt about George's waspishness and affectations, but I knew Vic was right. For the sake of general harmony we had to get along.

George and I were both paying-working passengers, aboard, more or less, on sufferance. If either of us didn't "fit in," or did less than our share of work, it was understood that we would leave the schooner. We were both outsiders, but George had none of the humility of an outsider. His assumption that he was doing the crew (to whom he honestly seemed to feel superior) a favor by helping them out in the absence of Yvor, and his indifference toward the schooner, infuriated me. George's presence aboard never failed to strike me as incongruous. That Yvor had been recalled by the Navy, that George had had nothing whatever to do with his leaving, made no difference. I regarded George as a usurper, and at the back of my mind (but not so very far back, I'm afraid) was a desire to show him up, to humiliate him. My dislike for George and my pleasure at being back aboard the *California* were feelings which coexisted without displacing each other. George's presence aboard affected the surface life of the schooner, but it was astonishing how little his presence mattered to the interior quality of the schooner. Only sometimes, as on that first day out on our way to Cyprus, I noticed a change, so faint I could hardly put my finger on it, a sense of hollowness in the familiar, like a well-loved song played slightly out of key.

But no one, nothing, could alter my love for the *California.*

Walking along her windward side, leaning against the wind, de-lighted that I was able to walk without slipping in that funny, angling way, as if my left leg were inches shorter than my right, I went forward until I could lie on the deck and, reaching out, hug the beautiful tapering bow. I rested my cheek on the gunwale and watch the frothing sea dip up and down, framed in the rope squares of the bow basket. A light southwesterly wind sent us gently on our way north. We were sailing under all canvas, the Genoa jib billowing out before us. Turning my head, I could read the stenciling on the foot of the foresail—Made by Mun Sang—followed by two rows of Chinese characters—8 North Canal Road, Singapore.

The sea was empty, sea and sky held together by the dark seam of the horizon, the sun being sucked slowly down into the sea. There was the schooner's creaking cadence and the cozy putt-putt-ing of the generator and the faint sea smell and the stronger boat smell of tar and mold and oil. A moon pale as smoke showed in the late afternoon sky. Hal had come on watch. I could hear the sad, reflective tone of "Tune X" played on the harmonica—an unidenti-fiable tune, mournful and sweet.

After a while Vic shouted through the skylight that chow was on. It was good, as it always was the first day out, when there was plenty of everything and everything was fresh. The icebox made it possible to have fresh butter—real butter instead of waxy mar-garine out of a tin, an unheard-of luxury aboard—and salad, with lettuce that was crisp and cold, and a gelatine dessert made from the plum juice which the colonel bottled on his farm and of which he had brought several cases as a good-by offering.

Art pushed his bowl across the table for some more dessert. "It certainly makes a difference having an icebox, even if it only lasts a couple of days," he said. "It's good to have a change now and then. The lounge certainly looks better since George fixed it up."

Perhaps it did. The supply cabinets had been fitted with new brass knobs. In place of a torn shirt, two clean dish towels hung on the nail above the sink. A brass tray, with a circumference equal to a truck tire, another of Art's Cairo purchases, was propped against the gun cabinet, and a pierced brass lampshade that George had bought in Beirut, and that I had also wanted but couldn't afford, stood beside it. The stone *tiki* from the Marquesas, a somber little figure with its fingers laced across its stomach, had been bracketed to a different spot on the bulkhead. They were all minor changes, to be sure, but I resented any alteration in the lounge. Every trivial feature of it had been impressed on my mind with the clarity with which one remembers a room in childhood.

Lingering over coffee, cigarette ashes piling up and turning green in the water at the bottom of the metal ashtray—the habit of putting water in the ashtray to prevent the wind from scattering the ashes had persisted even when there was no wind, although, perhaps, it made the ashtray easier to clean—Art typed out the log, and I riffled the pages of the *Boatman's Manual*, skipping the unintelligible bits about engine repairs and sidereal hour angles. The book was filled with provocative phrases such as *scandalized jib* and *unintentional gybe*. I read until Vic, putting the last plate back into the cabinet, advised me to hit the sack. "You take the same watch you had before—0400 to 0800—and it's your Cook Day tomorrow. Go on," he said, giving me a smack across the bottom—this, and calling me Matey, was a sign of particular affection.

When Art called down to me from the chartroom hatch that I was on watch, it was still dark. A square of night illuminated the top four rungs of the ladder. Reaching up with my foot, I switched on the light with my toe. I dressed, straightened the bunk and switched off the light. A sudden roll, and I crooked my arm about the base of the mast for support. It was good to know where everything was, to stretch my hand out and feel the comfortable solidity of the mast.

On deck it was lighter, and the sails were like sheets of pewter in the star-shine. "Hold her at three twenty," Art said. It was very warm and clear, the sea calm and black and vitreous. The schooner rocked gently, while Vega's diamond point of light described an

eccentric orbit around the mainmast. Cyprus was somewhere ahead
in the northeastern corner of the Mediterranean. The sun came up
at a little after five, and at seven I was still holding the dial steady
in the binnacle at 320. But then my mind wandered. I wondered
what I should cook for breakfast. Pancakes? Skillet biscuits?

Vic popped up from the main hatch like a jack-in-the-box.
"Watch it," he snapped. "Where the hell d'you think you're going?
Egypt?" I looked at the compass dial. I was eleven degrees off.
I eased the wheel back to the point again. There was the sound of
the generator being turned on. It made little barking and coughing
noises, and I could hear Vic snarling curses at it. George came up
on deck to take over the watch. He had an inflamed patch on his
chin from shaving. "Gracious," he said sarcastically, taking in my
untidy hair and the sweater, which I was suddenly aware was inside
out, "don't we look well groomed this morning." I started to frame
an irritating remark, and then, thinking better of it, said nothing
and went below to get breakfast started.

While the water for the coffee was on to boil I set the table.
I was glad that it was calm and that the plates stayed put. The
overhead was dappled with the reflection of the sun on the sea.
Following the directions in the *Joy of Cooking,* whose pages were
egg-stained and fingerprinted with grease, I stirred up a biscuit
batter. Skillet biscuits were easier than pancakes. You could make
them four at a time in the frying pan, and they would be done
before the coffee got cold—an important consideration because,
unless the Diesel stove was on (which was a battle I didn't feel
like fighting), the Primus stove was the sole heating unit. I washed
five eggs and lowered them with a spoon into the water heating for
the coffee. When the water was ringed with bubbles, I waited for
two minutes by the twenty-four-hour clock, removed the eggs from
the percolator and put in the metal coffee basket. There was a
beetle in the sugar jar. I lifted it out with the edge of the towel
and flipped it to Scupper, who caught it in mid-air. He thumped
his tail on the deck and whined eagerly for more. I called out that
breakfast was ready and that everyone should hurry before the
eggs got cold.

The crew filed into the lounge: Hal, dark and bearish as he
always was in the morning, pushing a barrel seat beneath him and

sitting hunched over the table; Art, clean and brisk, teeth white, cheeks pink, eyes brightly blue, with all the shine but none of the slickness of a junior executive; and Vic with his spry, sailorly gait, grubby sweatshirt torn around the neck and a crooked grin bringing out the sun wrinkles fanning from the corners of his eyes.

"The biscuits are sexy," Vic said. Sexy was Vic's universal epithet of approbation—"We came in and made a sexy mooring at this sexy little yacht club, and then . . ."

The crew grumbled among themselves about the carburetor or the generator, which was on the blink, and about the Diesel engine, which was leaking oil. "If it didn't leak so badly," Art said, "we could have powered and been in Famagusta by now."

I didn't care if we reached Famagusta that day or the next week. Time meant nothing to me. On board I was a prodigal with time. I felt as if I had all the time in the world. I felt as if we were all immortal.

The wind dropped and shifted to the north. We made little headway. It was hot—not the burning heat of the tropics, but hot. Every hour I heaved the line attached to the bucket over the side and slowly swung the full bucket back aboard again to wash down the deck, but the water evaporated quickly, and as I pattered across the deck barefoot I felt as if I were walking on embers. The Khedivial mail steamer from Egypt passed us, the passengers and crew crowding about the deck rail and focusing binoculars on us. Then the sea was once more calm and vacant. Hal put a spare carburetor on the generator. I made iced lemonade and sandwiches for lunch, a tossed green salad and meatballs for supper.

The schooner sat in the water and barely moved. "As idle as a painted ship upon a painted ocean. Coleridge." George addressed the overhead. "Why doesn't that terrible little engine work properly? It's a hundred miles from Beirut to Famagusta, and here we are, still *miles* away."

Vic shrugged. "We'll get there," he said flatly.

The following afternoon the wind came up from the southwest, filled the sails and sent us skimming along, heeled so far over that the lee rail was awash. The sparkling emptiness of the sea, its ultimate blue, was annealed to the paler, pristine blue of the sky. There was nothing else to be seen. No boats. No clouds. The sultry

afternoon, empty as on the first day of creation, edged into evening
and then night. When I went on watch, the decks were white in the
moonlight, and wet with spray. At sunrise, far off on the port side,
I saw the violet contours of Cyprus, the Cythera of ancient times,
the birthplace of Aphrodite, an island which now, according to
Sailing Directions, was enjoying a moderate export trade in asbestos, barley and false teeth.

As the heat grew with the day, we glided toward the medieval
fortress port of Famagusta. In a manner not unlike a print in a
photographer's developing solution, the gray stone of Venetian ram-
parts came up out of the mist of heat and took on the shape of
walls, bastions and towers. Set on a slope dotted with date palms,
the Gothic cathedral of St. Nicholas overlooked the harbor. It was
very quiet and still. There were only a few bluff-bowed fishing boats
riding at anchor alongside the quay.

"Fire up the engine," Hal said. With the clangor of a brass
foundry we powered into the harbor and tied up with the anchor
forward and the stern in close to the quay. We exchanged our boat
clothes for our shore clothes. Art removed the fiddle boards from
the table and covered the table with the jaguar skin, on which he
placed a Coleman lamp and a tridacna shell to be used as an ashtray. George used the last of the ice to mix a batch of dry martinis,
and, having plumped the pillows on the couches, he straightened the
pipes in the pipe rack, turning the stems so that all the bowls faced
in the same direction. Standing in front of the mirror in the yo-yo
room putting on lipstick, I could see him glancing censoriously
about the lounge. Apparently, all was in order, for he came into the
cabin and stood behind me.

"Why don't you go and encrust your nose with powder?" he
asked. "It's bright red."

"Powder would make it purple." I concentrated on outlining my
lower lip with a lipstick brush.

George reached in front of me, jogging my elbow, and picked up
my eyelash curlers. He held them up, clicking them rapidly open
and shut. "Sh'd think you'd get your eyelids caught in them."

"Look," I said, "you made me smudge my lipstick. For heaven's
sake, go away."

"Well, you don't need to shout. I can't bear women who raise their voices." He tossed the eyelash curlers back on the shelf.

At that moment there was a thump on the deck, and the doctor and the port captain, who was also the customs man and pilot, came aboard.

"Have a martini," George said, as they came down the companionway. "They're madly dry."

The English port captain and the doctor sipped their martinis appreciatively and invited us to join them for dinner at seven at the Acropole in Varosha, a new township a mile south of Famagusta.

The Acropole turned out to be a tearoomy little nightclub with a violinist and a Sephardic Jew who strummed sadly on an upright piano. Our faces transfigured by the ghastly light pouring down from the fluorescent tubes, we considered the possibility of *beccafico* —larks pickled in white wine—but the port captain said they were inedible, so we passed them up.

"What's there to do here?" Vic asked.

"Nothing," the port captain said. "There's sweet blow-all to do but look at ruins."

"No dancing girls?"

The port captain pursed his lips and shook his head.

A look of disappointment crossed Vic's face. "Well," he said, "that being the case, we might as well push off tomorrow or the next day."

But after examining the engine the next morning, all hopes of an early departure were abandoned. The leaks in the engine pumps were serious, and the pumps had to be taken off the engine and sent to the government workshop to be repaired, a job which we were told would take at least ten days. The gas line on the generator also had to be repaired. The staysail needed to be patched, and a sailmaker had to be called in to resew the mizzen.

Since I could be of no assistance with these chores, I volunteered to do the marketing. I walked the hot, dusty mile to Varosha and spent most of the morning in the central market place, where things were sold by the liter and the dram and by the Turkish measure of the oke. There were trays of wrinkled black olives, barrels of honey aromatic with thyme, bowls of cumin, sesame and aniseed, creamy wheels of goat cheese, mounds of apricots hovered over by blue-bottle flies. Flayed carcasses of kid and lamb, vivid as anatomical drawings, hung by strings of smoked sausages. There were ropes of sugared nuts, heaps of eggs and pans of golden butter.

Perhaps I was case-hardened, for in the midst of this sensual abundance the image of an A&P grocery, complete in every detail of its hygienic convenience, suddenly presented itself to me. Lugging the heaviness of my picturesque basket with its precarious handle, I longed for a pushcart. I yearned for paper bags instead of newspaper spillets, for things tinned and bottled and packaged and done up in plastic wraps and cellophane, for the marvel of prepared mixes and food frozen and immaculate.

After I had returned to the boat, I went to the one fresh-water tap on the quay and washed the dust out of my hair. The fishermen, who sat about with a cheerful indifference to purpose, eyed me inquisitively, but the inhibitive Oriental code of behavior still prevailed, and they studied me in silence, not laughing among themselves or making funny remarks, as Italians might. I meekly got out of the way when they came to fill their buckets, and they, seeing that the stern of the schooner had drifted away from the quay, brought a plank and held it for me so that I could get aboard. And when I came on deck again to stand on the stern, found the plank gone and did not quite dare to jump, one of them got up from mending his net and offered me his hand, averting his eyes to show that he was not being familiar.

I picked my way across the quay and, passing through the harbor gate, entered the walled area of Famagusta. The scene was pleasant rather than exciting. The immensely thick walls, the bastions, the Land Gate with its vaulted interior and dungeons, the Sea Gate with its iron portcullis guarded by the winged lion of St. Mark, the rock-hewn fosse, were all much as they must have been four hundred years before.

But of the private mansions and palaces of the once fabulous and scandalous city there was little trace. White-muzzled donkeys were tethered to the crumbled stone of ruined churches, and children full of games and laughter ran shrieking about piles of stone cannon balls. A sober little boy with a shaven head walked up and down a path of hen-scratched dust flying a yellow kite but not looking at it. Camels and goats cropped the withered grass along the walls. A few blue-tufted thistles and squills pushed themselves out of the drought-cracked earth. The Turkish families who lived within the walls existed quietly in their flat-roofed shacks, tended their kitchen gardens, sipped coffee in the shade of ragged date palms and black-podded carobs, played *belote* and attended prayers at the Cathedral of St. Nicholas, which had been converted into a mosque by the addition of a minaret to one of the Gothic towers and by a general redecoration of its interior.

Outside St. Nicholas a swarm of goldfinches had settled in a syca-more tree, and beneath the drooping leaves a woman sat knitting. Her necklace of gold coins sent white circles of light spinning on the ground. I stamped out my half-smoked cigarette in the dust— whatever else the Cypriots did, they fabricated a nasty brand of cigarettes called Joy—and, taking off my shoes, I went inside, slip-ping with relief from the haze of the sweltering afternoon into the cool whiteness of the mosque. Light filtering through foliated win-dows and quatrefoils fell on Koranic inscriptions and candelabra. A man with a white turban wrapped around his tarboosh—a sign that he was one learned in Koranic law—piloted me about this place where the Lusignan kings had been crowned kings of Jeru-salem. He swept across the Frankish tombstones lying at the foot of the Islamic pulpit, while I superstitiously stepped around them.

There was about Famagusta and the land around it a sense of calm—not so much the calm of tranquillity as the calm of ex-haustion, a sun-soaked torpor. It was as though the tumultuous squall of the past which had broken across the island and receded, leaving behind a litter of historical driftwood, had washed away all the forces of vitality and creativity. What there was that was new had been built out of necessity and for convenience—a mess of shod-diness huddling close to the comminuted remains of history.

CHAPTER TWENTY-TWO

Along the Anatolian Coast to Rhodes

TWO WEEKS AFTER WE HAD ARRIVED, we left Cyprus in the late afternoon and headed southeast. The sea was flat and smooth, with a light northwesterly wind. We rounded Cape Greco at eight, and Cape Pyla later on in the night. This was Wednesday. Thursday morning the wind fell. It was hot, and we were encompassed by clouds. At ten that night we picked up the Cape Kiti light. At noon on Friday we were off Cape Gata. At sunset we were still there. We tacked and beat our way along the southern coast of Cyprus; our progress was almost imperceptible. From time to time we switched to power, but the languid clanging of the engine did not seem to speed us on our way at all. The leaks in the salt-water pump had been successfully repaired, but the leak in the oil pump persisted. Hal morosely took the generator fuel system apart, cleaned it, and installed new fittings. On Saturday we had reached the western tip of the southern coast, and we were off Paphos Point. The sea was the dark, radiant blue of a Ceylon sapphire, the sphere of the sky a flawless ultramarine. I visored my eyes with my hand so that I could see Paphos Point more clearly. I asked Vic if he knew that Paphos was the place where Aphrodite had risen from the foam. "It's also the spot where Pygmalion's Galatea came to life," I added, pleased with myself for remembering.

"God *damn*, Hadley, you know a lot of useless things," Vic said. "I wish the wind would steady so we could sail on one tack."

With the charming caprice of good fortune, almost immediately the wind steadied from the southwest. We rushed ahead, the wake folding behind us in glistening furrows, fusing far off into a lighter, satiny blue.

We pulled away at last from the Cyprus coast, and Hal went below to make some fudge to celebrate. When it was cool, he divided it methodically, precisely, all the squares the same size, five squares to a person. George and I, inattentive of the overstuffed, thirsty feeling that was sure to follow, self-indulgently ate our allotment all at once. Art moderately ate two squares, placed the remaining three squares in an envelope, and put them away in his top bureau drawer to eat after supper. Hal wisely followed the precaution of hiding his share, and Vic, after sampling one square, did the same. The next morning he couldn't find his fudge supply.

"Come on, now, who's the dirty bastard who's swiped my fudge?" he belligerently demanded at intervals throughout the day. For a while he wore a deliberately pained expression of gloom and injury. Then the matter was forgotten until the fudge was finally discovered, a moldy mound, behind one of the sail bags in the lazaret.

"There, you suspicious bastard," Art said gloatingly, "that should teach you to remember where you put things!"

I had long since amended my first judgment that Art had no idiosyncrasies. He had: he was always right, and if he weren't, he never owned up to it. It was a ship's joke that Art had once charted a course across a peninsula and had poured maple sirup into the engine instead of lube oil, but whenever he was faced with these accusations, Art dismissed them as ludicrous—"*I* do a thing like that? You're all off your rocker!"

In Singapore I had regarded the crew as heroes who could do no wrong. It was a belief that I still hugged to myself. Even though I realized their shortcomings, I stubbornly chose to overlook them, wanting the crew, as I had my first love, to be a symbol of perfection unblemished by any reservations. Sometimes this wasn't entirely easy. But not then, not that fudge-making Saturday, when the weather was perfect and the day golden. Then even

George seemed likable enough. Basking in an ambience of well-being, I had a long chat with him about Dylan Thomas, T. S. Eliot and Shakespeare, each of us happily showing off to the other how many quotations he could recite.

Sunday was also clear and calm. Taking advantage of the weather, we washed our clothes by wetting and scrubbing them on deck, rinsing them over the side, and then knotting them to any gear where they might hang free to dry. Art shampooed Scupper— a ritual more than a necessity because Scupper only smelled clean and soapy for a few hours and then went right back again to smelling pungently doggy. Just before sunset the Turkish coast thickened the horizon ever so slightly, like a faint blot on a pen line.

That night the moon was pale and veiled with filmy clouds. In the phantom gleam of dawn the distant Taurus mountains were only a hint of land, a faint, amethyst monochrome. At breakfast Vic announced that we were two hundred and forty miles from Famagusta. "And still," Hal remarked irascibly, "a hundred and forty miles away from Rhodes." The delayed passage got on Hal's nerves. He liked actuality to have an uncompromising exactness.

The wind fell. The sky sagged with heat. Shutting my eyes on all the useful things I might be doing, I went below to the chart-room. A panel away, the throbbing convulsions of the engine obliterated all thought, and I dozed through the morning. When I came on deck again, the mountains sprang splendidly from the sea —ancient, steep, stiffly pleated with erosion, fawn-colored, black-clefted, wild and upreaching in the burning sunshine. Ridged and ruddy claws of rock raked the sea. Sometimes there would be a few white dots between the claws. It was difficult to focus my mind to the consciousness that these dots were the houses of a fishing village. Who, by choice, would live there? Wondering what it must be like to live in such harsh remoteness, I felt elated in my own freedom.

A variety of stinging horsefly descended upon us. A scourge of Ulysses-like proportion, they buzzed and whined everywhere. There was no escaping them. They were horrid creatures, slow moving and obstinate, with fuzzy legs like bits of poppy stalk. Scupper raced about the deck, jumping up to pick them out of the air. I struck at one crawling along my upper arm, then saw with disgust that its carcass, like a bloodied bit of charred marrow, still stuck to my reddened skin. After that, I tried to brush the flies away, but they seemed to prefer death to dislodgement.

Tuesday morning, the flies and the mountains and the heat were still with us. The wheelhouse was damp with heat, and everywhere I looked there were flies unattended and pairs of flies nervously reproducing themselves. There was a mating couple on the rope Turk's-head on the wheelspoke, and these I lifted off with a piece of Kleenex. Holding the balled tissue vibrating in my palm, I felt a brittle, bristling resistance against my closed fingers. Too queasy to deliver the death squash, I relaxed the press of my fingers and threw the Kleenex over the side. But the wind returned it to the deck, fluttering the corners open, and the flies, released, buzzed away toward the bow.

It was a day when everything went wrong. After fourteen hours of powering, the oil leaks in the engine, in spite of the repairs in Famagusta, were as bad as they had ever been. Hal, suspiring on the hatch, mumbled that we needed a new engine and new fore-rigging. This conversational bone was picked up and worried about by Art for the rest of the morning. "I told you in Cairo that the forerigging was shot. Now the forestay is so loose that the fores'l leach isn't tight. And I'm sure I don't know where the money's coming from." Art addressed Hal, who was stretched out at his feet, and Vic, who was sitting, tailor-fashion, close by, studying the chart. Hal crooked his elbow over his eyes, in such a way that his upper arm rested against his right ear, his right hand cupping his left ear, as though he wanted to shut out all further unpleasant communications.

"We'll scrape through somehow," Vic said equably. "We always have." The words were confident, the tone rather weary.

George had a boil on his thigh and limped despondently about the deck. Two of our last five eggs turned out to be rotten, so we had meager portions of scrambled egg for lunch. The supply of cigarettes ran out. In my diary I recorded the time and the place that I smoked my final, mildewed-sour Joy: "Time: 6:57 P.M. Place: Off the Lycian Taurus coast of Turkey, rounding Caledonia Point, the southernmost tip of land to the west of the bay of Antalya Korfezi, about eighty miles northeast of Rhodes."

Supper was a somber affair. The last of the bottled fruit juice
had been drunk. The last of the straw-swaddled bottles of Cyprian
wine, the sweet Commandaria and the Aphrodite George insisted
on describing as an "agreeable little white wine," had been drunk.
There was nothing fresh left. No vegetables except onions and potatoes. No meat. No cheese. No eggs. No fruit. George, troubled
by his boil, had put the least possible effort into cooking. In the
hot fly buzz of the lounge, we ate our tinned hash and metallic-
tasting pineapple chunks in silence, rocking back and forth over
the table, with the *tiki* bracketed to the wall surveying us and
swaying slowly from side to side.

We sat there, diminished by familiarity, each knowing the other
too well. Too frequently had we raked over the common ground
of our less interesting thoughts. Knowing each other's responses by
what had become an almost telepathic sense took away the incen-
tive to "make conversation." When Vic suggested on Wednesday
morning that we stop off briefly at the island of Kastellorizo, which
was on our way to Rhodes, and only a few miles distant, even Hal
seemed enthusiastic about the idea.

The chart showed Kastellorizo as the most easterly of the Do-
decanese islands, and one of the smallest, a hilly, irregularly shaped
island, four miles square, two miles off the Anatolian coast and
about seventy miles northeast of Rhodes. Searching through the
schooner's library, I found nothing more than a repetition of these
statistics. The island was off the tourist track. I leaned against the
wheelhouse and stared at the ancient, pine-dotted mountains. I saw
nothing of Kastellorizo except its steep, rocky hills until we were
almost inside the horseshoe-shaped harbor, which was rimmed by
white houses with balconied windows and arched doors. Waves of
gray-gold rock with craggy crests curled back above the houses. The
engine sounded thunderous in the quiet. It was only as we came
nearer that I saw that the town had been heavily bombed and that
many of the houses were empty shells. We passed one that evoked
a childhood recollection of a cardboard doll's house, with its white
paper coat torn in patches so that the gray underneath was exposed.

When the engine was cut off and the anchor chain paid out over
the windlass, a crowd of men and children, squinting against the

sun, lined up on the flagstone quay to have a look at us. A few women, holding the shutters ever so slightly away from the windows, peered out of second-story windows. They were, apparently, too cautious or too shy to come out on the balconies whose delicately carved wooden tracery was repeated on the rose windows below, and again on some of the grilles over the street-level shutters.

We lowered the dinghy and ferried ourselves and Scupper to the quay. Scupper, a solid barrel of a dog, tough and muscular, bounded ashore. With his nose thrust forward, he trotted busily away in pursuit of cats. Among the five of us there was a moment's irresolution; then Hal went off to look for a place where he could have a beer, George accompanied Art on a quest for something photographic, and I tagged along with Vic.

Children clustered about us on the quay side. They were curious, polite, asking for nothing, just looking hard, as though they were memorizing us. I stopped to light a cigarette, and a man who was standing in a near-by doorway took this opportunity to present himself: Stephen Hondros, assistant to the Mayor. He knew a bit of English and from him we learned that Kastellorizo had been bombed during the second World War by both the Germans and the Allies, and that most of the islanders, their houses ruined, had returned to their native Greece to get a fresh start. Of the twenty-five hundred pre-war inhabitants, less than five hundred remained, and these were mainly old people to whom it didn't matter where they waited for the end of time. I asked how they lived, and Mr. Hondros said that everyone somehow got by with a vegetable patch and a few goats.

There was only one provision store on the island, he said, that sold coffee and flour and nails and such things. If one had other needs, one sent to Athens. Sometimes people made a little money selling fish and goat's milk cheese to the Athens mail steamer which visited Kastellorizo twice a month. There were a few men—not as honest as they might be, he added hastily—who supported themselves by smuggling (he pronounced it *smoggling*) along the Turkish coast. He didn't know what it was that they smoggled, and he found it hard to believe that God would let them prosper from such an evil trade.

Vic and I walked along the narrow, flagged byways between stone houses that were so many shades of white: the chalky white of a bleached bone, the white of milk, of natural silk; houses of white verging into cream and ivory, of bluish white and grayish white, like the sheen of moss, and of white rosy from the bricks beneath. The byways and alleys and stone paths had been freshly swept. In this forlorn white town there were houses whose entire façade had been sliced away, houses that were stripped to foundation brick, houses that had crumbled, but nowhere was there a house that had suffered the further desecration of being used as a garbage dump. No one had heaped tins or bottles onto the rubble, and because there was no litter, the buildings had the aspect of tended and respected historical ruins.

We passed a house overlaid with the lacework of shadow cast by a sycamore tree, with a pot of basil on the window sill and a home-made bird cage with a lark inside hung above the door. An old woman, smiling the thin, enigmatic smile of the toothless, sat on the doorstep winding wool onto a spindle.

"Very picturesquey," Vic said. "Come on, kiddy. I want to climb up the hill."

Leaving the town, we climbed to the crest of the eastern spur of the surrounding rocky hills. Vic rubbed his perspiring forehead with the flat of his hand. I raised a small boulder, looked beneath it to be sure there were no scorpions there, let the boulder fall back in place, and sat down. Vic hooked his thumbs in his belt and remained standing.

The bombing had been the worst on this side of the slope. All the houses had been shattered. Looking down inside the honey-comb of fractured walls, I could see several hearths edged with painted tile and a white tile floor with a rippled black pattern. The *California,* floating in the blue-black, silver-reflecting harbor, was reduced to the size of a lucky charm in a birthday cake. Behind us, the ridge fell off and sloped steeply into a sheltered cove of apple jade touching on the calm depths of indigo that swept away to the yellowish mountains of Turkey.

We started back, following no particular path, but strolling diffidently on until we came to a lonely church which was built along the massive lines of most Greek Orthodox churches in the Byzantine style. We strayed inside. Rugs of sunlight were scattered across the dark stone floor. Candelabra stuck with heat-bent tapers hung from the vaulted whitewashed ceiling, and there was a great gilded iconostasis painted with flying angels, black-eyed cherubim and pale saints gazing heavenward. We wandered out into an astonishing courtyard. Broad and long, stepped to different levels, it was entirely paved with domed, black and white sea pebbles. Each touching the next, not a stone out of place, the pebbles were set into perfect and intricate designs—a tessellated strip beneath a colonnaded walk, a border of chevrons, a border of rippling vines, a wheel ringed with curlicues and an all-over curlicue square like the pattern of a wrought-iron gate. I took off my sandals and delighted in the feeling of the sun-warmed pebbles softly knuckling the soles of my feet with a nuzzling, warm pressure as I walked.

Pink slashed the gray, late-afternoon sky, the tamarisk tree in front of the church darkened, and our shadows pulled and stretched away from us. "Come on, Matey," Vic said. "It's getting late, and your old Uncle Willie wants some chow."

We walked slowly away from the church and the courtyard. Walking downhill toward the quay, I had to push my toes hard against my sandals to keep them from falling off.

The only store on the island was also the only restaurant. A small chamber which smelled of spices and the sea, it was not so much a store as a storehouse for nail kegs and flour, and not so much a restaurant as a place to have coffee and read the two-week-old Athens newspaper. By lantern light the crew, George and I ate highly seasoned rice wrapped in grape leaves and munched thick slices of black bread spread with goat's milk cheese. Scupper, sated with the joys of cat-chasing, padded restlessly around in ever-narrowing circles and finally slumped on the tamped-earth floor beneath the table.

Hal, who had found ouzo a tolerable substitute for beer, poured his fourth tumblerful. The measure of ouzo in the glass was sharply fragrant of anise, and it looked like water until water was added to it, when it then turned smoky. Released from trifles, released from insistence, I felt myself smiling an unbidden smile, as if a smile were the easiest expression for my mouth to take. I tilted back in my rickety chair and surreptitiously scratched my fly bites. I concentrated on scratching them just enough so that the itching would be mitigated and the welts wouldn't bleed. Glancing through the doorway, I could see the *California* riding at anchor, her sails folded cocoonlike along her booms, her lovely clipper bow gleaming in the moonlight, and her ratlines laddering up into the night.

We sailed for Rhodes the next morning. George was below tidying up, and the crew were on deck hoisting the sails. There was a certain numinosity about the crew—scarlet Polynesian *pareus* wrapped about their thighs, their backs bare and brown as they pulled on the lines. I could hear George scream like a bluejay below when he hit the boil on his leg against the table edge. Then the sails were lifted, and we were off.

Hal eased himself into the wheelhouse, moved his head experimentally against the cushion, then settled back, the sun sharpening the planes of his profile. A moody pipe drooped from his mouth. "I wonder if the engine will hold out," he said, and then embarked on a long, gloomy accounting of all the reasons why he didn't think it would. Luckily, his pessimism was confounded. The engine sputtered feebly along, but the wind and the current were with us, and we sighted Rhodes early the following day.

The classic tag aboard on first sighting landfall was: "Well, we found another one." Having made this statement, Vic hustled below to change his *pareu* for what he called his "sexy yachting outfit"— white duck trousers, white shirt and a khaki baseball cap. Art, as usual, was the first dressed, and George was a close second, coming up on deck brushing off invisible specks of dust from his white Brooks Brothers' shirt with the button-down collar.

Art, looking through the binoculars, was the first to spot an American destroyer anchored in the roadstead. This unexpected sight produced a flurry of excitement. Binoculars passed from hand to hand. Hal and Art and Vic speculated on the chances of getting engine repairs made. Somewhere in the midst of the discussion, Hal left off listening. "American chow," he said. He gave a mighty sigh. "I suppose it's a childish desire, but I have a craving for good old Navy home cooking. And it would be damn pleasant for a change to talk to someone who isn't a gook."

"Maybe it wouldn't hurt if we just swung alongside and said hello," Art said.

"I guess it would be okay," said Hal, "but they'd probably think we were Sunday yachtsmen or rich Americans or something and they'd say hello and that would be that."

"*Rich* Americans? Ha. This hardly looks like a yacht," George said, with a superior smile.

"Well, let me tell you, it would look a damn sight better without you aboard," I snapped. "You and those insane little mats you've put all over the deck so we won't track dirt below. I mean, you might as well put up lace curtains over the portholes—"

"Easy there, lady." Hal cut me short quite sharply. "Remember we're all one big, happy family."

"Oh, gracious, I don't mind what she says," George said, flicking his head back, the way singers do on a last note. Vic and I had a sympathetic meeting of glances behind his back.

"If only we could get a chance to talk with them," Vic began hopefully, and then he looked at me with a calculating eye. "Hadley," he said. "Hadley, our little glamor-puss. Hadley!" he roared. "Go curl your eyelashes and put on your tightest sweater."

"Vic, you're a genius," Hal said. "Okay, Hadley, let's go. Put on the black corduroy shorts you said had shrunk."

"And don't braid your hair. It looks like hell that way. Let it loose," Art chimed in.

"Now's your chance, Mrs. H. You too can be a *femme fatale*. You too can wreck, rake, reek, whatever-it-is havoc in men's minds. You'll be an absolute sensation, my dear!" George whinnied with laughter.

"Oh, shut up," I said. "Look, what *is* all this? You don't think I'm going to be some sort of corny decoy, do you? If you do, you have another think coming. You're absolutely crazy if you think I'm going to bat my eyelashes at a destroyer. Isn't there some other way you can make friends with it?"

"With *her*." Art automatically corrected me.

"Go on, lady, go down below, put on some lipstick and get duded up," Hal said dispassionately. "We've got to meet them somehow. They're Americans and they're the only people this side of Malta who can set us straight on our engine. There's no time to yak now. Go get dressed. We'd appreciate it if you'd make it snappy."

Alternately harassed and cajoled, I made up and changed to a dark blue sweater and white linen shorts. Vic eyed me critically. "Jesus, kiddy, don't you have any falsies or some damn thing?" he asked.

"No, I don't," I said, stating the fact in the same tone I would have used had he asked me if I had a cigarette. The peculiar boat level of intimacy on which we all lived was an atmosphere in which false modesty and pride fared no better than they do in a hospital ward or an army induction center. If I felt anything, I felt apologetic that I didn't live up to Vic's bosomy expectations.

"Well, you don't look very pneumatic," he said. "But I guess you'll do."

"Yop, lady, you look okay," Hal said, observing me rather narrowly. "Now just wander about and try to look like the sophisticated New York type you were when we met you. You know, sort of dopey and *Harper's Bazaar*ish."

I obediently sauntered about the deck and, at artistically spaced intervals, struck what I hoped were poses of sufficient languor and sophistication to be consonant with the tradition of *Harper's Bazaar*, but when we drew close to the destroyer and I saw the decks lined with men peering at us with and without binoculars, I lost my nerve completely and started to go below.

"Oh, no, you don't," Art said, suddenly materializing at the foot of the ladder. "Now's the crucial moment."

I backed up the ladder and walked self-consciously to the wheelhouse. Hal was at the wheel. Someone on the destroyer whistled, and a disembodied voice sang out, "Hey, honey. *Bay*-bee!"

"Why, Hadley, you're blushing," Hal said, delighted. "You ought to be flattered. Some idiot over there is breaking all Navy regulations by giving you the old whistle like that. If I were the OD, I'd give him a hell of a chewing out."

We were about fifty yards away from the destroyer when a man in a khaki uniform yelled through a megaphone for us to come alongside. Lines flew overhead like lassos at a rodeo, hawsers were secured to cleats, and somehow or other we were moored a few yards away from the gray steel cliff of the destroyer's hull. Scupper barked frenziedly.

A dozen men in khaki scrambled down the ratlines and leaped aboard. They were all officers, whose status was recognized by the crew but not by me, and there was an immediate discussion on a high technical level about the fouled engine and pumps. George scampered about being a barman with a tray of martinis, and within minutes a block of ice was lowered onto our deck, and more officers came aboard. Three machinists' mates started working on our engine pumps and two portable air-cooling blowers were installed, one in the engine room and one in the lounge.

Someone handed me a package of ground beef for Scupper, and someone else gave me a carton of Chesterfields when he saw that we had no cigarettes aboard.

The commodore sent word that the crew, George and I were to have lunch with him. "All right, Hadley, on the double now. Change to a dress and do up your hair," Hal said. The chartroom, the lounge and the yo-yo room were jam-packed with sailors in white jumpers and officers in khaki uniforms. The head was so small and cramped that it was hardly suitable for a dressing room, but, clutching my shoes and dress, I squeezed myself in. I rescued and dried a shoe that fell into the toilet bowl and, taking off one set of clothes, put on another. I emerged, feeling awfully conspicuous and discomfited by all the surrounding stares and maleness. I tried to be poised, but I kept tripping over machinists.

The deck, which had been familiar even in the dark, was now an obstacle course of lines and crates. I looked up at the face-lined deck almost on a level with our mast tops. "Where's the gangplank?" I asked. "I mean, how do I get aboard?"

"You climb," Hal replied grimly. "And for God's sake don't disgrace us by falling into the drink." He pointed to my high-heeled white sandals. "You'd better give me those."

I took them off reluctantly, knowing without looking that the soles of my feet were a mixture of calloused yellow and grease-stained gray.

Hal threw my sandals to the watchful sailors on deck. I climbed up the ratlines until I was level with the destroyer's deck. Clinging to the ratlines, rocking back and forth, I looked down at the strip of swirling water between the great and little hulls. Gritting my teeth, I turned around on the ratlines so that I faced the deck. A line of sailors watched me solemnly. The ones closest appeared fairly eager to be helpful, and I leaped forward at them, nearly knocking one of them down.

The thought flashed through my mind that the sailors were extraordinarily quiet, and then one of them whispered urgently into my ear, "The commodore is waiting, ma'am." I scrabbled around for my shoes, and then there was the commodore introducing himself, and all the sailors saluting, and Hal saying, "Yes, sir," and "No, sir," and "Thank you very much, sir." Flustered by all the goings-on, I mistook a lieutenant for the commodore and shook hands with him. The mistake was corrected, with everyone concerned smiling vigorously.

We had lunch in the commodore's cabin. The commodore, a brisk, clear-eyed man, told us that he owned a ranch in Big Pine, California, had a beautiful wife who had just built the best split-rail corral in Inyo county, and that he was the father of two young daughters. He was intelligent and kind, the sort of American, Hal said later, who was a fine ambassador for the U.S., the "good type" of American we had seen too few of in the consular and diplomatic services. I liked him very much but was petrified by his importance. I kept looking at the crew to see if I were saying the Right Thing, but their expressions were undecipherable.

Art asked if it would be possible for us to take showers aboard the destroyer, and the commodore said that of course it would be all right, but what about me? Was I also expected to bathe in an open shower stall?

With four men, the commodore said, he supposed I could manage to bathe with a little privacy, but not with over three hundred men. That would be difficult.

"Very," Hal agreed, helping himself to another piece of steak.

"The only solution," the commodore said grandly, "is for her to use *my* shower."

So that was settled. The commodore pressed a bell and a steward was dispatched for clean towels and a bath mat. After lunch, the commodore and the crew and George went off on a tour of the destroyer, and I was left to enjoy my shower. On his way out, Art hissed at me to remember to clean up, and not to, for God's sake, step on the bath mat with dirty feet.

I had a lovely time in the shower. There was a full jet of hot water, and the soap could be worked into a lather as thick as whipped cream. After the cold sea water and Dreft ministrations on the *California*, this was a heavenly experience. I washed my hair, and washed and scrubbed myself, completely forgetful of time, until, above the roar of the water, I could hear the surprised voice of the commodore coming through the wall ventilator asking if I were all right.

"Fine," I called back, turning off the shower. The bathroom was smoking with steam. The bath mat was sopping; the floor was awash; the towels were wet; and all my clothes were moist and splashed with water. Water, dribbling down the mirror-faced door of the medicine cabinet above the washbowl, ran off onto the commodore's wooden-backed military brushes and pooled around a cake of Palmolive soap, making it white and gummy.

Working with feverish quickness, I blotted the floor with the towels, wrung them out in the shower and kept on blotting and wringing until the floor was almost dry. I swabbed the walls, but the ceiling and the spots I couldn't reach still dripped. I wiped off the mirror, but it misted again almost instantly. I tugged on my clothes, which felt tight and sticky. I did up my hair in a dark and dripping knot. I shuddered at the thought of going forth to meet the commodore. I dried off his brushes and the soap, and then washed the green soapy stickiness out of the towel.

I wiped the mirror with the palm of my hand and saw my face flushed and dripping with perspiration, my hair raked with white comb marks. I kept sucking in my breath in anxious little gasps, wondering what I could do to fix things. I wrung the towels out for the last time, straightened them on the rack, and hoped that by some miracle they would regain their fluffy whiteness. But they hung there, gray, matted and sodden. As I opened the door, I realized that my shoes had made gritty tracks on the still-damp floor, but by then it was too late to do anything about it. There was the commodore. And there was his cabin as befogged with steam as the bathroom.

"Oh," I said wretchedly. There were no words. "Oh," I said again weakly. I wanted to close my eyes and drown the image of myself, the bathroom, the cabin and the commodore.

The commodore looked at me thoughtfully through a mist of

steam. "What a mess. My God, what an unholy mess!" he said. He stared at me and then began to laugh. He laughed until his face was as flushed as mine. He wiped the tears from his eyes, and seeing me standing there, stricken and dim-witted, he told me not to worry, that it was all right, that it was just the damndest mess he'd ever seen, that was all, even worse than the bathroom at home when his daughters had finished with it.

"Please," he said, breaking through my apologetic burbling, his face still lighted up with amusement, "just sit down and cool off." He rang the bell for the steward, who brought fresh towels and went to work with a bucket and a mop. I dried my hair and put it up again. People kept coming into the cabin, saluting and thrusting papers into the commodore's hand. I implored him, in between people and papers and salutes, not to tell the boys on the *California* about the hideous mess I had made. "They wanted me to make a good impression, you know, and . . ." I trailed off, not knowing how to continue. But there was no need to explain to the commodore, who was several jumps ahead of me.

"I know," he said, nodding. "I'll make a point of telling them how charmed I was with your company, and in the morning you and I will go off sight-seeing, which will give my officers a chance to fix up the schooner's engine and rustle up any supplies you may need which they'll feel freer to do if I'm not around." He scraped his chair back. "Now," he said, "you come with me, and we'll walk once around the deck, so that everyone can see you're an honored guest. Then you go back to the schooner and tell the crew that it's an order from me that they eat all their meals in the wardroom as my guests." He opened the door for me, and I followed him down the companionway and out on deck, where everyone saluted and snapped to attention. I tried to adjust my expression to one of serenity, but I felt trembly and ill at ease, the object of much staring and curiosity and whispered comments.

"You're doing fine," the commodore murmured out of the corner of his mouth. "If I weren't here, everyone would whistle."

I muttered something noncommittal. I felt dulled by the concentration it took to keep pace with the commodore and to keep my skirt at a genteel level, for with every passing breeze, the hem line fluttered ominously, threatening to fly over my head. When we drew level with the ratlines, I prayed that I would fall and break my leg on the deck of the destroyer and have to be lowered in a sling to the deck of the *California*. But nothing dramatic happened, and I climbed down as I had climbed up, hating every minute of it, dreading the slip, the uncertainty of footing that would send me crashing onto the deck or into the sea. Looking up at the destroyer made me self-conscious. On every deck there were crowds of men leaning over the rail watching. Looking down made me dizzy. I fixed my eyes on my hands as they moved jerkily and implausibly, like the badly manipulated paws of marionettes, down the lines.

While we were moored alongside the destroyer, I must have performed this climbing feat two dozen times. Toward the end, I must say that I got to be pretty good. I even managed to toss off a teeth-clenched smile, although every time I was sure I was going to fall.

The destroyer was the most intimidating institution I had ever run into. The aura of protocol and discipline scared me stiff. The crew, worried that I would disgrace them with my first encounter with the Navy, tried to impress on me the distinctions of Naval etiquette, but their drilling only heightened my confusion.

Naturally, I committed the unpardonable sin of being late for my appointment with the commodore the next morning. I thought that I had plenty of time to get dressed, but suddenly all my clothes were wrong. Either the skirts were too tight for climbing or were not to be counted on to resist wind gusts. I finally settled on an apple-green linen dress, and sewed a handful of small stove bolts to the inside of the hem to act as anchorage. The only mirror aboard was one the size of an average windowpane screwed onto the bulkhead in the yo-yo room. I rolled in one of the barrel seats from the lounge, and by alternately kneeling, standing and twisting about, I was able to see myself square by square like an architect's drawing pattern. I felt someone was looking at me. Then, for confirmation, I looked up and was appalled to see that all my preening and prinking, visible through the skylight, had drawn a crowd of sailors to the destroyer's lower deck. With a whispered flow of unladylike words, I scuttled off to the head, which afforded more privacy. By the time I was satisfied with my reflection in my compact mirror, which showed one feature at a time through a crackled pink and green iridescence, I was already ten minutes late for the commodore.

"My God," Art said irritably, "aren't you ready *yet?* The gig's waiting, the officers are waiting, and the commodore is waiting."

"The gig?" I asked blankly. "What's a gig?"

"The gig's the goddamned ship's motor launch, and for Christ's sake get on the goddamn thing!" He shot me a blazing look as I dashed out of the yo-yo room.

That evening the commodore invited me to join him at eight, so that we could go ashore for dinner. At five minutes before eight a message boomed out over the destroyer's loud-speaker system: "Now hear this. Now hear this. Mrs. Hadley lay up to the commodore's stateroom on the double!" My consternation, and the broad nuance of the word *lay* set the crew and the sailors lining the destroyer's rails into fits of hilarity. Art gleefully recorded the incident in the log:

"As Hadley was to join the commodore and go ashore at 8:00 P.M. and, as always, would never be on time, I thought of a good joke. At five minutes before eight we passed the word over the loud-speaker system. . . . The results were as expected, and all that were in on it gathered around to watch. She literally jumped and yelled, with her hair flying all over and trying to get lipstick on, etc. Of course we played dumb and told her to hurry up, that our clock must be slow, etc. About that time the commodore came aboard and we all had a great laugh on Hadley. The destroyer's crew got a hell of a charge out of it, and I'm sure will talk about it for some time."

Being moored alongside the destroyer was like being at the receiving end of the horn of plenty. We were given cartons of American cigarettes, two cases of condensed milk, camera film, gallon containers filled with raisins and chocolate bars, thick coils of line, non-skid deck paint, spare parts and all the tools and soap and toothpaste we needed. The ship's doctor lanced George's boil and gave all of us booster shots of anti-tetanus vaccine. We ate our meals in the wardroom, and Scupper, surrounded by dog-lovers, was fed in monarchical fashion. The crew of the destroyer spent most of their free time working aboard the *California*. They overhauled the pumps and the engine, repaired the radio, insulated the Diesel exhaust with asbestos, and saw to it that our tanks were topped off with fuel. Even though theirs were the eyes that con‑ stantly bored into my back and theirs the voices that chanted, "This is the way we scrub the deck," when I mopped up after Scupper, I had to admit that I had rarely seen a more likable, generous and hospitable group of men.

"But what did you expect?" the commodore asked. "We're *Ameri‑ cans.*" He went on to say something about what a good country America was, and didn't I think so, and I said yes, it was—it really was. America was no longer dulled by familiarity. It was a place I wanted to go back to, and I missed it very much.

We were moored next to the destroyer for four days. "What peaceful, good days," Hal said, heaving one of his great long sighs.

"This may sound slushy," Vic said, leaning forward against the wheelhouse roof, resting his left foot on the ledge between the deck and the cushioned seat, "but those guys have been so damn decent to us, it makes you realize just how great the old U.S. is. You've got to hand it to the Americans. No matter how goofy and mixed up they are, they're a wonderful bunch when you really get down to it. It's one of those things you don't think about very much, but when you do, it really hits you, doesn't it?"

"It sure does," Art said.

We left for Crete at the same time the destroyer sailed for Tur‑ key. When she weighed anchor, we cast off, rounded her stern, came along her starboard side, set all sail and headed out of the bay. The destroyer caught up with us, steamed past and circled tightly about us. She dipped her colors, and we dipped ours. Then over the de‑ stroyer's loud-speaker the commodore's voice rang out, "So long, *California.* Good luck and good sailing!"

"Well, there she goes," Hal said. "We're all on our lonesome again."

"No kidding," Vic said. "I've got a lump in my throat as big as an ostrich egg."

CHAPTER TWENTY-THREE

Voyage to Crete and Malta

THE MERMERIS STRAITS stretched languidly before us, and the morning was clear, with a gentle wind. The waves danced toward us in serried rows, then fell behind, and the *California* skimmed along imperturbably. Unexpectedly, Art's sharp voice rang out, "Hadley, check the chartroom. Batten everything down. We may be in for bad weather."

I went below to the chartroom and stuffed my shore clothes into a duffle bag and heaved the bag into the lazaret. I collected all the loose notebooks and pencils and papers and rusty paper clips from the chartroom table and put them into a drawer. I removed a packet of hairpins and my lipstick from the lid of the chronometer case and stowed them away in the foot-square cubbyhole by the bunk. I bent over the chart table and glanced at the chart which had our course from Rhodes to Crete marked out from departure to arrival with a penciled line that swept confidently between the black, printed markings of islands and shoals and reefs across a smooth, white paper sea. At the moment, the chart held no more interest than most other sheets of printed directions. Mileage and degrees of latitude were negligible factors in the measure of distance traveled, and the reduction of time, space and a small, creaking schooner to a line so exact and so absolute, a line so complete in itself, called for a finer adjustment of fact and fancy than I was capable of.

When I climbed the hatch ladder and came on deck again it was chilly and the wind had sharpened. The waves had lost their look of order, and their blue-black peaks rose and fell with erratic rapidity, like the felt hammers on a furiously played piano. I felt somewhat surprised, not by the perversity of the weather—the weather predictions of the crew were unfailingly accurate—but by the suddenness of the change.

"Gracious!" George exclaimed as a cloud of spray hissed over the bow. Hal scowled at the sea and sucked on his pipe. "It looks like it's going to get pretty mean," he said, kicking shut the chartroom hatch.

The waves smacked viciously against the hull, and the *California* began to bounce and roll. Waves of icy spray showered over the wheelhouse, and now that Art had rolled down the rear and side canvas flaps, the wheelhouse was a damp and stuffy cabin. George glanced at the water trickling through the corners where the canvas was laced together. "Gads," he said petulantly, "it's like being in a leaky convertible."

Art gave an eloquent snort and then turned to me, "Fair weather gale. I told you so," he said. I smoked the cigarette I had crawled into the wheelhouse to have. The giddy instability of the schooner and the inhalation of a strong American cigarette just beginning to go moldy had a dizzying effect. There was the low whistle of the wind rushing through the rigging, and the sharp smacking chorus of the waves dashing against the hull, and the softer chorus of unidentifiable boat sounds.

The sun set with a display of brilliance. The sky darkened. For a while one sun-illuminated cloud glowed on the horizon, gradually fading away, and the darkness deepened. There was no moon, and we spent the night anxiously threading our way past the small islands that lay all around us. The stars were obscured by clouds. Coming up on deck, I could see nothing but blackness and shades of blackness.

Sleep was impossible. The overhead of the chartroom leaked badly, and as we were sailing by dead reckoning, the charts had to be consulted frequently. After Vic had stumped up and down the ladder three times, I lay awake listening to the clumping of feet and incoherent shouts on deck voicing gibberish like a distant radio.

Ashamed of doing nothing, I got up and went to the lounge to
make a fresh pot of coffee.

It seemed an eternity before the dawn came and the cold, slow,
sluggish beginning of a new day. My eyes felt prickly with tired-
ness, my thoughts disconnected. The horizon was fuzzy, the wind
strong, the skies clear and bright. Waves of spray still washed over
the deck, but the short, choppy waves of the day before had been
replaced by high, rolling seas. It was my Cook Day, and I lurched
about the galley getting breakfast ready, my thoughts retreating
from everything save the problem of keeping the Diesel stove going
and the coffeepot from tipping over.

Occasionally my mind opened to receive a fragment of conversation—Art grieving over the staysail that had blown out during the
night; Vic saying that it sure had been a hell of a balloo all right,
and George saying something idiotic about that being an inventive
use of tmesis. Hal, when he came down from the wheelhouse, was
moodily silent. I don't think he said anything except "Salt," and
"Jam," and "Here," as he passed the garbage bucket through the
hatch up to the deck for me to empty.

Tirelessly, and with patient splendor, the *California* climbed and
descended the waves' great, white-crested slopes. Frequently, the
waves moved too swiftly to be climbed, and then there would be a
jarring concussion below and a hissing rush as a hill of water exploded against the bow and sent a cascade of water streaming in-
board. Somewhere over the waves' summits were islands, but I
didn't see them. Half closing my eyes against the sharp wind, and
tingling with the iciness of the crystal spray, I felt as though I had
just been born in the center of an uncluttered world of bright sky
and clear, racing hills of water.

But when I went below again to the lounge, the sea relinquished
its paramountcy and grandeur, and frittered away to dark blue
water sloshing about three small portholes. I was soaking wet, and
miserably aware of being so, and my nose was running from the
cold. I thought of getting a handkerchief, but that seemed like
a colossal amount of trouble to go to. Sticking up from the bookshelf was a back cover, advertising cigarettes, torn from *Time*,
Atlantic Edition, and I scratchily blew my nose with that. The
water outside the portholes might just as well have been stationary,

canceling all the nobility of the schooner's progress through the gale. There was no suggestion of forward motion; only a constant staggering lurch that set everything rattling and crashing in the cabinets. Every action I performed was laborious and tentative. To prepare three meals and to wash up the dishes and pots took up most of the day. If there were memorable moments, they came when I went up on deck briefly, to fetch the vegetables from the vegetable locker, or to take coffee to whoever was on watch, when I was able to stand for a little while with my arm crooked around a shroud, looking at the sea, switching to another strength, another being.

When Crete was sighted, I was cutting the eyes and the pale green sprouts out of old potatoes, and when the engine was turned on and we entered the harbor of Heraklion, I was wiping up the mess of a broken bottle of tomato ketchup.

We sailed from the noisy commotion of the gale into the tranquillity of the harbor. The sudden calm and quiet were eerie and strange, and the booming of the sea against the breakwater gave an unreal, almost trancelike focus to the unaccustomed stillness. By the time the sails were dropped and furled, it was dark, and the officials who could have given us clearance to go ashore had all gone home.

In the morning, after breakfast, we sat around doing nothing in particular, waiting for the port official to come and clear us. Vic was up on deck. Hal, George, Art and I were below in the lounge. George was leaning against the galley sink talking and smoking. Hal was lying on his side on the couch opposite him, his chin resting on his fist. Art and I were sitting on the other couch and using the lounge table as a deck. I put the letter I had just written to Kippy in an envelope, licked the flap, sealed it by rubbing my fingers along the edge and settled back to listen in to George's and Hal's conversation.

"Why, yes," George said, "because Europa had a *béguin* for bulls, Zeus disguised himself as one, and to make a long story short, they were married. One of their children turned out to be King Minos, but, of course, Minos is only a semi-mythical figure. The Palace at Knossos attributed to him dates back to about four thousand years ago, when the Minoan civilization was at its peak. And according to Sir Arthur Evans, the stone throne of Minos is the most ancient in Europe. . . ."

Hal's clear, coffee-colored eyes traveled on past George to a box of Dreft on the ledge of the galley porthole. "Well," he said abruptly, "I suppose it's interesting as hell, but the whole thing depresses me. The Mediterranean is filled with places like Crete. Everything's in the past and the best is over and there's no future and just sort of an exhausted present with everyone sitting around half dead drinking ouzo. They ought to industrialize. A couple of hundred factories would put this place back in business again."

George smoked his cigarette carefully, holding it between his third and fourth fingers. "Yes," he said, sighing, "there's an indefinable sadness about the Mediterranean. The present always seems to have a lingering ache of the past, an indefinable sadness."

"Look," Art interrupted, "I'm making out a list of provisions. What do we need? Do you suppose things will be cheap? What about meat?"

"Let's get some veal," George said. "I adore veal."

"Hey, you guys," Vic shouted down the skylight, "the port official's here."

After the port official had gone through our papers and departed, I went back to the chartroom, got ready to go ashore and then discovered that I had no money at all, no drachmas, no piastres, not even a stray dinar that I might have saved and forgotten about. Not certain how long we would stay in Rhodes, I had cabled for money to be sent ahead to me in Malta, which, I reflected, did me no good whatsoever because we wouldn't be in Crete long enough for me to send a cable and receive a reply. The schooner's cash assets were so low that we all had agreed that there was to be no borrowing from them at all. Nothing at all, Art had stressed, not even a penny; it was a matter of principle.

Neither Hal nor Vic had money to spare—they had about a dollar between them. I didn't want to ask any favors from George, and Art, I knew, would object to lending me fifteen cents' worth of drachmas on the theory that going without might teach me a lesson in foresight and thrift. In the hope that I might be able to sell them, I dropped two packs of American cigarettes, left over from the days of the destroyer, into my leather shoulder bag, and then, as an afterthought, and just to be on the safe side, I slipped into the yo-yo room, and when Art wasn't looking, pocketed a handful of change he had left on the bookcase. I felt guilty—not very, but enough to say to myself that he wouldn't miss it and that I would pay him back in Malta.

I walked briskly down the quay past all the fishing boats and stopped at the first eating house I came to. It was filled with men drinking coffee, and all of them lifted their heads and stared at me as I stood in the doorway, hesitating on the brink of male territory. I felt my embarrassment rising, as it frequently did in the East when I felt I should make a public apology for being so barefaced, so barelegged, so conspicuously female in a world where women masked their femininity in public and would never think of intruding on their menfolk in a public place. But I sailed in, sold my two packages of cigarettes to the startled proprietor, asked him where the bus to Knossos stopped, darted out again, asked four other people where the bus stop was, finally located the bus and boarded it.

I settled back on a lumpy seat. Wedged tightly between a woman hugging a hen in a wooden cage and a woman hugging a basket of pears and mulberries, I looked out the open window, delighting in the traffic signs that said STASIS instead of STOP. We rumbled through the dusty, shabby neutrality of Heraklion and nosed out into an unremarkable landscape of parched fields stretching away to scrubby, gray hills and a few dramatic peaks that spurred the heat-filled belly of the sky. Dun-dreary countryside, picked out here and there with the gleam of an olive tree and the stiffened darkness of cypress; a flock of goats grazing by the roadside; a man in black and white costume leading a frail-legged donkey, and the donkey braying—a hoarse, retching squeal—as we rattled past.

I wanted something that I felt was being withheld. Hal often spoke of the diminishing returns of traveling, and although it was senseless, and I had argued sharply with him, for a dispirited moment I knew what he meant: to travel, expecting always to see something new and fresh, and to feel disappointed, almost gypped, when one didn't. I held the caged hen so that the woman next to me could stretch her legs. The hen pecked irritably at my fingers.

I was trying to see if I could hypnotize it by staring at it when the conductor told me we had reached Knossos.

I was the only person to get off the bus. At first all I saw was a roadside provision store and coffeehouse, and then, on the other side of the road, on the knoll of a hill, with more hills in the background, I saw a cluster of buildings and I walked slowly toward their rust-red columns—slowly, because I didn't want to miss anything; slowly, because I wanted to make the thrill of discovery last as long as possible.

But once there, in a courtyard that glimmered in the sultriness of the morning, past the turnstile, the custodian in his barred sentry box and the porcupine that had scurried across my path, there was no more holding back. With the tense, expectant excitement of a child unwrapping Christmas presents, I flew from one place to another, trying to take everything in all at once. The Minoans had a predilection for irregular building sites, and the ruins were all up and down, the roof of one chamber serving, in many cases, as the terrace for another. The partially restored ruins covered an area possibly no larger than one and a half city blocks. No more the immensity and the mystic grandeur of the Orient— this was a palace scaled to the proportions of men and menlike gods where only the jars for oil and treasure were sizable. Along scarred gray gypsum walls, voluminous earthenware and stone pots stood in rows. Banded with ropy patterns of a fine design, voluptuous as if still pregnant with the riches of the past, they were so tall that only by standing on tiptoe could I peer down their swollen dark insides.

I walked up and down handsome, sun-saturated staircases, through cool, tenebrous rooms speared with sudden steeples of light and thrust with columns. I wandered about a partly paved court bounded by broad flights of stairs, and I felt a respectful wonder for it, sentimental wonder really, for if there weren't a chance that this was the dancing floor which Daedalus had built for Ariadne I should have passed it by, looking at it casually, as one might any empty courtyard.

I stood for a long time, leaning against a column, looking at Minos's throne, "the most ancient in Europe," I could hear George saying. But it's sweet, I thought—so little, so completely unsuitable for Minos, who would have chosen, I imagined, a far more pretentious affair, and not this narrow, gypsum chair with its chiseled, scooped-out seat and its prim, high back as gently crenate as the leaf of a Swamp White Oak.

Happily bemused, limply moving in the heat and fly drone of the House of Frescoes, I wandered among portraits of tiny-waisted, large-eyed women with sinuous hair and chalk-white breasts neatly dotted with red-currant mammillae; among butterflies and delicate flowers; among goats with swept-back, curving horns; among beautiful bulls as flowing and free as the ones painted on the rocks at Altamira.

I stayed at Knossos until my head ached from hunger and the heat, and then I took the bus back to the center of Heraklion. I headed for the nearest outdoor café, where I ordered coffee and a plate of rice and bits of mutton done up in grape leaves. This was not the cheapest offering on the menu, and when I paid my bill I had left over only the price of an admission ticket to the museum. Feeling slightly relieved that the last of Art's guilt-tinged change would be gone, I bought the ticket.

The museum was the old-fashioned sort—cluttered, dusty, dimly lighted and filled with the faded fragrance of the past. Slowly I walked past the fingerprinted glass cases filled with things that had miraculously survived the passing of four thousand years. Vases of black marble veined with red and white, pottery swirled with trumpet shells and the spiraling coils of cuttle fish, cylindrical cups and fluted cups and beaked jugs with looped handles, seals of jasper and the oval bezel of a gold signet ring carved with birds, a cat eying a frieze of birds on a dagger blade, an octopus that looked at me from a polychrome vase. Standing among seashells and libation cups, there was the famous snake goddess, a lovely little figure in pearl-pale faïence, with a note propped up against her stiffly flounced skirt exposing her in three languages as an impostor, as only a casting from the original, which was in the British Museum. But she was beautiful, and that she was an impostor didn't matter, and it was she that I looked the longest at.

In the late afternoon the fishing boats put to sea. The crew and George returned from Knossos and the market. Vic glanced at the fishing boats casting off from the quay. "The gale's over," he said. "Guess we'd better get going, too."

"Christ," Hal said, thumping the market basket down. "I'm tired. Hate shopping for food."

"Well, the meat was cheap," Art said, slapping his pockets to find a cigarette. "But the butcher should have paid me for showing him how to cut chops." He slipped his hand into his trouser pocket and drew out his wallet. He frowned as he riffled through the bills. Then he shook the change and counted it, whispering to himself, "Ten, thirty, sixty, eighty . . ."

"I wish I had your dough," Vic said rather absently.

Art replaced his wallet and, with an intent expression, checked through the notebook in which he wrote his expenses.

"Did you like Knossos?" I asked.

But Art's attention wasn't to be diverted. "Picturesque," he said, still scanning his notebook. "I'm sure I had ten thousand drachmas more. I didn't buy anything or I would have written it down. I don't know where it could have gone to. I mean it's almost a buck . . ."

"Sixty-five cents," I said.

"Sixty-six and two thirds cents," Hal said. "Don't get into a sweat about it. It'll probably turn up somewhere." He was sitting loosely bowed forward on a bollard, his knees apart. He reached down and examined the fraying cuff of his khaki trousers. "Hadley," he said, "I wish you could sew."

"Look," Vic said, "let's not stand here yakking about sixty cents. Let's pack up our toys and get the stuff put away and get going."

"All right, all *right*." With suppressed annoyance and sudden action, Art grabbed up the Moses blanket filled with vegetables and blood-stained packages of meat. "Here, Hadley, put it away."

I was glad of the chance to be useful. No task was too trivial for me not to feel that it was an offering of affection for the *California*. As I put the vegetables away, feeling the grittiness of the potatoes and the satiny smoothness of the marrow, I felt the satisfaction of contributing to the schooner's routine, and I could imagine Hal saying in some indeterminate future, "Hadley really was a help, even if she couldn't sew or pump the bilge."

Art's spurt of irritation was dissipated in the activity of departure. Whistling "Way Out on the Desolate Billow," he mashed the supper potatoes. We left Crete at six. Heraklion was a filigree in black against the coral bands of sunset. There was a light west wind, and we sailed out into a calm, lustrous sea—wine-dark now, as Homer had seen it.

The moon hung in the sky like a hunter's horned trophy. We headed north and, sometime during the night, passed the invisible boundary between the Sea of Crete and the Aegean Sea.

"Next stop, Malta," Vic said. "Five hundred miles. We should do it in four days." We did it in ten.

It was a strange voyage, plagued with freakish seas and wanton weather. The first night out there was a sudden chill and a sickening, rolling swell. By the time we had left the bay and powered clear of a few small islands, the slight oil leak in the engine developed into a bad one. As our oil supply was low, the engine was shut down. Under sail, we made little headway. The Genny had been insecurely tied, and in the heavy pitching it filled with water, tore, and parted the port-whisker stay. Lying on the chartroom bunk and laxly responding to the pitching sea, I was asleep when a gust of wind blew out the flames in the running lights, and I never knew if it were true, as Vic insisted it was, that we had barely missed colliding with a Greek caïque.

The following day was coldly hazy—a withered, dead day, pressed between a heavy sky and a flat sea. The sails fluttered and flapped forlornly, like sick birds. Art tinkered with the engine and ventured to start it up again. Instantly the engine was seized by a paroxysm of coughing and couldn't catch its breath. A few minutes later it gave a throttled gasp and sighed away.

Glancing down to rest my neck, I saw a sponge floating past beneath the surface of the water and wondered how it could have fallen overboard. I suddenly realized that it wasn't *our* sponge that we used for dishwashing but a *live* sponge, and I called excitedly to everyone to come and see it. But only Vic and Hal bothered to come, and Vic said, "That's a real, live sponge, all right," and Hal said that a sponge was a very low marine order, and that if I saw any more, I was to try to catch hold of them because they were useful and expensive as hell.

By the next day, Monday, we were off Cape Malea, one of the stuggy fingers of the Peloponnesian peninsula. It was a cloudy morning, a pale light covered everything, and by the afternoon, the gray-purple clouds weighing down upon the peninsular mountains flashed with lightning. Scupper looked at us all reproachfully as though he believed we were tormenting him on purpose with the thunder.

Tuesday we sailed from the Aegean to the Ionian Sea, through the Elaphonisos Channel between the Peloponnesian peninsula and Kithira island. The sun rose and died, and it was wretchedly cold. The clouds above Cape Malea were like a swollen roll of bruised flesh. At noon the wind veered, there was a violent squall, and the rain came down in a torrent. I was in the galley when a massive sea hit us broadside. The gunwale went under and the galley exploded with a flying eruption of pots and pans and small provisions.

A barrel seat struck me in the shin, and, losing my balance, I fell against the seat ledge and cracked my head sharply just above my ear. It hurt so much that I was savagely indignant that my head didn't bleed, so that I could have appeared as wounded as I felt. For the remainder of the day the portholes were under and the galley seesawed crazily.

That night it was bitterly cold. There were not enough blankets. Water sieved through the overhead of the chart house.

By Wednesday we had passed the finger of Cape Matapan, the land vanished, and we were in open sea. Greece to the north, Libya to the south. It was a bleak day, smurred with rain. George's spectacles fell off the wheelhouse ledge and broke. There was a running swell, and I was conscious of little else but the monotonous repetition of the bow leaping upward, pausing in a moment of suspension, and then falling back on the sea with a shattering impact and a hissing burst of spray.

"The sunny Mediterranean, my eye. It's colder than a bastard," Vic grumbled.

At last a day came when the chill went from the air. The day started much as any other since we had left Crete. I sat in the wheelhouse with stiff, unthawed limbs, my eyes feeling pinched and my throat tight from smoking too much. But as the morning progressed, the air seemed sweeter and warmer than usual. By noon the sun was dazzling and cloudless. Land reappeared on the sky line— the southeast coast of Sicily. The day went by, a long moment of infinite content. Even the beans at supper tasted good. Vic, as a last resort, had sprinkled them with rosemary and oregano. I saved a cupful of them to eat when I went on watch. I needn't have bothered, because Vic took over my watch for me, and when I woke up it was almost breakfast time.

"Look," Vic said, pointing a black-rimmed finger at a sandbank on the horizon. "Malta. We found another one."

CHAPTER TWENTY-FOUR

Malta

THE BRITISH CROWN COLONY of Malta drew nearer, a small island, lion-colored and treeless, with Valletta, its fortressed capital, a lofty mound of smoked topaz, bare and proud and somewhat somber. The pilot's launch came coursing out to meet us. Art kicked our sick little engine to a start, and we panted along behind the launch, past the breakwater, past the fine yellowish fort of St. Elmo, past Ricasoli Point, and into the stateliness of the harbor. Inside the Grand Harbor, with the quick-flying gulls flashing overhead and the tugs chuffing past, we made our way slowly about the barges and the steamers and the flittering, painted brightness of the water taxis, and turned at last in the oil-filmed water to moor with our stern against Lascaris Wharf.

There weren't many people on the wharf: mostly men loading coir-colored cargo bales onto trucks, and men leaning against lodging-house entries, assembled in groups, talking, shading their eyes with their forearms, gazing out at the harbor. The lodginghouses looked as if they would be dark and sour-smelling inside, but their united façade was singularly pleasant—tawny, faded stone beetling with balconies, the balconies narrow and enclosed with dusty glass and exterior shutters. Neither latticed like true Arabic moucharabies nor shaped like English bay windows, these orphaned bits of architecture reminded me later of so much of Malta, which, lost between Europe and Africa, belonged to neither and nowhere.

Above doors painted red and blue and green were the lodging-house signboards: OLD LAND AND SEA, IRON DUKE, CROWN AND ANCHOR,

DREADNOUGHT, BONNY PRINCE and GOLDEN FLEET. The Golden Fleet was opposite to us. GOOD AND CLEAN BEDS, it proclaimed in slightly crooked capitals on the arch above its crimson door. Then in the foreground, as if the whole scene were a neatly designed piece of stagecraft, the touches of color were repeated in leaves and lozenges on the rims and spokes of the high-wheeled, horse-drawn carts that rattled by.

"Quaint," George said wearily, looking as if he didn't approve of what he saw at all. We stood about on the deck all dressed up in our shore clothes, waiting in the hot sun until the port officials came and liberated us.

"Now for the mail," Art said. One after the other, jumping off the stern onto the wharf, like children playing Follow-the-Leader, we set off to get the mail.

On our side of Valletta—the west side—the wharf was the only thoroughfare at sea level, and the quickest way to get to central Valletta was to take the lift opposite the Customs House up to the Barracca Gardens. The lift turned out to be two freight elevators housed in a black iron tower braced against walls of weathered limestone. Hal lent me twopence to buy a ticket. We queued before a turnstile and waited for the top elevator to come down, so that the elevator at the bottom could go up. The man behind me buried his nose in the nape of my neck; his breath was moist and tickling. A tiny boy, with round, solemn eyes and a slimy patch between his nostrils and his crusty upper lip, edged up to me and thrust out a sheet of Lotto tickets, but Hal said no one ever won anything in weekly lotteries and wouldn't lend me a shilling to buy a ticket. "No," he said curtly to the child. The child shrugged and marched back to the end of the queue holding the sheet of Lotto tickets in front of him and swinging his free arm with exaggerated defiance.

The elevator came down, and the gates of the upgoing one clanged open. We were penned in with suffocating closeness. Standing in the cataleptic trance that elevators generally induce, I could see the wall of the embankment inching by on one side and, on the other, the harbor sinking and the boats diminishing. I fixed my eyes on two framed advertisements above Art's head— SUNLIGHT SOAP, lemon-yellow background; OXO BOUILLON CUBES, red background.

The vertical journey clattered and swayed to a close, and we trooped out into the Barracca Gardens, a rather tatty little park with a refreshment stand and a fleet of green benches on which knitting nursemaids and old, tired people sat. A brief glimpse of the pale lacquer-blue harbor from this high promenade, and then we turned through the palm-shaded gateway, past the Garrison Church of England into Castille Square, which was dusty and gave off an amber shimmer in the heat. We walked through part of the old town where the sidewalks arrowed to the harbor in long, descending flights of stairs, where every street corner had its guardian marble saint arbored in light bulbs and every house its brass dolphin door knocker. The people were dark, but without glamour or liveliness, their darkness dim and blurry as that of figures in an underexposed photograph. Medium sized, neither conspicuously lean nor conspicuously stout, the Maltese seemed to have no distinguishing racial features at all. Their very clothes seemed to be without personality—a covering, that was all, like a dog's pelt.

We found the American Consulate, picked up the accumulation of three months' mail, and then the crew and George went along to the bank with me to cash the two rent checks sent by the tenants of my New York apartment.

I left the bank feeling enormously rich. Having paid the crew what I owed them, I still had two hundred dollars left over. "Let's go to the best hotel and have everyone wait on us hand and foot, and let's eat everything there is except rice," I said. "I'll pay, of course," I added grandly, the two hundred dollars already burning a hole in my pocket. Peering in a shopwindow, I saw a tea cloth of white lace. I wanted it.

"Whatever for?" George asked. "Maltese lace is awfully coarse." But I felt quite incapable of discrimination. I wanted to buy something, anything at all, just for the absurd pleasure of spending money on something I could quite well do without.

"I feel frightfully *nouveau riche*," I said apologetically as the tea cloth was being wrapped up in brown paper, but secretly I felt what happy people the *nouveau riche* must be.

Before I pocketed the change, I gave Art six shillings. "What the hell's that for?" he asked.

"I stole it from you in Crete," I said coolly, very much in com-

mand of the situation. "Consider the extra shilling as interest." The
satisfaction I derived from Art's expression was, in a well-chosen
word, exquisite.

Walking was completely out of the question. We must, I insisted,
drive to the hotel. George summoned a carriage, meant for four,
but when Hal sat on the edge of the seat there was room enough
for us all. The driver tipped his tweed cap and stuffed away the
newspaper he was reading. "To the Phoenicia. *Allez! Avanti!*"
George said. George always made a point of knowing the names of
the best hotels everywhere.

The carriage had a wonderful artificial fragility, an eighteenth-
century delicacy, its black-lacquered wheels and frame curiously
frail, and its seats, covered with cream-colored linen, bounded by
little thin brass arms. There was a brass lamp by the driver's seat,
and a canopy, scalloped with maroon velvet, with cream-colored
curtains that could be pulled all around.

Off we went, spanking lightly along, the red tassels bobbing on
the jingling harness. A warm wind flowed from the harbor and
ruffled the panache of pheasant feathers between the horse's twitching ears. We jingled up Kingsway, passed beneath a bridge, jingled
a little bit farther, and, as we rounded a bend, the big white Phoenicia Hotel, plumped in a garden of palms, came into view. I
didn't have any idea how much the carriage ride had cost. Although
the driver's slurred, salivary Maltese sounded vaguely like Arabic,
I couldn't understand what he said. I held up a handful of shillings
and half crowns and gestured to him to take the proper sum.

"He'll cheat you," Art said. I didn't think he would, and even
if he did steal a little, what did it matter? I was Lady Bountiful
for the day.

When we returned to the schooner, we were visited by a few
officers of the British Navy, for whom the *California* appeared to
have almost the same fascination as it did for me. In fact, the
personnel of the entire British Navy, or at least a mighty segment
of it that was stationed in Malta, professed themselves ardent
schooner enthusiasts, and in no time at all we were invited aboard
every destroyer and submarine in the harbor and kept in that
peculiarly turbulent state known as a social whirl. Of course, there
had to be return parties aboard the *California,* and George bustled

about with the pep of a social director making arrangements for them, brewing enormous quantities of gimlets and martinis and heaping the Damascened brass tray Art had bought in Cairo with carrot curls, cubes of cheese wrapped in bacon and rounds of toast spread with mock paté.

Every day, though, brought with it a smaller party, a gathering of Navy types in the lounge, and for hours the lounge would be filled with hilarious laughter as uproarious boasting went on and innumerable anecdotes were told relating to sex and excretion. From the chartroom I could hear chance phrases:

"So I said, 'My ship's the fastest ship in Her Majesty's Navy, and by God, it's got the fastest skipper too . . .'"

"I'd been on leave and I had a bad case of Delhi belly and Di said . . ."

"I thought that this little hussy looked ready for a bit of a slap and tickle, and I . . ."

"Have another gin, you old sod . . ."

Whenever I appeared, everyone was very polite. Stilted conversation would be substituted for the group enjoyment of obscenity. I fled from the schooner. I left in the early morning, and returned at dark, often to an empty ship, for the crew and George would have gone off to a naval party somewhere.

The early mornings were cool and enveloped in a milky haze. From where I stood on the gently rocking schooner, the shore always looked ragged and forlorn. (We had moved from Lascaris Wharf to a mooring between two buoys in Marsamxett Harbor so that we could be closer to the British destroyers anchored there.) Signaling for the water taxi to come, I would cup my hands about my mouth and call, "Dghaisa! Dghaisa!" And "Die-uh-sa, die-uh-sa," I could hear my call echoing, far away and mournful.

The bright-painted dghaisa would approach noiselessly, the eye of Osiris on its gondolalike prow suddenly there, looking up at me. The boatman would row me swiftly across to the shore, and I would wander for a bit along the old waterfront section breathing in its lemony, tarry, cumin-seed smell. Then up through the English resort section to catch a bus, a quite ordinary bus, except that it had a shrine up by the driver's seat that was lighted by a tiny Christmas tree light bulb. The slow drive to Valletta was through the old suburbs of Sliema, past the weary, dust-yellow, square-faceted houses. There were people about, and yet there was the feeling that everyone had gone away. It all appeared so forsaken and weary and bare and treeless.

In Valletta, the main topics of interest still seemed to be the bombings of World War II and the Great Siege of 1565, when the Knights of St. John had driven Dragut and his Ottoman armada from Maltese shores. Like Tithonus, the poor old Knights had not been allowed to die and were forced to live on in a sort of weary agony of remembrance. Their portraits were reproduced on post cards, and the floor of the Cathedral was paved with their emblazoned tombstones, beneath which they lay, all alike in death, with their feet crossed to show that they had seen the Holy Land. Their barracks had been carefully preserved, and the museum was lined with their earthly metallic shells—armor so cunningly contrived that it no longer looked man-made or artificial, but as if, like armadillos, the Knights had been born complete with carapace. All things considered, Valletta was a gloomy and depressing town.

And yet I waited on in Malta, postponing the day when I should have to say good-by to the crew and sail back to New York.

I didn't know what I would do when I got back to New York. Faces of the people I had missed while I had been away offered themselves to my mind, and my thoughts ranged idly over New York, as if I were already there, with all the things to do and see and hear and buy and eat spread before me. I both wanted and did not want to go home again.

"What's your hurry, kiddy? Why d'you have to leave now? Why don't you come along with us to Naples, spend a couple of months kicking around Europe and then go back? You're welcome to sail with us across the Atlantic if you want. What's another year?" Vic was stretched out on the couch in the lounge, lying on his back, with his hands clasped behind his head, his legs drawn up as a prop for a thick anthology of essays titled *From Confucius to Mencken.*

"I've got to get back to Kippy," I said. "He's sitting in New York with my mother and Mrs. Greig, and maybe it doesn't make much difference to him whether I come home now or a year from

now, but I like to think it does, and, anyway, I miss him. I promised him I'd be back for Christmas. He says he wants me to see
him in his school play. He's going to be one of the Wise Men, the
one that carries the myrrh—m-e-r, myrrh, he wrote."

"Well, I'm sorry to see you go," Vic said. He tapped the anthology shut and it slid to the floor. He didn't bother to pick it up.
"Do you want to go back? What the hell are you going to do when
you get there? Go back to being a New York so-phis-ti-cate? Get
married to some idiot, or what?"

"I haven't a clue what I'm going to do," I said. "If it weren't
for Kippy, I don't think I'd go back for a while yet because I love
traveling around—not to get anywhere in particular. Just for its
own sake. Someone or other once said he'd like to spend the whole
of his life traveling if he could just borrow another life to spend at
home. I couldn't agree with him more only I wish that I could do
all my traveling aboard the *Cal*. I don't think I've ever been as
happy as I have here on board."

Thinking back on those early days from Singapore to Ceylon, I
felt myself filled with a great wave of love for the schooner. "I'll
never forget the time I first came aboard and sailed with you to
Ceylon," I said, hoping Vic would want to talk about those days
which were set apart from all other days I had ever experienced.
But all he said was that it was a crying shame Yvor had had to
leave in Ceylon. Then he got up, walked over to the stove and, with
his finger, tested the side of the coffeepot for warmth.

"Why don't you write to Yoke when you get back? I got a letter
from him today. He's out of the Navy now. Tell him how we are
and everything. That we miss him like hell. That it's not the
same without him. You know." Vic sighed. There was a long pause
while he fished around in the cabinet for the coffee mugs. "What
ship are you taking out of here?" he asked in a more cheerful tone.

"I don't know," I said. "I guess I'd better get busy on it. What's
it cost, do you suppose?"

"About two hundred bucks, I guess. Here's your coffee."

"It can't," I said, reaching out for the cup. "I've only got about
one-seventy."

I had precisely one hundred and sixty-seven dollars and fifty-nine
cents, and in the morning I set out to find a steamship company

that had a sailing on which I could book passage for this amount. I was assured by half a dozen travel agencies that this was a ridiculous and impossible quest on such short notice. Fetched up at last in the run-down, water-front office of an Italian steamship company, I anxiously repeated to the clerk that there must be some way I could get to America on the money I had.

Mumbling to himself, he pulled his forefinger down a grubby page of rate columns and sailing dates. And then, "Eh!" he said. "Ah!" There was a way. I could travel steerage on a small Italian ship, registered under the Panamanian flag, sailing from Valletta on Wednesday of the coming week. That would cost one hundred and sixty-two dollars. But *di terza classe*—he pursed his lips and shook his head—that was not very nice, not nice at all. Whatever the prospects were, they would have to do, I said. There was no other alternative.

"*Allora*," he said, smirking in a rather unpleasant, patronizing sort of way. "*Come desidera*. As you wish." And with a great many *alloras* and *vediamos* and a final gloomy *ecco fatto*, he wrote out my ticket.

On the afternoon of the day before I was to sail, Hal helped me to put my luggage on board a small, old-fashioned, dirty, one-funneled steamer, whose wooden walls were wrinkled and scabbed with the paint layers of five decades. "Judas Priest! What a firetrap," Hal said with disgust. "I've never seen such a stinking ship. Sure you don't want to change your mind and come back with us, lady?"

"No," I said abruptly, feeling my eyes fill up. "When will you be back in the U. S.?" I was very close to crying, and the sickening odor of hot salt water and garlic in the corridor made me feel sick.

"C'mon, let's get off this clunk. When will we be back? God, I don't know. Maybe a year, maybe less. Once we get to Panama, that'll mean we've made it around the world. Then we'll go through the Canal and wend our way homeward." We walked down the gangway onto the wharf.

We took a *dghaisa* out to the *California*. Vic scribbled a statement on a sheet of the *California's* stationery—which, from dust and mildew, had a scorched look all around the edges—to the effect that I was signed off the schooner with the Captain's permission, with all my financial affairs and personal credentials in good order.

George and Art went off to a party on a destroyer. Then Hal and Vic and I were left alone. After we had eaten a supper of bacon and eggs and olives we sat for a while in the lounge, Hal playing "*Isa Lei*" on the harmonica, and Vic accompanying him on the cocolele. The Coleman lamp was lighted, and it threw a golden circle on the overhead and on the jaguar skin covering the table, leaving the rest of the cabin in semidarkness. A beam of light from one of the destroyers filtered through the porthole and fell on a patch of bulkhead below the bookshelf, where Scupper's paw mark was clearly imprinted. Looking up at the stone *tiki*, I could barely make out the place where its fingers were firmly laced across its rounded stomach.

There was enchantment in the cabin. When I had first come down into that cabin from the East Asiatic Docks in Siam, I had felt that I had stepped into someone else's dream, and now, sitting there in the semidarkness, I felt that it was my own dreams that enfolded me. I had waited for a revelation, a portent, a moment that would send me in a new direction. And that moment had come—not really when I had first seen the *California*, but sometime later, a moment, perhaps, when I had been on watch at dawn somewhere between Singapore and Ceylon, a moment unplaceable in time, but irrevocable, when I had crossed a boundary my old self couldn't cross, when I had turned to another direction, not necessarily better or worse, but different from what it had been before.

And there was no going back. I had advanced into happiness, the sort that in its pleasure of immediacy evoked the knowledge of future nostalgia, an experience whispered through by the thought that it would never be so wonderful, that it would never be quite the same again. For a while, time had seemed, like the lamp light on the table, a golden circle encompassing the pattern of my life. But now there would be no more illusion of staying the passage of time, and the pattern of living would change again, to what new form I didn't know, to what degree I wasn't sure, but change it must, for in some indescribable way, I felt myself altered to a new frame of being. It was a strange sensation, like being in the depth of a dream and, half-waking, feeling my dream self slipping away, and being able to do nothing about the real self that was taking over.

To part from the *California* at dawn the next day seemed to me to be parting from all the happiness in the world. With a shout, Hal hailed a *dghaisa* for me.

"Please don't come to the ship with me," I said. "I can't bear to say any more good-bys. But say something nice so I'll feel better."

"You look pretty," he said. "That's a nice hat with the beads."

"No, something better than that. Something that isn't true or that I'm not, like I'm a good sailor or something."

"You can't sew and you can't pump the bilge and you can't hoist a sail, but I guess you're a good sailor," Hal said. The sound of his voice gave his presence a solidity in the shadowy, hazy world. I hugged him good-by, and I hugged Vic and Art.

"Don't wake up George," I said. "Just tell him good-by."

The boatman came and rowed me away through the haze to the gleaming wetness of the dock.

CHAPTER TWENTY-FIVE

Home

THE VOYAGE FROM Malta to New York was meaningless to me, a pause between feeling—nothing more. I watched the misty contours of New York draw nearer imperceptibly. There was the Statue of Liberty beckoning and majestic, and the sky line of New York with its curious Gothic delicacy that grew higher and higher until it fell behind the pier sheds of Hoboken. And then, on the dock, a crowd of faces, out of which I picked, as if no others existed, the welcoming faces of my mother, my father, Mrs. Greig and Kippy. I was home again after an absence of a year and a half.

My mother and father had hired a Carey Cadillac in honor of the occasion, and the Cadillac and liveried chauffeur cast into sharp focus my third-class arrival, making it seem less adventurous than ignominious. "You youngsters," my father said, smiling his incomprehension. "It beats me the way you travel around. Why didn't you let us know? We would have cabled the money to you wherever you were. I don't like to think of you traveling around with all the *hoi polloi*." He put his arm around my shoulder. "Well, anyhow, no matter how you got here, it's wonderful to have you back all safe and sound."

"Now you sit here and I'll sit here and Kippy can be in the middle," my mother said, bustling us into the car. "And you'd better have a nice hot bath when you get home. I've had your old room all fixed up for you so you'll be nice and comfortable until those people move out of your apartment."

"Back to Seventy-second Street," my father directed the chauffeur. "Now, darling," he said to me, "let's hear all about this trip of yours."

There suddenly didn't seem to be very much to say.

During the next few weeks I found I had less and less to say. The first question my friends asked was "Well, how was your trip?" But before I got as far as Manila in the telling, I could see their attention wandering, and after a while I just said, "Fine," and let it go at that. Even James, who had urged me on my way, appeared inattentive, willing to hear about the places he himself had been and no more. It was useless to try to tell him about the schooner. It was plain that he wasn't interested. "Now, what are you going to do?" he asked.

"I don't know," I said apologetically. I had vaguely imagined that travel would have a therapeutic value, that the stimulus and the absence from the familiar would act upon me in such a way that, on my return to New York, I would feel fresh and eager, filled with drive and purpose to take up my life where I had left off. It distressed me to discover that I felt nothing of the sort. Like love, travel is absorbing. Everything else withdraws to make room for its emotional demands and the expansion of one's senses. Now that my wanderings had come to an end, I felt sluggish and apathetic, as if, like some creature emerged from a chrysalis, I had suffered metamorphosis in reverse, a butterfly become a caterpillar.

"How does New York look to you?" Mrs. Greig asked.

"Fine," I said. There was a winsome extravagance about the shops along Fifth and along Madison and about the number of well-dressed and good-looking people. As a city, New York was a model of beauty and comfort. "It looks fine," I repeated. "Just the same." Perhaps that was why it seemed a little dull, a little flat: the city was as I remembered it; it was without the complex of fascination of a new place.

I went to see Kippy in his school play. He was an excellent Wise Man. He knelt before the Mother and Child without tripping over the tasseled cord of his robe, he looked suitably solemn, he didn't push any of the angels or knock their tinseled wings askew, and he recited his lines as if he knew what they meant. After the play was over we walked home together along Lexington Avenue, turning west toward Park at Seventy-second Street. Kippy had changed to navy blue ski pants and a leather jacket, but his face still bore traces of stage make-up. "Was I good?" he asked.

"You were wonderful," I said.

"D'you think Vic and Hal and Art and Yvor would've thought I was good?"

"Sure they would. I bet they would have said you were the best of all."

"I liked them," Kippy said. "I liked the *California*."

Those days aboard the *California* seemed infinitely precious to me. Over the rumbling and rushing of the traffic, I suddenly heard superimposed the clear sweet sound of Yvor playing "Way Out on the Desolate Billow" on the guitar and Hal accompanying him on the harmonica. I got my normal hearing back within seconds, but I was still feeling lightheaded and somewhat shaky when we entered the lobby of the apartment house. The doorman touched his cap and held open the elevator door for us. The elevator seemed to take an abnormally long time to reach the fourth floor. I burst into the apartment, told Kippy to go and watch television, went into my room and closed the door. I dropped my coat and hat on my bed, sat down at the desk, and began to write a letter to Yvor. I remembered Vic saying that the trip hadn't been the same without him. "Tell him we're okay. Tell him we miss him like hell." I began with that, but the rest of the letter was hard to write. I balled up several abandoned attempts and dropped them into the wastepaper basket.

I went into the hall, picked up the telephone receiver and dialed for the long-distance operator. "I want to speak person to person with Yvor Smitter, s-m-i-t-t-e-r, Pasadena, California," I said. "No, I don't know the number." I gave the operator his address and sat down on the straight-backed gilt chair that my mother—no lover of lengthy conversations—had placed by the telephone.

"Please make a note of the number. Sycamore seven-six-oh-five-three," the operator said in a metallic voice.

I wrote the number down on a small white pad stamped with DON'T FORGET in red block letters across the top. I could hear the telephone ringing on the other end. A woman's voice answered.

"Mr. Ida Smithers? I have a call for you from New York," the operator said.

"Just a minute. I'll call him."

"Hold on," the operator said to me. In the background I could hear a female voice, and a male voice saying, "Okay, I'm coming, I'm coming."

"Hello?" That was Yvor's voice.

"Is this Mr. Ida Smithers?"

"Yeah, I guess so," Yvor's voice sounded deeper than I remembered it.

The operator said, "Go ahead, please," at the same time I said, "Hello, Yvor?"

"What?"

"Yvor, it's me, Leila Hadley. How *are* you?"

"Hadley? Well, I'll be damned. It's great to hear your voice. When did you get back to New York?"

"About three weeks ago," I said. "How *are* you? Are you okay?"

"Yeah, I'm fine, I guess." Yvor's voice quickened as he asked, "How's the *Cal?* How was the trip across the Med?"

"It was all right, but it wasn't the same without you." I hesitated for a second, hoping that I didn't sound too soppy. "Why didn't you write me? I wrote you from Beirut, but you never wrote back."

"I'm sorry, pal. I didn't have much time. You know I don't like writing letters, don't you? How's the *Cal?*"

"She's wonderful. They're going to put in a new engine when they get to Gibraltar, I think."

"The old one finished, huh?"

"Yes," I said, reaching out for a cigarette and lighting it with one hand.

"Hadley?"

"I'm here. I was just lighting a cigarette. Look, Vic said for me to tell you they miss you terribly."

"Yeah, they're a hell of a good bunch of guys. What are you doing in New York? How's old Kipperoo?"

"We're both all right. I'm not doing much of anything here. Honestly, I feel like flying back to Malta and getting on board the *Cal* again. You know something? I really feel lonely here."

"Yeah, I know—" Yvor broke off. "It was a letdown, wasn't it,

getting back and all. Everyone asked me how the trip was and how
many storms we had, and then they started yakking about teevee
or their goddamned secretaries or some silly—"

"Your three minutes are up. Signal when through please," the
operator interrupted.

"Okay, okay," Yvor said. "What are you doing, Hadley?"

"Oh, I don't know, not much. I've seen a lot of plays and people, done some shopping. I've just come back from Kippy's school.
He was a Wise Man in the Christmas pageant. Right now, the
Wise Man's in the living room glued to television. What are you
doing?"

"Well, let's see. Just before you called, I was sitting in my room
listening to the record player. Not on hi-fi. Hey, what is all this
hi-fi business, anyway? Are people as crazy about it in New York
as they are here? People I know here will sit and listen all day to
an electric razor or a vacuum cleaner or anything as long as it's
on hi-fi."

I giggled appreciatively. "Oh, Yvor, it's so good to hear you. I
wish you were here. Maybe I'll get used to everything in time, but
I feel so lonely. Remember how we all used to sit around talking
on the *Cal?*" A catch was released in my mind, and my memory
spun back to the *California's* lounge, radiant in the tropical light.
I paused for a second. The mind's time is faster than ordinary time,
and that second's pause was long enough for me to recall and savor
again that moment when I had leaned against the wheelhouse and
peered across the gap of calm green-blue water at the island of
Nancowry, with its shaggy huts and the white beach running down
to the lagoon. "Do you remember the Queen of the Nicobars,
Yvor? And that little girl, Sophia, who collected shells for me? Do
you remember Thaipusam and the day all the flying squid leaped
aboard and Kippy used them for water pistols?"

"Keep on talking, Hadley, it's good to hear you. Why don't you
come out here so I can talk to you? I'm staying with my grandmother at the moment. She'd love to have you. I've told her a lot
about you. I was thinking of going to New Guinea. It would be
great to see you before I went. Come on out here."

"All right," I said. "All right. Would your grandmother mind
putting me up for the week end? I'll fly out tomorrow."

"Hadley, you're great." I heard him sigh. "This call must be costing you a fortune. Send me a wire what plane you'll be on and I'll meet you. Do you really mean it? Will you really come?" "Cross my heart," I said. "I'll be there."

I flew to California the next day. Three days after I had arrived, Yvor and I were married in the Church of the Lighted Window in La Canada, near Pasadena. "Well," Mrs. Greig said afterward, "at last you've come to your senses and married a good man." "Yes," I said. "I really think everything is going to be all right at last."

Instead of going to New Guinea, Yvor returned to the university to get his Ph.D. in geology. The following September the *California* successfully completed her round-the-world voyage, and Yvor and Kippy and I went down to Panama City to welcome her on her arrival.

Two months later, at the end of November, our daughter was born, and we named her Victoria California.

Johannesburg, 1957

Afterword

AFTER VICTORIA WAS born and christened, with Hal, Vic, Art, Mrs. Greig and Carol Saroyan, now Carol Matthau, as her godparents, I worked on shaping my notebooks into a travel book for which I received an advance and a contract from Simon & Schuster while I was in Bangkok. That I had money to pay for the repairs necessary for the *California* after her sails had been blown out by a typhoon in the Gulf of Siam was the *real* reason, I'm sure, that the crew relented and let Kippy and me come aboard as passengers. The *good* reason, the article proposed by a friendly magazine editor in Singapore, I now expanded and sketched in as a major part of my travel book.

Yvor and I had been married for almost a year, living in the suburbs of Los Angeles, when he was awarded a Fulbright scholarship to get his doctorate in geology and to do hydrological and other research at the University of the Witwatersrand in Johannesburg, South Africa. We planned to drive from California to New York where we would meet up with Kippy who was visiting his grandparents, then sail away on a passenger-carrying freighter to Durban where we would pick up a Land Rover and drive on to Johannesburg. Warned that pilferage and stealing were unusually heavy at Durban, where our household possessions would be unloaded before they were trucked to our new living quarters, we decided to take not only our necessaries, but our most cherished belongings with us, stowing them in a U-Haul trailer since the back of our car was already filled with crib, bottle sterilizer, formula, baby food jars, cuddly toys and all the other paraphernalia Victoria required.

Yvor packed his collection of treasures: a chamois pouch filled with pearls from the Northern Cook Islands, a repoussé silver bowl from Bangkok, black-lipped pearl shells from the Tuamotus; an intricately carved canoe paddle from the Marquesas, the skin of a jaguar he had shot in an Ecuadorian jungle; an ornithological specimen bird of paradise from Indonesia; six rifles, two pistols, cartons of ammunition, and much else.

My choices: my travel notebooks, several beginning chapters of my travel book on which I was working, reference books, family photographs, family treasures, antique silver whatnots. My clothes, including the Oriental finery of Chinese wedding skirts and silk brocade coats, Indian saris, Siamese silk dresses woven with two colors so that the purple flickered scarlet, the green flashed blue and the blue shimmered green. A mink coat given to me by Victoria's godmother Carol.

Jewelry boxes. Boxes lined with turquoise silk and covered with Swatow embroidery; a box of Florentine leather with there, in the top tray, Victoria's blue-beaded hospital identification bracelet that had circled her wrist when she was first brought in for me to see, all swaddled, with a tuft of hair caught up in an absurd ribboned bow; a brass chest for all the jewelry I had bought on my recent around-the-world travels. Heavy silver and gold-dipped pieces, pearls, coral, turquoise, and pieces set with semi-precious stones. Dramatic, massive and extraordinary adornments that brought to mind markets, bazaars, souks; each piece a memory, an image, a scent, a jingle of another world of which I had wanted to be a part.

A silver belt I could buckle on and see the naked-tailed rats in a lane in Chiang Mai in Siam, now Thailand, where I had almost stepped on a venomous banded snake, and would have, if I had not been pulled back by a coolie. A necklace I could fasten and see again the vista of a beach the color of an ancient bronze mirror, the sampans and junks in Hong Kong's harbor. Earrings I could put on and hear a muezzin's cry. A bracelet which flashed in my mind's eye images of Ceylon's, now Sri Lanka's, Temple of the Tooth, and an ocean red with algae with the catamarans surfing on to the beach beyond Colombo. A silver cross I could hold in my hand, which brought back a white-washed church near a donkey path in Santorini. A brooch I could pin on and hear a child singing a missionary hymn in an up-country lane near a Philippine church with windows made of *lapiz* shell. Toe-rings I could clasp on and feel the heat of India like a lover's embrace. I've always loved the synaesthesia evoked by jewelry, its *aide-mémoire* effect. Yvor used to say I could wear Europe around my neck and wrists and clasp my hair with Asia and let North Africa fall from the lobes of my ears.

There it all was in the trailer and the car, all the tangible memories of travel, all the things Yvor and I most valued, with Yvor driving and I beside him with Victoria in her basket on my lap. Yvor and I joked and laughed as we left Los Angeles and headed east. We talked about what we might expect to find in South Africa. The sun set as we were crossing the Mojave Desert, and as the sky darkened, I began to feel cold. Trucks juddered past us. One of their drivers must have flicked a still-burning cigarette on to our U-Haul because strange reflections of light suddenly appeared on the windshield. Turning my head to look back, I saw flames behind the rear window. Our U-Haul, with all our cherished possessions, was on fire.

Yvor kicked the blazing U-Haul free from its attachment to our car before the flames reached the gas tank, sending it toppling from the road onto the desert just as the flames reached the boxes of ammunition. Shells exploded in sharp crackling bursts, detonating like fireworks. Bullets whined above our heads. Gusts of wind caught glowing scraps of paper and clothing and tufts of burning fur that looked like bouquets of sparks and sent them whirling in the night air above the ghostly desert stretching out on all sides.

Hours went by. Frightened and cold, I hugged Victoria closely to me as I watched much of my past disappear in smoke and flying sparks. The tangibles of memories I treasured most were burned, gone. Except for Carol's mink coat and a few pieces of jewelry, nothing was insured. But what did it matter? A diminished self in the desert, I felt myself growing the carapace for a new self in an Old World, a world I had never seen. I turned my back against the wind and looked away from the fire with Victoria warm in my arms, my sweater wrapped around her. Yvor took off his tweed jacket and caped it around us.

We managed to get to New York, board the passenger-freighter, the Robin Wentley, and arrive in Durban as expected with no further problems.

I had pictured South Africa as somewhat dark and jungley, in part a remote and barbarous Zululand, peopled by noble savages carrying assegais, hunting masses of zoo animals, surrounded by a countryside of farmland and vineyards tenanted by Boers, or Afrikaners of Dutch descent, and English settlers, interspersed with towns featuring all modern conveniences, gold mines and a constellation of promising authors, among them Alan Paton, Laurens Van der Post, Nadine Gordimer. Since I had been forewarned about the inverted weather— Christmas, the peak of the hot season, good for picnics on the open grasslands of the veldt, July dead cold with sharp winds—I was warmly dressed when we docked at Capetown, then Port Elizabeth, and finally Durban. After Durban, with its touristy, costumed rickshaw men, Yvor drove several thousand feet up the escarpment of the great African plateau to Johannesburg with its trapezoidal mine dumps and contemporary urban sprawl. Once there, we ensconced ourselves in an apartment, and enrolled Kippy in Pridwin, a boys' day school where he quickly made friends, did well as a student, enjoyed playing soccer and rugby.

Yvor and I were busy as bird dogs dealing with the travail of travel. Unpacking our household belongings from barrels and crates. Building bookcases from bricks and planks we painted white. Getting a telephone installed. Buying adaptors for our record player and Waring blender and toaster so that they would work on direct current instead of alternating current. Buying extra school uniform caps, shirts, blazers, knee stockings for Kippy. We coped with lengthy Must Do lists as time consuming as the *California* crew's lists of chores to be done when ashore. We found our way around and about Johannesburg. We registered with the American Consulate, checked out the United States Information Service, located a pediatrician and a Scottish nanny willing to look after Victoria and Kippy if Yvor and I wanted to get away for a few days. We looked up people to whom we had letters of introduction, among them, Nadine Gordimer, whose second collection of critically acclaimed short stories had recently been published in America by the same publisher to whom I had a commitment to turn in a travel memoir.

I felt guilty that I was procrastinating getting back to work on my book. I wrote postcards and letters to friends and family. I kept a notebook of scribbles about African game and bird life Yvor and I saw from time to time on day trips to rural areas where Yvor was studying plant life and rock formations. The birds and animals we saw were sometimes beautiful, sometimes bizarre, splendid, striking, astonishing, dreamlike. The comic, cocky briskness of a warthog with its upright flag of a tail, the whimsical ballerina gait of an ostrich, a troop of baboons racing away to leap into a big-bellied baobab tree, the feeling of connectedness with the natural world which came over me as I watched scene after scene was dazzling, restorative and prompted me to scribble, scribble, scribble. But I wasn't in the mood to write about the *California,* and those other days of travel. I felt I wasn't *ready* to write about that voyage I knew had transformed my way of being and thinking. If it hadn't been for that voyage, I'd never have met and married Yvor, a scholar and a scientist unlike any man I'd ever met in New York, as were Hal and Art and Vic. Being with the crew, identifying with them, wanting to merge with them, wanting them to approve of me had stretched my mind so that it never could return to the dimensions it had been before I met them.

I longed for that heightened sense of being I'd felt on board the *Cal.* Now, I just felt a sort of comfortable workaday blur, I told Yvor. He said I needed a change of scene, that I should join him on a three or four day jaunt to Zululand. Wonderful. I'd read enough about Zululand. It was time to go there, see it, write about it. I bought myself a spiral notebook and some extra fountain pens for the trip.

So, on Boxing Day, the day after Christmas, Yvor and I jounced along in our Land Rover to Nongoma, some 300 miles south in Zululand, a territory about the size of Maryland, where Yvor was collecting fossils and rock samples, and where we were lucky to be granted an impromptu audience with Cyprian, the Paramount Chief of the Zulus. Lacking the circlet of scarlet loury plumes crowning his head, the leopard cape of royalty, the sweeping kilt of furtails and the roughly polished diamond earplugs I had imagined, his earlobes were undrilled, and he was wearing an olive drab coverall and black wing-tip shoes, without socks. Ngonyama Cyprian Bhekuzulu Nyangayezizwe ka Solomon Zulu Paramount Chief, as he was styled on his deckle-edged calling card, spoke knowledgeably with Yvor about soil conservation, stock control, annual cattle sales, and asked him what the "Negro situation" was in America, warning him not to speak with cream on his tongue. While he and Yvor were talking and I was scribbling in my notebook, a young Zulu man crawled on his knees and elbows through a curtained archway. In his left hand he held aloft by one leg a small varnished table with a crocheted doily on its top. With both elbows and knees he propelled himself across the floor, holding the table leg so steadily that the tabletop hardly wavered.

"*Bayete, Nkosi* (Hail, Chief)," he murmured as he crossed in front of Cyprian to deliver the table to the space between Yvor's chair and mine. Crawling backwards, he retired, nearly colliding with another servant holding up a tray in his left hand who also elbowed and kneed his way across the room. The second servant negotiated a path around the feet of Bengu, the Chief Secretary and Royal Interpreter; Cyprian's First Wife, characteristically full-bosomed and full-bottomed as most Zulu women, who was wearing a beige tam, a floral-printed dress and shiny black patent leather low-heeled pumps; Cyprian's mother, Ndhlovukazi, the She-Elephant, a courtesy title conferred on all Zulu queens, and unkindly apt in this instance, dressed in clothes matching those of her daughter-in-law. The servant halted near Cyprian's feet to mumble a submissive "*Bayete, Nkosi*," and then deftly placed the tin tray bearing a glass pitcher of kaffir beer, a drink of fermented sorghum, and six jelly glasses on the table, before he crawled backward out of the room. Lukewarm, Ovaltine-colored, the kaffir beer tasted the way mildew smells.

I tried to enlist Bengu's help in kindling a conversation with Cyprian's wife and mother, but each attempt fizzled out. "Too much shy," Bengu explained, and went back to saying "*Ay hay*," and "*Hau*," and "That is true," in his deep bass voice whenever there was a pause in Yvor's and Cyprian's conversation. Yvor wanted to do a little more rock chipping and collecting around Mtubatuba that afternoon, and so we excused ourselves after presenting Cyprian with a tin of English biscuits and a combination red leather clothes brush and manicure set I had fossicked from the Land Rover's glove compartment for an obligatory Boxing Day offering. Cyprian presented us with a meat-serving set of three bowls carved from marula wood, stained with shoe black, joined together so that they rested somewhat crookedly on twelve stubby legs, the sort of native artifact you could pick up for a few shillings in any curio shop. Then in came the two servants zigzagging in short staggering steps, carrying between them a freshly butchered ox leg covered with wet reeds to keep off the flies.

"We are hospitable peoples," Bengu said, gesturing toward our parting present.

Cyprian smiled, his cheeks pushing against his bloodshot and bulging brown eyes. "As we Zulus say, 'We leave through a nice gate. May you grow old and walk with a stick'," he said. "We part as friends."

In the front yard, our Land Rover looked half the size, dented and dusty, in comparison with Cyprian's shiny new Chrysler. As we drove away, Cyprian, Bengu, Ndhlovukazi and Cyprian's First Wife grouped themselves together and saluted us with a big-voiced benedictory farewell. "*Hamba gahle!* (Go you well!)"

We called back the traditional reply, "*Sala gehle!* (Stay you well!)"

Even though we shouted, our voices sounded dim and pale.

All the way to Mtubatuba, my head aching from the kaffir beer, I sat holding the three-bowled meat container in my lap. Most pronounced changes of thought slip away unnoticed, but now the dark jungles of Zululand that quivered for so long in my imagination were supplanted with views of lush round-shouldered hills and valleys filled with the tumult of tropical vegetation. Stopping to collect samples, shielding our eyes from the afternoon sun, Yvor and I gazed at the green and lovely landscape, seeing the rolling hills around us sprinkled with Zulu kraals, a haze of wood smoke drifting above clusters of stockaded, pale brown, beehive-shaped huts, the margin of a shallow valley beneath us, and valleys beyond green-black with the press of aloes and feathery acacias.

As Yvor drove, old men clustered along the roadside saluted us with the Zulu greeting, *Sakubona!* (We see you!) Many wore knee-length kilts of goatskin twisted into tassels, this traditional tribal dress complemented with leather belts and anklets studded with a mosaic of colored metal nail heads and punch holes. Wearing many-stranded necklaces of wire, beads or bottle caps or a mix of the three, they carried knobkerries, heavy carved sticks with big round tops that could serve as clubs or canes or direction pointers when Yvor asked about villages along the way. Some elders had what looked like black deck-tennis quoits or holders for large pots on top of their heads that Yvor told me were rings of polished fungus to designate their status of district headmen. Almost all the old men had earlobes plugged with carved and painted thick wooden cylinders as wide as silver dollars. The earlobes of the few who had removed these ornamental discs sagged like empty rifle slings.

Women appeared, striking and splendid in brilliant patterned blankets and leather aprons, worn as lightly in the heat as though they were gauze, their necks and full rounded limbs coiled with white beadwork woven with primary colors. Married women had done up their hair in an ochreous red Nefertiti-like coif. Unmarried girls had also forcibly straightened their hair and divided it into scores of braids no longer or wider than a wooden kitchen match: autochthonous dreadlocks. Further to proclaim their maidenhood, young girls left their full and often exquisitely pointed breasts uncovered, a sight novel to me, unfamiliar and unexpected outside the pages of *National Geographic* in those conventional times of the mid-1950s.

Several women carried water pots on their head, big and round as beach balls, with designs picked out on their lustrous black surfaces with small embossed ovals, circles, fish motifs and diamond shapes. When I travel, I buy things, collect artifacts and souvenirs. Amassing tangible memories of places I've relished, foreign places, out of the way places, almost amounts to an addiction. Some things delight me for only a little while until they are dimmed by the obscuring glaze of familiarity. Other things, like most jewelry, retain their evocative appeal for years. So be it. Nothing would do but for me to examine all the pots in sight and enter upon the formal ritual and complicated negotiations of settling upon a mutually satisfactory purchase price, bargaining less playful, less game-like, more matter-of-fact than the Asian kind of haggling I was used to. I was startled, when I held up my compact and got a handkerchief out of my tote bag to remove a gnat lodged in the corner of my eye, that women bunched behind me to peep in my mirror at their glistening, round-as-a-pocket watch reflections. There were whoops of laughter and an obbligato of "*Hau! Hau! Hau!*," that indispensable Zulu expletive which may mean practically anything according to the tone in which it is spoken. With low, sonorous, rolling volleys of "*Hau!*" and "*Ay hay*," simulating understanding, old men watched Yvor chipping rock samples and labeling plastic packets.

Whenever we stopped near a village, children attached themselves to me to guide me around the circle of *rondavels*, the Afrikaans term for the beehive-shaped, windowless huts which each housed a family. Stepping around a roaming menagerie of pigs, goats, bantam hens, donkeys, and brindled, whippet-like dogs with upward curving tails and long, bony legs, I dodged curtains of air-cured biltong, salted strips of a variety of antelope flesh that had been hung out like laundry to dry. I tripped over hunting assegais propped against hut walls of wattle and thatch. I inhaled the rank odors of human sweat, urine and excrement, of sour beer and the pleasurable scent of wood smoke. Sometimes a bare-breasted or blanketed woman would edge forward, clapping politely before she accepted with cupped hands an offering of herbal candies, candied ginger or fruit drops from my travel tote bag.

I was fascinated by the large three-legged black iron cooking pots that were prototypes of the cartooned cauldrons in which missionaries and pith-helmeted hunters are boiled. As I entered a hut I would be met with a cloud of flies and by a smoky darkness flecked with light specks filtering through the arching roof. Rush sleeping mats were always piled in a corner of a cow dung floor that had been pounded to a smooth polish. Off to one side would be a slightly sunken fireplace, usually a clay oven, a few home-made wooden spoons and footed wooden bowls; baskets filled with dried herbs, edible roots, corn meal; calabashes filled with souring milk, earthenware pots filled with kaffir beer in various stages of fermentation, an occasional quilt of goat and springbok hides hanging on a peg; somewhere a shelf set aside for pots and little bottles of *muti,* foul smelling and horrid looking medicines.

The huts were so out of my ken that I was seized with the sense of being present in some preposterous double exposure of time, across which there was no bridge, no connection. Going from one kraal to another, I felt queerly self-conscious always to be at the end of the glance of a woman, a young child or an old man with such a breach between us. Apart from Cyprian's young male servants, I seldom even glimpsed a young man in the countryside. We were told in *Fanagolo,* the lingua franca of southern Africa, that all the young men had gone off to work in the gold mines of Jo'burg.

Before we left the piedmont, the sound of our car engine flushed an unsuspected population of guinea fowl from the heath-like scrub edging the road. Tiny heads down, they scurried before us, chittering with agitation, their pear shaped bodies in a befuddled rush of gray-and-white speckled feathers. A minute later, we came upon a troop of about a dozen baboons lounging in the shade of a wild fig tree. They watched us approach with sherry-colored eyes squinting beneath the curiously human scowl of their brows. Then, when we were almost within touching distance of them, they departed in a bravura flourish of acrobatics, the females running tipsily on three legs, gripping their babies to their breasts, and the males loping after them. Somewhere a loury cried "Go 'way, go 'way," the sound piercing as a birth wail.

In traveling, there are certain chance moments when you seem to cross a boundary. The familiar and the commonplace so completely drop away that you are assailed by a sense of purest wonder, and are overtaken with delight by the immediacy of the moment itself and by the knowledge of retrospective pleasure that will be distilled from it. Looking at the wings of lilac rollers flashing in turquoise streaks across the bright vacant blue of sky, I knew then an engraving of this and other moments of that Boxing Day were being bitten into my memory, and that for a very long time afterward, print after print could be struck off with every line sharp, every color fast as it had been in that clear African light.

Returned to our apartment, I wrote a long piece, incorporating Zulu history with a memoir about Boxing Day, which I titled

"Sakubona, Zululand." Having written that, I had the satisfaction of giving back life to an experience, written words becoming as tangible memories as the Zulu pots resting then on the top of our bookcases, and the three-bowled meat dish given to me by Cyprian, Paramount Chief of the Zulus, holding paperclips, elastic bands and erasers on my desk.

This satisfaction prompted me to start to work again on my travel memoir. Even though all of my notebooks and best photographs had burned, I had some negatives and other photographs, scraps of notes and carbons of letters I had saved as extra packing material for some of the china we had brought with us. Art sent me some photographs of life aboard the *California*. My mind contained a reservoir of memories. Yvor could check for accuracy what I remembered about the *California*. I couldn't let down my publisher.

I began to write, transporting myself into time past. I was no longer in Johannesburg, but driving on dirt roads with newspaper editor Suchitr, looking at ancient Siamese temples, as Suchitr told me about art and Buddhism. I was in Ceylon, where a Buddhist monk wrote Romanized versions of mantras for protection and healing in my notebook, and told me that joy was not in the accomplishment of a task but in the doing of it. I was in Bombay, now Mumbai, listening to Mulk Raj Anand's stories of his childhood in a Bengali village, asking him about the differences in sculpture from Gandhara and Gupta dynastic sculpture, listening to him explain about the iconography in Hindu art, what various *mudras* (hand movements) meant, what *ushnishas* (Buddhist top-knots) indicated. Then the editor of one of the greatest art magazines in the world, Mulk is now ninety-eight and still writing. "Creative people never have time to get old," he'd said. I was in a luxurious Peugeot, sitting beside Halim Gargours, the Chief of Police of Beirut as he drove me from one end of Lebanon to the other, showing me every place he found beautiful. The man I called James, the famous satirist, humorist and wordsmith, S.J. Perelman, my longtime friend Sid, who had urged me to board that passenger-carrying freighter and sail to the Far East, wrote me not to worry about writing a book, but just do it, write everything, then edit later. Even though I knew he was miffed that I had married Yvor and not him, he still wrote me funny, loving letters encouraging me to write.

Nadine Gordimer was also encouraging, although she told me to keep to the point and not pile paragraph on paragraph like crocodiles heaped on each other for a communal sunbath. I thought Nadine's writing was perfection. Years later, I was elated but not surprised when she was awarded the Nobel Prize for literature. Nadine and I chatted on the telephone almost every day, and became such good friends that when my son Matthew was born in July 1956, a month after her son Hugo was born, I asked her to be Matthew's godmother.

Matthew was a year old when I sent my finished manuscript and some photographs in three cardboard boxes to Simon & Schuster. I knew I had written twice, almost three times, as many pages as I'd been asked to do, so it was no surprise when I heard that a lot would have to be cut and whittled from my book. It was my first book, and it was alive in its entirety in my mind, as I had written it. When I re-read it years later, I was appalled to see how much had been cut and chopped and pruned away.

I continued to share Yvor's passion for travel, his enjoyment of the natural world, his interest in the rare, strange, beautiful, curious and lived with him for four years in South Africa, traveling in the country and out of it while he searched for water-indicating plants in the Kalahari desert and fossils, and traveled just for the joy of seeing and exploring places off the beaten track. Kippy, Yvor and I bounced around Bechuanaland in our Land Rover. Several times we shot crocodiles in Maun with Bobby Wilmot as our guide, a wild young man who liked to ride a zebra across the veldt and join the herds of wildebeest that raced past the Okavango swamps to a lake which was pink as watermelon juice until the flamingos swimming on its surface flew up with clattering wings into the misty white bowl of the sky.

On our many trips to Bechuanaland, Yvor and I were always fascinated with the birds we saw. Solitary widow-birds, with foot-long black tail feathers fluttered in slow, swimming flight over the level savannas of the veldt. Weaver birds flashed red and gold in the scrub thorn which was belled with their pendant, upside-down nests. A retinue of tick-eating egrets, suave and gleaming against the dry, rough grass, accompanied each and every drove of rust-colored and black-and-white cattle. Hornbills, uttering melancholy, whistling cries, glided and dipped across the dirt road, and where there was a camel-thorn tree, there was usually a tawny hawk or a harrier eagle perched sentinel on its crown.

Once we witnessed a fight between a secretary bird and a ringhals, a spitting cobra, which could blind you with its venom. The back of the bird's head was plumed with a panache of black quills, which looked enough like feather pens to have suggested its clerical designation, but there was nothing suggestive of a clerkly mien about the bird, nothing meek, nothing domesticated. It stepped deliberately across the veldt as it had stepped across the plains of time, aware of us, unafraid. One scaly leg lifted, stretched forward from a bulbous knee socket and descended. Pause, the other leg lifted, stretched, descended, and the great eagle-headed body advanced in a movement of majestic stealth. Suddenly, the bird spread its black-fringed wings and began to hop and lunge, wheel and whirl in a queer dancing rhythm, one massive wing curved across its breast, the thick feathers a solidly protective shield against the striking snake.

To kill its adversary, the secretary bird delivered jabbing thrusts with its beak. Balling its left claw into a club, it soundlessly began to flail the ground. Implacably, the weird and savage attack continued. Yvor and I sat mesmerized in the Land Rover, watching. Then, with wings folded back, the ribboning body of the ringhals clutched in its beak, the secretary bird strode away over the stillness of the veldt.

Sometimes, ostriches would run along the road parallel to us. Yvor clocked them running about thirty miles an hour, slower than a rogue elephant which once detached itself from the herd around him and came thundering and bellowing—a terrible BWAAANK sound—after us. The elephant came so close to the back of our Land Rover that I could feel the earth shaking beneath us on the road. For at least a mile, this terrifying chase continued until at last the elephant slowed down, and we outdistanced him.

A professor of Yvor's at the University of the Witwatersrand told

Yvor that it wasn't to worry, elephants wouldn't bother you when you stopped in a car, you just had to honk your horn and they would go away. Not so. An elephant burned its trunk on the hood of this same professor's truck, backed off, and charged, pinning the professor in the driver's seat between its tusks. Shaking its head, trying to loosen its tusks, the elephant turned the truck over on its side. The professor had to spend eighteen months in the hospital before all his bones could be reset, mended, reattached, his muscles stitched, a shattered hip socket rebuilt and he could walk again.

On our way back from Zululand, we drove through Hluhluwe, a game reserve for white and black rhinoceroses. There we saw crashes of rhinos, seemingly molded on prehistoric armatures, looking as though they were melting in the sun with their clay-colored hides dripping from them in rippled folds. I saw here, for the first time, a herd of lowering Cape buffalo watering themselves at a pan. Yvor said they were mean-tempered, nasty brutes, belligerent, able to gore you through and kill you in one swift thrust of their horns, but they looked peaceful enough, their pelts the color of baking chocolate, their heads more bull-like than the buffalo heads on the tail sides of nickels, or the heads of buffalo I had seen roaming the grasslands out west when I had got my divorce from Kippy's father. Months later, Yvor braved a wounded Cape buffalo in the bush that a friend of his had shot. A wounded buffalo is a menace to human beings and wildlife in its vicinity. Yvor managed to shoot the buffalo before it killed him. People said Yvor was lucky to have survived, an event which conferred on him the status of a white hunter had he wished to join that profession which, happily for me, he did not.

Outside the game reserves, most of the wild life in Africa had disappeared in South Africa, subject to the mass-slaughter of game and meat-hungry Africans, except for little frequented areas like the protectorate of Bechuanaland. Bumping along the bush tracks in the Kalahari Desert, we saw enormous herds of plump-rumped zebras and high-shouldered blue-grey wildebeest cantering along the roadside. We saw browsing kudus with spiraling horns, sable antelope kneeling to drink at the edge of a lake, a lone loping giraffe floating across a clearing, or sometimes, a herd of them. We saw prides of lions but only a few leopards. We glimpsed suede-smooth duikers, bearded nyalas, springbok as they arced across our path. Elsewhere, baggy-eyed warthogs, their tails looking like little flagpoles, trotted briskly along narrow, dusty roads. Sometimes, when we stopped to watch a troop of baboons, we would meet a distinguished primatologist studying them, such as the renowned Dr. Washburn from the University of Chicago, who regaled us for almost an hour about baboons' habits and peculiarities.

When we took Kippy with us to see the magnificence of Victoria Falls, in Rhodesia, now called Zimbabwe, we also took a trip to see hippopotami at close range. Neither Yvor nor I were aware at the time that the hippos could easily have tipped us into the Zambesi where there were crocodiles lazing on the banks, which we hadn't seen until we were rowed close to shore. Happily, we landed safely. Innocent idiot that I was, I once threw an elephant turd like a giant Frisbee at a crocodile dozing in the Okavango Swamp near Maun in Bechuanaland so that I could get a better photograph of it. The crocodile raced after me on its stuggy little legs so fast that I was terrified it would outrun me. But again, Yvor and I seemed to be surrounded by guardian angels, and no harm came to me.

Whenever we were more than forty miles away from the nearest town or butcher shop, Yvor had a permit which allowed him to shoot game for us and the African men who often traveled with us to help Yvor in his search for water-indicating plants. Yvor shot guinea fowl, which were filled with parasites and beautiful antelopes I couldn't bear to eat. In remote areas, we came across settlements of Herrero women, many six feet tall, and far taller with their turbans, who were strongly scented with herbs and who wore long-sleeved turn-of-the-century missionary styled dresses.

Bechuanaland of the 1950s was far less populated than Botswana is in the millennium, although we often were hailed by nomadic river Bushmen, pygmy-sized, the women usually bare-breasted with tattered hide skirts which didn't hide much, Yvor joked, and the men either covered with swatches of animal skin or wearing ragged shorts and tee-shirts. Most of the women were steatopygous. Their buttocks stuck out so far in back you could put a butterplate on them, as Kippy once observed.

Less primitive, and greater in number, were members of the

Bamangwato tribe, who lived in dome-shaped *rondavels*, unlike the river Bushmen who lived in lean-tos made of acacia branches covered with skins or tattered trading-store blankets or canvas. I noticed that the Bamangwato had marvelous pale, polished, heavy wooden milkpots, each shaped somewhat like an elephant's knee and foot in miniature, with a leather thong piercing a knob on the side to make it easy to carry. At a kraal near where Yvor and I had stopped for lunch, I traded a mirrored metal compact and a few shillings for one, and wanted to acquire others, but there weren't any. Only dirty yellow plastic pails. I shrugged, started to leave, but a woman tugged at my denim skirt, gesturing to me to sit down on a stone she rolled toward me. She then opened her mouth and shouted so loudly that I felt my ears go numb. There was an answering trill of sound far away. One of Yvor's Johannesburg work crew officiously came to translate what the woman next to me was saying. "She say sit, wait, more *kamelos* (milkpots) coming, coming soon." Yvor smiled. "You've just heard the bush telephone," he said to me. "Let's wait and see what happens." Within half an hour, four women ran into the settlement, each carrying one or more wooden milkpots. Yvor's workman said they had come from "too much kilometers." Naturally, I bought them all. Nadine, who had come to refer to Yvor and me as Mr. and Mrs. Artifact, said they would make nice lamp bases, but I liked them plain, just as they were.

Once, I traded a magnifying glass and a pair of sneakers for a river Bushman's quiver of love arrows. The Johannesburg workmen Yvor took with us to follow our Land Rover in a truck, were of no use in the bargaining procedure. They treated the Bamangwato people like underlings, but they were terrified of the Bushmen whom they considered evil-minded sorcerers. The quiver was made from the scrotum of an eland, the arrows had tips of varying poisonous strengths: to alert a woman of a male's interest, to daze the woman to tractability, to stun the woman into near insensibility, to knock out the woman for a problem-free sexual assault, with time for a little undisturbed sleep. I later traded this in Johannesburg for a witch doctor's kit for fortune telling, filled with flat squares and strips of bone carved and incised with patterns comprising circles, dots, stripes; and some cowrie and cone shells.

The room-boys in the apartment building where we lived were sure I was a witch doctor, not only because they saw the kit I had bought, but also because I had brought a basket of selections from my collection of seashells with me, several golden and spotted cowries among them, symbolic of women in African eyes, and some cone shells I was told by the room-boys were "man's thingies." The roomboys pleaded with me to tell their fortunes, prophesy the future, often offering the equivalent of a month's pay for me to do so. Needless to say, I kept the moral highroad, not at all tempted, except to "cure" servants' fears and ailments. Our Zulu and Xhosa maids often trembled with fear because they had a *tokoloshe*, an evil spirit, on their shoulders, or they had broken out in hives because they knew someone had put a spell on them.

All right, let's see what the "bones" had to say about that, I would tell the victimized one, and I'd stop everything, get out the witch doctor's kit, invert it, carefully regard the position of bones and shells, and make up some comforting balderdash. Looking at my watch, I'd set the watch ahead to a convenient time and prophesy that by then the *tokoloshe* would be gone, the spell's power dispersed, and offer assurances that their hives would disappear the next afternoon, if not sooner. With the provision of an aspirin or a cup of tea with milk and honey, all spells and evil spirits would be routed.

Yvor had had one year of medical school, but that was enough to enable him to play a real doctor. He was called upon in the bush to perform all sorts of operations on river Bushmen and their children. Armed with little more than a bottle of aspirin, a pair of tweezers, bandages, band-aids, a darning needle and dental floss, eye drops, a bottle of peroxide, a roll of cottonwool and a sharply honed blade on his Swiss knife, Yvor would remove splinters from suppurating infections, set broken fingers and arms, lance boils, remove an insect embedded in an ear or grit from behind an eye, stitch up wounds and rips and tears in flesh. He would be rewarded with rare-as-gold chicken eggs, biltong, lion claws or teeth, elephant hair woven into a bracelet for me.

I returned to America with Kippy, Victoria, and Matthew six months before Yvor had finished his Ph.D. dissertation in order to be on hand when my book was published. Nadine had provided an appropriate title, "Give Me the World," from a poem by Yeats, and I was surprised to see quarter-page advertisements for my book in the *New York Times*, captioned, "The Girl Who Did What Millions Dream of Doing," illustrated with a glamorous picture of myself. I was relieved that the reviews were filled with praise. I was described as looking like "a bird trying to charm a snake," when I was interviewed on the Jack Paar Show, the antecedent of the Johnny Carson Show. I was pleased that *Give Me the World* was included in the *New York Times* list of Notable Books of the Year in 1958 and to be a Foyle's Travel Club awardee in England where *Give Me the World* was also published. But, I remembered what the Buddhist monk in Ceylon had told me, that "joy was in the doing," and I knew him to be right, both in the content of what I had written about and in the writing process itself.

When Yvor completed his doctoral dissertation on water-indicating plants in the Kalahari and additional research on fossils for a scientific journal, he joined Victoria, Matthew and Mrs. Greig who was helping me look after them in an apartment I had sublet in New York. By then, Kippy was enrolled in Groton, a boarding school in Massachusetts, where his father had gone.

That a Hollywood producer had optioned *Give Me the World* for ten years with the promise of making it into a film—although the promise was never realized—gave me hope that I might become a professional writer, a convenient occupation since Yvor's and my travels alone and with children had already provided material for several magazine pieces I had no trouble getting accepted.

Yvor wasn't sure what he wanted to do until an opportunity came up for him to teach in Jamaica. Neither Yvor nor I had ever been to the Caribbean, and the prospect of living in the West Indies appealed to us as well as to Mrs. Greig who longed to get away from the cold to an island famed for its butterflies big as hummingbirds and its hummingbirds as bright as butterflies.

We settled into an attractive house with a garden visited, as Mrs. Greig had anticipated, with many large butterflies and brightly colored hummingbirds, which flew through our open lighted windows at night, sometimes got entangled in my hair and then had to be carefully unsnarled. Set to rest on the windowsill until morning, they would emerge from a seeming coma and fly off on invisible wings, hovering to sip nectar from urns of hibiscus around the patio. The house had an upstairs bathroom with a balcony opening into the boughs of a tulip tree with luscious orange flowers the size of the silver porringers given as customary baby presents in the late 1950's when my fourth child, Caroline, was born in a local hospital. My hospital room was on the ground floor with open French doors through which dogs, cats, chickens and an occasional goat wandered on occasion.

Bougainvillea standards, like huge gaily-colored lollipops were planted in a circular island on our driveway. There was a hedgerow of sky-blue plumbago, the orange-flowered tulip tree, plus several garden beds where I had the satisfaction of pressing in a bulb, a leaf, a root and seeing it sprout into a plant in a few days, an inspiration to learn all I could about gardening, which in time prompted me to write articles about gardening and eventually led me to write a book about gardening by the sea.

Although Yvor's teaching job didn't live up to his expectations, we were so delighted with life in Jamaica that he took on several business ventures that allowed us to stay there for four years, before we returned to New York.

When we came back to New York, a friend of mine who was a reporter for the *New York Times* interviewed me about traveling with children. I disagreed with Robert Benchley's well-known quotation that you either travel first class or with children. I said I thought it was much more fun to travel with children than without them, particularly in Europe where you could skip a lot of sightseeing in favor of offbeat attractions more entertaining for children as well as for yourself. When published, the interview attracted considerable attention. Walker Publishing Company asked me to do a four-volume set of guidebooks about traveling with children in Europe which went on to become a single large guidebook published by William Morrow, which in turn became *Fielding's Guide to Traveling with Children in Europe.* I succeeded in establishing myself for a decade as an expert in family travel both in the United States and in Europe.

I also wrote travel articles, book reviews, celebrity profiles and articles on food and cooking. I was given a job as an editor on *Diplomat*, a magazine where I produced and wrote a gallimaufry of monthly articles, and from there, went on to work as a women's editor and cartoon editor at *The Saturday Evening Post*. Getting paid to do what I liked doing—editing and writing—was a joy. I liked being back in New York seeing friends, meeting writers, editors, artists. Victoria, Matthew and Caroline enjoyed their New York schools and visiting museums and playing in Central Park on weekends.

Yvor, in the meantime, having lost money in Jamaica with business ventures, looked around for other projects to develop. When he felt dull and stale, when ideas failed to jell, he longed to escape, to get away, to travel. I understood this siren song of travel. The joys of travel were unfailing. There was always a heightened sense of seeing, feeling, hearing the new, tasting new food, sleeping in new places, speaking in English, or mastering the rudiments of a totally new language, or trying to improve my French or Spanish; I felt recharged as Yvor did, a fresh sense of life, of feeling alive, alive-oh!

Travel for me, with its adventures, mishaps, surprises and joys always is both an experience and an education. The more you know when you go, the more you come home with, I would admonish the children, urging them to bone up on the countries and places we visited. For Yvor, travel was more of an escape, getting away from what he didn't like, and going somewhere else. He didn't like New York, and lured by a business project, he took off one day for the Philippines, saying he would be back in several weeks. He returned four years later with Hodgkin's disease, from which he recovered in a few months. We divorced, and not long after, he died an untimely death from a heart attack, in California, at the age of fifty.

To have the experience of traveling ambered in the pages of a book is a great satisfaction. To have those who care to read the book is a greater satisfaction. But to have readers write, or readers at book signings and book readings ask what happened to Art, Vic, Hal, Yvor, Kippy, myself and to that enchanting heroine, the *California*, and to Scupper is the greatest satisfaction.

I will try to answer some of the questions I was asked.

Having graduated with a Masters degree in Business Administration from Stanford University, Art became a Director of an organization involved with aerospace and electronic equipment. His management concerns ranged from precious metals to missile guidance to bartering oil for rice in Indonesia, to defense contracts and fighter planes. Of all the crew, Art traveled the most, with business and pleasure trips to Malaysia, Japan, Taiwan, Israel, France, Italy, Germany, the United Kingdom, Sweden, Pakistan, India, Mexico, China.

The circumnavigating voyage of the *California* gave him "a tremendous sense of accomplishment. All the odds were against us." He feels that the five-year, 42,000 mile trip changed his life, giving him confidence and the assurance that he could succeed in whatever it was he wanted to do. In 1994, for distribution among his friends, he organized the production of a videocassette in color, "World Voyage of the Schooner *California*," with photographs, narration and a musical score from the Sea Symphony by Vaughn Williams. Married to his late wife Barbara for many years, Art is the father of two daughters and a son. Retired in Arizona, he lives with one of his daughters, two German Shepherds and a Himalayan cat in a large and attractive hilltop house overlooking Sedona's extraordinary red rock formations.

Hal Dane McCann said that if the voyage on the *California* changed his life, he was not aware of it. "I think my life would have followed the same pattern had I not gone," he said. "I was an engineer when I left California, and I've been an engineer ever since I got back. If I ever said the trip was the ultimate escape, perhaps it was, but it was damned hard work. *Damned* hard work." After the world trip was completed, he worked with an engineering and construction company located in Los Angeles, where structural and innovative engineers like himself designed edge-of-the art support systems for the National Aeronautics and Space Administration (NASA) and other organizations.

He married Dorothy, an attractive fashion model, and they became parents of three tall and beautiful daughters one of whom is a close friend of Vic's elder daughter who lives nearby.

Lean, long-legged, six and one-half feet tall, Hal has always found plane travel uncomfortably cramped. He prefers cars and trains as transport. He and Dorothy have visited London and Paris, driven through Scotland, toured Canada by train, but apart from obligatory business trips to a handful of American cities, Hal traveled little during the past fifty years. Dorothy told me Hal really didn't like to travel much. I suppose I was aware of that from the way Hal was aboard the *Cal.* I remembered that he had little interest in foreign languages, spoke of the diminishing returns of travel, and often opted not to go ashore but to stay aboard and read a few more chapters in Burton's *Anatomy of Melancholy.* He still remains a voracious reader, but now his recreational reading consists mostly of scientific journals devoted to physics and mathematics. I know no one except Hal whom I would believe if that's what they told me, but Hal is too reticent to waste time telling me something that isn't true.

For William Ward Vickers, circumnavigating the world as the titular skipper of the three-masted schooner *California* was " the fulfillment of a lifetime dream." A former Marine pilot, Vic steeped himself in academia to get his doctorate in earth sciences, and has spent his working career involved with atmospheric physics, oceanography, glaciology and meteorology. He traveled and lived in Scandinavia, chartered a ketch to explore coastal and inland Mexico, boated on the Danube and the Yangtze, traveled in China with his wife Vivian, and went fly fishing with her on Vancouver Island off southwest British Columbia.

Over the course of some twenty-five years, whenever he has had the time and the inclination, Vic has been writing and working on a definitive, detailed, illustrated volume about the *California,* her crew, and their adventures. Vic's daughter Heather, acting as his agent, is now helping him look for a compatible publisher.

"Everyone knows that travel broadens your horizons, informs you about cultural differences and world politics, apart from all the benefits you derive from the travel experience itself," Vic once said to me as we sat at a handsome dining-room table fashioned from a giant slab of mahogany he had acquired in Colombia, South America, where the crew had stayed several months to make enough money to continue their trip across the Pacific. "I don't mean the table," he said. "Although I'm damn proud of that table, I meant other benefits, like memories of good times."

After he retired, Vic and Vee sold their house in Pride's Crossing, and moved west to California, where Vic and Hal developed and ran a commercial avocado-growing business for a few years, then sold it, and moved south to San Diego. They found new places to live within a twenty-minute drive from each other. Vic and Hal get together frequently, and keep in touch with Art whom they see on a regular basis.

I've never been out of touch with Vic, Hal and Art. They kept me posted about news of George, who lived in Colorado and northern California, became an architect, married a "socialite Roosevelt," according to Vic, had a son, and died in his mid-seventies of a heart attack. I rarely get a chance to see or visit Hal, Art or Vic and their families, but they always live in my mind's house as they were in the 1950s, their bodies toned, fit, tanned to the color of cinnamon with *pareus* knotted around their waists, their expressions and movements intelligent, alert, trustworthy, and as they are now, older, but totally recognizable, still focused and aware, their voices unchanged, resonant, speaking with humor and intelligence.

Their goddaughter Victoria California, when she was twenty-five, traveled to Dharamsala in India, where she translated Sanskrit into Tibetan at the Library of Tibetan Works and Archives. I visited her there and later wrote *A Journey with Elsa Cloud,* a memoir about my travels with her in India.

And Kippy, my six-year old son, the former cabin boy, what happened to him? First of all, he is no longer Kippy, but Arthur, as he firmly styled himself at Groton. He went on to Yale University, then to Tulane Medical School where he trained as a thoracic surgeon while he was inducted into the U.S. Army. From Arthur Twining Hadley III, he progressed rapidly to Colonel Dr. A. T. Hadley. He married a young Norwegian woman, Karen Gotaas, and was stationed in Berlin with her when his daughter, Holly Hildegard Hadley, was born, September 1, 1975. Holly, my beloved eldest grandchild, is getting her doctorate in forensic psychology.

Arthur returned from Berlin for a year's training in pathology at Walter Reed Hospital in Washington, D.C., divorced Karen, spent two years as an Army flight surgeon in Korea, and returned to a residency to train in aerospace medicine at the Army Air Force Base in San Antonio, Texas. From there, he went on to the Lyndon Baines Johnson Space Center at the National Aeronautics and Space

Administration (NASA) in Houston, Texas to become an astronaut candidate. Finding the lack of gravity harrowing as a working condition, he spent a year as a student at the Command and Staff College at Fort Leavenworth, Kansas where he married Texas-born Beverly Bludworth and flew to Germany where he was put in command of a station hospital in Mainz. As a Hospital Commander, he was posted in America, Germany and Saudi Arabia's Hospital Desert Storm. He described his stint there as lots of camels, but hardly Camelot.

Rather than wait around to be appointed General, he resigned from the Army to set up private offices as a bariatric specialist, making people thin and healthy in Houston, Texas, where he is now also a medical legal consultant specializing in hospital practice.

He told me recently that he remembers our voyage together. "And, of course, the *California*, the places we stopped at, the crew, Scupper, everything." He and Beverly have fished in Scandinavia, toured South America and Europe. "I like traveling. I'm always curious about things. I like visiting art museums, tasting regional wines and food, checking out foreign medical procedures. I remember everything that interests me." I've got Cicero's quotation pinned on my mind's bulletin board: "Memory is the treasure and guardian of all things." Perhaps having a good memory is simply a matter of attention. I never had to tell him when he was a child to pay attention. He always was attentive to what was going on around him. His half-brother, my son Matthew, who is now a large-animal veterinarian, is the same way, observant, quick to find a hummingbird's nest or to remember where he first saw a painting. I thought this trait of memory and observance might go hand-in-hand with both my sons' predilection for doctoring where memory and attentiveness are a *sine qua non*; just as they are, I think, for exploration and travel, traits you need to get the most out of what you are seeing, feeling, hearing, doing, smelling, tasting.

Scupper? That marvelous sea dog was given to a Navy ship which supplied the Navy stations of the Channel Islands off the coast of Santa Barbara, California. He lived a long, comfortable and happy sea-going life. In the ears of my mind, I can still hear his toenails clicking as he trotted along the deck of the *California* with a flying fish in his mouth.

The *California* was anchored in San Diego's harbor after the crew returned to America from Panama in 1953. Two years later, when Yvor and I were in Africa, Art, Vic and Hal realized they could no longer afford to maintain their cherished schooner. They sold her to T. S. Applegate, a schoolteacher, who sailed her to Hawaii. He arranged for her to be filmed along Maui's coastline for the early episodes of "Captain David Grief," a short-lived television series based on Jack London's collected short stories, "A Son of the Sun," which aired in 1957. The same year, on a dark June night, six teenagers boarded the *California*, hauled up her anchor, fired up her engine, and managed to sneak away from her dockside mooring in Honolulu only to ship-wreck her on a nearby coral reef, where she foundered and sunk.

When the *California* was repaired and re-floated, Applegate leased her both to a local oceanographic group as transport for scientific research in the South Pacific area, and for private sailing and fishing charters. On one occasion, he leased her to a film studio for an historical adventure feature with Spencer Tracy in the lead. One side of the *California's* hull was painted black to represent the piratical bad guys' vessel, and the other side painted white to represent the good guys' ship.

Rescued from this sacrilege by two enterprising young men, and repainted, the *California* went on to become a popular sunset-dinner boat cruising along the coast of Waikiki for some twenty years.

She then returned to the mainland with a new owner to be refitted as a San Diego-based whale-watching vessel. In 1981, she ran aground in a fog on Point Loma, and was pulled off the reef in a battered condition. This time, the gallant lady, beautiful even in her old age, did not survive.

As a comforting postscript, Anita C. Mason, daughter of naval archi-tect Al Mason—who was a seventeen-year-old high school senior when he designed the schooner/barkentine which was to become the *California*—has a sizable collection of notebooks, blueprints and other memorabilia concerning him (about whom she is writing a book) and the original owner/builder, John Polkinghorne.

Polkinghorne grew up in Cornwall, England. His reason for building the *California* was to sail her from San Francisco back to Cornwall after he retired from Mare Island Naval Shipyard, west of Vallejo, California. By the time Polkinghorne had sailed as far as Tahiti, war broke out in the South Pacific, forcing him to race back to San Francisco. Anita Mason is as pleased as I am that Vic, Hal, Art and Yvor fulfilled her father's and John Polkinghorne's dreams.

About the Author

LEILA HADLEY has been traveling since she was six months old. She is the author of many magazine articles and eight books, including *A Journey With Elsa Cloud,* a critically acclaimed travel memoir set in India. She is married to Henry Luce III and lives in New York City and Fishers Island.

SELECTED TITLES FROM ADVENTURA BOOKS

No Hurry to Get Home: The Memoir of the New Yorker Writer Whose Unconventional Life and Adventures Spanned the Twentieth Century by Emily Hahn. $14.95, 1-58005-045-X. Hahn's memoir captures her free-spirited, charismatic personality and her inextinguishable passion for the unconventional life.

The Unsavvy Traveler: Women's Comic Tales of Catastrophe edited by Rosemary Caperton, Anne Mathews, and Lucie Ocenas. $15.95, 1-58005-058-1. Twenty-five gut-wrenchingly funny responses to the question: What happens when trips go wrong?

A Woman Alone: Travel Tales from Around the Globe edited by Faith Conlon, Ingrid Emerick and Christina Henry de Tessan. $15.95, 1-58005-059-X. A collection of rousing stories by women who travel solo.

East Toward Dawn: A Woman's Solo Journey Around the World by Nan Watkins. $14.95, 1-58005-064-6. After the loss of her son and the end of a marriage, the author sets out in search of joy and renewal in travel.

Dream of a Thousand Lives: A Sojourn in Thailand by Karen Connelly. $14.95, 1-58005-062-X. The award-winning account of a young woman immersed in the heart of Thailand.

Journey Across Tibet: A Young Woman's Trek Across the Rooftop of the World by Sorrel Wilby. Foreword by the Dalai Lama. $16.95, 1-58005-053-0. An inspiring story that captures the sensibility of a remote land and its people.

The Curve of Time: The Classic Memoir of a Woman and her Children Who Explored the Coastal Waters of the Pacific Northwest, second edition by M. Wylie Blanchet, foreword by Timothy Egan. $15.95, 1-58005-072-7. The timeless memoir of a pioneering, courageous woman who acted as both mother and captain of the twenty-five foot boat that became her family's home during the long Northwest summers.

Seal Press publishes many outdoor and travel books by women writers. Please visit our Web site at **www.sealpress.com**.